Tigers of
Tammany

Tigers of Tammany
Nine men who ran New York

Tigers of
Tammany

Alfred Connable and
Edward Silberfarb

Holt, Rinehart and Winston
New York   Chicago   San Francisco

Designer: Ernst Reichl
81535-0117
Printed in the United States of America

Contents

To the

Bosses and Reformers

Long may they rage

Alas! and must the chieftain die,
Who led the ranks of war?
Dear woods . . . soft breezes . . . the moon's pale light . . .
These, these are sweet; but not to me
So sweet as is my Tammany.

—*The Songs of Tammany*

Chapter 1

Tamanend and the Evil Spirit

"To public views he added private ends,
And loved his country most, and next his friends."
—*Ode to St. Tammany*

In the Great Wigwam on the Island of Manhattes two columns of fiercely painted braves stood silently, their eyes fixed on the closed curtain. Behind the curtain, the Sagamore of the tribe, tomahawk in hand, the badge of a soaring eagle over his heart, interrogated a trembling paleface.

"Are you a citizen of the United States?" the Sagamore asked in perfect English.

"*Etho,*" the captive replied, hoping to curry favor through his knowledge of the Indian tongue.

"Are your intentions friendly and honorable?" the Sagamore persisted.

"*Etho.*"

"Are you a lover of freedom?"

"*Etho.*"

9

The tribe's Wiskinkie, a surly looking brave with two large keys hooked to his belt, walked behind the curtain. He too wore a badge, this one depicting a great Eye over a door with the words inscribed: "No Slave nor Tyrant enters."

After a moment the Wiskinkie reappeared from behind the curtain and moved quickly to a door at the opposite end of the Wigwam.

"John Morton!" the Wiskinkie shouted to the door.

From behind the door a deep voice acknowledged the name of the white stranger. The Wiskinkie returned to the curtain and whispered to the Sagamore. A moment later the Sagamore emerged and walked between the two columns of braves to the door. He knocked three times. Two knocks sounded in reply. The Sagamore returned to his prisoner behind the curtain.

Suddenly the Wigwam resounded with voices raised in song:

> "Sacred the ground where freedom is found
> And virtue stamps his name;
> Our hearts entwine at friendship's shrine
> And union fans the flame.
> Our hearts sincere
> Shall greet you here
> With joyful voice
> Confirm your choice
> *Etho! Etho! Etho!*"

The curtain was rapidly drawn aside. The man named John Morton was pushed forward; his path between the two lines of braves was lighted by two men carrying torches. Behind them came the Sagamore bearing a Cap of Liberty perched on a tall staff.

As John Morton walked the gantlet toward the distant door, three men stepped forward to block his way. The man in the middle, the Father of the Council, raised his tomahawk above the prisoner's head. The tomahawk came crashing down.

In the nick of time the Sagamore deflected the blow of the tomahawk with his Liberty staff.

"*Sago, Sago*, Sagamore?" asked the Father of the Council, raising the tomahawk to strike again.

"*Sago, Sago, oly*," the Sagamore replied.

"Is this stranger worthy of a seat among us?" the Father of the Council asked in English, still brandishing his tomahawk.

"*Etho*," said the Sagamore.

"Does he love freedom?"

"*Etho*."

"Will he unbury the tomahawk from beneath the Great Wigwam before his country's good requires it?"

"*Yaughta*."

"Will he bear adversity, torture, and death in defense of liberty, like a true Son of Tammany?"

"*Etho*."

The Father of the Council dropped his tomahawk to his side.

"Conduct him, Sagamore, to our Grand Sachem."

The small procession of torchbearers, Sagamore, and frightened stranger, continued along its way between the two columns of braves to the door.

"Grand Sachem," the Sagamore addressed the door, "this stranger has given the fullest assurance of his sincere intention to support the harmony, reputation, Constitution, and Laws of this Society, and it is therefore recommended that he be adopted as a Brother."

The door opened. The Grand Sachem, mightiest of the tribe, stepped out. A hush fell over the Wigwam. The Grand Sachem glared at the paleface. Then he spoke softly.

"Friend, the favorable reports given of your character and intentions have recommended you to the acceptance of this Society."

The Sagamore handed the staff with the Cap of Liberty to the Grand Sachem, who held it over the head of John Morton.

"John Morton," intoned the Grand Sachem, "you do freely declare that you will support the harmony, reputation, Constitution, and Laws of this Society, and preserve inviolably all its secrets from the knowledge of others."

John Morton raised his left hand. "*Etho!*" he replied.

The Grand Sachem turned to the assembled braves.

"Brothers, are you satisfied with the declaration and obligation of the candidate?"

The braves stamped their feet in unison. "*Etho!*" they cried.

Now the Wiskinkie walked over to John Morton and bent toward him expectantly. Morton whispered in his ear: "Liberty is our life." The Wiskinkie whispered back: "May you ever enjoy it."

John Morton placed his left hand over his heart and the Wiskinkie repeated the gesture. Then Morton extended his left hand and interlocked forefingers with the Wiskinkie in the Tammanial Grip of Brotherhood.

The Grand Sachem spoke: "I now confirm you as a Son of Tammany and member of the Columbian Order."

The new brave was led to a leather-bound volume where he signed "John Morton" to the Constitution of the Society of Saint Tammany.

It was now two hours past the setting of the sun on the third day of the Second Moon, Season of Snows, the Year of Discovery 347, of Independence 63 and of the Institution 50.

The Grand Sachem turned once more to his tribe.

"Would you now be willing to lose this Brother?"

The braves stamped their feet. "*Yaughta!*" they cried.

This was the elaborate initiation ceremony which was repeated hundreds of times by the only private club in American history to function through the years as a major political-party organization. The prescribed details of the ritual, previously unpublished, are part of a treasury of Tammany arcana donated to Columbia University in February 1965, by New York Democrats anxious to discard the traditions and taint of Tammany Hall.

Such bastardized "Indian rites" sound little more than collegiate today; but to the early men of Tammany, pioneers in the Democratic Party, they were deeply meaningful symbols of the hard struggle for liberty in the new republic. They stand in stark contrast to our contemporary political rituals, flattened and dehydrated by the demands of electronic news media and the sophistication of the modern electorate. An occasional campaign hootenanny still stirs up our rural countryside or gold balloons enliven an otherwise predictable national convention. But in the great cities, where the chaos and color of ward politics once had a special urgency, a dull quiescence has settled over the scene. America's urban politicians, in tune with the colorless era of automation, have now succeeded in substituting "great debates" for torchlight parades, skillful mediators for crusty old bosses, scientific polls for backroom hunches, issues for bread-and-butter, images for outright lies, legalized dishonesty for graft, civil servants for hangers-on, poverty centers for clubhouses, smiles of complacency for scowls of outrage, and cautious brainpickers for candidates.

If the quality of government has improved, the spice of political drama has almost disappeared, and with it many of the immigrant virtues which propelled the idea of democracy beyond the wildest dreams of the founding Puritans. In the arena of politics there are few unashamed rascals left to corrupt us nor truly outraged reformers to save us.

The only relief from this ennui continues to be found in the fact and myth of Tammany Hall. Everybody has heard of Tammany Hall and nobody is sure exactly what it is. From year to year it can be re-discovered in one of two familiar conditions: omnipotence or banish-ment. It is the oldest continuous political organization on earth, the best known, least loved, and most successful villain this side of Transyl-vania. Whether a candidate is running for Governor in New York or Justice of the Peace in California, he can ensure his safety by running against Tammany Hall. Tammany is the sole creator and perpetuator of all civic ills.

Whether it leads to victory or defeat, the anti-Tammany campaign is always a comfortable strategy. Defeat for the anti-Tammany candidate means that he has fought a gallant, impossible battle against a many-tentacled monster rooted in original sin. Victory means that he has vanquished and obliterated that monster, wiped it off the pages of history—until the next election.

Unfortunately, however, there will always be a small group of spoil-sports who remain unconvinced that Tammany Hall is extant. They will tell you, for example, that there is no such place as Tammany Hall, which is true; or that nobody belongs to Tammany Hall, which is al-most true. Perhaps the height of such sacrilege was reached during the 1960 presidential campaign when a Kennedy organizer laughingly told author Theodore White: "Why, do you know that Lyndon actually thought Carmine DeSapio and Tammany controlled New York!"

The war on Tammany has nonetheless continued unabated. "Do you really believe that the Tammany machine has been broken?" Barry Goldwater asked the 1963 Young Republican Convention. The reply was a resounding, "No!" And in the spring of 1965, when New York's beleaguered Mayor Robert Wagner was mulling over his prospects for a fourth term, one newspaper sympathetically noted: "Mr. Wagner may feel the time has come to turn the town over to someone whose political and official hands will be free to do as Mr. Wagner might do if Tammany's handcuffs weren't locked on his wrists." Another paper predicted at the time that continuing Democratic Mayors in office would be "reconsigning New York to the Tammany maw."

Everyone knows that, handcuffs, maw and all, "Tammany always takes care of its own." But few realize how consistently beneficent it has been to its adversaries: New York's most famous Republicans—John Lindsay, Nelson Rockefeller, Thomas Dewey, Fiorello LaGuardia, Theodore Roosevelt—were all swept to power and national celebrity on the strength of fighting campaigns against the "boss rule" of Tammany Hall. An honor roll of indignant Democrats has also profited from Tammany's hostility: DeWitt Clinton, Grover Cleveland, Franklin Roosevelt, Herbert Lehman, Mayor Robert Wagner, and Senator Robert Kennedy.

Each of these gentlemen, and hundreds more, has earned the distinction of single-handedly dealing the final, fatal blow to Tammany Hall. The most recent of these wallops, expertly delivered by Republican John Lindsay, was perhaps the unkindest of all. In the course of his remarkable winning campaign in a solidly Democratic New York City, Lindsay shattered a cherished tradition by attacking "clubhouse hacks" rather than "Tammany parasites." The implication of this wording was that Tammany no longer existed, a slight which Mayor Lindsay could later have cause to regret. For there is nothing Tammany enjoys more than gloating over its own obituaries.

When Tammany Hall's first autocrat, Aaron Burr, mortally wounded Alexander Hamilton, the Tammanyites went into hiding. Their honor, it was said, was stained for all time. Curiously enough, only a few months later anti-Tammany Mayor DeWitt Clinton was openly wooing their support. Tammany died again when the New York *Times* revealed that colleagues of Grand Sachem William Marcy Tweed had made clerical errors amounting to some $200,000,000. Reformers captured City Hall and it took the new boss, "Honest John" Kelly, all of two years to throw them out.

Near the close of the nineteenth century, Tammany was twice proclaimed dead, and twice Richard "The Squire" Croker led his braves back into power. Still another burial took place at the turn of the century with the election of reform Mayor Seth Low. Boss Charles Murphy replaced him after two years of patient endurance.

During World War I yet another reform wave swamped the City. The war outlasted it. Then came a series of calamities from which Tammany could not possibly recover: Boss Murphy's death as he was guiding Al Smith toward the presidency; the Seabury Scandals and the forced resignation of Mayor Jimmy Walker; successive victories by

Fiorello LaGuardia, feebly resisted by a string of inept Tammany leaders; the population influx strengthening the once-subservient Brooklyn and Bronx political machines; and, worst of all, the New Deal welfare programs which undercut Tammany's neighborhood charities.

The word Tammany remained interred as a nostalgic epithet until its fond resuscitation by Carmine DeSapio in 1953 with the election of Mayor Wagner, the proudest boast of DeSapio's "New Tammany," capped the following year by the narrow victory of DeSapio's gubernatorial choice, Averell Harriman. Then, in 1958, Nelson Rockefeller, wearing the broad smile of ancient discovery, aroused the citizenry to the dangers of the Tammany revival and won Harriman's place in Albany by an overwhelming vote. The cue was thus supplied to Robert Wagner when he sought reform support for a third mayoral term in 1961. He had no recourse but to destroy his patron DeSapio and declare that he would forever rid New York City of the Tammany evil.

One of Tammany's more tranquil funerals occurred in the last week of 1965, when Wagner took leave of City Hall after miraculously surviving twelve years imprisonment in the nation's second most burdensome office. Tuckered out after 4,383 days of insistent urban crisis, Wagner had chosen to side-step a head-on collision with two buoyant young politicians whose dreams of the future embraced nothing less than the White House. Had he sought a fourth term, the Mayor would have been obliged to defeat Congressman Lindsay, the first conspicuous Republican candidate for the mayoralty since LaGuardia. And if he had outlived that challenge, which was far from certain, he would then have had to contend for control of the State Democratic Party with Senator Robert F. Kennedy, the newest of New York's Democratic leaders.

No man of reason would relish the idea of competing with two such ambitious matinee idols, and least of all that most reasonable of men, Robert Wagner, who, by his own public confession, had already grown "weary" and "stale." The Mayor decided to pick up his memories and leave the field, thus, with more of a whimper than a bang, bringing to an end another Tammany era in American political life. Wagner and his famous father were the last two popular candidates whose careers were spawned in the clubhouses of Tammany.

What, then, was Tammany Hall, and what remains of it today? It was and is many things, some mythical, some dormant, some active under less offensive names. Officially, Tammany Hall is the Executive Committee of the New York County Democratic Committee. After the fall of Carmine DeSapio, this group of party leaders from thirty-three districts in Manhattan preferred to be known as "Chatham Hall" after their meeting place in the Chatham Hotel.

By extension, Tammany has also come to mean the entire regular organization of the dominant party on Manhattan island and its sphere of influence in the other boroughs and at state and national conventions. Historically, Tammany is the birthplace of the Democratic Party, dating its origins to the Society of Saint Tammany, organized two weeks after George Washington took his oath of office. The Society, which held its last formal meeting more than a decade ago, began as a fraternal order with liberal interests, and was converted into a powerful political machine which has played a major role in electing mayors, judges, governors, senators—and Presidents, beginning with Thomas Jefferson in 1800.

At one time nearly all important New York City Democrats were members in good standing of the Tammany Society, subscribing to passwords, secret handshakes, and stoical rituals culled from Indian lore. The Society's anniversary and Independence Day celebrations were portentous political affairs. On these occasions especially, even Democrats who opposed the workings of the Tammany machine were careful to pay homage.

President Franklin D. Roosevelt, whose nomination Tammany had opposed, sent yearly messages of greeting to the Society. In 1936, he wrote to the Fourth of July celebrants: "Just as the Declaration of Independence was a protest against Tory oppression, so did the Society of Tammany come into being to preserve the hard-won fruits of the Revolutionary War, threatened then, as now, by the Tory interest. In this day, as in the days of its founding, the Society of Tammany is on the side of popular rights and against the exploitation of the many for the benefit of the few." Three years before, FDR had joined with Herbert Lehman, Jim Farley, and Bronx Boss Ed Flynn in entering a city ticket against the Tammany candidates, thus ensuring a Fusion victory for Fiorello LaGuardia.

Tammany's 1938 parade, led by Al Smith in high silk hat, was switched from Independence Day to Army Day to permit the Society's more affluent members to embark on summer travels. This break in a tradition honored since 1789 was compounded in 1944 by the elimination of all rallies and parades; they were replaced by a public dinner to which women were unprecedentedly invited. FDR's messages became a bit vague ("I trust the celebration will inspire all who participate with renewed appreciation of the blessings of freedom") and the gamut of heresies was completed the following year when a Society member, Judge Jonah Goldstein, ran on the Republican-Fusion ticket for Mayor.

There was a flurry of activity after the war when President Truman sent his greetings, thus at least acknowledging the Society's continued existence, and membership attendance increased substantially following the elevation of Carmine DeSapio to the Tammany leadership. But DeSapio began to neglect the Society's banquets about the time his portrait appeared on the cover of *Time* magazine. The other members, who had maintained their dues in order to socialize with "The Chief," lost interest. The meetings finally stopped at the request of Averell Harriman, who was anxious to de-emphasize the Tammany label on his gubernatorial candidacy.

The Society's 177th anniversary in May 1966, was a lonely one for Judge Edward McCullen, whose eightieth birthday fell that same month. Judge McCullen still fills the position of Tammany Scribe, once held by DeWitt Clinton. "A lot of people owe just about everything they've got to the Society," he says, "but I never hear from them anymore." Judge McCullen has been retired from the bench since 1956. He is the last remaining officer of the Society of Saint Tammany.

Is there any likelihood of resurrection? "There have been seasons of eclipse," the Tammany Society's official historian wrote in 1901, "when the star of Tammany was obscured; but, after a time, the clouds rolled by, and the old Wigwam came prominently into view, in full possession of apparently indestructible vitality."

Although Judge McCullen maintains there is still considerable coinage in the Society's wampum bag ("It's all in cash"), two problems remain: there are no active members and there is no Wigwam. During its first decade, the Society met in saloons, later it built a succession of massive halls to hold its nominating conventions. All but one of these buildings have been razed and the last is in the possession of the International Ladies Garment Workers Union.

The Tammany Museum, forerunner of the New York Historical Society, is no more. Most of its precious Indian relics were sold to P. T.

Barnum. The remainder are housed in the Tammany Society room at the National Democratic Club on Madison Avenue. The Charles Murphy Memorial Flagpole, dedicated at a great ceremony in 1926 on the 150th anniversary of the Declaration of Independence, still towers above Union Square across the street from the last Tammany Hall. Its bas-reliefs of Indians and early settlers are turning green and ugly in keeping with the decline of what was one of New York's fashionable neighborhoods. Other visible remnants of Tammany are scattered about the City: numerous statues and monuments, among them Grant's Tomb, to which the Society contributed substantial sums; and the bridges and parks built by old-time Tammany contractors. And at Gettysburg, a tall Indian monument on the south slope of Cemetery Ridge honors the fallen Tammany Regiment. Seven thousand men, led by Grand Sachem William Kennedy, fought for the Union under Tammany's banner. More than sixty-five hundred, including Colonel Kennedy, did not return.

Should the Society of Saint Tammany be revived and construct a new Wigwam, where could men be found today fit for the mission of delivering the famous "Long Talk" on Independence Day? Who could match the ornate rhetoric of Thomas Francis Grady, or William Bourke Cockran (whom Winston Churchill called the greatest American orator), or the homilies of Alfred Emanuel Smith and George Washington Plunkitt?

In New York City today, artists and intellectuals who dabble in politics frequently sign their names to anti-Tammany advertisements. But Tammany once boasted of its own literati: Aaron Burr's Princeton classmate Philip Freneau, whose long poem "The Prophecy of King Tammany" was a favorite at Society meetings. The youthful William Cullen Bryant, in later years a Republican convert, published a literary annual in league with the editor of the St. Tammany Magazine. Tammany proposed Washington Irving for Mayor and sent his brother William, a popular satirist, to Congress. Fitz-Greene Halleck, in recalling his youth, wrote of smoking a "segar 'mid the jovial throng" in Tammany Hall. The Irish immigrant Miles O'Reilly (Charles Halpine), renowned during the Civil War as a poet and journalist, was a member of Tammany's ruling committee.

In the days when democratic themes were fodder for both poets and politicians, Tammany was considered less anti-intelligentsia than anti-aristocracy. It was proud to originate the first celebration of Columbus Day, long before it became the province of Italian-Americans. The gay torchlight parades and block dances of Tammany's Fourth of July were also accompanied by prayers, sermons, and solemn readings of the Declaration of Independence. The platform of Tammany Hall was extended to Fanny Wright for lectures on free love and socialism; Tammany legislators fought for workingmen's suffrage and the abolition of debtor's prisons.

Tammany found jobs and homes for thousands of bewildered immigrants. It was the chief political power behind the administration of Governor Al Smith, which pioneered the social legislation now an integral part of our national life. The New Deal's program on Capitol Hill owed much to Senator Robert Wagner, Sr., a stalwart in the Tammany organization. In our century, Tammany, through both support and withholding of support, has helped push New York on the winning bandwagon in 15 out of 17 Presidential elections.

Yet throughout its history, and for good reason, Tammany has symbolized for most people the quintessence of corruption, greed, and evil in big city politics. It has attained world-wide notoriety as the worst example of the American political machine.

In its finest achievements, as well as its better known iniquities, Tammany epitomizes much of the conflict and paradox characterizing the thrust of America's fortunes into the modern world. Tammany's leaders and wardheelers, like Americans everywhere, have been alternately ruthless and softhearted, prone to both conscience and neglect, religious fervor and gross materialism, loyalty and hatred, liberty and tight discipline, hard work and easy money.

The story of Tammany centers on its arrogant Bosses, supremely self-educated and socially ambitious men, essentially lonely figures caught in the whirlwinds of conflicting cultures and values. In victory they have been, at best, comic rogues; in defeat, near-tragic innocents with little insight into the nature of their failure. The best of Tammany's tigers have been tormented and extraordinarily talented men who never quite came to terms with the world around them. Their careers subjected them to more humiliation than satisfaction. Their ultimate fates have rarely been pleasant.

Parapsychologists might trace the succession of downfalls to a hot July night in 1804 when the rowdiest of Tammany's first hurrahs rocked a tavern on Manhattan's Nassau Street. Round after round of toasts were proposed and drunk to the deadly marksmanship of Boss Aaron Burr, whose chief adversary, Alexander Hamilton, lay at that moment on a bed of pain, his life's blood trickling from a cruel wound in the right side.

Hamilton's ghost, smarting under the bad taste of these proceedings, has been wreaking vengeance ever since. Aaron Burr, the victor in a fair duel, became the only Vice-President in our history to be indicted for murder (though not the only Tammany Boss) and fled to European exile. His protégé Martin Van Buren, who won the high office which had eluded Burr, failed to convince the people that he was anything more than a shrewd Tammany politician, and was defeated after one term.

Fernando Wood, who gave New York City its greatest park, was deposed by a self-styled reformer named William Marcy Tweed. Boss Tweed, in turn, was sued for six million dollars and died a pauper in prison. His successor "Honest John" Kelly perished of a broken heart when his nemesis Grover Cleveland was elected President. Kelly's chief lieutenant and political heir, Richard Croker, was ultimately ousted by reformers, beset by blindness, and harassed by court suits from vindictive children. Croker did manage to ease his demise by spending his waning years in Ireland in the company of a stable of thoroughbred horses, a Cherokee bride fifty years his junior, and several million dollars.

In our own century, Charles Francis Murphy was dispatched by a fatal attack of indigestion as he was grooming Al Smith for the Presidential nomination. Smith died a bitter and disappointed man, as did his exuberant ally Mayor Jimmy Walker, who was exiled to Europe. In 1961 Carmine DeSapio was stripped of power by Greenwich Village rebels and sent naked into the local void, the only brand of punishment appropriate to the offender. DeSapio, a robust fifty, was too young to die, too clean to prosecute, and too provincial to export.

It remains to be seen what the ghost of Alexander Hamilton has in store for J. Raymond Jones and the other Tammany leaders of the 1960's, but if the ghost doesn't get them, the scholars will. Tammany Bosses have traditionally rated contemptuous treatment in the chronicles of our evolving democracy. Yet their lives, and the organization which they molded, are in many ways more demonstrative of our national character than the glowing legends of heroes and Presidents. "There is a certain satisfaction," Ralph Waldo Emerson wrote, "in coming down to the lowest ground of politics, for we get rid of cant and hypocrisy."

When Tammany men have set forth on masquerades, the result has been transparent and ludicrous. For the value of the pure politician, like the artist or the thief, is his disdain for lip service. Political bosses do not need popular acclaim to reach the top. They are usually there before we know it, and we are always a little surprised to discover them. Yet perhaps in that discovery we see ourselves more truly than in the images we worship at the polls and the box office.

There is something to be learned from the story of Tammany's tigers, about our country and about ourselves. That story, like our story, begins with a myth, long since tarnished, which was sung and danced around the campfire three centuries ago.

Among the Algonquin-speaking Indians in the East, the Delawares were the friendliest to the early-European settlers. Their wigwams dotted Pennsylvania, New Jersey, Staten Island, and Long Island. One of their subtribes, the Canarsie, sold Brooklyn to the Dutch. Their blood brothers in Westchester County, the peaceful Wappingers, unloaded a lovely forest island off their Yonkers encampment called Manhattes for twenty-four dollars worth of trinkets. Outlanders have been heard to remark that it is worth at least twice that today.

When William Penn met with the Delawares under the great elm tree at Shakamaxon to iron out trade and territorial squabbles, he encountered their ancient sachem, or chief, Tamanend. The name was later recorded as Tammany.

"I found him an old man," Penn wrote, "yet vigorous in mind and body, with high notions of liberty; not to be imposed upon, yet easily won by suavity and peaceable address." The boastful Quaker was thirty-eight; "Chief Tammany of Many Days" was at the very least one hundred fifty years old. "He never had his equal," wrote a missionary attuned to Delaware mythology. "He was in the highest degree endowed with wisdom, virtue, prudence, charity, affability, meekness, hospitality, in short, with every good and noble qualification." Tamanend, we must believe, was the first to plant beans, tobacco, and Indian corn. He domesticated the crab apple tree, baked corn bread, grew mandarins and onions, discovered snake-bite antidotes and a cure for syphilis, and carved out the first birchbark canoe.

Tamanend's signature appears on a contract with Penn dated April 23, 1683. Quite understandably, there is some dispute as to whether this is the same Chief Tamanend who was an advisor to the Aztecs before Cortes invaded Mexico, and who traveled to Peru somewhere between 1030 and 1250 to help Manco Capec, Son of the Sun and Sachem of the Andes, establish the first Inca government.

Legend may have fused two men. The early Tamanend lived with his tribe west of the Allegheny Mountains and is believed to be buried in the Indian fortress near Muskingum, Ohio. The Tamanend who flourished in the seventeenth century was reportedly born in Delaware, later establishing his wigwam on the New Jersey site now occupied by Princeton College. Following his dealings with Penn, he spent his years of retirement along the banks of the Schuylkill River and was buried near Doylestown, Pennsylvania. As a noble character in the fiction of James Fenimore Cooper, however, Tamanend speaks as a man whose life has crossed the centuries: "My day has been too long. In the morning I saw the sons of Unamies happy and strong; and yet, before the night has come, have I lived to see the last warrior in the wise race of the Mohicans."

Whether he lived to be two hundred or seven hundred years, Tamanend left no room for argument about his mastery of the art of politics. "His government was of the patriarchal kind," Professor Samuel Latham Mitchill of the College of New York assured the sixth-anniversary meeting of the Tammany Society, "and but that he was no shepherd, you might compare him to the venerable Abraham of Judea. There was no force, no violence in his measures, but general consent and concurrence of sentiment conferred on him all the authority he possessed. He disdained usurpation of power and would sooner have been bound, loaded with weights and cast headlong into the Lake than attempt any invasion of the people's rights."

Tamanend's most recounted political exploit was an exhausting, single-handed battle with the Spirit of Evil. In the words of Mrs. Euphemia Blake, the Tammany Society's official historian, "Never was such a fight on the earth since the war of the Old World giants in ancient Greece." A benevolent and peace-loving man, Tamanend was provoked into this climactic struggle by many years of harassment. The

Evil Spirit, angered at Chief Tamanend's just and felicitous government, had sent forth clouds of mosquitoes to sting the Delaware
squaws and papooses. When Tamanend chased away the mosquitoes
with his newfangled tobacco smoke, the Spirit retaliated by growing
poison sumach on the braves' hunting trails. Chief Tamanend, according to Professor Mitchill, then "set fire to the turf and consumed
the venomous plants, which burned with such rapidity that the EVIL
SPIRIT HIMSELF, who happened to be skulking about the spot, was
sorely singed by the flames."

As a last desperate maneuver, the Evil Spirit dammed up the Great
Lakes with clear intent to flood every Delaware village in the East.
Sprinting to Buffalo in a rage, crafty Tamanend gouged out a great
drain from Lake Erie to save his people. The most conspicuous evidence of his handiwork is known today as Niagara Falls.

Then he set off to meet the Spirit face to face in the age-old game
of decision by monarchical contest. What ensued was a no-holds-
barred wrestling match which lasted nearly two months and covered
hundreds of miles with the two champions of virtue and vice relentlessly stalking and striking. "They clinched," Professor Mitchill reported, "and dreadful was the crashing of timber which they trod in
the scuffle." During one far-ranging round of this battle between Mortal Good and Immortal Evil, enough trees were felled to create the
Western Prairies.

In time, as the antagonists reached the Ohio River (another of
Tamanend's good works, along with the Wabash, the Miami, and the
Allegheny), the Evil Spirit carelessly betrayed signs of fatigue. Tamanend, as pragmatic a man as the chiefs who would follow in his footsteps, judged it to be an even match on land, and with a mighty leap
knocked the Spirit down and rolled him toward the water. He was
stopped short by a massive boulder which, unknown to Tamanend,
greater spirits had placed in his path to perpetuate the balance of
nature. The bout was declared a draw, and Tamanend and the Evil
Spirit went back to their respective works. Political moralists have
discovered that the boulder is still there.

It was only a matter of justice that in the early 1770's a band of
rebels battling the Evil Spirit of England's King George III should
proclaim Tamanend their patron saint. The Sons of Saint Tammany,
like the Sons of Liberty, became a focal point for anti-British fervor,

using the American aborigine as a symbol of national aspirations. They were among the most famous of the rash of "Indian" societies which broke out after the French and Indian War. Some of its stalwarts are believed to have been guests at the Boston Tea Party, a late evening affair which successfully combined Indian ritual with polite revolutionary action.

The artist John Trumbull, whose paintings of revolutionary events decorate the Capitol rotunda in Washington, is often credited with prefixing the "Saint" to Tammany. But several years before Trumbull's suggestion, Saint Tammany's Day (May 1) was established in Philadelphia as an annual occasion for Indian pageantry and commemoration of "America's patron saint." Tamanend's apotheosis is no longer recognized except in Louisiana, where a county (or parish) on the northern edge of Lake Ponchartrain bears the name St. Tammany. The great sachem's eligibility for sanctification remains an open question: he was rumored to have died by his own hand, setting his wigwam ablaze while under the influence of firewater.

Most likely, the Sons of Saint Tammany used the sainthood as a jest at such counter-revolutionary Tory groups as the Society of St. George. With the coming of the Revolution, the Pennsylvania Militia proudly adopted Saint Tammany as its leader in spirit. "What country on earth, there did ever give birth to such a magnanimous saint?" asked a song in a Revolutionary drama. "His acts far excell all that history tell and language too feeble to paint."

After the Revolution, the "Indian" clubs were disbanded, but their members remained wary of the aristocrats who now threatened to make General Washington an all-powerful oligarch. Less than two months after the Federal Constitution went into effect, the Sons of Saint Tammany reformed their ranks and held a "Saint Tammany's Day" Parade in Philadelphia. A Pennsylvania Senator, who watched the event with some misgivings, noted in his diary that night: "There seems to be some kind of scheme laid of erecting some kind of order or society under this denomination, but it does not seem well digested yet."

Within the fortnight that scheme was indeed being digested by a group of New York libertarians convened in Barden's Tavern on lower Broadway. Their leader was William Mooney, a shrewd Manhattan furniture dealer who had appeared on the upholstery float in New York's Constitutional Parade costumed as the President's chair-maker.

It was said of William Mooney that he was also a deserter from the Revolutionary Army, but such gossip did not become credible until he was caught taking four thousand dollars from the City treasury to purchase, in his words, "trifles for Mrs. Mooney."

Thus, in the spirit of democracy and petty thievery, was the Society of Saint Tammany (called also the Columbian Order, for patriots with bad Indian experiences) founded by Mooney and his followers on May 12, 1789, primarily to represent the anti-monarchist middle-class. It dedicated itself to "the independence, the popular liberty, and the federal union of the Country" and "whatever may tend to perpetuate the love of freedom, or the political advantage of the Country." The New York *Daily Gazette* reported: "It is founded on the true principles of patriotism, and has for its motives, charity and brotherly love."

"Stand together," Chief Tamanend once told his tribe, "support each other, and you will be a mountain that nobody can move; fritter down your strength in divisions . . . let wigwam be divided against wigwam, you will be an anthill which a baby can kick over."

This precept has been stressed by Democratic leaders from Jefferson to Johnson. It is seldom taken seriously until Election Day. Whether the struggle is between Dixiecrats and Northerners, bosses and reformers, Bucktails and Swallowtails, Hards and Softs, or, in the earliest days, Burrites and Clintonians, the Democratic Party traditionally eschews the monotony of unity. In most cases the clamor and chaos of intra-party squabbling has provided an energizing and cathartic experience for all factions, strengthening their will to win against the common enemy.

At other times, when a "consensus leader" fails to come forward to salve the wounds, the results have been disastrous. During its modern period of estrangement from the liberal wing of the Democratic Party, Tammany Hall showed little enthusiasm, for example, for the late Adlai Stevenson's Presidential candidacy in 1956. As a result, Dwight Eisenhower easily carried New York. This dangerous game of political fratricide, of course, has no party limits; it achieved its finest hour in 1964 when the Republicans chose an outspoken faction hero to face a Democratic consensus leader, with predictable results.

Such diversions were not tolerated by Chief Tamanend, who was the concensus leader *par excellence*. We are told that his constituents "trusted him with power because they were confident he would not abuse it. He managed matters with such consummate prudence and circumspection, so mindful of each, and so provident for all, that the Community in submitting to Tammany did but consult, in the most perfect manner, its own true interest."

To ensure that his enlightened political machine was in constant touch with the grass roots, Tamanend divided his nation into thirteen tribes, with a sub-chief in each Wigwam directly responsible to Tamanend's Great Wigwam. Each tribe was designated by the name of an animal, whose attributes were fully described by Tamanend at the reorganization ceremony with fond hopes that they would be emulated. A point of interest for students of bossism is that after Chief Tamanend's death, all thirteen prospering tribes lost interest in political matters and were absorbed into other Indian nations.

Grand Sachem William Mooney of the Society of Saint Tammany followed the great chief's lead by dividing his organization into one tribe for each of the thirteen new states, and naming them after the animals prescribed by Tamanend. New York was the Number One Great Wigwam, headquarters for the national "Eagle" tribe. Pennsylvania was Number Eleven, the "Eel" tribe, a slight of sorts, for the Philadelphia Tammany Society had organized itself eleven days before New York. As other Wigwams formed in Pennsylvania, however, it moved up to Number Two, the "Tiger" tribe. After the Civil War, and down to the present day, the tiger became the symbol of the New York City Tammany organization, presumably because it was the emblem on Boss Tweed's fire engine.

Apart from New York and Pennsylvania, the most active of the original Wigwams were Rhode Island (Beaver) and New Jersey (Tortoise). The Tammany Society of Georgia (Wolf) exercised considerable influence in state politics during the early-nineteenth century. The other original Societies were:

> Massachusetts (Panther)
> Connecticut (Bear)
> New Hampshire (Otter)
> Delaware (Rattlesnake)
> Maryland (Fox)
> Virginia (Deer)
> North Carolina (Buffalo)
> South Carolina (Raccoon)

As new states entered the Union, they were dutifully given tribe names:

> Vermont (Moose)
> Kentucky (Elk)
> Tennessee (Porcupine)
> Ohio (Mammoth)
> Louisiana (Brant)
> Indiana (Squirrel)
> Mississippi (Alligator)
> Illinois (Lion)
> Alabama (Hawk)
> Maine (Seal)
> Missouri (Rhinoceros)

Wigwams were also established in Texas and, as late as 1887, in Portland, Oregon, but by this time the practice of assigning animal names had been abandoned, if only through exhaustion. None of the above groups was ever powerful and some were only paper organizations existing in New York City files. Tammany's claim to being a bona-fide national organization was accurate only in the first fifteen years of its existence, and even this organization was confined to a cluster of states on the eastern seaboard.

The center of the action was in New York City; the designation of tribes by states was largely wishful thinking. Mooney's New York tribe was itself divided into thirteen tribes, each headed by a local Sachem. As Tammany later developed into a political machine, the sachemships were mostly held by the Democratic ward leaders in Manhattan. With the exception of Boss Tweed, however, the coveted office of Grand Sachem was kept apart from the position of Democratic County Leader. This tradition of maintaining a separate leader in the Society was initiated by William Mooney, the first Grand Sachem, who turned over his duties after a year in office to William Pitt Smith, the faithful Tammany secretary whose minutes of the first meetings are still preserved.

By 1790, when he relinquished the Grand Sachemship, Mooney had become a minor power among the small merchants and workingmen of the city, and he yearned for the heady cigar aroma of the political backrooms. The organization he founded was in good working order, its hierarchy well-established. Its major feature was centralized control window-dressed by a democratic structure. The Sachems elected by the Society's American-born membership (adopted citizens were accepted as honorary "Warriors" or "Hunters" but could not vote) formed a Council of Sachems which selected the Grand Sachem, or "Supreme Executive of the Columbian Order." Thus at the outset one of the basic principles of successful boss control was institutionalized: the leader's immunity from the whims of a broad electorate.

Other officers elected to one-year terms by the Council were the presiding Father of the Council (later merged with the office of Grand Sachem), the Scribe of the Council, the Treasurer, the Sagamore, and the Wiskinkie. The Sagamore served as master of ceremonies at initiations, as keeper of the "Great Seal" for documents, and preventor of "any useless delay" at Society meetings. The Wiskinkie (sergeant-at-arms) swore an oath to preserve the Society from "intruders and eavesdroppers." He was paid one dollar per meeting to demand the password from each member on entrance. Tammany's last Wiskinkie, Hubert Kelly, served under twelve successive bosses from the turn of the twentieth century until his death at age ninety-two years. In the spring of 1962 he was mourned at a Requiem Mass attended by the City's old-line Democrats.

The framers of Tammany's constitution had the foresight to require a three-thousand dollar bond from the treasurer and the Grand Sachem's signature on all outgoing checks. This apparently was not enough to allay suspicions of any man who sought and received the office. A treasury watchdog committee was established at the first regular meeting of the Council of Sachems on November 9, 1789, composed of four trustworthy Sachems, including Grand Sachem Mooney.

Solidarity was the keynote of Tammany's founding document. The motto of the Grand Sachem was set down as: "Preserve by Concord. Harmony will render the Institution perpetual." If a Brother divulged a Tammany secret to an outsider, he had "approached the gates of infamy" and was liable to impeachment by a Judiciary Council. All proceedings of the Society were secret unless seven-eighths of the members voted to make them public. The Council Scribe, whose badge bore the word "Sacred," was instructed to "sacredly conceal" all records. In addition to the password, the Wiskinkie carefully checked for badges and the Tammanial handshake, by which "the Brothers will know each other in any distant region of the world." Meetings could not begin until the Wiskinkie announced: "None but Brothers are present."

Membership in the Tammany Society was open to adult males of "virtuous deportment" whose reputation as good Democrats was affirmed by one of the Brothers. A "good Democrat," of course, was some distance from our present conception. The Tammany member who proposed admission of a friend swore that the candidate was "firmly attached to the State Constitution as essential to prevent an undue consolidation of power in the General [Federal] Government." If this sounds like the manifesto of a Southern Democrat, it should be noted that a member had to be just as "firmly attached to the Constitution of the United States, at least so far as the same may tend to secure and perpetuate the equal and inalienable Rights of Man."

A Tammany initiate paid $1.25 as his entrance fee, attended regular membership meetings in the Great Wigwam twice yearly (second Mondays in January and July), and took part in numerous extra meetings, including the Society's Anniversary on May 12 and the Independence Anniversary on July 4. He was also allowed to attend, without voice, the monthly meetings of the Council of Sachems.

It was the Sachems' responsibility to turn out their tribes for all gatherings, particularly for the annual "Long Talk" on Tammany Anniversary Day. This was the moment of truth for the Society, the harangue of purple phrases which would propel them forward into a year of even greater virtue and achievement. Down to the days of Senator Robert Wagner, the Long Talker was Tammany's shiniest ornament, holder of an honor next only to the Grand Sachemship.

Considerable politicking was involved in the selection of the anniversary speaker. Nominations and election for next year's orator were held in October, giving him seven months to perfect his speech. The result of such efforts was always laudable, as witness this excerpt from the Long Talk of 1791: "Let ASIA extol her ZAMOLXIS, CONFUCIOUS and ZOROASTER; let AFRICA be proud of her DIDO, PTOLEMY, AND BARBAROSSA; let EUROPE applaud her NUMBERLESS WORTHIES, who from ROMULUS to CHARLEMAGNE, and from CHARLEMAGNE down to the present day, have founded, conquered, inherited, or governed states; and where among them all, will you find coercion so tempered by gentleness, influence so cooperative with legal authority, and speculation so happily connected with practice as in the INSTITUTIONS OF TAMMANY? Avaunt then ye boasters!"

Toasts on Anniversary Day were drunk to the President, the Governor, the Republic of France, Chief Tamanend, Philanthropy, Humanity, the Laws, Universal Emancipation from the Aristocracy, Revolutions ("may they never cease until the whole world be regenerated") and to America ("may her glory never be tarnished, may her national character never be stained with the vices and crimes that have disgraced the nations of the old world"). After this strenuous round, those who could still raise their glasses joined with the Grand Sachem in a final toast to: "The Day; may every returning anniversary find the Sons of Tammany more unanimous and more virtuous."

Then the braves crossed arms and linked hands, in the style of modern-day civil rights demonstrators, to form the "Chain of Union" and sing their closing song:

> "Are we not sons of Tammany
> That ancient son of Liberty!
> Bright are the links of our great chain
> Unsullied may they ever remain.
> The mighty calumet then prepare
> Its fragrant scent shall fill the air.
> Then pass the bottle with the sun
> To Tammany and Washington."

The peace pipe and the communal bottle were passed around while the date for the next meeting was announced in pseudo-Indian jargon. The year began with December and was divided into three-month seasons: Snows, Blossoms, Fruits, and Hunting. Months were "Moons" and years were calculated from the Columbian Discovery of 1492, National Independence in 1776, and the Founding of Tammany in 1789. Thus, for example, was the Tammany Society to have stirred itself for a meeting on February 1, 1967, the braves would have gathered on the First Day of the Third Moon, Season of Snows, the Year of Discovery 475, of Independence 191, and of the Institution 178.

Tammany's predilection for wine and song in the midst of serious business was constitutionally authorized. On any moon in all seasons the Society was empowered to vote itself into a committee of the whole known as the Committee of Amusement. This section of the meetings was devoted to spirited debates on political issues, "American and other anecdotes," and "patriotic and moral songs." The songs may have been fairly inclusive, for the bylaws provided: "While in Committee of Amusement, the Brothers shall have and are hereby granted the privilege of calling for such refreshments from the Great Spring at their own expense as they may severally desire."

More sobering tasks were undertaken by the Committee of Charity, which investigated Tammany braves who applied for relief. All members were required to donate at least one dollar a year to the charity fund. When a Brother died, the Society was responsible for the welfare of his widow and children. Sachems and their tribes turned up in force at the funerals, wearing black and white ribbons to symbolize the "extinction of life and the resurrection hereafter."

Among the first expenditures listed on the Society's ledgers are payments "for mending windows, for one box candles, and to the widow Smith." Tammany's charitable instincts, later the keystone of clubhouse philanthropy, were early engrained in the organization. When the Society was chartered by the New York State Legislature in 1805, its purpose was described as "affording relief to the indigent and distressed members of the said Association, their widows and orphans, and others who may be found proper objects of their charity."

But from the very beginning the Society of Saint Tammany also had urgent political goals. It was intent on combatting the Society of the Cincinnati, an association of former Revolutionary officers whose membership was maintained by primogeniture. The Cincinnati was not named after an Indian tribe, but after the Roman patrician general Lucius Quinctius Cincinnatus, a dictator who displayed flashes of virtue during his struggles against the plebeians in the fifth century B.C.

Tammany and the Cincinnati were natural enemies. The birthplace of Tammany was a city tavern, the motto of Tammany: "Freedom Our Rock." Most of its founders had been footsoldiers in the Revolution. The Cincinnati ("Omnia Reliquit Servare Rempublicam") was established by wealthy officers, six months before the Continental Army disbanded, at the Ver Planck Mansion, headquarters of the monarchist General Baron von Steuben, near Fishkill, New York. Von Steuben was a chief organizer and helped establish branches of the society in all thirteen states. The other leading figure in the Cincinnati was Alexander Hamilton, who became president of the New York chapter.

The two societies shared an interest in charity, patriotic celebrations, independence, and national union. In fact, there were a handful of Cincinnati members, such as Lieutenant Colonel Ebenezer Stevens (a member of the Boston Tea Party and later chief of the New York Militia), who were also active in Tammany. But the bulk of the Tammany membership considered the Cincinnati a neo-Tory menace to the expansion of democracy. The Cincinnati agitated for a strong Federal government, a lifetime Presidential term, and suffrage limited to landowners.

Alexander Hamilton's ascension in Washington was greatly disturbing to Tammany. He was considered the major influence, and probably the writer, of President Washington's attack on the creation of "popular societies," interpreted as a direct slap at Tammany. But Washington was also eager to enlist Tammany's services to the cause of the Union. In 1790, a year after the Society was formed, he called upon the braves for a diplomatic mission unique in the annals of fraternal organizations.

The Creek Indians, stirred up by the Spaniards, were raiding American settlements in Georgia and Florida. Who better to pacify them, reasoned the President, than New York's political Indians, who paraded annually through the streets, smeared with warpaint and clutching tomahawks? An invitation was sent to the Creeks for a pow-wow in Manhattan. Their chieftain, a belligerent half-breed named Alexander McGilvery, was delighted to accept.

Chief McGilvery arrived with a large band of Creeks in New York City to find the Tammany braves decked out in feathers and bucks' tails, sitting cross-legged in wigwams pitched along the Hudson River. The Creeks descended upon their hosts with great whoops of excitement, causing a score of the Tammany Brothers to run for their lives. But Grand Sachem William Pitt Smith, always a quick thinker, led the remaining braves in Indian songs to the delight of both tribes. Then he spoke of the spirits of the two Great Chiefs Tammany and Columbus walking through the Wigwam. The Creeks were impressed. They hailed Smith as *Tuliva Mico* ("Chief of the White Town"), and Smith and McGilvery smoked the pipe of peace.

During the next few days, the Creeks were feted at banquets, escorted to concerts and the theatre, and exposed to all the wonders of urban civilization. At the end of the week Chief McGilvery was overjoyed to sign anything with his jovial hosts, most importantly a peace treaty which was transmitted to President Washington, "the beloved Sachem of the Thirteen Fires." By this treaty, the new nation's vulnerable boundaries in the southeast were thenceforth protected from Spanish schemes.

Such finesse made a deep impression on men of politics whose ambitions were grander than delivering the Long Talk or playing the lead in the annual pageant "Tammany the Indian Chief." When diplomatic skill emanates from a group of men sharing similar social and economic views, the makings of a political machine are self-evident. Three men saw this in particular: one was Aaron Burr, a rising young Senator from New York and a good friend of William Mooney's; the other two were wealthy but progressive Southern gentlemen who badly needed friends to the North. All three were interested in electing a new *Kitchi-Okemaw* (Great Grand Sachem), or, President of the United States. It occurred to them that the Tammany Society might be the cornerstone for a new and powerful political party.

In the summer of 1791 the Democratic Party was born when those two ardent naturalists from Virginia—Thomas Jefferson and James Madison—came down the Hudson on what they described as a "botanical expedition." Among the fauna awaiting them on the banks of Manhattan were Aaron Burr and the braves of Tammany Hall.

Chapter 2

The First Hurrah: Aaron Burr's "Little Band"

> "How misunderstood! How maligned!"
> —*Woodrow Wilson at the grave of Aaron Burr*

During the 1960 Presidential primaries, the Junior Senator from Massachusetts was fond of relating the story put out by Thomas Jefferson and James Madison when they visited New York in 1791: they were looking for wild flowers and a rare species of butterfly in the Hudson Valley. "But I'm not looking for butterflies," John Kennedy told his audiences, "I'm looking for votes."

Jefferson was also looking for votes, five years in advance, for the election of 1796. He came to New York City to seek the active support of Aaron Burr, the newly elected Senator who was Madison's co-leader in the opposition party on Capitol Hill. In exchange for Burr's backing, Jefferson offered him the Vice-Presidency. This prospect emboldened Burr to establish the Tammany machine, building upon the foundation of his friend William Mooney's Society. The alliance thus formed between the Virginia "democrats" and the Society of Saint Tammany became the basis for the voting strength of the Democratic Party: the South aligned with the big cities of the North.

Aaron Burr was the guiding force in Tammany during the last decade of the eighteenth century. On the face of his credentials, Burr was an unlikely candidate for the distinction of being the first Boss of an anti-aristocratic machine. The genteel grandson of the Calvinist demigod Jonathan Edwards, he was a fourth generation Puritan, a prominent member of the Society of the Cincinnati, a generous patron and connoisseur of the arts, one of the most cultured men of his day.

But Burr was destined to frequent during his life-time the political backrooms and the courts of Europe, the rostrum of the United States Senate and a cell in Richmond City Prison; brothels and gambling halls, the salons of great novelists and painters, the battlefields of the Revolution, the campfires of Western frontiersmen, freezing Parisian garrets where he fought for life against starvation—vastly disparate worlds of luxury and terror, to all of which he brought an easy sense of belonging and a curious detachment. "The summary," he once told his daughter, "is that I am resolved to go, without knowing exactly why or where."

Modern politics began with Aaron Burr and he was to pay the price for being a supremely dispassionate tactician. "Never in the history of the United States," wrote Henry Adams, "did so powerful a combination of rival politicians unite to break down a single man." Had Burr been born in our time he would have been more successful. His colleagues would be less suspicious of his cool demeanor in the heat of conflict. But in an era when politics was a career of passion, with flowery elocution, screaming invective, and power maneuvers based on deeply felt principles, Aaron Burr was something of an oddity. Politics to him was an affair of the mind. He was in it for the "game," a word which professional politicians in the twentieth century use without embarrassment.

Working discreetly behind the backs of polite society, Burr developed close relationships with the Tammany Sachems who regarded him as their best route to power and prestige. Around William Mooney he placed his own aides, the "Tenth Legion," to transmit policies to Tammany. He converted the disenfranchised tenants of Tammany into landowners, thus creating a new electorate which threatened to topple the controlling oligarchy. Aaron Burr was the leading pragmatist behind the rise of democracy in post-Revolutionary America. Allied with Jefferson the philosopher, he began the struggle to give the people genuine access to the machinery of government.

There was good reason for New York's aristocrats to be alarmed by Burr's recognition that a workingman's society had great political potential. For more than a century under British Colonial Government a handful of wealthy dynasties had controlled the State. The Revolution did not break their grip; it merely eliminated the most flagrantly Tory families who had backed the wrong side.

The new State Legislature was elected by a small minority of the State's 180,000 inhabitants. Barely ten percent of the people could meet the property requirements demanded at the polls. Yet the State Legislature, in the name of the people, selected United States Senators and Presidential electors. And four State Senators, who comprised the Council of Appointment, named all State non-elective officers, which at that time included the Mayor of New York City. The City's government was little more than a branch of the State. The people of Manhattan could exercise limited political power only through election of State legislators and the Governor.

Gubernatorial elections were largely personal and economic wars waged within the upper class, a situation that continued to exist long after the rise of the middle-class and Aaron Burr's Tammany Hall. Banking and shipping families were later joined by railroad and oil dynasties. (Modern echoes of the early struggles were heard in Albany as recently as 1958 when the Rockefellers ousted Averell Harriman, and in 1962 when the Morgenthaus failed to oust the Rockefellers.) Early New York politics centered around the alliances formed and broken within a few families. The patriarch of the strongest combine won the governorship.

This was the position of General George Clinton, New York's first elected Governor. The prosperous Clintons were leaders of the Anti-Federalist Party, a States' rights organization which sought to maintain for New York a status of semi-independence from Federal jurisdiction. George Clinton was a popular figure with the middle-class and workingmen. His ambitious nephew DeWitt was Scribe of Tammany's Council of Sachems, a founder of the Tammany Museum, and the recipient of strong support from his Tammany brethren in a successful race for the State Assembly.

Governor George Clinton was present in the Tammany Wigwam when the Creek Indians came to call, and he was invited back to give a Long Talk. "Deprived of liberty," he warned the braves on that occasion, "independence is a mere name. While you guard against the encroachments of foreign powers, at the same time guard against the encroachments of your own government." Tammany's sympathies were clearly in the Clinton camp. The membership oath, as we have noted, required a firm attachment to the State Constitution as "essential to prevent an undue consolidation of power in the General Government."

The Schuyler family was anathema to both Tammany and the Clintons. Philip Schuyler, also a wealthy Revolutionary General, was the powerful paterfamilias. His son-in-law was young Alexander Hamilton, Tammany's arch-foe. His ally was John Jay, spokesman for the aristocrats at New York's first State Constitutional Convention. Schuyler, Hamilton, and Jay led the Federalist Party in New York. They believed in limited powers for the State under a strong Federal Union.

Political warfare after the Revolution was waged by the State's first families with the guidance of bright young Wall Street lawyers. With America in a state of virtual anarchy, the courts were crowded with complex and confusing law suits. Many of the old Tory barristers had closed up shop, to the distress of a lucrative clientele beset with legal problems. It was a favorable season, financially and politically, for fledgling attorneys. In New York City three lawyers were most in demand: John Jay, Alexander Hamilton, and Aaron Burr. It was in the courtroom that Burr and Hamilton, already rivals as war heroes, first found themselves in direct opposition and grew to dislike each other intensely.

Hamilton and Burr, both short, proud men of renowned grace and dignity, had been gallant officers of the Revolution with equally arrogant ambitions. Hamilton was originally an immigrant from St. Croix in the Virgin Islands, born of a common law marriage between a French Huguenot mother and a Scottish merchant. His marriage to Eliza Schuyler, member of the great Federalist family, served to erase memories of his origins and place him in circles of social eminence. He was a self-made man, a powerful orator, a profound political and economic philosopher.

Aaron Burr, at ease with his own family credentials, could deal comfortably with high society and with the Tammany ex-footsoldiers whom Hamilton feared and despised. He was the son of the Reverend Aaron Burr, Sr., Pastor of Newark's First Presbyterian Church and a founder and early president of Princeton College; and Esther Edwards Burr, daughter of the austere theologian Jonathan Edwards. As was the case with Hamilton, Aaron's parents died when he was a boy, he was taken to the home of relatives, and he ran away to sea. But he returned to enter Princeton, graduated at sixteen, went to law school in Connecticut, and at nineteen volunteered for the Army, distinguishing himself as an heroic soldier during the hardships of blizzard and starvation in General Benedict Arnold's "Death March" to Quebec.

At twenty, appointed aide-de-camp to General Washington, Aaron Burr made his first important enemy. Washington considered him an impulsive upstart who was constantly urging foolhardy actions against the enemy. Burr, in turn, had a complete lack of faith in the Commander-in-Chief's strategic sense. Through the services of John Hancock, Burr secured a transfer to the staff of General Israel Putnam, who was perched with half the Continental Army on the perilous heights of Brooklyn. When the British fleet cut off Putnam's forces, Burr saved his men from annihilation by organizing a retreat from Long Island, upstaging a nearby artillery captain, Alexander Hamilton. In response to his promotion to lieutenant colonel at the age of twenty-one, Burr's first official action was to send a message to Washington asking why the advancement had been so long in coming. The dangers of such arrogance were not lost on Hamilton, who had become Washington's private secretary and would remain in his confidence for the rest of his career.

Two years after Hamilton married a patriot's daughter, Aaron Burr took as his bride Theodosia Prevost, the prominent widow of a British colonel. She was ten years Burr's senior and had five children by her late husband, two of them in the service of His Majesty's fleet. But she had powerful friends, among them Washington and James Monroe, who had protected her property from seizure by the Continental Army. And she had the learned interests and esthetic appreciation which made marriage tolerable for Aaron Burr.

In 1783 Burr and Hamilton established law practices in New York City. Burr was a brilliant technician in the courtroom, scoring points through broad legal knowledge and attention to detail, rather than appeals to a sense of justice. Most infuriating to Hamilton was the fact that Aaron Burr never lost a case. In personal confrontations between the two men, Hamilton was always affable; in letters about Burr to friends he was vituperative. Burr, on the other hand, gave Hamilton no direct signs of either friendship or hostility in his presence or out of it. His only hypocrisy was silence.

The political battle lines in New York were now drawn between Philip Schuyler's Federalists and George Clinton's Anti-Federalists. Alexander Hamilton, the Schuyler family's strategist, became a principal architect of the Federal Constitution. Although its final formulation was too radical to suit him (he favored life tenure for the President and Senators), he ensured the success of the new Constitution by winning over the New York ratifying convention from the Clinton forces.

Aaron Burr was elected to the State Assembly where he distinguished himself as an outspoken abolitionist. To the voters, he was striking in appearance but relatively colorless as an orator, reluctant to display the slightest sign of emotion. An enemy wrote of a Burr speech to the voters of the Sixth Ward: "It was of an icy nature, it was frigid and inanimate; it did not so much as make one drop of blood run from the heart with more than ordinary velocity." Politically, Burr began as an independent. He avoided taking a firm position on the most urgent issue of the day: how much power should be vested in the new Federal Government. He was never deeply committed in the great debate on this theme which would be conducted for fifteen years by Alexander Hamilton and Thomas Jefferson. Burr was first and last a professional politician.

Disagreement over the extent of Federal power was only the public aspect of the contest in New York between the Federalist Schuylers and the Anti-Federalist Clintons. The basic personal issue that divided them was of a simpler nature: the Clintons wanted New York for the Clintons, the Schuylers wanted it for the Schuylers. For either family to exercise dominance in the State, they were compelled to woo those clans which held the balance of power, including the Van Rensselaers, the Van Cortlandts, the Knickerbockers, and—most influential of the "swing" families—the Livingstons, scions of a Scottish immigrant who had settled in Albany on a 160,000-acre estate a century before. In Burr's day the patriarch was Robert Livingston, one of the five framers of the Declaration of Independence and America's first Secretary of State. Robert Livingston was also an early member of the Tammany Society.

Aaron Burr, though he was the highest-paid lawyer in New York

City ($12,000 a year), did not have a family fortune behind him. But Burr's work in the State Assembly convinced Governor George Clinton that he might be the bright young man to supply the Clintons with the brains and youthful skill that Hamilton was providing for the Schuylers. Consequently, in 1789, although Burr had supported a personal friend against Clinton in the previous year's gubernatorial election, Clinton named Burr as State Attorney General. In that same year George Washington was inaugurated as President, Alexander Hamilton became Secretary of the Treasury and engineered Philip Schuyler's election to the United States Senate, and William Mooney established the Society of Saint Tammany.

Burr was now in a perfect middle-of-the-road position. He had backed the losers against Clinton and been rewarded by the victors. He was beholden to no one. He was officially recognized as the State's foremost legal authority. He was not identified in the public mind as a spokesman for either the Federalists or the Anti-Federalists. He was still on good terms with many aristocrats and at the same time had developed an independent following among workingmen for his liberal positions in the State Assembly. The Tammany Sachems regarded him as a true friend to the downtrodden.

When Philip Schuyler came up for re-election to the Senate in 1791, the task confronting George Clinton was to find a candidate strong enough to defeat his old rival. With Hamilton ensconced as President Washington's chief advisor, the Schuylers were becoming increasingly influential. Fortunately for Clinton, however, the powerful Livingston family had become disenchanted with Hamilton for urging more Schuyler men on the President than Livingstons. Particularly discomforting was the choice of Federalist John Jay as first Chief Justice of the U.S. Supreme Court, a post which Robert Livingston had fully expected for himself.

The Clintons and the Livingstons went into caucus. For the Senate race, the Clintons would not accept a Livingston, the Livingstons would not accept a Clinton. What they agreed upon was a moderate with popular support who owed allegiance to neither dynasty. Aaron Burr was the logical compromise candidate. With the Clintons and the Livingstons behind him, Burr decisively beat Philip Schuyler and became United States Senator from New York. This was the victory that marked the beginning of Alexander Hamilton's fears for his own career.

That same year, the Jefferson-Madison "botanical expedition" arrived in Manhattan to confer with Burr and his friends in Tammany. In that meeting the ideological, political, and personal links which gave birth to the Democratic Party were forged into a national Anti-Federalist alignment. The Federalist cause, which then prevailed under the leadership of President Washington, Vice-President John Adams, and Secretary Hamilton, could be crushed, its enemies felt, if Secretary Jefferson could come to terms with other opposition leaders—Senator James Madison of Virginia and Senator Aaron Burr of New York.

Alexander Hamilton correctly feared that the "contemptible hypocrite" Jefferson, the gravest threat to his own national power, might very well be able to put together an overpowering alliance if Burr and Clinton joined with him. Hamilton knew he would have to tear apart the new coalition before it was firmly cemented. In 1792, when Governor Clinton was up for re-election, Hamilton sought to prevent Burr from becoming an entrenched power in the State. He prevailed upon Chief Justice John Jay to step down from the Supreme Court and battle for the governorship.

Among the Anti-Federalists, as Hamilton knew, there was widespread talk of running Burr for Governor instead of Clinton. These rumors may well have originated with Burr and his Tammany associates to establish his role as kingmaker. George Clinton came to Burr for a pledge of support, thus giving tacit acknowledgment to Burr's status as New York City's new political Boss. Burr and Tammany threw their support solidly behind George Clinton.

The Tammany Society was one of several fraternal groups, most of which were less politically minded, that Burr pulled together into a grass-roots organization. Although rigid restrictions on suffrage limited the Society's leverage in this first political contest, the braves were effective in mobilizing small merchants and property-owners behind the Clinton banner. The campaign was the first direct test of political strength between Burr and Hamilton. When the votes were in, it was so close that the outcome was thrown into the State Legislature. There, on the basis of a legal brief drawn up by Burr, a slew of Jay ballots were invalidated on technicalities and George Clinton was re-elected. Senator Aaron Burr, at thirty-five, thus emerged as an important figure in what would be called, taking the cue from a Federalist epithet, the "democratic" party. Nine years after establishing his first law practice, he was nationally famous, and the Tammany Society had made its entrance into the political wars.

The first Boss of Tammany Hall was a small, handsome man, five feet six inches, meticulously groomed, "as composed and immovable as one of Canova's living marbles," Winfield Scott wrote of Aaron Burr, "he wears the same aspect in all times and situations." Other observers were struck by his eyes, dark hazel, intense, spell-binding ("the eyes of a lynx," an enemy wrote). Women found him irresistible. Young Washington Irving, who covered Burr's treason trial, reported "not a lady, I believe, in Richmond, whatever may be her husband's sentiments on this subject . . . would not rejoice on seeing Colonel Burr at liberty." Food and drink sent to Burr's prison cell during his ordeal was provided by the prosecutor's mother-in-law.

Burr's affairs were major scandals in the press. He wrote lightly of them to his daughter, gleefully checking off daily seductions. His need for love was insatiable, his prowess astonishingly durable. In his early seventies he carried on a tumultuous love affair with a girl fifty years younger and fathered two illegitimate children. Throughout his career he frequently slept in bordellos, rising early the next day to don his black silk suit, carefully brush back his locks from his high forehead, and walk out erectly and soberly to visit his friends in high society.

Aaron Burr was a tough man, with a strict code of honor by his lights and fidelity to friends of his choosing, but with no moral base to guide his actions, and with the impenetrable reserve which would become the hallmark of successful Tammany Bosses. Children loved him and he adopted and brought many to live with him, to be educated according to his theories. "I never ask and never answer an impertinent question," one student reported; "I was brought up in the Burr school."

Burr was a lavish, often anonymous, patron of youthful lawyers, writers, and artists. The early American painter John Vanderlyn studied on a Burr "scholarship." To carry out his work, Burr was always in debt to friends and law clients. Although much of his life was consumed by the struggle to borrow from one to pay back another, he always placed his deepest interests above his obligations to creditors.

While by nature Aaron Burr was more a technician and manipulator than an original thinker, he had a great thirst for knowledge and was extremely responsive to creativity in others. His idol was the English writer Jeremy Bentham, the utilitarian philosopher who defined moral actions as prescribing "the greatest happiness for the greatest number." Voltaire and Chesterfield, on the other hand, appealed to Burr's strong streak of cynicism. He was also fluent in the histories of Herodotus, Gibbon, and Plutarch. A book which bore great influence on his educational theories was Mary Wolstonecraft's *Vindication of the Rights of Women.*

Burr was the first prominent spokesman for Feminism in America. He saw in his daughter Theodosia, his only child in wedlock, the grand opportunity to improve Womanhood: "I hope, by her, to convince the world what neither sex appears to believe—that women have souls!" Theodosia was placed on a rigorous schedule, trained in stoical ideals, languages, singing, dancing, the harp, horsemanship, stylish dressing, precise speech, and (with the aid of a mirror) the art of subtly conveying and concealing emotions with facial expression, in the Burr tradition. In Burr's rigid plans for Theodosia's cultivation was an extension of the ideal image that he held of himself. She was a true believer in the private myth of Aaron Burr: "You appear to me so superior, so elevated above all other men, I contemplate you with such a strange mixture of humility, admiration, reverence, love, and pride, that very little superstition would be necessary to make me worship you as a superior being."

Somewhat different sentiments were expressed about Aaron Burr by the leading public figures of the day. Although Burr was extravagantly adored by those who knew him best, he was hated by a larger group of countrymen as no American has ever been hated. "I feel it a religious duty to oppose his career," Alexander Hamilton said of this "embryo Caesar." George Washington wrote more cautiously to John Adams: "By all that I have known and heard, Colonel Burr is a brave and able officer. But the question is, whether he has not equal talents for intrigue." And Thomas Jefferson lamented: "No man's history proves better the value of honesty. With that, what might he not have been!"

Burr's supreme pride, which frightened the greatest names of his era, prevented him from achieving the stature in history he desperately wanted—this in an age when vanity was honored. Hamilton, Washington, Jefferson were the haughtiest of men. But Burr's conceit was greater, so much so that he could never bring himself to answer his attackers. "I leave it to my actions to speak for themselves," he said, "and to my character to confound the fictions of slander." He would not "condescend to refute a calumny," except twice, by polite invitation, in duels. "Revenge," he said, "is not in my nature."

As a politician, Aaron Burr moved his chessmen with no grand design, but he was remarkably adept at limited gambits. He had one of the quickest minds, though certainly not the deepest, of his times; a brittle, pragmatic mind, yet always receptive to the stuff of imagination which appeals to the intelligent gambler. "There is about his actions a cunning, a sort of legerdemain, which, while it defies conclusive proof, eludes the most acute research," wrote the most active Burr researcher, James Cheetham, a New York journalist who detested Burr. "In everything, therefore, which relates to this gentleman," Cheetham hedged, "no higher a species of testimony ought to be expected than that of a circumstantial or presumptive nature."

If he were talking one plan with a friend, or friendly enemy, the odds were that Burr had already undertaken another. He was quite obviously a difficult man to trust. "Habituated to intrigue, and distinguished by the secrecy and celerity of his movements," Cheetham wrote, "one of his primary political maxims is never to converse on an important subject in the presence of two men." Burr avoided communications in writing on political subjects, even to confidants. But if he rarely revealed his true intentions in any situation, it was probably because they were rarely firm.

And, too, Aaron Burr lacked full confidence in his own judgment. His freest confiding was in the presence of his longtime friend and Tammany Sachem, Matthew Davis, "so remarkable for his chattery," a contemporary noted, "that it has always appeared strange that Burr should trust him with his secrets." On occasion the Boss would characterize himself as a virtuous innocent surrounded by vengeful mortals. He could be surprisingly naïve about the motives of others. "Burr is as far from a fool as I ever saw," his friend Andrew Jackson said, "and yet he is as easily fooled as any man I know." In politics he was known for his cunning, yet just as often he was too-trusting, encouraging those who could martyr him. When an associate betrayed him, he wrote in his journal, "I am sick at heart, having made the most afflicting of all discoveries, the perfidy of a friend."

There exists in our political history no man of such mystery and duplicity. "He is the ancient Stoic and the primitive Epicurean fused into a live unity," a Burr pupil said. As a man, Aaron Burr will always remain an enigma. Much of his correspondence was burned by

Matthew Davis, his first biographer. As a political Boss, however, Burr's meteoric rise revealed an extraordinary talent for party organization and electioneering. It was in the arena of practical politics that all the facets of his remarkable personality were applied most successfully, and his contributions as a pioneer made an enduring mark.

When Burr began the task of shaping the Tammany Society into a political force, his work was made easier by several ready-made advantages: the Tammanial hierarchy molded by William Mooney and the founders of the Society; the rapidly expanding membership, which drew on friends and relatives of the original braves; the virtuous reputation for patriotism and philanthropy; the communality of fierce political beliefs; the core of frustration and anger against disenfranchisement; the attraction of the Society not only for workers, merchants, and tavernkeepers, but for a number of social luminaries as well. This last asset was a vital one. It is unlikely that the Tammany Society, even with Aaron Burr's covert leadership, could have developed into a party machine without members who brought with them good connections and political experience.

Contrary to a common impression, there was not, in the beginnings of our political parties, a complete polarization of economic interests and background. Just as the Federalist Party was led by New England shipbuilders and bankers, and families of New York's Dutch aristocracy, so did the Democratic-Republican Party look to liberal southern plantation-owners and northern patricians for guidance. Two years after Tammany was established by Mooney and his coterie of ex-footsoldiers, members of distinguished families began to join the Society: Clintons, Livingstons, Van Rensselaers, Van Cortlandts, Roosevelts, Pierponts, and Van Nesses. Their unity as Anti-Federalists, of course, was not to be assumed. Then, as now, there was nothing New York Democrats found more invigorating than attacking one another. The aristocrats needed Tammany for support and Tammany needed the aristocrats for window-dressing. Some, like DeWitt Clinton, were active members. But none was able to build a personal machine within the organization which could match Burr's, primarily because Aaron Burr held a special fascination for the leaders of Tammany; he had about him an aura of great power and ambition unfulfilled which exactly matched the mood of the Tammany braves.

Until 1796 Burr's Tammany "machine" could better be described as a following, for he spent most of his time in Washington, maintain-

ing an informal relationship with the Sachems through couriers. To
the delight of the men of Tammany, he publicly opposed John Jay's
appointment as ambassador to England, attacking him as too favorable to British interests. The Senators were enraged, for Jay was a
popular figure on both sides of the aisle, but Burr was reflecting his own
sympathy with the French spirit as well as the sentiments of the rank-
and-file Tammanyites who admired the French Revolution. Cash from
the Wigwam Treasury was sent to France at the height of the Revolution. Tammany's ceremonial use of the French Cap of Liberty was
maintained for more than a century.

When war broke out between England and France, Senator Burr
clashed with the neutralist posture of President Washington by demanding an embargo against England. The President was further angered
to discover that Secretary of State Jefferson was allowing Burr to
examine important State Department documents during the crisis.
Washington quickly brushed aside Burr's name when it was presented
as a possible choice for Ambassador to France, and he named James
Monroe. He also refused Burr's promotion to Brigadier-General when
a war scare developed over the French sinking of American ships in
retaliation for the Jay Treaty, which Burr had adamantly opposed.
Alexander Hamilton, having proved his military skills to Washington
by suppressing the Whiskey Rebellion in Pennsylvania, became the
President's military aide during the hostilities and blocked Burr from
participation. John Adams, the unsuccessful proponent of Burr's promotion, remarked that Washington had elevated "the most restless,
impatient, artful, indefatigable and unprincipled intriguer in the
United States, if not in the whole world, to be second in command
under himself, and now dreaded an intriguer in a poor brigadier."

Few of Adams' fellow Federalists felt as charitable toward the brash
young Senator from New York. Burr had taken his Senate seat at the
expense of Philip Schuyler; he had prevented John Jay from becoming
Governor of New York, and attempted to derail his ambassadorship; he
had attacked the President's foreign policies; he had worked for the
liberalization of bankruptcy laws (an interest Burr could easily share
with the less privileged); and, most aggravating of all, Aaron Burr had
won his battle to open up legislative sessions to public scrutiny. With
each step he took in his appeal to the "commoners," Burr alienated
the conservatives of both parties in Washington and New York State.
The Anti-Federalist leaders grew fearful of his increasing popularity

with the disenfranchised masses. Disturbed by the widespread publicity accorded Burr's Senate speeches, Governor Clinton sought to silence him by offering to take him from the Senate and install him in the State Supreme Court. This was an honor without future which Burr quickly refused.

For immediate support, Burr had to rely on Tammany, which had yet to flex its biggest muscles, and on the pro-French South, which was suspicious of all Northerners. If this was a thin power base, Burr nonetheless determined to take the long chance by siding squarely with the Southern Democrats, the Eastern workingmen and shopkeepers, and gamble on an influx of new backing from the West. When Tennessee applied for statehood, he was among its most ardent supporters. He helped that state's first Congressman, Andrew Jackson, learn Washington politics, and the two men, totally dissimilar in personality, formed a life friendship. In later years Andrew Jackson was one of the very few politicians who refused to turn their backs on Aaron Burr.

Election year came once again to New York State in 1794. Governor Clinton and Lieutenant-Governor Pierre Van Cortlandt (whose Congressman son was a Tammany brave) decided to step down after eighteen years in office. John Jay made his second try on the Federalist ticket for the governorship, enlisting Stephen "The Patroon" Van Rensselaer as the lieutenant-gubernatorial candidate. DeWitt Clinton's associates claimed that Burr had been angling for both the Federalist and Anti-Federalist nominations and, having failed to receive either, stayed neutral during the campaign. Indeed, there was little sign of conspicuous activity on Burr's part during the contest. Jay's election seemed a foregone conclusion after the choice as running-mate of Van Rensselaer, one of the most powerful of upstate aristocrats as well as a popular politician in the City. Van Rensselaer, like Hamilton, was a son-in-law of Philip Schuyler, but he was also an early member of Tammany. He resigned from the Society to make his cause with the Federalists and assisted Jay to victory.

Burr's apparent apathy toward this development was pure realism on two counts: he saw little hope in stopping the Jay-Van Rensselaer bandwagon; and he needed Federalist votes, particularly those in the sphere of influence of such families as the Van Rensselaers, to become Vice-President. He concentrated on building his national backing in Washington, withdrawing for the moment from the factional fights in

New York. He had no desire to do battle with the Clintons for control of the Democratic Party at this juncture. One goal was in mind: that all unite behind Jefferson for the Presidency in 1796, for Jefferson had promised Burr Southern support for the Vice-Presidency. But the electoral vote that year surprised both Jefferson and Burr: 71 votes for John Adams, 68 for Thomas Jefferson, 30 for Aaron Burr. Jefferson, the Democrat, became Vice-President to Adams, the Federalist "three-vote President." The Federalists swept the New York State Legislature, which in that era chose Senators as well as Presidential electors, and Burr consequently lost his Senate seat to his old opponent, Philip Schuyler. Alexander Hamilton thus returned to dominance in the State.

Aaron Burr turned his full attention back to New York politics. He was content to win election back to the State Assembly, along with George Clinton's nephew DeWitt. He befriended a number of upstate Federalists who assisted him in the passage of bankruptcy and anti-slavery measures, small steps in opening up ultimate political power to the mass of the populace. Tammany, fervently abolitionist, came to look upon him as the Tammany Assemblyman. The issue of slavery, to the men of the Society, was inextricably tied to the rights of the workingman and universal suffrage. ("It was a maxim of conduct with this sagacious savage," a Tammany Long Talker said of Chief Tamanend, "far more refined and excellent than prevails among most of our civilized, enlightened, and Christian legislators, that . . . a fellow man ought never to be degraded to the condition of a slave.")

Despite the disappointment of 1796, Burr recognized that he could emerge as the kingmaker in the Presidential election of 1800 if he could secure New York City for the Democrats. Vice-President Jefferson, who had so brilliantly articulated the power of the people in the Declaration of Independence, was a gentleman farmer, more at ease with his father's slaves than with the vulgar tenants of the urban North. Once again he was counting heavily on Aaron Burr to swing New York, the pivotal state between Federalist New England and the Democratic South. Burr now had three years in a Federalist-controlled State to rally support for a Jefferson victory. He had run out of money and, by now, had made more enemies than friends among the political leadership. But he did have the most important qualification for a political Boss, in the words of a Southern politician who had watched him operate in the Senate: "He has an unequalled talent of attaching men to his views, and forming combinations of which he is always the centre."

In preparation for the Presidential election of 1800, Burr pushed through the State Assembly a bill cutting up New York State into districts where the voters could directly choose the electoral college. This legislation, however, was killed in the State Senate and the choice of electors remained in the Legislature. Victory in New York for the national candidates, therefore, would hinge on the elections for the State Legislators in 1800. This was the chief concern of the Tammany Sachems who visited evenings at Aaron Burr's mansion at Richmond Hill.

In early New York City, when Times Square was upstate and the metropolis was confined to the southern tip of Manhattan, the estate of Richmond Hill was rolling, wooded countryside with a spectacular vista of the Hudson River. When Abigail Adams lived at Richmond Hill in 1790 she wrote:

"The house is situated upon an eminence; at an agreeable distance flows the noble Hudson—fields beautifully variegated with grass and grain—the venerable oaks and broken ground, covered with wild shrubs—give a natural beauty to the spot which is truly enchanting. A lovely variety of birds serenade me morning and evening . . . The most delicious spot I ever saw."

John Jacob Astor later bought the estate cheaply, sliced it into lots, and made a fortune. Today it is a flat area of cement and drab warehouses near the Holland Tunnel in downtown New York.

Aaron Burr first visited the mansion at Richmond Hill when it served as General Washington's headquarters during the Revolution. After he began practicing law, Burr (who owned a townhouse at 4 Broadway) took over the lease of Richmond Hill from John Adams. The country home which Burr shared with his wife and daughter was noted for its splendid library, expensive wines, paintings, and continual redecorating projects, the last, courtesy of Grand Sachem William Mooney. A minor fortune was owed to Mooney for the furnishings he supplied Richmond Hill. He was never able to collect the money. Burr entertained lavishly in his home, borrowed and lent indiscriminately, and saved never.

Richmond Hill was the scene of brilliant social gatherings, a port of call for Talleyrand, Louis Philippe, and scores of European notables.

Burr's wife Theodosia enchanted international society with her vivacity and quick wit. Burr insisted that their daughter bear his wife's name. He trained young Theodosia to emulate, and eventually exceed, her mother in mind and grace. "The happiness of my life depends on your exertions," he told her, "for what else, for whom else do I live?"

Theo was eleven years old when her mother died. Burr's careful planning served to assuage his melancholy at the passing of his wife. (Enemies charged that he was in the company of a prostitute at the time of her death.) Young Theodosia, plump and pretty, with insight and humor far beyond her years, became the mistress of Richmond Hill. She served as her father's hostess at dinner parties, entertaining nobility, kings of industry, and powerful politicians of both parties. She became internationally famous for her poise and accomplishments. To be invited to Richmond Hill in the 1790's was deemed as great an honor as attendance at a European court. The bitterest of Burr's enemies, even Hamilton, were entranced by Theo as each year she grew more beautiful.

The most important gatherings at Richmond Hill, however, took place not at the dinner table but long after Theodosia was tucked away for the night. These were the frequent meetings between Aaron Burr and a group of earnest gentlemen who were not on the official guest list: Grand Sachem William Mooney; Sachem Matthew Davis; attorney William Van Ness and his brothers John and Cornelius; the Swartwout brothers—John, Robert, and Swendon; and Burr's stepson John Prevost. All were active members of the Tammany Society. This was the Tenth Legion of Tammany, or Aaron Burr's "little band." They formed the cadre, referred to by present-day machines as "the boys," directly responsible to the Boss, always trustworthy in their accounts of intermediary dealings.

"Versed in the art of hocus-pocus," an unfriendly journalist wrote of Burr, "while sitting in his state room waiting the entrance of his political tools into the anti-chamber, his mandates fly through the union . . ." Through these "tools," Burr handed down instructions to the Tammany braves who convened in a less ostentatious environment —the "Long Room," a dimly lit hall attached to Abraham "Brom" Martling's Tavern at the corner of Nassau and Spruce (the "Pig Pen," Federalists called it). The purpose of all Burr's edicts was to whip the Society into a cohesive political team. For his ministrations, which became an open secret, Burr was attacked in the press as "exercising an amiable superintending care over the poor ignorant multitude," a phrase in which any successful Boss would take great pride.

Burr developed a technique which is still used by well-managed party organizations, particularly in big-city political clubs, and perhaps most strikingly by union committees for President Truman's upset victory in 1948. He maintained an elaborate card index of all voters in the City, containing their political histories, states of health, idiosyncrasies, how best to approach them, how to make sure they arrived at the polls. The one drawback was that the file did not have enough cards to suit Burr. Most of the workers, being tenants, were not entitled to vote. The obvious remedy was to convert them into property owners. Burr called upon affluent Democrats to finance their political brothers in the purchase of land as joint tenants, with legal ownership of separate parcels.

This was the maneuver that forever changed the nature of American politics. To accomplish it, however, Burr needed more money than individual contributions would raise. Alexander Hamilton had established a "national bank" with the Federal Government as majority stockholder. Apart from the deeper issues thus raised between Hamiltonism and Jeffersonism, this measure, passed by the Federalist Congress, enabled Hamilton as Secretary of the Treasury to oversee the banks in New York State. The Federalists thereby gained enormous political power. They refused to issue any new bank charters, and they added many Anti-Federalist merchants to their roster of supporters by refusing them credit unless they backed Federalist candidates.

Jefferson was unable to halt these inequities on a national scale, but Aaron Burr brought about a substantial coup in New York State. New York City was plagued by bad water and yellow fever. To meet the crisis, Burr steered through the State Assembly a bill establishing the new Manhattan Company, chartered by the Legislature to supply safe water in greater quantity. The legislators acted quickly after heavy pressure from all but morticians for speedy action. In their haste they overlooked a sleeper clause in the bill providing for a branch of the Manhattan Company which could undertake banking functions. For the first time, bank loans could be made to Anti-Federalists by a non-federal bank.

Nurtured by dollars, the Democratic organization grew spectacularly in New York City. In the old Federalist neighborhoods, the aristocrats suddenly awoke to find land-owning Democrats all around them, organized in precinct groups, well-furnished with leaflets, posters, and speakers, canvasing house-to-house for more money and votes. The men in the Tammany Pig Pen, now citizens of property, fanned out into the City's seven wards to establish campaign headquarters for the Jefferson-Burr ticket.

Confident that the City was now all but in his pocket, Aaron Burr put out feelers to the Federalist friends he had cultivated upstate. He needed them more than he had realized, for to his dismay he found that outside the City the Democrats were split far apart. Burr had been depending on the Livingstons, his former patrons, whose hatred of Hamilton and the Schuylers was now implacable. But the Livingstons had renewed their old feud with the Clintons, now that George Clinton was out of power. Quarrels had sprung up between other important factions of the party as well.

With the odds overwhelmingly against conciliation, the unification of the New York Democratic Party by Aaron Burr in 1800 emerges as one of the exceptional feats in political party history, an accomplishment which Senator Robert Kennedy hoped to duplicate in the 1960's. To achieve it, Burr banked on the temperament of Alexander Hamilton, the adversary he had studied closely over the years. He waited cautiously for Hamilton to draw up the Federalist ticket for the new State Legislature which would name New York's Presidential electors. Hamilton feared that if Jefferson and his New York ally were to win, the cause of Federalism, with the nation still in embryo, would be dealt a devastating blow, and he himself would lose all influence. It was an understandable act of desperation, then, that he placed on his slate for the Legislature not the most prominent Federalist leaders in New York, but loyal, lackluster followers who could absolutely be depended upon to vote against Jefferson and Burr. John Adams described Burr's reaction to this decision: "Burr, who had friends in all circles, had a copy of this list brought to him immediately. He read it over, with great gravity folded it up, put it in his pocket, and, without uttering another word, said, 'Now I have him all hollow.' "

Standing before the party workers in a meeting place on William Street, Aaron Burr read his own ticket for the State Legislature. It was the calculated risk that Hamilton had shunned. On it were well-known candidates from all over the State, from every rival branch of the Democratic Party, including a Clinton, a Livingston, a Tammany choice, and others not even on speaking terms, many of questionable loyalty to Burr. As Burr began reading, gasps of surprise greeted the names, and then, as he finished, the room resounded with cheers. The Boss had done the impossible. As in all organizations where the Boss has earned the faith of the rank-and-file, the nominations passed without a dissenting vote.

On Tuesday, April 29, 1800, the polls opened in New York City for the election which would be crucial for Jeffersonian democracy, as well as for Alexander Hamilton, Aaron Burr, and Tammany Hall. During the three days of voting, Burr prodded his Tammany aides to turn out the City vote. Hamilton, mounted on a white charger, galloped furiously between the polling places, urging on the Federalist forces. At twilight on Thursday the polls closed. Aaron Burr's ticket had carried New York City, the neighboring rural areas, and enough upstate votes to capture both houses of the State Legislature. A slate of New York electors was guaranteed for the first Democratic President. It was a stunning defeat for the long powerful Federalists. The United States Senate adjourned in consternation.

From the viewpoint of the Federalists, many of whom believed Thomas Jefferson to be an anarchist, it was nothing less than a national emergency. "The Democrats," Chief Justice John Marshall wrote, "are divided into speculative theorists and absolute terrorists. With the latter I am disposed to class Mr. Jefferson." Philip Schuyler charged that Jefferson was "pervaded with the mad French philosophy." Burr's always efficient espionage network came upon a letter from Hamilton to Governor John Jay urging him to reconvene the New York Legislature, under the lame-duck Federalists, to deprive the new Legislature of the right to choose electors because of "the extraordinary nature of the crisis." Hamilton's strategy was to adopt the Burr proposal, which the legislators had killed, to allow the people to choose the Presidential electors directly. This maneuver was unacceptable to Governor Jay ("It would not become me"). Next, Hamilton tried to dump the Federalist incumbent, President John Adams, fearing that he was too weak a candidate to stand up to Jefferson and Burr. Again Burr's spies intercepted the telling document from the printing shop, even before it had reached Hamilton, and leaked it to the newspapers. Adams forthwith dismissed Hamilton's men from the government and the Federalist Party cracked down the middle.

Under Article II, Section 2, of the United States Constitution, the candidate with the highest electoral vote would be named President, the second highest, Vice-President. This electoral system had resulted in 1796 in the split-party rule of Federalist President John Adams and Democratic Vice-President Jefferson. Each state, under the Constitution, determined its preference. In 1800 New York gave Jefferson its highest total, Burr its second highest. But there was no way of accurately foretelling how the combined totals of all the states would juggle this ticket.

When Pennsylvania split its vote between Jefferson and Adams, Burr had cause for concern. The danger now loomed that Jefferson and Adams would be first and second in the voting, leaving Burr out in the cold as he had been four years before. Burr knew that Jefferson could not deliver the Vice-Presidency. Of the thirty votes that Burr had received in 1796, only one had come from his supposedly strong allies in Virginia. This time he knew he would have to carry the South. He began his campaigning in South Carolina, where first votes looked secure for Jefferson but second votes appeared to be going to a Federalist favorite son. Burr's work paid dividends; South Carolina went to Jefferson and Burr without a wasted ballot. So skillfully, in fact, was Burr maneuvering for the Democratic ticket, it began to appear he had overstepped. There was now the possibility that in addition to beating Adams, he might beat Jefferson too. Burr secured a promise from the Governor of Rhode Island that he would vote for Adams instead of Burr, decreasing chances of a deadlock between Burr and Jefferson. As it turned out, the Governor did not vote at all; his alternate cast his ballot for Burr.

"It is highly improbable that I shall have an equal number of votes with Mr. Jefferson," Aaron Burr wrote to a friend, "but if such should be the result, every man who knows me ought to know that I would utterly disclaim all competition." The convoluted nature of this disclaimer, typically Burritian, gives indication that he was not above answering whatever call might come. Indeed, his Tammany aide William Van Ness, dubbed Burr's *valet de chambre* by one newspaper, was working far harder for Burr than for Jefferson.

The results of the electoral voting were: Aaron Burr—73; Thomas Jefferson—73; John Adams—65. It was the first great victory for the Democrats, brought about, as are so many elections, by a handful of key votes (less than 300 ballots in New York City which Tammany had swung for Burr's State Legislature ticket). At the same time, for Jefferson it was a Pyrrhic victory, perhaps more of an embarrassment than Adlai Stevenson would have faced if in 1952 he had tied with his professional backer, Chicago Boss Jake Arvey. Thomas Jefferson, the Virginia gentlemen and eloquent philosopher of Democracy, was now deadlocked for the highest office in the land with the Boss of Tammany Hall. It was a moment of humiliation he would never forget.

Whether Jefferson or Burr should become the first Democratic President was now a matter for Congress to decide. For Hamilton, who hated both men, the choice was not an easy one, but he concluded that Burr's skill as a politician was more dangerous than Jefferson's moral fervor. If Burr were elected, he predicted, the Presidency would be held by "a man who will possess the boldness and daring necessary to give success to the Jacobin system, instead of one, who for want of that quality, will be less fitted to promote it." But a number of Federalists liked Burr personally and felt him to be relatively moderate, less of a threat than a dedicated theoretician. Some of these were men close to Hamilton and had, in fact, been sent by him to make overtures to Burr. Hamilton explained his initial strategy: Burr "is bankrupt beyond redemption, except by the plunder of his country . . . Yet it may be well enough to throw out a lure for him, in order to tempt him to start for the plate, and then lay the foundation of dissension between the two chiefs."

To Hamilton's surprise this tactic backfired and many Federalists fell to supporting Burr in earnest. Hamilton flooded the mails with letters, using different, often contradictory, approaches. He threatened to withdraw from public life if Burr were elected. He appealed to the strong current of anti-French feeling among Federalists by painting a portrait of a man heavily in debt, promiscuous in private life ("a voluptuary by system"), revolutionary in thought, all symbolized by a corrupt, blood-soaked France.

"I have myself heard him speak with applause," Hamilton wrote, "of the French system, as unshackling the mind, and leaving it to its natural energies." Burr, he said, had quoted in his presence a favorite saying of Napoleon's: "*Les grand ames se soucient peu des petit moraux.*" ("Great souls care little for small morals.") "Will any prudent man," asked Hamilton, "offer such a President to the temptations of foreign gold?" The Boston *Centinel*, one of many Federalist papers which preferred Burr to Jefferson, retorted: "He is the grandson of the dignified Edwards, the great American luminary of Divinity, and a son of (Princeton) President Burr who was also a burning and shining light in the churches." Said Hamilton: "He is as unprincipled

and dangerous a man as any country can boast—as true a Cataline as
ever met in midnight conclave."

   If Burr had deliberately contributed to the deadlock with Jefferson,
once the electoral votes were announced he was reticent to push his
luck. He instructed Tammany Sachem Matthew Davis that the effort
to support Jefferson must be a full one. To Jefferson he wrote, "I set
down as calumny every tale calculated to disturb our harmony." And
a Federalist Congressman noted, "Had Burr done anything for himself,
he would long ere have been President." The fact remains, however,
that Burr did not remove his name from consideration.

   On Wednesday, February 11, 1801, a bitterly cold day in Washington, outgoing Vice-President Thomas Jefferson, in his role as President
of the Senate, read the tied electoral totals to the assembled legislators.
Burr stayed away from the scene, as he did throughout the voting. The
Federalists caucused and decided en masse to support Burr against
Jefferson. The first ballot came at 1 P.M. Burr had 55 votes to Jefferson's 51.

   But a unit rule was in effect which bound each state by the majority vote of its Congressmen, requiring the winner to pick up nine
out of the sixteen states. On this basis, Jefferson had eight states, Burr
six, and two were tied. A number of Federalists heeded Hamilton's
pleas for Jefferson and voted against their own caucus, hoping for a
continued deadlock until a compromise Federalist candidate could
come forward. Balloting proceeded all day and night, twenty-seven
rounds in all with no shifts in strength, until the exhausted Congressmen, at 8 A.M. Thursday, adjourned for a few hours' sleep. They were
back at noon to confirm the first ballot result, and so it continued for
the next four days. One vote would give Jefferson his ninth state.
Three votes were needed by Aaron Burr to become the third President
of the United States. An approach was made to Burr through Hamilton's law partner to see if he would co-operate with the Federalists if
they elected him. He refused.

   In Sidney Kingsley's Broadway drama of 1943, *The Patriots*, Alexander Hamilton and Thomas Jefferson, in idealized characterization,
confer after the twenty-seventh ballot. Hamilton produces documents
alleging that Burr has financial backing from Napoleon and plans to
become a dictator. Out of conscience he offers the Presidency to Jefferson if he will promise not to purge Hamilton's friends in office. The following dialogue ensues:

"JEFFERSON (*He crosses to his desk, crisp and final*): I shall not compromise, General Hamilton. You can do whatever you choose. I cannot compromise on this.

"HAMILTON (*holds out his hand. It is shaky.*): Since the fever took me, I can't hit the side of a barn with a pistol. Burr is cool as a snake, and one of the best shots in America. I've fought him for five years now. If I cross him in *this*—he will challenge me. I have no doubt of that. I am a dead man already. But at least you are honest. I shall urge my friends to break the deadlock. You will be President. Your victory is complete."

Although poetic license assists a compelling scene, the hard truth is that, unlike Burr, Jefferson did indeed make concessions to the Federalists, and on the 36th ballot, taken Monday, February 17, a current of excitement swept through the legislative chamber when a Vermont Congressman broke the deadlock by withholding his vote. The Presidential election drew to a close as two states tied, four went to Aaron Burr, and ten to Thomas Jefferson.

The Federalist floor leader, James Bayard, was angered at Burr's refusal of Federalist offers: "Burr has acted a miserable paltry part. The election was in his power, but he was determined to come in as a Democrat, and in that event would have been the most dangerous man in the community." But Bayard, in a letter to Hamilton, paid unwitting tribute to Burr's fidelity by attacking his lack of "political skill": "The means existed of electing Burr but this required his cooperation. By deceiving one man (a great blockhead), and tempting two (not incorruptible), he might have secured a majority of the States. He will never have another chance of being President of the United States; and the little use he has made of the one which has occurred, gives me but an humble opinion of the talents of an unprincipled man."

Bayard's prophecy, at least, was correct. Burr had reached the pinnacle of his national influence, though he would rise higher in notoriety. He had frightened Jefferson and could now add the new President to a growing roster of enemies who were jealous of his successes and suspicious of his methods. Hamilton and the Schuylers were now determined to finish Burr with the aid of the fence-jumping Livingstons. Burr held the empty position of Vice-President. The only remaining political support came from his friends in Tammany Hall.

But to Burr's great disappointment, patronage allotted to Tammany was small compared to the crucial vote it had secured for Jefferson. John Swartwout was appointed a Federal Marshal and a few small plums were dispensed to the Burrites. Particularly hurtful was the President's refusal to name Tammany Sachem Matthew Davis as Naval Officer in the New York Customs House, "the only request I have ever made," in Burr's words to Jefferson. The appointment went to an upstate Congressman. Jefferson funneled all Federal patronage in New York through Governor George Clinton, who had returned to office in the Democratic landslide of 1800 and was grooming his nephew DeWitt to take over the State. DeWitt Clinton, newly elected as Senator, viewed Burr as his principal rival in this quest for leadership. The Clintons froze the Burrites out of State jobs as well.

To sustain his organization, the Boss must be able to deliver the votes to the candidates and the jobs to the party faithful who produce the votes. Some Tammany supporters who had followed Burr as a route to power and cash felt betrayed and became his enemies. Money for the Burr organization was as difficult to come by as patronage. Because of debts, Burr was forced to sell his stock in the Manhattan Company, and DeWitt Clinton maneuvered Burr and John Swartwout off the company's board of directors. It is a reflection on Burr's powers of personal persuasion that, with little money or patronage at his command, he was successful in keeping most of his Tammany followers from the blandishments of the Clinton-Livingston forces. He prevailed upon Mayor Edward Livingston to appoint his stepson as City Recorder but he received little else.

Jefferson, while formally expressing regrets that Burr's talents could not be used in the cabinet, allowed him no duties other than the constitutional function of presiding over the Senate. Burr was snubbed by the Virginia Democrats and Northern Anti-Federalists he had helped weld together for the election. They were convinced that he had sought the Presidency for himself. "Little or no consequence is attached to him in the general estimation here," Senator DeWitt Clinton wrote, "and he will soon appear to every age in his true colors."

As a result of the Jefferson-Burr deadlock, Burr's circle of friends in the capital now included more Federalists than Democrats. At a Federalist banquet commemorating Washington's birthday, Burr made a surprise appearance to toast "The Union of all Honest Men!" Informed of this conciliatory gesture in the enemy camp, Hamilton wrote to a fellow Federalist, "If the story be true, 'tis a good thing, if we use it well. As an instrument, the person will be an auxiliary of some value; as a chief, he will disgrace and destroy the party."

An intensive campaign of vilification was launched in the press by Burr's enemies, seeking to purge him from the Democratic Party. Leading the attack was the New York *American Citizen*, edited by James Cheetham, an immigrant whom Burr had helped start in the newspaper business but who was now allied with DeWitt Clinton. Cheetham attacked the Burrite faction in Tammany as "the little band of disappointed office-seekers—wretched in talents—worse in principle —and most of them destitute of all the attributes of respectability."

Burr issued no public reply to a long series of broadsides, but he did find it necessary to establish the New York *Morning Chronicle*, a largely ineffectual journal under the editorship of Washington Irving's brother Peter, a man of grace and good humor whose refutations of the attacks on Burr lacked the ferocity to which readers were accustomed. The only widely read publication on Burr's behalf was a sensational pamphlet by "Aristides" (pseudonym for Tammany's William Van Ness), a savage diatribe against the Clintons and the Livingstons.

New York City's Democratic Party suffered the first in a long series of bitter splits. It was the start of the great New York Democratic sport of battling other Democrats; struggles with Federalists, Whigs or Republicans have never seemed to have the same appeal. Tammany sent its Burrite delegation to the party's City Convention in 1802 with the intention of assuming control. Burr pushed for a nominating committee of twenty-one men, three from each of the City's seven wards. His assumption was that he could win a majority of the seats. Mayor Livingston and the Clintons favored forty-nine members, seven from each ward, in order to diminish the power of the Burrites. It was this plan that won. Burr's Tammany faction won only a dozen seats on the committee. When the committee met to choose a mayoral candidate, it was immediately broken up into Burr and Clinton wings. DeWitt Clinton won the nomination for Mayor and was elected.

Early in 1804, Vice-President Burr received the news that he was to be dumped from the Democratic national ticket and replaced by George Clinton. Jefferson wrote in his memoirs that he was approached soon after by Burr for a government appointment but turned him down flatly. On the brink of being shoved completely off the political stage, Burr worked desperately to construct a maverick State organization, building on his narrowing Tammany-based Democratic support in the City and nearby counties plus scattered upstate Federalist allies. On the weekend of February 18, a rump convention of insurgent New York Democrats met to nominate Aaron Burr for Governor. The following Monday the Clinton organization convened to name as their candidate Morgan Lewis, Chief Justice of the State Supreme Court, brother-in-law of Robert Livingston, a Princeton classmate of Burr's, and an early member of Tammany.

The ensuing campaign was unparalleled in invective, though never between the principals. The *American Citizen* called Burr "a disgraceful debauchee who permitted an infamous prostitute to insult and embitter the dying moments of his injured wife." (This charge, referring to Burr's absence from home when his wife died, was never proven and never denied.) The public was also reminded of Burr's "treachery" in the election of 1800. The 12th Amendment, specifying "distinct ballots" for President and Vice-President, was adopted after its earlier introduction in the Senate by DeWitt Clinton. It was reported that Vice-President Burr trembled as he read the proposed amendment to the Senate. The press also carried the first public utterance of Hamilton's "despicable opinion" of Burr: "He is a dangerous man and ought not to be trusted." Hamilton, now dwarfed by Jefferson in the nation, was determined to kill off Burr and regain influence in the Federalist Party. His main effect was to discourage Federalists from defecting to Burr in the State election.

In New York City, Burr ran up a narrow plurality to reach a statewide total of 22,000 votes. But Morgan Lewis swept the upstate areas, taking a total of about 30,000 votes. It was Aaron Burr's last election. He was forty-eight years old. Four times he had been blocked from important offices: Minister to France, Brigadier-General of the Army, President of the United States, and now Governor of New York. The prime agent in all these defeats had been his old courtroom rival Alexander Hamilton.

William Van Ness of Tammany Hall entered the Manhattan home of Alexander Hamilton on Monday, June 18, 1804, and silently handed him a message from Burr. The letter, which attached clippings of Hamilton's published opinion of Burr's character, requested full retraction. In replying through Van Ness, Hamilton inquired what specific charges Burr had in mind. Burr answered in part: ". . . political opposition can never absolve gentlemen from the necessity of rigid adherence to the laws of honour and the rules of decorum. I neither claim such privilege nor indulge it in others." He asked for a general withdrawal of "expressions derogatory to the honour of Mr. Burr." Hamilton, who had spread too many such expressions among too many acquaintances, could not back down. On June 27, Van Ness transmitted Burr's formal challenge for a secret duel to be waged on the west bank of the Hudson near Weehawken, New Jersey.

The showdown at Weehawken, where Hamilton's eldest son had been killed in a duel three years before, was the climax of one of history's bitterest political rivalries. It had been foreshadowed in violence on several occasions. James Monroe had asked Burr to be his second in a duel with Hamilton which never transpired, thanks to Burr's mediation between the two men. The issue was Monroe's disclosure of an adultery scandal involving Hamilton, full details of which Hamilton then courageously published. Later, Burr's Tammany lieutenant John Swartwout was wounded in a duel over the "Aristides" pamphlet, and Robert Swartwout was wounded by DeWitt Clinton. The only previous duel that Burr himself had fought was with Hamilton's brother-in-law, who fired a shot that missed Burr by inches, then before the second round apologized for his insults to Burr.

On the Fourth of July, 1804, a week before the date set for the Burr-Hamilton duel, the Society of Cincinnati gathered for its Independence Day banquet. Among those in attendance were the Society's New York president, Alexander Hamilton, and Aaron Burr, the Tammany politician who continued his role as Cincinnati gentleman. Others at the gathering reported that Hamilton, in the presence of his enemy, laughed manically throughout the evening and at one point jumped onto the banquet table to render a song. Burr sat silently, his chin resting on his hand, looking straight at Hamilton, as if to take the measure of his nerve. He left early. There was work to do. He sent Theodosia, now the bride of a wealthy South Carolina planter, instructions to burn all papers that could harm his reputation should he be killed ("This is particularly applicable to the letters of my female correspondents"). To Theodosia's husband Joseph Alston, he wrote, "I commit to you all that is most dear to me—my reputation and my daughter."

Early on the morning of July 11, John Swartwout, who had been fired by Jefferson as Federal Marshal because of his loyalty to Burr, awakened Vice-President Aaron Burr in his home. Another member of the Tammany "little band," William "Aristides" Van Ness, who would serve as Burr's second, accompanied his boss in the boat across the Hudson. As soon as they landed on the New Jersey side, Burr and Van Ness shed their coats, cleared away the foliage from the field, and awaited Hamilton. Alexander Hamilton came onto the field shortly before 7 A.M. Burr and Van Ness lifted their hats in salute. Van Ness and Pendleton, Hamilton's second, measured ten paces between the principals and cast lots for choice of position and who would give the word to fire. Pendleton won. The pistols were loaded. Pendleton asked the men if they were ready. Both said yes. Pendleton gave the word to fire. Both men slowly raised their pistols. Burr took aim and fired.

Instantly Hamilton raised up on his toes, turned slightly to the left, fired over Burr's head, then staggered forward, and fell hard to the ground where he lay in convulsions. Burr advanced toward Hamilton with a look of astonishment and regret, but before he could reach him, Van Ness stepped between the two men, concealed Burr's face with an umbrella, and hurried him away so that the attending doctor, who was approaching the field, would not be able to swear to his presence. The physician ran to Hamilton, who was lying in Pendleton's arms. "This is a mortal wound, Doctor," Hamilton said. The bullet had cut through the liver and lodged in the spine.

Alexander Hamilton lay in agony throughout the day and night as the men of Tammany staged a wild celebration at Brom Martling's Tavern. He died at two o'clock the following afternoon. Years later, when Aaron Burr had finished reading Laurence Sterne's *Tristram Shandy*, he told a friend: "Had I read Voltaire less, and Sterne more, I might have thought the world wide enough for Hamilton and me."

"Tammany Hall has never had any toleration for traitors, either national or those professedly working within its own ranks. For mere seceders and factionists breaking away from the organization, on the contrary, there is always a way open to return, if the fight has been an open one and fairly conducted. But when Tammany drops a man for disloyalty to the party that is the end of him. So it proved with that distinguished soldier and early patriot Aaron Burr. . . ."

In these words, Tammany's official historian disowns the Society's first political chieftain. As in all official histories, of course, the attention is less to niceties of truth than to an object lesson of current use to the institution. Burr is berated for "lack of patience to await his time," a gentle reminder to impatient organization men that a good party functionary must wait his turn in line. "Jefferson was chosen," the Tammany historian concludes, "and Tammany had no further use for Aaron Burr."

Although the Clintons and Livingstons had turned on Burr, it was actually three years after Jefferson's election that Aaron Burr and Tammany came to a parting of the ways, not on account of political infidelity but because of public reaction to the death of Alexander Hamilton. Playing on a growing public revulsion to dueling, the Clintons claimed with great effect that as Hamilton fell, Burr acted the part of a stage villain, laughing fiendishly and rubbing his hands with glee. Hamilton was instantly transformed into a beloved martyr. A ballad set to a Scottish tune gained wide popularity: "Oh! wo betide ye, Aaron Burr / May mickle curse upo' ye fa'! / Ye've killed as brave a gentleman / As e'er liv'd in America." Thousands of tearful mourners came to watch Hamilton's burial, complete with military honors by the Society of the Cincinnati and a moving oration by Gouverneur Morris, who recorded in his diary that the job was difficult inasmuch as Hamilton, in his opinion, was born a bastard and died a vain monarchist.

A coroner's jury reported: "wilful murder by the hand of A. B." Burr quickly packed his bags. In a letter to Theodosia, he was ostensibly more concerned about leaving behind a lady love than the harrowing experience he had just survived: "If any male friend of yours should be dying of ennui, recommend to him to engage in a duel and a courtship at the same time." With his Tammany secretary, young Samuel Swartwout, Aaron Burr fled to Georgia. The Sachems of Tammany went into hiding. Tammany Hall, its Boss a killer in flight, fell into that disrepute from which it would never fully recover.

In the South, Burr was greeted by friendly Democrats, frontiersmen anxious to meet the gunman who had slain the symbol of the oligarchy. When the lame-duck Senate opened for business that autumn, Vice-President Aaron Burr made a surprise appearance at the rostrum. "It certainly is the first time," a Federalist Senator observed, "and God grant it may be the last, that ever a man, so justly charged with such an infamous crime, presided in the American Senate. We are, indeed, fallen on evil times." The Democrats in Washington, however, were surprisingly cordial to Burr, and Jefferson sought him out. Several of Burr's relatives suddenly turned up with important appointments in the new territory of Louisiana.

It was not, of course, a matter of friendship. President Jefferson, at odds with the Federalist judiciary under stubborn Chief Justice John Marshall, needed Burr's help to institute impeachment proceedings in the Senate against the judges who were hindering the Administration's power. It was a rash move, more impulsive than the abortive attempt by Franklin Roosevelt, a far more skillful politician, to "pack" the Supreme Court. The initial defendant selected was Justice Samuel Chase, an ill-tempered Adams appointment who had made a practice of waging personal attacks against Jefferson from the bench.

Thomas Jefferson watched approvingly as Burr theatrically decked out the Senate chamber with colorful flags and desk covers for the historic contest between executive and judiciary in the national legislature. But when the impeachment proceedings opened, the President was dismayed at the impartiality which Burr showed from the chair. None of the Senators, in fact, knew whether or not he favored Justice Chase's impeachment. For the second time that Jefferson had to depend heavily on Burr—the first was the election of 1800—he had no idea where he stood. "Against Burr personally," Jefferson said later, "I never had one hostile sentiment. I never indeed thought him an honest, frank-dealing man, but considered him as a crooked gun, or other perverted machine, whose aim or shot you could never be sure of."

Chase was acquitted. Three days later Aaron Burr's term as Vice-President expired and he rose to address the hushed Senate: "This House is a sanctuary; a citadel of law, of order, and of liberty; and it is here—it is here, in this exalted refuge; here, if anywhere, will resistance be made to the storms of political frenzy and the silent acts of corruption; and if the Constitution be destined ever to perish by the sacrilegious hands of the demagogue or the usurper, which God avert, its expiring agonies will be witnessed on this floor."

He spoke calmly and extemporaneously, with little trace of passion, but with an earnestness that deeply affected his colleagues, most of whom had worked against all his ambitions. John Quincy Adams, then Federalist Senator from Massachusetts, recorded that when Burr finished speaking, he immediately stepped down from the rostrum and walked out of the Senate silently and alone. "The whole Senate were in tears," the Washington *Federalist* reported, "it was half an hour before they could recover themselves to come to order." A resolution was unanimously adopted by the Senate praising Burr's "impartiality, integrity, and ability." A Federalist Senator wrote to his son: "This man, but for his vices, might have held the first office in the gift of the Nation. He certainly is an able man—he is ambitious—But he is fallen and I much doubt if he can ever rise again. . ."

Two years later Jefferson instituted the case of the People of the United States against Aaron Burr. The charge was treason. The star government witness was General James Wilkinson, a Princeton classmate of Burr's and the Jefferson-appointed Governor of Louisiana Territory, long suspected by George Washington of being on the Spaniards' payroll. Not until access was gained to papers in the Spanish archives in the 1930's was he exposed as a double-agent, better known to Madrid as Don James Wilkinson. The documents indicated that he originated a plot to invade Mexico in which he apparently tried to enlist Burr's participation. But Exhibit A at the Burr trial was a cipher letter, partly forged, by Wilkinson's own admission, which had been delivered to Wilkinson by John Swartwout, former Scribe of the Tammany Society. The letter announced that Burr was coming down the Mississippi to join forces with Wilkinson.

Wilkinson's response to the letter was curious: he sent Swartwout to Washington in chains; he wrote Jefferson that a force of seven thousand men under Colonel Burr was about to attack New Orleans; he demanded from the Spanish Viceroy a huge sum to defend Mexico from Burr's attack; he prevailed upon Jefferson to issue a Proclamation condemning the "Burr Conspiracy" in order to arouse public opinion; he instituted a reign of terror in New Orleans through his secret police, which served to eliminate some old enemies; he spread panic throughout Louisiana as the mighty Burr forces grew nearer.

The army against which Wilkinson was prepared to "spend my last breath in the cause of my country" consisted of a handful of men, women and children (including Andrew Jackson's seventeen-year-old son), packed into houseboats, some supplied by Jackson, sailing to settle on some Louisiana land that Burr had purchased. In the face of General Wilkinson and the United States Army, the families on the houseboats dispersed. Burr fled through the wilderness on horseback disguised as a frontiersman. Andrew Jackson, as Commander of the Tennessee Militia, was ordered by the White House to arrest

Burr, but he allowed his friend to proceed through Tennessee untouched. In Mississippi, Burr surrendered to civil authorities and was acquitted by a Grand Jury, just as he had been cleared earlier by a Kentucky Grand Jury with the aid of defense attorney Henry Clay. Again he took flight, but he was captured by the Army in Alabama and sent to Richmond, Virginia, for trial with Chief Justice Marshall presiding.

At one point in the Grand Jury sessions preceding the trial, all but two of the jurors were ready to indict the braggart alcoholic Wilkinson rather than Burr. "Wilkinson," said the foreman of the jury, Congressman John Randolph, "is the only man I ever saw who was from the bark to the very core a villain." But Jefferson could not afford to heed the strong sentiment building against the man he had entrusted with the governorship of Louisiana. He needed Wilkinson to destroy Burr, which he hoped would unite the nation behind his Administration. The indictment was brought in under heavy pressure from the President.

From his prison cell Burr wrote calmly to Theodosia in reply to her ardent protestations of his innocence: "You have read to very little purpose if you have not remarked that such things happen in all democratic governments. Was there in Greece or Rome a man of virtue or independence, and supposed to possess great talents, who was not the object of vindictive and unrelenting persecution?" Burr's defense attorney, Luther Martin, reflected this notion in his summation: "Socrates was made to drink the hemlock, and Aristides was banished by the people . . . Jesus Christ himself was crucified by the people."

The final verdict was unsatisfactory to both Jefferson and Burr: "We of the jury say that Aaron Burr is not proved to be guilty by any evidence submitted to us. We therefore find him not guilty." It was an equivocal decision, tantamount to expressing "reasonable doubt" in both directions, and perhaps an accurate summation of the career of Aaron Burr.

At night in Richmond the "Burr Conspirators" were hanged in effigy. Burr and Samuel Swartwout, one of the few remaining loyalists in the Tammany Tenth Legion, fled to Philadelphia under police protection. Whatever had been the exact blueprint for Burr's western adventure, soon after his long ordeal in prison and the courtroom he was back at the drawing board, noting dryly that he now had "a more perfect knowledge of our men." He sent Swartwout to England to seek support for "X," the cipher he designated to Theodosia as the conquest of Mexico, but which emerged as meaning any scheme for empire in which Aaron Burr could emerge as leader. Swartwout's mission failed and he returned to New York to devote himself to Tammany politics, which, as we shall see, proved a good deal more remunerative than his exploits with Aaron Burr.

Burr thereupon embarked for Europe himself. In Britain he was the house guest of his great idol Jeremy Bentham; here, he met two of his admirers: Charles Lamb and Sir Walter Scott. He was also a frequent guest at debtors' prisons and was finally deported by the embarrassed British Government. In Germany he was welcomed by Goethe and the Weimar nobility. But no progress was made with "X." When word reached Burr that Napoleon had spoken in favor of freeing Mexico from Spain, he hurried to Paris where he startled the French diplomatic corps with a variety of proposals, involving, at various times, Mexico, Louisiana, Canada, and the West Indies. The common denominator of all his plans was an alliance between America and France against England and Spain. Napoleon declined. Burr was crestfallen. He had exhausted all possibilities for "X." From Theo he received the advice, "Go to New York. Make your stand there. If you are attacked, you will be in the midst of the Tenth Legion."

It was a romantic notion. With the exception of the Swartwout brothers and Matthew Davis, the Sachems of Tammany no longer acknowledged Aaron Burr. When Theo went to New York to gather support for her father's return, William Van Ness—Burr's second in the Hamilton duel and the Tammany Aristides who had fiercely defended him—refused to see her. To secure appointments in City Hall and Albany, Tammany had split between Mayor DeWitt Clinton and Governor Morgan Lewis. Burr's political isolation was complete. No party, no state, no country wanted him.

After four years of exile Burr finally reached Boston, masquerading as a bewhiskered Frenchman named Adolphus Arnot, without a penny in the pockets of his stylish garments. He tried to sell the rare collection of books he had treasured for a lifetime to his old Boston Federalist friends. All refused him. A reprieve came at last when Harvard President John Kirkland came to his aid and bought the books, enabling Burr to board a ship to New York, captained by a cousin who failed to recognize him. Once in Manhattan, Burr hid in the house of the Swartwout brothers until, assured that no harm would come to

him, he borrowed ten dollars and put up his attorney's shingle outside
a tiny room on Nassau Street. On the first day, to his astonishment,
the room was mobbed; five hundred people in all came to assure him
of their devotion.

Ecstatically, Burr wrote to Theo of his new life's beginning. The
reply came as a stunning blow: Aaron Burr Alston, Burr's eleven-year-
old grandson, "he who was to have redeemed all your glory," was
dead. And Theodosia, overcome with grief, was severely ill. Not yet
thirty, Theodosia packed the private papers which Burr had entrusted
to her and boarded the *Patriot* to sail to New York and join her father. Nearing Cape Hatteras the ship sailed into stormy seas.

It was reported that for months and years thereafter, each day
Aaron Burr walked the Battery, searching the harbor for the first signs
of the ship. He refused to believe that he would never again see his
fondest hope for immortality. Alexander Hamilton, born out of wedlock, dead at forty-seven, left seven children and would have distinguished progeny into our century. For Aaron Burr, grandson of
Jonathan Edwards, there would be not one descendant to do him
honor. That had been his greatest ambition. But the *Patriot* never
arrived.

Chapter 3

Tammany Takes the White House: The Van Buren Regency

> "To Martin Van Buren, the Grand Sachem of the Eagle Tribe—
> the Great Spirit . . . smiles graciously upon the sages and warriors
> of the tribe who aim to elevate their chief in 1836 to the highest
> station in the country."
>
> —A *Tammany toast, 1832*

Among the ebullient well-wishers who greeted Aaron Burr's return to the practice of law there were few who carried political weight. Sachem Matthew Davis and the Swartwout brothers remained as personal friends, but Tammany and most Democrats had turned to greener pastures. Even Burr's old friend Henry Clay, on encountering him in New York one day, passed him by without recognition.

Burr was deeply touched by those who did feel a sense of loyalty and he tendered them all the favors in his power. He worked for the elevation of Andrew Jackson to the Presidency (twelve years before Jackson was finally elected), a lonely campaign in which he vainly sought the support of Theodosia's widower, Governor Joseph Alston of South Carolina: "You owe it to yourself, you owe it to me, you owe it to the memory of the dead." When Luther Martin, Burr's brilliant defense counsel at his treason trial, stumbled onto his door-step one night, penniless and dissipated by drink, Burr took him in and sheltered him until Martin's death at eighty-one.

In his late seventies, Aaron Burr married Madame Eliza Jumel, star alumna of a Providence bordello and the richest widow in New York City. And he continued to practice law. Clients were steered to him by rising young attorneys whom he had assisted during their appren-ticeships. Chief among those who seized this opportunity to repay their old mentor was Burr's most talented and cunning protégé, Mar-tin Van Buren. It was in large part through Van Buren's efforts that Aaron Burr was able to make of his twilight years a productive vocation.

Martin Van Buren, the New York *Tribune* noted, was a "favorite of that wily and unscrupulous politician by whom he was initiated into the system of party tactics of which he was a conspicuous and successful representative." A Southern Senator succinctly described the basic tactic which Van Buren learned from Burr: "He rows to his object with muffled oars." (As another observer put it, "He was the first to make his way into the White House in gumshoes.")

The object of Van Buren's discreet oarsmanship was the Presidency of the United States, a goal which Burr had missed by three votes. Van Buren sought to vindicate what was then called the "Burritian School of Politics," synonymous with shrewd opportunism. He valued his Machiavellian sobriquets—"The Little Magician," "The Red Fox," "The American Talleyrand"—although he would have liked equal credit for political courage. He was a man of great personal integrity with one overriding political conviction—that party rule was the bul-wark of democratic government. To many of his contemporaries, Van Buren's spoils system appeared less a principle than a ruthless method of self-advancement. Not until a quarter-century after his death did historians begin to treat Martin Van Buren as something more than an astute Tammany Boss.

Van Buren learned his first lessons in politics in the rowdy at-mosphere of his father's tavern in Kinderhook, New York, more than a hundred miles north of Martling's Long Room but close in spirit to that Tammany Pig Pen. Abraham Van Buren, a Dutch farmer and tavernkeeper of modest means, was a Revolutionary veteran, an ardent Jeffersonian, the town clerk of Kinderhook, and embroiled in the local politics of the little Rip Van Winkle village on the banks of the Hudson. He encouraged young Martin to study the foibles and issues of humanity in grand abundance at the tavern, but took scant interest in his son's formal education. Martin Van Buren would be one of nine Presidents (among them: Washington, Jackson, Lincoln, and Truman) who never attended college.

As a boy, Van Buren hurried from the village schoolhouse each afternoon to tend bar for his father and eavesdrop on the earnest conversations of sodden Democrats plotting for power. Little escaped him. He was fluent in Dutch and precocious in political understanding. He quit school at fourteen, worked for six years in the office of a Kinderhook attorney, and before he was twenty-one had moved to New York City, met Aaron Burr, tried a case in court (standing on a bench so the jury could see him), participated as a delegate at a political convention, and joined the "Little Band." Van Buren took an instant liking to Burr and was convinced that his political godfather remained a loyal Jeffersonian. Based on his conversations with New York Congressmen, he always believed that Burr had not lifted a finger for his own candidacy in 1800.

Like Burr (and Hamilton) Van Buren was short (five feet six inches), bright-eyed, and erect in bearing. He had Burr's knack for ingratiating friends and straddling political fences, though he was less devious beneath the deferential exterior. He was a warmer human being, which made his intrigues somewhat more palatable to his associates. An affable, red-haired country boy, his polychrome tailoring exposed him as a *nouveau* city slicker: white-duck trousers, snuff-colored broadcloth coat, bright orange tie, pearl vest, and yellow kid gloves. Dressing like a swell has always endeared important politicians to the men of Tammany, particularly when it represents a successful escape from plebeian beginnings. Even as a young man, Martin Van Buren looked the part of a nineteenth-century Tammany Boss.

Most importantly, Van Buren early displayed the politician's meticulous attention to prudence; his loyalty did not embrace political suicide. After serving a year as William Van Ness's legal apprentice, he was formally admitted to the New York bar, thanks to the ministrations of Burr and Van Ness, and returned to practice in his Hudson Valley birthplace. In 1804, as Burr embarked upon his desperate campaign for the governorship, William Van Ness wrote to his former pupil: "Mr. Burr is the intended victim of villainy and persecution against which it is the duty of every friend to sustain him." Van Buren replied: "The support of Col. Burr would not under existing circumstances be proper." Any man who could, at twenty-two, so readily distinguish between personal gratitude and public posture was a young politico to be watched. Burr himself must have been impressed, though hardly overjoyed, at how well his teachings had taken hold.

Another fundamental lesson which Van Buren learned from Burr was a basic mode of operation: influencing Tammany from the outside. With the exception of Burr and Van Buren, the tigers of Tammany have all been members in good standing of the organization, rooted in the politics of New York City wards and precincts. Even leaders who rose through the ranks to national fame, such as Richard Croker and Carmine DeSapio, lost their power when they neglected to mend neighborhood fences. But Aaron Burr shaped Tammany from his mansion at Richmond Hill, working through a coterie of trusted associates, never himself venturing into the Society's meeting hall. Van Buren was not so reluctant to enter the Wigwam; in fact, he was treated there as an honorary Grand Sachem. Yet throughout his career he preferred to construct his initial power bases—in New York City, in Albany, and in Washington—through a series of regencies. This penchant for rowing with "muffled oars" from a distance was first revealed in his decision to return to the small town of Kinderhook rather than remain with his new masters in the clamorous arena of New York City. With frequent trips back to the City he was able to maintain his Tammany connections without being branded a Burrite.

Had Van Buren stayed in the City, the pressures from his superiors, appeals to gratitude and promises of advancement, might well have been irresistible during the Burr campaign of 1804. Instead, he was able to reject Van Ness's plea from afar and give his support to Morgan Lewis, candidate of the Livingston-Clinton wing of the Democratic-Republican Party, which had become the regular organization. This proved to be a wise move. Morgan Lewis won and Aaron Burr lost all support after the duel with Hamilton in the summer of that year. Van Ness, Burr's second in the duel, was not fit political company so long as the public memory was strong. But Martin Van Buren emerged as a leading Democrat in his home county of Columbia, a Federalist stronghold. He married a local Dutch girl, built a lucrative law practice and, at twenty-five, was appointed County Surrogate. For a decade he remained publicly aloof from the Tammany Society. This, too, proved fortuitous, for Tammany was fast developing a reputation for corruption amidst the hoopla of patriotic rituals.

There was, for example, the grizzly case of the bones at Wallabout Bay. These were the remains of more than eleven thousand American prisoners who had died aboard British ships during the Revolutionary War. The bones were discovered along the marshy shore of Wallabout Bay (site of the Brooklyn Navy Yard) in the vicinity of property owned by Tammany Sachem John Jackson. Recognizing the value of martyrdom, Jackson donated some of his land to Tammany for the erection of a memorial to the war dead, and set about gathering the bones and raising funds for a tomb. With the assistance of his Tammany Brothers, Sachem Jackson managed to collect twenty hogsheads of bones, constructed a suitable vault, but failed to raise enough money for the planned memorial.

It was decided nonetheless to hold a cornerstone-laying ceremony in the hope that the general citizenry would rally behind the project. On April 13, 1808, the braves of Tammany set sail for Brooklyn in thirteen open boats, one for each tribe, each bearing a huge coffin draped in black. Then, through the crowd-lined streets of Brooklyn, the Brothers marched in funereal procession carrying a model of the monument-to-be. On its panels were inscribed mottos calculated to "Remember the British." Tammany youths were symbolically costumed as the Seven Virtues. The bones were locked in the vault after considerable speech-making by the master of ceremonies, Grand Sachem Benjamin Romaine, and numerous City fathers, Congressmen, and military officials.

Romaine finally secured one thousand dollars from the State Legislature to erect the monument. Five years later somebody noticed that the monument was nowhere to be seen. This aroused the curiosity of the frugal legislators, but their investigators were never able to determine what had happened to the money. A gentle breeze of suspicion tended to waft toward Romaine, inasmuch as he had been removed as City Comptroller on charges of stealing land belonging to the people of New York.

Other Tammany Sachems turned out to be equally hazardous risks in the public service. Jonas Humbert, the City Bread Inspector, was forced to resign following accusations that he was extorting fees from subordinates. Collector of Assessments Abraham Stagg, who succeeded Romaine as Grand Sachem, was found to have misappropriated one thousand dollars in City moneys. He later repaid it. Alderman John

Bingham, a Tammany Sachem since 1791, was charged with conveying City land to his brother-in-law and then repurchasing it himself.

Perhaps the most poetic bit of thievery occurred when about one
thousand dollars worth of City supplies, as well as vast amounts of
rum, gin and brandy, unaccountably vanished during William
Mooney's term as Superintendent of the Almshouse. The founder of
the Tammany Society was paid a City salary of one thousand dollars a
year with five hundred dollars expenses for his troubles. An investigation revealed that he had appropriated some four thousand dollars
above this sum to purchase, in his words, "trifles for Mrs. Mooney."
He was fired by Mayor DeWitt Clinton but his brothers in Tammany
rendered him a consolation prize: a return to the office of Grand
Sachem which he had first held twenty-two years before.

The chief result of DeWitt Clinton's efforts to win over Tammany
through patronage was a growing public distrust of his administration.
He was widely attacked as a ruthless spoilsman and opportunist. "The
meekness of Quakerism," Clinton retorted, "will do in religion, but not
in politics." As scandal diminished Tammany's jobs, the Society
joined in the growing righteous furor against Mayor Clinton's methods. As a personality, Clinton was an easy target. He was haughty
and overbearing, of patrician tastes, intolerant of criticism, demanding loyalty from others without offering it in return.

It remained only for positive proof of political treason to convince
the braves that DeWitt Clinton, once the Scribe of Tammany, must
be drummed out of the Society. That evidence came with the news
that Clinton was plotting to run in 1812 against incumbent President
James Madison, a revered founder of the Democratic Party. The braves
angrily assembled in Martling's Long Room to pass a resolution:
DeWitt Clinton "was cherishing interests distinct and separate from
the general interests of the Democratic party, and determined to establish in his own person a pernicious family aristocracy; devotion to his
person had been in a great measure made the exclusive test of merit,
and the only passport to promotion." The Tammany Brothers concluded that if Clinton would not support Madison for a second term,
they "could no longer consider him a member of the Democratic
Party."

DeWitt Clinton defected to run on a Federalist-backed "Peace
Party" ticket against President Madison. The Tammany Society helped
carry New York City for the President, but with the upstate Federalist

vote Clinton won New York State and the North, with the exception of Vermont and Pennsylvania. Had he won Pennsylvania, he would have been the fifth President of the United States.

In that same election of 1812, thirty-year-old Martin Van Buren campaigned against the bankers and landlords and was elected to the State Senate (by 200 votes out of 20,000 cast) over Edward Livingston, former Mayor of New York. Once in office he denounced Clinton as a party traitor and made clear his aim to pursue a common goal with Tammany: the political extermination of DeWitt Clinton. For the first and only time in its history, Tammany looked to an upstate Democrat for its leader. "Bucktails," the nickname for the Sachems who wore bucks' tails in their hats at Society gatherings, was the new name applied to all Democrats who supported Van Buren in his fight against Clinton. The course of that struggle would run until Clinton's death.

Martin Van Buren was the first political leader to dominate Tammany since the fall of Aaron Burr ten years before. The New York Democratic Party, which Burr had united in the State Legislative elections of 1800, was now hopelessly splintered into factional followings of the Clintons, Livingstons, and Burrites. Governor Morgan Lewis, a Livingston man who broke with Clinton during his term of office, attempted with little success to bring Tammany into his dominion. His New York City supporters met with the Sachems in Martling's Long Room for a great feast and offered toasts to a mutual hatred of DeWitt Clinton. Some of the Burrites, however, preferred to bury the tomahawk temporarily in exchange for City jobs from Mayor Clinton.

An attempt was also made at a secret meeting between the leaders of the Burr, Lewis, and Clinton groups to forsake their differences and rally behind the Tammany banner. This alliance, too, was stillborn. On another occasion DeWitt Clinton went so far as to seek out Burr's secretary John Swartwout, with whom he had once fought a duel. His appeal for Swartwout's support was fruitless.

Adding to the Democratic disunity was the changing complexion of the Tammany Society itself. Aaron Burr's efforts to enfranchise the braves by converting them into property-owners had been all too successful. Tammany members became solid, solvent, thoroughly middle-class citizens with a decided disinterest in expanding suffrage to the

landless, particularly the foreign born. Just as in our day a number of
trade unions have erected barriers to Negroes, Tammany was the
classic example of the private liberal institution seeking to monopolize
hardwon gains. And just as the civil rights movement relentlessly
pushes ahead today, so was the tide of early nineteenth-century immigration a force too powerful to resist.

DeWitt Clinton recognized this as a young Senator when he introduced a bill to cut the naturalization period from fourteen to five
years. But Tammany stood by its constitutional prohibition against full
membership for the foreign born. It viewed newcomers, mostly Catholics from Ireland and the German Rhineland, as the vanguard of a
popish plot to conquer the New World. The Society also inaugurated
"Buy America" campaigns to eradicate the influx of foreign goods.

At the beginning of the nineteenth century there were less than
60,000 New Yorkers living in the City's seven voting wards. Moving
north in Manhattan there was a gradual decline in economic status.
The wealthiest of the city-dwellers lived along the Battery, the Tammany *nouveau riche* several blocks above them. At Reade Street, near
City Hall, the transition began to the squalid slums. Into this northern
area (of what is now downtown Manhattan) streamed thousands of
poor, uneducated Irishmen who posed a threat to the wage levels of
American-born workers. Here was born the traditional American rationale for immigration restrictions—fear of labor competition.

The Germans, though largely skilled and better-off economically on
arrival, spoke a strange tongue and clung to odd customs. The "in-
dolent and effeminate" Italians and Spaniards came under attack in
an early anniversary Long Talk by Tuenis Wortman, a celebrated
Tammany intellectual. In a learned philosophic discourse on "The
Influence of Social Institutions upon Human Morals and Happiness,"
Wortman argued, to the pleasure of the Wigwam, that systems of
jurisprudence and forms of government are the determinants of ethnic
character.

This was the premise on which Tammany was forced to rely
when, after two decades of stubborn resistance, the Society supported
Patrick McKay, the first Irish State Assemblyman. The premise was
simple: if they bother you too much, teach them the right brand of
politics. The Irish immigrants, instantly antagonistic to the pro-British
Federalists, gravitated naturally to the Democratic Party. Perhaps,
Tammany Sachems reasoned, McKay's election would serve to pacify

the ruffians until they were civilized enough to become good Tammany Democrats a few generations hence.

The hope was shortlived. On the night of April 24, 1817, hundreds of wrathful Irishmen massed at Dooley's Tavern and marched down to the Tammany Wigwam. This time they would not be satisfied with a token Assemblyman on the Tammany ticket. They wanted Thomas Addis Emmett, an Irish patriot exiled to New York by the English, nominated for a seat in the United States Congress. The Wiskinkie hastily barred the doors but the Irishmen smashed through the windows and invaded the convention hall. In the melee that followed, furniture was broken into bits and scores of Tammany braves were beaten senseless. Total destruction of the tribe was imminent when old-stock reinforcements arrived to rout the Irish back to Dooley's. Thomas Addis Emmett, a brilliant attorney and orator, eventually became State Attorney General. Tammany had been served fair warning that the days of Protestant domination were numbered.

For the purists within the Society, the prospect of initiating naturalized citizens was the climax in a whole series of blows to the original Tammany mystique. The Wigwam which was nearly demolished by the Irish was not the dark, smoky Long Room in Brom Martling's Tavern. It was a five-story building at the corner of Nassau and Frankfort Streets, officially called the Tammany Hotel (bedrooms on the upper floors were rented). This Hall (which headquartered Tammany from 1812 to 1868) had been a dream of the Society since its inception. Ten dollar shares for its construction were authorized in the early bylaws. This was raised to sixteen dollars with the issuance of four thousand shares for the construction of "A Hall with a View" by the Tammanial Tontine Association in 1792. Other funds were raised by lotteries, by Sachem Jacob Barker, a wealthy shipbuilder and banker, and by the Tammany Building Committee, headed by Sachem Matthew Davis, Burr's closest friend. The new Tammany Hall (later known as the Sun Building) opened with appropriate Indian ceremonies led by Sachem Abraham Valentine, a Tammany police magistrate who lost his job on charges of stealing money from prisoners.

Once ensconced in their new quarters, however, some of the braves were nostalgic for the convivial barroom atmosphere which had prevailed in Brom Martling's little wooden inn. A certain congeniality and informality in the game of politics was forever gone from their lives. This loss was compounded when the Tammany leaders, in keeping with their prestigious surroundings, and bowing to public opinion in the aftermath of Indian aid to the British in the War of 1812 (Tammany had contributed three generals), began to mute the Indian motif in public ceremonies. The travesty was effected despite strong pleas from charter members, some of whom resigned in protest. "We see that the Society is rapidly diminishing," Cheetham's *American Citizen* reported, "and that the more civilized of the savages are beginning to associate with tamed and tutored men." In fact, Tammany's membership was increasing, but the Society was searching for respectability as a political organization.

A more significant heresy occurred when the Society accepted for membership fifty Federalists, including the entire Livingston clan (four Livingstons, including Robert and Edward, were already members). The older Anti-Federalist braves saw no reason to welcome opposition party members, who were specifically denied eligibility by the Society's constitution. But the political sagacity of the Sachems prevailed over the patriotic fundamentalists. Tammany was now, first and foremost, a party institution. In the mass defection of aristocratic opponents it was pleased to acknowledge the death rattle of the Federalist Party in New York State, a development which had been inevitable since the passing of both enemy chieftains, Alexander Hamilton and Philip Schuyler, in 1804.

By 1815, Tammany Hall had become the headquarters of the Democratic-Republican Party in New York City. The party's General Committee was ruled by a directorate interlocked with the Society's Council of Sachems. Acting on the Sachems' recommendations, the General Committee met in Tammany Hall to nominate City candidates. It was at a series of such meetings that DeWitt Clinton was denied renomination as Mayor and as Lieutenant-Governor (a post he had held simultaneously with the mayoralty). Clinton retired to Long Island to till his farm, drown his sorrows in drink, and contemplate an idea he had been toying with for five years—the digging of a great canal between the Hudson River and Lake Erie.

The Tammany Bucktails successfully backed a reform Governor who appointed their leader, State Senator Martin Van Buren, as Attorney General. In this post Van Buren, at thirty-two, won national attention as a skilled prosecutor (he tried General William Hull for the "treasonable" surrender of Detroit in the War of 1812) and as the consummate "Man of the Party." Van Buren deplored the fact that "the country was overrun with personal factions" and called for "two great parties, arrayed against each other in a fair and open contest. . . ." Van Buren could be an equivocator on social issues but never on party principles. He believed that battle lines and loyalties must be clear-cut. The attainment of Jeffersonian Democracy would be impossible, in his view, until the establishment of true party discipline. Thus Van Buren became the first American politician openly to reconcile the democratic philosophy with the political machine. To indicate the force of his intentions, he offered a wondrous creature known as the Albany Regency.

The Albany Regency was the first full-fledged political machine in the United States. It was designed to perpetuate the continuity of Democratic power in New York State and to carry that influence into the national party councils, regardless of who might come and go in the governorship and the mayoralty. From its urban power base of Tammany to party headquarters in the rural western counties of New York State, the Regency maintained its influence for thirty-five years, through the regime of Governor Horatio Seymour and until the election of Mayor Fernando Wood, Tammany's first avowed City Boss.

The pattern of patronage and control established by the Regency was the forerunner of the Tammany structure solidified half-a-century later by "Honest John" Kelly. Everything hinged on commanding obedience at the lowest level. Van Buren traveled throughout the State putting into operation party headquarters in every county and hamlet. Essentially this was the embryo of the County Committee system, with little Tammany Halls in every locality. The Albany Regency was the State Committee and Van Buren the State Chairman.

The Regency was crucial to Martin Van Buren's success in weathering the strong political comeback of DeWitt Clinton, and maintaining control in New York during the years of his absence as Senator and President. The three basic building blocks of the Regency were patronage, party newspapers, and the legislative caucus. The structure stood because of Van Buren's success in assembling a brilliant and conscientious staff of lieutenants who were fanatically dedicated to the principle of party discipline. Among them was a group of talented New Englanders who migrated to New York and were recruited by Van Buren, including young John Adams Dix of New Hampshire (who finally reached the governorship in 1875 at the age of seventy-five). The most publicized of Van Buren's intimates in the Regency were two other future governors, both natives of Massachusetts: Silas Wright, who began his political career as a twenty-one-year-old Congressman, and the prominent Troy attorney and newspaper editor, William Marcy, namesake of Boss William Marcy Tweed.

The Regency's record in opposing political corruption was generally a good one, but its fierce partisanship became so notorious that Marcy was driven to defend its policies on the Senate floor during a debate with Henry Clay: "It may be that the politicians of New York are not so fastidious as some gentlemen are. They boldly preach what they practice. When they are contending for victory, they avow their intention of enjoying the fruits of it. If they fail, they will not murmur. If they win, they expect to reap all the advantages. They see nothing wrong in the rule that to the victors belong the spoils of the enemy." Silas Wright in an equally candid if less memorable statement, confirmed the Regency's forthright policy on appointments: "Give them to good and true and useful friends who will enjoy the emolument, if there is any, and who will use their influence to our benefit. This is the long and short of the rule by which we act."

Allegiance to the Regency was established by exploiting at the local level the vast appointive powers of the Legislature and, in good years, the Governor. Even an unfriendly Democratic Governor had to appoint Regency men to maintain a semblance of party unity; they in turn hired local party workers on their staffs. The judiciary was a constant source of strength to the Regency. Its personnel was dictated right down to the justices of the peace, who wielded great influence with the rank-and-file voters. In evaluating a candidate's qualifications for the judiciary, the Regency placed one criterion above all others: party loyalty. This tradition is still very much alive in New York, where most judgeships are awarded as a form of political gratitude, and justices of the peace do not even need a law degree.

Any Regency appointee who had questions about the current party line was urged to consult William Marcy's newspaper in Troy, Tammany's *National Advocate*, or the *Albany Argus*, a vital organ of the body politic skillfully edited by Edwin Croswell, whom Van Buren had lured from the *Catskill Recorder*. The *Argus* was to the Regency as *Pravda* and *Izvestia* to the Politburo. One could be certain in scanning its columns that doctrines emanated from the top and were to be accepted accordingly. Van Buren considered it a primary weapon in the quest for party unity. With the *Argus* in circulation, he said, the

Democratic Party could "endure a thousand convulsions"; without it, "We might as well hang our harps on the willows." There was little cause for him to fear that the *Argus* would fold. Its circulation was ensured by anxious party workers throughout the State; its advertising was bolstered by the insertion of the State's voluminous legal notices.

In addition to press and patronage, the Regency's success was all but guaranteed by the State Legislative caucus. This was Van Buren's method of securing party-line votes on every issue. With the decline of the Federalist Party, the Democrats dominated both the State Senate and Assembly. There was, however, a vast feeling of indifference among the lopsided majority toward their party. The legislators' loyalties were to various economic interests, geographical districts, and splinter group leaders. With the institution of the legislative caucus, the Bucktails whipped the dissident senators and assemblymen into line for a public show of unity. The Tammany-Van Buren wing of the party outnumbered the Clintonians and pressed for a vote in caucus. Once the vote was taken, the party was then bound by decision of the caucus, factional squabbles ended, and a unanimous party vote ensued on the floor of the Legislature for the bill or candidate in question. Should any legislator miss a meeting of the caucus, he could simply follow the guiding principle of decision-making as enunciated by Regency philosopher Silas Wright: "Act as your judgment and the advice of friends shall dictate."

Before each caucus the leaders of the Regency would generally meet with a select group of Bucktail legislators, including Tammany Sachem Ogden Edwards, to work out policies in advance. These councils of war took place in New York City, Albany, Kinderhook, or sometimes in nearby New Lebanon at the home of Van Buren's friend Elam Tilden, Postmaster and local Democratic power. Van Buren grew extremely fond of Tilden's son Samuel who showed a precocious interest in politics much as had young Martin Van Buren. "Sammy" Tilden was allowed to eavesdrop on the important adult talk in his father's parlor.

As Van Buren worked to build a bright future for his party, he was haunted by a shadow from the past—DeWitt Clinton, who had a dream of far more appeal to the people than a party machine. The Erie Canal was more than a patronage empire. It would mean thousands of jobs for laborers and seamen, fattened coffers for merchants and traders, a way West for restless settlers, and a new boost to the entire economy of upstate New York and the port city of Manhattan.

In 1816 Clinton came out of political retirement to push the Canal scheme at the most opportune moment: the Bucktail Governor Daniel Tompkins was running for Vice-President with James Monroe. Monroe and Tompkins won, the Governor resigned to move to Washington, and Clinton took his case to the people. Van Buren and the party leaders were willing to push for the Canal but, over the strong opposition of Tammany, they had to suffer Clinton in the bargain. Clinton won the governorship, and the State Legislature immediately appropriated seven million dollars to begin construction of the first Canal section between Utica and Rome. Within eight years the Canal would be open along the 363 miles from Troy to Buffalo, built by sweat and muscle at a cost of twenty thousand dollars per mile.

DeWitt Clinton's triumphant scheme (which Van Buren had the political sense to support in the State Senate) aroused the wrath of Tammany, that institution of prophets which scorned the Canal as "a ditch to bury its author in." The clash with the Governor, who now rode a new wave of popularity, would have to be re-directed toward a revival of anger at aristocratic rule. In 1818 Tammany legislator Ogden Edwards introduced a resolution calling for a constitutional convention to abolish the old Council of Appointment, the Governor's patronage fount which the Albany Regency sought to supplant. Clinton withheld approval of the convention, knowing it would be controlled by the Bucktails. By the time he agreed to it a year later, Tammany was agitating for a convention with far more sweeping powers to end discriminatory suffrage, to redistrict the State Senate, and to do away with the Council of Revision, a Federalist relic which held veto power over all legislation.

"I am in favor of a convention properly and fairly called," the Governor said, "but not for one got up precipitately for bad purposes, under bad auspices, and with a view to shake society to its foundations in order to sustain bad men." Van Buren and Tammany, seeking a critical victory over Clinton, aroused public opinion to the dangers of continuing government under a document established by the Federalist oligarchs. The Clintonians were maneuvered into an agreement to a referendum. The vote was overwhelmingly in favor. The only remaining question was whether radical or temperate reform would prevail in rewriting the State Constitution.

On August 28, 1821, the delegates gathered in the spacious Assembly chamber of the State Capitol. U.S. Vice-President Daniel Tompkins was chosen president of the convention. As he peered down from the rostrum, he saw three forces arrayed before him. On one side were the radical Democrats led by Peter Livingston and Erastus Root, whose tirades put the fear of the guillotine into the privileged classes. The conservatives—Clintonians and Federalists—were guided by Stephen Van Rensselaer, the erudite Chancellor James Kent of the New York Court of Chancery, and Elisha Williams, a brilliant trial lawyer who had been Van Buren's chief courtroom rival in Columbia County.

Caught between these two elements was Tammany Hall, the reluctant dragon in the struggle for the rights of new Americans. It was inevitable that Tammany, with its own privileged class of newly prosperous mechanics and shopkeepers to protect, and yet with its craving for a new source of power from the immigrant masses, should become the spokesman for moderate reform. Van Buren, speaking softly and smiling benignly, led the Tammany forces, eventually gaining control of nearly all the Democratic delegates, and building a smooth bridge to the moderate Federalists in the camp of Senator Rufus King. Working with the caution and serenity which were his trademarks, Van Buren gradually gathered the entire convention about him.

First target of the reformers was the veto power vested in the Council of Revision, which consisted of the Governor, the Chancellor, and the Supreme Court Justices. The Council of Revision, charged the reformers, was an impediment to social progress and a clear violation of separation of powers. But to the conservatives, the Council was the last stronghold against the radical doctrines of the Jeffersonian Democrats. "I see the axe laid to the root of the tree which our fathers planted, watered and defended," a proud judge declared, "a tree which yielded much good and wholesome fruit, and has long afforded us shade and shelter. I confess, sir, that I witness its destruction with no ordinary emotions."

Van Buren and Tammany Sachem Ogden Edwards led the Bucktails to victory against the Council of Revision, but The Little Magician pulled in the reins before the veto could be abolished altogether. Despite the cry of Peter Livingston's radical wing to "keep the power with the people," Van Buren moved for a compromise, which prevailed: a Governor's veto that could be over-ridden by a two-thirds majority of the Legislature. Having taken a half-step backward, Van

Buren then moved forward quickly to annihilate the Council of Appointment, the oldtime patronage autocracy which gave four State Senators the right to appoint all non-elective officers of the State, including the Mayor of New York City.

The Council of Appointment was replaced by a system of gubernatorial appointments (with legislative confirmation) for officers with state-wide duties, and local control over the selection of local officials. Thus, for the first time, New York City was empowered to elect its own Mayor, although indirectly by appointment of the City Council.

The conservatives, led by Chancellor Kent and Stephen Van Rensselaer, then rallied to protect the Governor's three-year term. The radicals fought for a yearly rotation of the office to assure popular control. Once again Van Buren called for compromise and won it with the approval of a two-year term. (The term was lengthend to four years in 1938.)

The stage was set for the bitterest struggle of the convention on the issue of suffrage. Tammany had already coined the slogan: "We would rather be ruled by a man without an estate than by an estate without a man!" The upstaters, fearful of the City's landless masses, argued that only property-owners are suited to vote and to rule; those who inherit property are free of avarice and have the leisure to develop governmental skills; those who acquire property thereby demonstrate talents befitting proper voters and office-holders.

The prospect of universal manhood suffrage aroused "no ordinary emotions": for the conservatives, a fear of being engulfed by foreigners, and anxiety over the quality of plebeian-controlled government; a fundamental philosophic issue for the uncompromising reformers, who viewed man's right to govern himself as the most precious of divine gifts; and, to Tammany, a potential source of overwhelming political power which could sustain the Democratic machine into the centuries. The stakes were high for all, the decision was a momentous one, and each speaker sought to outdo the last in grandeur or acerbity.

Into this fiery congregation, as it wrestled with the doctrines of Plato, Locke, and Rousseau, came a terse recommendation from the convention's committee on suffrage that the vote should be extended to every white, male, adult citizen with six months residence in his district who either paid taxes, had worked on the public roads, or was a militia veteran. Then Chancellor James Kent rose wearily to deliver what one delegate called "an elegant epitaph of the old constitution":

"By the report before us we propose to annihilate, at one stroke, all property distinctions, and to bow before the idol of universal suffrage. That extreme democratic principle has been regarded with terror by the wise men of every age, because in every European republic, ancient and modern, in which it has been tried, it has terminated disastrously, and been productive of corruption, injustice, violence and tyranny. Dare we flatter ourselves that we are a peculiar people, who can run the career of history exempted from the passions which have disturbed and corrupted the rest of mankind? If we are like other races of men, with similar follies and vices, then I greatly fear that our posterity will have reason to deplore in sackcloth and ashes the delusion of the day."

The radicals smelled victory in the air. "Domineering aristocrats!" Erastus Root shouted. "I trust the old names of Aristocrat and Republican will persist till the former shall be bound to the footstool of the latter!" Root and Livingston proposed that suffrage be extended even beyond the limits of the committee's recommendation. This appealed to Elisha Williams and the shrewder of the Federalists on the theory that the voters would then reject the entire constitution as an absurdity. Van Buren spotted this tactic lurking beneath the oratory of his old courtroom adversary and took him to task on the floor of the convention, thus splitting the Federalist-radical coalition. New amendments and counter-amendments were put forth. By the end of September, the convention was in such confusion that votes taken one day were reversed by the same majority the next. Finally, on October 29, Van Buren and Tammany's Ogden Edwards succeeded in steering the resolution for broadened suffrage through the convention by a vote of almost 2 to 1.

The following year, 1822, the new constitution was approved by the voters. Tammany staged a city-wide celebration with great parades, flag-waving, the firing of artillery, a banquet at the Wigwam, and the ringing of bells sounding the final death knell for the Federalist Party and rule by the well-born. A toast to the future was drunk at a Wigwam banquet: "to the young and rising politician, may integrity and principle guide him."

The results of the new power shift were immediate. Federalists were ousted from their seats of authority in many local communities. Bucktails replaced Clintonians in Albany. DeWitt Clinton, fearing that

Van Buren and Tammany could now defeat him, declined to run again for Governor. New voters flocked to Tammany, giving the Hall control of the City Council, which picked New York's first elective Mayor, William Paulding. As Tammany ruled New York City for the first time, the Albany Regency now reigned supreme in the State. Its creator, thirty-eight-year-old Martin Van Buren, was elected to the U.S. Senate, and departed for Washington as the champion of the new democratic constitution.

For all the zeal of its newly empowered rulers, New York in the 1820's was a city in decay. Streets were strewn with garbage and overgrown with grass. The water supply was polluted. Yellow fever and cholera struck once again. The municipal debt mounted dangerously, while the Tammany councilmen sold off City land to meet the deficits.

Tammany Brothers continued to appear at the center of scandals. Sachem Jacob Barker, who had raised twenty-eight thousand dollars for the construction of Tammany Hall, was indicted in a multimillion dollar stock swindle along with Grand Sachem Matthew Davis and Sachem Henry Eckford, a prominent shipbuilder. Burr's old friend Davis was acquitted, but Barker and Eckford were convicted and fled the country.

Within the Tammany Wigwam, ethnic animosity threatened the Indian comradery of old. Protestants clung to their sachemships in the Irish wards with the same tenacity that Irish district leaders would later display in Jewish and Italian neighborhoods. Anti-Catholic feeling ran high, despite the recognition that the new immigrants were responsible for Tammany's growing hold on the City's politics. Anti-Semitic forces were led by Benjamin Romaine, the Grand Sachem who had consecrated the bones at Wallabout Bay. A particular target of Romaine's was Mordecai Noah, a tall, broad-shouldered Sephardic Jew who was an ardent supporter of Martin Van Buren.

Noah was a prolific playwright, an Hebraist, historian, and active Zionist. He had served as American Consul in Tunis, where he negotiated the release of a group of American sailors captured and enslaved by pirates, but he was removed from his post by then Secretary of State James Monroe on religious grounds. Later he attempted to establish a Jewish state, with himself as chief, on Grand Island in the Niagara River. He called it Ararat, which would indicate that he was not hampered by diffidence, but his scheme went no further than the laying of a cornerstone.

Tammany's attraction for Mordecai Noah may have coincided with his theory that the American Indian was one of the lost tribes of Israel. At any rate, he came to New York City and attracted Van Buren's attention as the editor of the *National Advocate*, a literate, partisan journal which espoused the Tammany cause in general and Martin Van Buren in particular. Van Buren steered Noah's name for Sheriff through the Tammany General Committee, despite a roar of opposition that a Jew should not be placed in a position to hang a Christian. Noah retorted: "Pretty Christians to require hanging, at all."

With Van Buren's assistance, Noah got the job, but in 1822 when his name was placed before the Committee for renomination, Benjamin Romaine and the anti-Semitic faction seized control of the convention and put up a rival candidate. Noah and his supporters rushed from the Hall, claiming that the nomination was already his. The following day he and his opponent both set up campaign headquarters in the Wigwam, a situation that often occurred when the sachems could not agree on a candidate. This time Noah lost, but he remained to become a power in Tammany: the first Jewish Grand Sachem.

While in Washington, Van Buren's dominion over the New York Democratic Party was firm but it could never be absolute. Communication and transportation were slow. And there were times when the impulsive Tammanyites were quite happy that the voice of reason was off in Washington. While Senator Van Buren was acting as campaign manager for Secretary of the Treasury William Crawford, rounding up Capitol Hill support for the 1824 Democratic Presidential nomination, a Tammany-Regency resolution was rammed through the State Legislature in Albany ousting ex-Governor Clinton from his only remaining public office: unpaid member of the Canal Commission.

Van Buren was not consulted for a simple reason: it was a reckless move which he would have immediately blocked. But hatred of Clinton, and fear that he would garner all the credit for the new Canal, compelled the Bucktail legislators to press their luck in an attempt to retire Clinton completely and permanently. The result of their efforts was precisely the opposite.

The Erie Canal had captured New Yorkers' imagination. Tammany called it "Clinton's Folly" but the Irish "canawlers" were making a great dream come true, digging with pick and shovel through rock, sand, and swampland, swigging whiskey from barrels placed along the canal route by local townspeople anxious to move the proceedings another mile ahead. Tammany said that even the Almighty Clinton could not make water run uphill, but the Irish were building locks in their "Canawl." Tammany leaders claimed that enough boat traffic could never be attracted to pay for the building of the Canal, but a fifteen-mile section between Rome and Utica was already a thriving success. Tammany hoped that Clinton would fall on his face in his mighty ditch, but the people of New York State had never, and have never, hoped so hard for one project to succeed.

Outrage swept the State when DeWitt Clinton was fired as Canal Commissioner. In New York City an angry mob of ten thousand assembled to protest the interference of politicians in the people's future. To Van Buren the upshot of the State Legislature's anti-Clinton maneuver was painfully predictable. He himself had gained popularity when Clinton abruptly removed him from the office of Attorney General. Now, too late, he watched the transformation of his rival into an heroic martyr. The bandwagon was rolling to return DeWitt Clinton to the Governor's mansion.

The year 1824 was not a red letter one for Martin Van Buren, champion of party unity. As Clinton's fortunes rose spectacularly in New York State, in the nation the "Era of Good Feeling," over which President James Monroe had presided for seven years, was coming to a bitter end with the clash of sectional factions splintering the party of Jefferson. Monroe, seeking political retirement at sixty-six, refused to promote a successor, thus inviting attack from Van Buren for abdication of party leadership. Working with the Bucktail Congressmen, Van Buren had ousted the pro-Clinton Speaker of the House, but he failed to win Monroe's support in an unsuccessful attempt to block ex-Federalist Congressman Solomon Van Rensselaer from the office of Albany Postmaster. The President's indifference to matters of party discipline and patronage was to Van Buren a heresy.

In the scramble for the White House, Van Buren believed that Secretary of the Treasury William Crawford, a Virginia native and former Georgia Senator, could be a unifying figure. The other contenders were more popular leaders in their own right: Secretary of State John Quincy Adams, who had renounced his Federalist past; Senator Andrew Jackson, hero of the Battle of New Orleans; Speaker of the House Henry Clay; and Secretary of War John Calhoun. So well-distributed was their strength that when Van Buren called together a Congressional caucus to nominate the Democratic candidate, half the Congressmen stayed away and the cry was raised: "King Caucus is dead."

While Van Buren made frequent trips across the Potomac, seeking to restore the old Jefferson-Burr axis (then known as the Albany Regency-Richmond Junto), his pro-Crawford leader in Tammany, John Van Ness, was encountering strong rivalries. Most of the old Burrites leaned toward Calhoun, a powerful proponent of States' rights. Robert Swartwout was pushing for John Quincy Adams, and for good reason. In his post as Navy agent, Swartwout was caught embezzling $68,000 in Federal funds. He was saved from a prison sentence when Secretary of State Adams asked the government to accept a mortgage on Swartwout's property in restitution.

Yet another faction in Tammany was led by Robert Swartwout's brother Samuel, who found vigorous Irish support in the fight for Andrew Jackson. "Old Hickory," the son of Irish Presbyterian immigrants, more than matched Tammany's anti-British sentiments (from the age of thirteen he had borne scars inflicted by a British officer's saber). He was also the first eminent politician to talk of equal rights in America without condescension. Tammany had long been worshipful of Jackson as a "common man" and a military hero, although none of the Bucktails could forget, and some could not forgive, the General's *faux pas* when he visited the Wigwam during DeWitt Clinton's first term. Two years after Jackson had repelled the British invaders from Louisiana, he received an invitation from Grand Sachem William Mooney in the rococo style dear to the hearts of Tammany braves:

> Columbia's voice in peals of iron thunder proclaimed the dread feat of that eventful morn! Terra was drenched with human gore! The perturbed elements were hushed! Mars and Bellona retired from the ensanguined field! And godlike Hero resumed her gentle reign. . . . We approbate your noble deeds and greet you, hero. Scourge of British insolence, Spanish perfidy and Indian cruelty—these, sir, are the sentiments of the sons of Liberty in New York who compose the National Institution of Tammany Society No. 1 of the U.S. Here, sir, we guard the national flame—"preserved by

concord"—its effulgence in a blaze of glory, shall surround and accompany you to the temple of interminable fame and honor.

Needless to say, Jackson did not refuse the invitation. The night of the banquet, Tammany Hall was overflowing with Bucktails all aglow with firewater. A rousing toast was raised to Old Hickory: "To General Jackson, so long as the Mississippi rolls its waters to the ocean, so long may his great name and glorious deeds be remembered!" Cheers rocked the Hall, then all was silence as the braves stood, glasses held high, awaiting the General's flattering response. Summoning up his finest military timbre, Jackson thundered: "To DeWitt Clinton, Governor of the great and patriotic State of New York!"

The General drank alone in silence. Suddenly, to his great puzzlement, the Hall broke into an uproar. Shouting threats and curses, the braves threw their glasses to the floor. Jackson was amazed. Had he not made the safest possible toast to the Governor of the host state, a leader of the great Democratic Party of which Tammany was a conspicuous institution? Bewildered and angry, he stalked from the Hall.

In time, however, most of the Tammany Sachems put aside hurt feelings and sympathized with Jackson's naïveté. After all, who but a New Yorker could appreciate that New York Democrats have always hated each other? In preparation for the national election of 1824, Jackson partisans were picked for local office by a majority of the Tammany nominating committee. On the night when the ticket was to be presented to the membership for confirmation, the committee took the precaution of arriving early at the Hall, called a quick aye vote under Samuel Swartwout's watchful eye, and quickly adjourned. The exit was delayed by pro-Adams leader Robert Swartwout, who leaped to the chair amid shouts of "Liar!" and "Traitor!" and a grand fist fight ensued.

If Tammany was no marvel of unity in the elections of 1824, neither was America. Andrew Jackson won a plurality of both the popular and electoral vote, John Quincy Adams was a close second, John Calhoun was elected Vice-President, Henry Clay took a majority of New York's thirty-six electors (chosen by the State Legislature), and Van Buren's candidate William Crawford came in at the bottom of the scramble. All professed to be Democrats, running under various faction labels such as "Democratic-Republican," "National-Republican" and just plain "Democratic." By the time the candidates' friends, including

Van Buren, had finished bending the New York electors' ears, Henry Clay's votes had mysteriously evaporated. With no candidate having a majority, the election was thrown into the House of Representatives. It was apparent that New York, with its delegation now split evenly between Crawford and Adams, would be the pivotal state.

Van Buren focused his blandishments on Congressman Stephen Van Rensselaer, the proud patroon who had led the Old Guard at the State constitutional convention. The night before the Congressional vote, the two men ate dinner together at the boarding house where both lived in Washington. Van Rensselaer, wavering from one moment to the next, finally promised a vote for Crawford. But as he walked to the House chamber the next day he was intercepted by Massachusetts Congressman Daniel Webster and Henry Clay, now out of the running; they bombarded him with pleas for Adams. By the time Van Rensselaer had reached his desk, however, he reassured Van Buren that his vote was safe for Crawford. The ballot box was passed through the chamber. After a moment of hesitation, the old patroon, prayerful and trembling, dropped in his vote. With that single slip of paper, John Quincy Adams became the sixth President of the United States.

The Albany Regency was thus denied a patron in the White House. And DeWitt Clinton, martyred hero of the Erie Canal, won back the governorship by an overwhelming vote. The following year he boarded the Canal boat *Seneca Chief* in Buffalo for an historic first journey from Lake Erie to the Atlantic Ocean. At the end of the voyage he dumped a barrel of pure Erie water into the briny sea. From that moment on, money flowed from Clinton's Folly.

The Canal earned seven hundred thousand dollars a year. The cost of overland freight between Buffalo and New York dropped from one hundred to ten dollars. The two-week stage coach ride from Albany to Buffalo was cut to four days by horse-drawn packets. Along the Mohawk Valley, towns prospered into cities, the salt fields of Syracuse found their market, Buffalo emerged from the wilderness, settlers poured into the Midwest, and New York City became the leading recipient of Western goods. Five years after Clinton performed the rite of the "wedding of the waters," property values in Manhattan had soared sixty percent.

The phenomenal success of Clinton's gamble, a happy-ending adventure story which had become totally identified with his person, should have placed him on the road to the White House and destroyed Martin Van Buren as a power in New York State. But the ways of politics have never been known for logic and smooth momentum. The usual ingredients of a successful political career are 20 percent substance, 20 percent hypocrisy, 20 percent timing, and 40 percent luck. Clinton's good luck had come when Tammany overreached its strength to fire him as Canal Commissioner. His bad luck was that the Van Buren Regency had already taken hold on the State Party, saddling the Governor with an unfriendly Legislature, hostile State officers such as Comptroller William Marcy, and a grass-roots organization which thrived on small pieces of patronage. And DeWitt Clinton's bad luck turned to tragedy in 1828 on a winter's eve in Albany when, at the age of fifty-eight, he sat down for a quiet dinner with his family and was suddenly stricken by a fatal heart attack.

In a eulogy delivered before the New York Congressional delegation, Martin Van Buren praised Clinton's zeal and talents which had created "the greatest public improvement of the age." He and Clinton had endured "collisions of opinion and action" but "our political differences have been wholly free from that most venomous and corroding of all poisons—personal hatred . . . I, who whilst he lived never, no never, envied him anything; now that he has fallen, am greatly tempted to envy his grave with its honours."

Historians have valued these remarks as a sincere tribute to a respected political antagonist. "Because the Senator was unfamiliar with 'corroding' personal hatred, which normally attended political battles, he could speak in this manner without fear of criticism," notes Robert Remini, a close student of the period. "Nor need he ever have blushed with embarrassment at the thought of others reading his comments. New Yorkers studied them and were moved by their eloquence. It was fitting, they agreed, that he should have uttered them." Van Buren's eulogy was also an effort to clear the air of intra-party bitterness. He was hailed as "the master joiner" of splits in the party woodwork. With the death of DeWitt Clinton, the patient, pragmatic Fox of Kinderhook emerged without rival as the Democratic party leader of New York.

The Adams-Jackson schism within Tammany and in Washington was too wide to be bridged by Van Buren, but it could be exploited for a new realignment. When Henry Clay was appointed Secretary of

State, Jackson and his supporters made charges of a "corrupt bargain" which had secured Clay's votes for President Adams. Calhoun and Crawford joined the Jackson legions and Van Buren made a special trip to the Tammany Wigwam to advise the braves that the party must now unify behind Andrew Jackson.

Robert Swartwout and his pro-Adams faction were enraged. They cited the "danger and absurdity of confiding the destinies of the country to a mere arbitrary soldier." Although Jacksonians dominated the Tammany General Committee, the vocal minority carried on a pitched battle to bar them from Tammany Hall. One day they succeeded by locking the doors of the great meeting hall. The Jacksonians retreated to the cellar where they drew up a slate of pro-Hickory candidates for local office. On Election Day, gangs of immigrants, many of them still aliens, were carted from ward to ward, depositing Jackson ballots as they went. Pro-Adams "native Americans" arrived at the polls to find Tammany inspectors guarding the proceedings with hickory branches. Such tactics were successful because the secret ballot was unknown. The voter was required to ask for the ballot of his choice. Bribery was wide spread and fraud was easy. With no State regulations governing elections, the parties established their own controls.

The local Jacksonian slate carried the City by 5,000 votes and Robert Swartwout and the Adamsites were forever banished from the Wigwam. Prominent among the new office-holders were first-generation Irishmen, the new wave of Tammany Hall. From its early days of chauvinism, Tammany had come full circle to woo the immigrant masses in earnest. Special meetings were arranged for Irish, German, and French constituents in their native languages, to urge their entrance into party activity. Tammany legislators, eager to recruit new voters almost as they stepped onto the pier, pressed for the reduction of the five-year naturalization period.

But Democratic strength in New York City was offset by the sudden upstate development of the new Antimasonic Party. It was a coalition of farmers, workers, religious leaders, and small-town pillars of civic virtue who were skillfully woven together by agents of Adams' National Republican Party, forerunner of the Whigs and Republicans. Initially, the group was mobilized after the kidnapping of a Freemason defector near Rochester who had threatened to publish the hallowed secrets of the Order of Masons. Rumors of his murder spread, a search was impeded by the Masonic leaders, and liberal upstate politicians found an electrifying cause in the attack on Freemasonry. Fifteen Antimasonic candidates were elected to the State Assembly in the fall of 1827. The following year a full-fledged State party convention was held to collaborate with the National Republicans against the Van Buren-Tammany Jacksonians. New York State, which Jackson had considered safely in his corner, became the leading question mark in the Presidential campaign against Adams. To secure the votes of straying upstate Democrats for Jackson, Van Buren consented to run for Governor, although he had no desire to leave Washington.

Tammany was aware that victory in the election of 1828 would mean the Hall's first opportunity to control Federal patronage in New York City. With Jackson in the White House and Van Buren in Albany, the Sachems were confident of their own omnipotence in New York City. The election was also the first in New York State which would give the voters a direct choice of the Presidential electors. Thus the campaign carried a new sense of national urgency into the neighborhoods, and new excesses of hoopla—campaign songs, buttons, parades, posters, and handshaking tours.

Van Buren pushed his cause through the Tammany workers in the City, concentrating his personal appearances in the upstate counties, chatting with the farmers, singing with churchgoers, seeking out the old Clintonians to win them over to Jackson. He also traveled in other states on behalf of Jackson's candidacy, fulfilling his role as the first national campaign manager in American politics. He took charge of scheduling, publicity, fund-raising, and all aspects of organization and imagery. To Jackson's campaign biographer, he wrote: "Does the old gentleman have prayers in his house? If so, mention it modestly."

On Election Day in the City the usual cries of fraud rang out at the polling places. Illegal voting was heavy on both sides, but apparently the Jacksonians had more skillful mathematicians. Tammany gave its first Irish hero a 6,000 majority out of 25,000 votes cast. Martin Van Buren, running against two opponents, won a plurality and the governorship. He helped Andrew Jackson to victory in twenty of the State's thirty-six electoral districts. Daniel Webster remarked that Van Buren had done more for Jackson's victory than any ten leaders. In every section of the country save New England, Jackson crushed incumbent President Adams, cutting across class lines, amalgamating interest groups and political factions which had defied compromise. The Democratic Party, born in a previous century as an infant coalition between Tammany Anti-Federalists and Virginia Jeffersonians, had come of age, tutored and whipped into shape by Martin Van Buren, united behind a new and hugely popular President. "Martin Van Buren," Remini has noted, "put together a splendid organization and then gave it to the people."

The people wanted jobs, and Tammany people wanted all the Federal jobs in New York City. They were not disappointed by President Jackson, a vigorous practitioner of the spoils system. (Contrary to exaggerated accounts, however, it should be noted that during his eight-year Presidency, Jackson's patronage affected less than twenty percent of Federal job-holders.) Governor Van Buren was pleased by Jackson's principles of patronage and the *carte blanche* delivered to Tammany Hall. He had grave doubts, however, about the official suitability of Samuel Swartwout, who received the lush post of Collector of the Port of New York. As it turned out, Jackson would have been wise to heed Van Buren's objections.

Samuel Swartwout, through all his years of service to the lost causes of Aaron Burr, had received few rewards and was hungry enough to become the first of the great Tammany pirates. It was, in fact, an astonishing feat of self-control that Swartwout so diligently attended to his collectorship duties for the space of eight years before he packed $1,225,705 (and sixty-nine cents) of public moneys in his trunk and sailed from his beneficent port to Europe. There he was joined by a fellow Tammany brave, William Price, U.S. District Attorney for the Southern District of New York and a piker. His take was $72,124 (and six cents). Few remembered Billy Price. But for decades afterward, anyone who embezzled public funds was said to have "Swartwouted."

The largest slice of Bucktail patronage was awarded to Van Buren, whose run for the governorship had been designed primarily to swing New York to Jackson. After two months in Albany, Van Buren resigned and returned to Washington as Secretary of State, leaving the Regency to control the affairs of New York. This in itself was a record of sorts in exalted musical chairs; within twelve weeks, one man served as U.S. Senator, Governor of New York, and Secretary of State.

Whatever respect Van Buren commanded in Washington, however, resulted purely from his successes as a party leader, and particularly from the power he wielded in Albany and New York City. He was greatly admired by most of the old Jeffersonians and young Jacksonians for having held together the splinters and fragments of the old Democratic-Republican Party. Others regarded him as a charming manipulator, an urbane Tammany Boss whom Jackson had entrusted with the task of bringing the spoils system to bear on the entire Federal Government. Both assessments were true. As Secretary of State, Van Buren undertook a role more befitting a modern Postmaster General, dispensing patronage, strengthening the organization, and acting as liaison between the President and the Democratic leaders on Capitol Hill. But he was also a successful statesman, applying his diplomatic skills very effectively in his new world of international politics, resolving trade disputes with England, negotiating agreements with France, and bringing into being the first treaty with Turkey to give American ships access to the Black Sea.

Van Buren became Jackson's closest advisor and the most influential member of the cabinet, which earned him the enmity of Vice-President John Calhoun. The two men split over a variety of issues, chief of which was Calhoun's fear that Van Buren was easing his way into the position of Jackson's heir apparent. Acting on this fear, the irate Calhoun brought about a self-fulfilling prophecy. Faced with an opponent who had a long record of successfully exploiting opposition errors, Calhoun proceeded into the trap. His first mistake came in the Peggy O'Neill affair, which became something of an Irish-American cause célèbre.

Peggy O'Neill was the daughter of a Washington tavernkeeper, a lady of thirty-three years and considerable charm with a hint of scandal in her past. Her first husband died in 1828 and the following year, with what Washington social circles felt to be considerable haste to climb the ladder, she married Jackson's new Secretary of War John Eaton. The second Mrs. Eaton (his first wife had been a ward of Jackson's in Tennessee, where the President and the Secretary of War were early friends) was immediately snubbed by the wives of her husband's colleagues, and it soon became official cabinet policy to avoid contact with both Eatons.

Van Buren would have no part of this edict and made a pointed display of treating Peggy Eaton with kindness. Rumors were circulated by the Calhoun camp. Van Buren was a widower with four sons (his wife Hannah died of consumption after twelve years of marriage, and he never remarried). But the crucial basis of his friendship with Peggy Eaton was actually political and never romantic. She was a favorite of the President's, as a charming dinner partner and the wife of a close friend. Those who snubbed her could now be considered the President's enemies.

It was suggested that Van Buren used Mrs. Eaton in an effort to discredit Calhoun and gain further favor with President Jackson. Whatever his motives, this was precisely what occurred. Under pressure from the cabinet members, Eaton was forced to resign, despite Jackson's intervention. Van Buren announced his own resignation in protest, thus giving Jackson the opportunity to shake up the entire cabinet and toss out the Calhoun allies who had pilloried the Eatons. The new cabinet members were not only pro-Jackson but they favored Martin Van Buren as the man to succeed him. Among them was the old Son of Saint Tammany, ex-Mayor Edward Livingston, who had opposed Van Buren in his first State Senate contest in Columbia County. Livingston had become a Jacksonian while serving on the General's staff at the Battle of New Orleans and he developed a close friendship with Van Buren.

Van Buren relinquished his post as Secretary of State to Livingston and accepted Jackson's designation as Minister to England. The Little Magician was now the possessor of three regencies: Albany, Tammany Hall, and the national cabinet. "He has so surrounded the President with his creatures," Calhoun bemoaned, "that his affairs can be safely administered in his absence." But Calhoun had not lost hope. After Van Buren left for England, Calhoun secured the support of Henry Clay and Daniel Webster in a move to block Senate confirmation of Van Buren's appointment as Minister. The Senate convened and voted itself into a deadlock. Calhoun, presiding, cast his vote to break the tie, confident he had cut short the political career of Martin Van Buren. "It will kill him, sir, kill him dead," Calhoun gloated, "he will never kick, sir, never kick."

Van Buren was in no mood to kick. He was enjoying the leisurely life of the London embassy, where the Secretary of his legation was his Bucktail comrade Washington Irving. The news of the Senate action reached him during a fancy ball at Ambassador Talleyrand's. The statesmen, nobles and their ladies were indignant, but Van Buren smiled serenely. It was far from a disappointment to a politician who had once chastized Tammany for overplaying its hand against DeWitt Clinton. Van Buren nodded politely when a gentleman at the ball tried to reassure him: "It is an advantage to a public man to be the subject of an outrage."

"Although I had ardently desired it," Martin Van Buren said of the Senators' defiance of a Presidential appointment, "I could not persuade myself to believe that their passions would drive them into a measure the inevitable results of which might have been seen by a schoolboy." The press in both England and America attacked Calhoun and his cohorts for playing a cynical game of politics with the affairs of state. President Jackson was enraged and prepared for vengeance. Missouri Senator Thomas Hart Benton, measuring the outcry, remarked to a Senate colleague: "You have broken a minister, and elected a Vice-President."

"Van Buren for Vice-President!" was the theme of a mass indignation meeting staged by the Bucktails at Tammany Hall. Mayor Walter Bowne, official Grand Sachem of the Tammany Society, was among the leaders who toasted Van Buren as the honorary "Grand Sachem of the Eagle Tribe," lauding his "faithful support of the Great Grand Sachem of the Nation." "Van Buren for Vice-President in '32, for President in '36!" the braves shouted. Then came nine cheers and the boom for Van Buren was on.

The first Democratic National Convention was held to publicize party solidarity behind Andrew Jackson and to choose a new Vice-Presidential candidate. It came as little surprise when the President presented Van Buren's name to the delegates as his hand-picked running mate. Before he had landed on American shores from his return journey from England, Martin Van Buren had already received the nomination to preside over the Senate which had rejected him.

The Democratic Convention, which was actually a public show of unanimity in the style of the 1964 LBJ pep rally, replaced the Congressional caucus over which Van Buren had presided. The new method was made necessary by the failure of the 1828 caucus; more immediately, it was prompted by a national convention the previous September of the Antimasonic Party which nominated former Attorney General William Wirt, the prosecutor of Aaron Burr, for the Presidency. The National Republicans, who dubbed themselves Whigs in order to characterize the Jacksonians as Tories, also convened in Baltimore to formalize the anti-Jackson alliance of Calhoun, Clay, and Webster. Henry Clay took the nomination.

On May 31, the Tammany General Committee officially approved the Democratic slate and throughout the summer Tammany drummers summoned the faithful to Jackson-Van Buren rallies at the Hall.

A great ceremony was held in front of the Wigwam to plant a Hickory Tree. Tammany barkeeps rolled up huge kegs and moistened the roots with good Democratic beer. Competition from the Whigs pushed the price of neutral voters up to five dollars. On Election Day Tammany dispatched burly goons to the polling districts. As in the 1828 election, fraudulent balloting was a commonplace on both sides. The Jackson-Van Buren ticket carried New York City and the nation. In New York State, control by the Albany Regency was bolstered with the election of Van Buren's confidant, William Marcy, as Governor.

One of the key issues in 1832 was President Jackson's veto that year of a bill to recharter the Bank of the United States. The charter was not due to expire until 1836, but anti-Jackson Congressmen pushed through the rechartering measure early to present Jackson with a political dilemma: sign and disenchant Tammany and thousands of anti-Bank Democrats; veto and appear to be endangering the national economy. Jackson's enemies knew that he favored a reorganization of the existing bank, but this position would be difficult to justify after a veto of the charter itself. The President decided to veto. In his message he charged that "the rich and powerful too often bend the acts of government to their selfish purposes." It proved to be a popular position with a great majority of the voters.

After the election, the Bank's president Nicholas Biddle took measures aimed at forcing Jackson to choose between recharter or a financial panic. President Jackson responded by depositing Federal funds in banks scattered throughout the nation, nearly all of them operated by loyal Democrats. Van Buren, a militant foe of the big bankers since his first campaign for the State Senate, gave full support to the President's actions (despite their inflationary effect on the national economy). From the floor of the Senate, Henry Clay pleaded with Vice-President Van Buren to intervene with the President and save the nation from economic disaster. Van Buren listened carefully to every word and nuance of Clay's long, impassioned oration. When the speech had ended, he stepped down from the presiding chair, walked straight to Clay's desk, smiled broadly, bowed, and said: "May I bother you, Senator, for just a bit of your fine old Macceboy snuff?" He took a pinch, raised it to his nose, bowed again, and walked out of the Senate.

Van Buren's refusal to acknowledge any criticism of Jackson's bank policies was applauded by the Tammany leaders, who had their own private banking interests to promote, and by the workingmen of the Society. A few of the Tammany merchants, however, joined with the Whigs in support of the Bank of the United States, fearing that unless it were sustained the economy would collapse. The "bank war" became the overriding issue in the New York City elections of 1834, the first in which New Yorkers voted directly for their Mayor.

For the mayoral nomination, Tammany passed up Sachem Gideon Lee, the incumbent Mayor and a banker, for Cornelius Lawrence, whose financial instincts were less well-developed. As an early Tammany historian described him: "Lawrence had the habit of strolling the streets, glasses in hand behind his back, ogling all the pretty girls till one tangled him in a plot much to his financial and mental distress." The Whigs were confident of beating Lawrence and concentrated their fire on the thirty-two City Council seats. Each of the ward campaigns was used as a forum to attack Jackson, Van Buren, and the bank veto, with the hope that Congress would be influenced by Whig victories on the issue.

On Election Day, rain poured down on the voters lined up at the polls, but the ardor of the "bank war" prevailed. Knife fights tested the political courage of Whigs and Bucktails. One man of unidentified political persuasions was stabbed to death. The Whigs organized counter-goons to keep away Tammany voters. In the "Bloody Ould Sixth" Ward, a populous district north of Park Row and east of Broadway, Tammany poll watchers were irked at the size of the Whig vote. They began to tear up the offending ballots.

A mob of fifteen thousand Tammanyites marched on the Whig bastions. Lame-duck Mayor Gideon Lee rushed to Masonic Hall, headquarters of the Whigs, and called down from the steps for order in the streets. A well-aimed paving block placed him temporarily out of the action. The Whigs ransacked gun shops along Broadway, then moved to the State arsenal at Franklin and Elm Streets in search of more weapons. A garrison of citizen volunteers fought them off until the militia arrived. Meanwhile, the cavalry scattered the Tammany rioters, and the ballot boxes of the Sixth Ward were carted off to City Hall under armed guard. The results of New York City's first experiment in democracy were mixed. Tammany's Cornelius Lawrence squeaked through by 181 votes out of 35,000 cast. But the Whigs captured a seventeen to fifteen majority in the City Council, thus gaining control of some one million dollars a year in patronage.

The banking issue was kept alive through the 1830's and became a rallying point for the most vigorous reform movement of the decade. Tammany, ever liberal in its yearnings, had allowed the Scottish reformer Fanny Wright to lecture in the Hall against banks, religion, private schools, private property, war, slavery, female subjugation, large families, and the bonds of matrimony. To the chagrin of the prospering Sachems (who had intended merely to give the braves a chance to let off steam) Miss Wright's Democratic followers broke away from the mainstream and formed their own faction. The political danger came stunningly clear when a candidate of the new Workingman's Party defeated a Tammany man for the State Legislature.

In an attempt to absorb this threat from the left, Tammany took the lead in pushing a series of progressive measures through the Legislature to protect workers' rights, outlaw debtors' prisons, and reform the State military draft. The Workingman's Party yielded to the less extreme but more effective Equal Rights Party, which centered its attacks on banks, paper currency, and monopolies. As these were the same demons under fire from Van Buren and Jackson, the Equal Righters were welcome at Tammany meetings. It soon became apparent, however, that the benevolence of the Sachems would not satisfy the radicals. At one meeting Sachem Gideon Lee turned over his gavel to a banking colleague, Preserved Fish (so christened by a New Bedford fisherman who rescued the infant Fish from the sea). Chairman Fish rapped for attention. The anti-bankers hooted him down and the meeting was adjourned on the verge of riot.

A second meeting was set for 7 P.M. on October 29, 1835, in hopes of reconciling the hads and had-nots. The doors of Tammany Hall swung open promptly at seven. The reformers trooped in, only to find that the regulars were already on the platform preparing to nominate Isaac Varian, a mayoral hopeful, as chairman. The Equal Righters nominated their own chairman. Varian refused to leave the chair until the catcalls of the Equal Righters drowned out his reading of the election slate proposed by the Tammany nominating committee. With the Hall in an uproar, Varian and the Old Guard retreated to the Pewter Mug, a nearby tavern on Frankfort Street, to complete the nominations.

The Equal Righters took over the platform and were in the process of passing a resolution condemning the Bank of the United States when a clever Tammany loyalist slipped into the basement and turned off the gas lights. An observer commented at the time: "It is halfpast seven, and the darkness of midnight is in Tammany Hall. Nothing but the demon spirit of monopoly, in its war upon humanity, could have been wicked enough to involve such an excited throng in total darkness." But the ingenious Equal Righters whipped out from their pockets loco-focos (self-igniting matches) to illuminate the meeting room. The Loco-Focos (as the press nicknamed the faction) went on to name their own candidates. But Tammany won the local elections and recaptured the Hall, gaslights and all.

Tammany's ward committees stole much of the Loco-Focos' thunder after the Great Fire of December 16, 1835, which destroyed forty-five acres of buildings in downtown Manhattan. With the cost of food and coal pushed beyond the means of most immigrants, Tammany ward leaders celebrated the Christmas season by distributing money, fuel, clothing, and baskets of turkey and pies. These hand-outs were stepped up in quantity and frequency as the campaign began to roll for the next Presidential election.

It was clear that the ailing President Jackson, anxious to avoid the sin of divisiveness committed by James Monroe, would name his own man before he stepped down. Van Buren's credentials as a temperate, deferential, but strong party chieftain, which failed to stir the Loco-Focos, were exactly the qualifications which Jackson sought in his successor. The Loco-Focos loudly deplored Van Buren's role as Boss of the Tammany regulars and the Albany Regency. And they charged that his comments on Equal Rights principles were too evasive to warrant liberal support.

Van Buren's caution gave rise to a tale about a Tammany Sachem and a Loco-Foco, who were riding near the Vice-President on a Hudson River sternwheeler. The Loco-Foco, snorting at the thought that a Tammany Boss could be a national statesman, challenged the Sachem: "I'll bet you the price of your passage that you can't go over to him now and get a straight answer to the simplest question you can ask." The Tammany brave, an ardent Van Burenite, took the bet and approached his idol, confident of victory. "Don't you think, sir," he inquired of Van Buren, "that the weather is fine?" "Well," Van Buren replied, "that is a relative term and ..."

This story had little effect on the second Democratic National Convention which met at the First Presbyterian Church in Baltimore and unanimously nominated Martin Van Buren, the pride of the Bucktails and the choice of the President. To rope in the Loco-Foco vote, ex-Kentucky Senator Richard Johnson, a hero of the Equal Righters, was named for Vice-President. The Loco-Focos tendered a hearty endorsement to Johnson and indicated, although they could not share Tammany's jubilation, they would support the national ticket, while fielding their own local candidates in the New York City elections.

At fifty-four, Martin Van Buren climaxed his political career by winning the Presidency, but it was not a national sweep for a popular hero. He carried New York City by a little over 1,000 votes (compared with 6,000 for the Jackson-Van Buren team) and his electoral plurality of 46 (over four opponents, including Congressman William Henry Harrison and Senator Daniel Webster) was a sharp drop from Jackson's 170. It is doubtful, however, that any other successor to Jackson could have held together as many diverse political elements.

Locally, Tammany candidates who sought to ride Van Buren's coattails did not fare well. Only six out of thirteen survived the wrath of the Loco-Focos. Tammany was once again pronounced dead.

Martin Van Buren was the first President born under the American flag and the first machine politician to reside in the White House. His triumph signaled the close of the Jeffersonian Tammany era in American politics. Ahead of President Van Buren, the last of Jefferson's disciples, lay a disastrous financial panic, a resurgence of Federalist strength in the new Whig and Republican parties, and the paramount issue of slavery, which once again split the Democratic Party.

The election of 1836 marked the high point of Tammany's direct influence on the White House. It would be half a century before another strong Democratic President emerged. And even then, Grover Cleveland was an arch-enemy of Tammany Hall.

After 1836, New York City and State remained as critical factors in every Presidential election, but Tammany Hall was emulated in cities throughout America. Tammany's leaders, unlike Burr and Van Buren, were never completely comfortable in their national aspirations. Their greatest rewards came in reaping the riches of their own backyard. Following its first half-century as a unique center of power and change in a small, youthful nation, Tammany would now turn inward to New York City, a nation in itself, with new empires to be gained in each generation from the ships of the immigrants and the wards of the slums.

Chapter 4

Fernando Wood,
The "Model Mayor"

"The people will elect me Mayor though I should commit a murder in my family between now and election."

—*Fernando Wood*

"I never yet went to get a corner lot that I didn't find Wood had got in ahead of me."

—*William Marcy Tweed*

Financial panic struck the nation in 1837. Jackson's banking policies, as his enemies had predicted, prompted speculations and a disastrous inflationary spiral. The outgoing President's edict that gold or silver must be paid for all public lands led to a run on the Western banks. Unable to meet the demand, the banks closed and the failures spread to the East in time to greet Martin Van Buren at his gala inauguration.

The new President called Congress into special session to authorize the transfer of government funds from State banks into an independent treasury. Many conservative Democrats switched over to join the Whig opposition. The Whigs depicted Van Buren as a cold aristocrat eating from gold spoons in the White House while the country was plunged into poverty.

In New York City, insurance companies collapsed under the weight of seventeen million dollars in property claims stemming from the Great Fire, which had destroyed 530 buildings in the 17-block heart of Manhattan's business section, including the Merchant's Exchange, the last of the City's seventeenth-century Dutch houses, and scores of warehouses stuffed with food and clothing. Savings accounts were wiped out overnight. Hundreds of firms went bankrupt. The insurance company investors, many of them widows who had found a safe cache for their savings, were ruined. The City was recovering from a severe cholera epidemic in which thousands died and half the population (100,000) had fled in panic. At least one-third of the City's manual laborers were jobless. Ten thousand persons were living in utter poverty.

A month after President Van Buren's inauguration, the Loco-Focos massed in City Hall Park to protest the rule of the monopolists, which they contended had brought on the crisis. "Bread, Meat, Rent and Fuel!" a poster proclaimed. "Their prices must come down! The voice of the people shall be heard and shall prevail!" At the climax of the rally a man leaped up onto the makeshift speaker's platform and cried: "Hart's flour store! Offer a price! If he refuses, take the flour anyway!"

But Eli Hart, a prospering Tammany district leader, had the wisdom to escape from his flour warehouse before any price was offered. Hundreds of the Loco-Focos fashioned clubs from the tree branches in City Hall Park and marched through the streets to Hart's establishment, smashed through the locked doors, and scattered five hundred barrels of flour and one thousand bushels of wheat along Washington Street. Tammany Mayor Cornelius W. Lawrence and a contingent of police arrived on the scene, only to be turned back by a fusillade of stones and vegetables. In search of rifles, the mob moved on to a National Guard arsenal, where, after a hard fought battle, they were dispersed by the militia.

The Flour Riot was the first in a long series of mass raids on food warehouses, which led to the ouster of Mayor Lawrence in the 1837 elections. But the new Whig Mayor, Aaron Clark, whose splendid patent leather pumps earned him the nickname "The Dancing Mayor," was no more successful in turning back the rising tide of poverty. Tammany, busily passing out baskets of coal and groceries, accused the Mayor of total indifference to the plight of the poor. A counter-investigation revealed how Tammany could afford its own generosity. It was charged that $600,000 had been extorted from gamblers, thieves, and ladies of the evening and their customers, by Tammany judges and jailers who put in the fix and turned the fees over to the Hall for its charitable activities. In addition, City employees indebted to Tammany for their jobs were required to kick back six percent on each pay check.

Such revelations were important issues in Whig Mayor Clark's barely successful campaign for re-election in 1838 (mayoral elections were then yearly), despite his having quadrupled the City budget and presided over an administration as wasteful and corrupt as anything Tammany could offer. Mayor Clark's re-election—by a margin of 519 votes out of 39,341 cast—was equally the work of ousted Tammanyite Robert Swartwout, who imported 200 thugs from Philadelphia to vote Whig "early and often" and attack Swartwout's old comrades on their way to the polls. Tammany also imported assistance from the City of Brotherly Love, but the Whigs' price won the day ($22 for the first vote, $8 for each additional vote).

By the following year, the Loco-Focos had moved back into the fold, recognizing with their brethren that the Whig menace could be eradicated only by a united Tammany. Sachem Isaac Varian beat Mayor Aaron Clark by 1,000 votes, bringing in with him a Democratic City Council slate. Varian was a popular politician with a valuable memory for the names of constituents which failed him only once. After reading a newspaper reference to Old Boreas, the North Wind, sweeping the streets clean, he remarked in amazement: "I thought I knew every Democrat in New York! I never heard of him." Mayor Varian was able to survive two years in office at a time when Tammany scandals were becoming so commonplace as to produce public apathy.

To replace Burr's onetime secretary Samuel Swartwout as Port Collector, President Van Buren appointed longtime friend and Tammany Sachem Jesse Hoyt, who was either more honest or less adventurous than the great Swartwout. During his term of office, Hoyt's illegal stock transactions resulted in only thirty thousand dollars of judgments against him, which was less than one-fortieth of Swartwout's take, and twenty thousand dollars less than the concurrent acquisitions of a mere teller at the Tammany-dominated Manhattan Bank. The Manhattan Bank, founded by Aaron Burr to purchase property for Tammany braves, had become a huge depository for Federal, State, and City funds. A considerable sum of this money ($1,300,000, according to one investigation) found its way into Tammany war-chests through loans and the bank's own political expenditures. The courts dragged in a hapless cashier for destroying the records, dispensed a fifteen-day jail sentence and a $250 fine, and in the commotion a fellow employee vanished along with $50,000.

As the campaign of 1840 began, however, local scandal was not the greatest threat to Tammany Mayor Varian. A far more serious drag on the ticket was at the top, in the person of President Van Buren. After all, corruption in New York City was a moral issue of enduring interest to few but Protestant Puritans. The immigrant voting force was far more concerned with jobs, homes, food, and simple hospitality in a strange new world. Tammany Hall established a special bureau to help acclimatize new Americans; Tammany judges conducted mass naturalization ceremonies with little regard for legal niceties; and Tammany district leaders placed their new charges in menial City jobs or on the ballot for minor offices. The Whigs' organizational efforts to attract new voters were half-hearted at best; they concentrated their attack on Van Buren as the symbol of Tammany hypocrisy, an autocrat masquerading as a Democrat, the villain responsible for all the economic woes of the City and the nation.

Despite a costly war in Florida with the Seminole Indians, clashes between Maine and Canada, and war clouds drifting over from Great Britain, Van Buren's hold on the national party was as yet secure, and the Democratic National Convention nominated him unanimously for a repeat match against Whig Congressman William Henry Harrison. The ensuing "log cabin and hard cider campaign" marked the first widespread use of reverse-imagery, now a major staple of political skirmishes. The technique involves a simple assessment of the protagonist's greatest vulnerability and the antagonist's greatest asset, and then a barrage of publicity to reverse the impression.

Van Buren had won office as the political leader of the plebeians; Harrison the Whig represented the party of property. The solution was simple. Whigs depicted Van Buren as an effete dandy lolling on arabesque divans in the Blue Elliptical Salon of the White House, spraying himself with Parisian perfumes, sipping exotic wines and gloating over the furnishings with which he had surrounded himself at public expense. Whig songwriters, sloganeers, and ballyhoo artists then went to work on Harrison's victory over Tecumseh's brother at Tippecanoe River, Indiana, twenty-nine years before, placing him in the Jacksonian tradition, a rough and ready frontiersman, a man of the people who lived in a log cabin instead of a town house and swigged hard cider instead of champagne. The Democrats countered with the slogan "Three Cheers for O.K." (Old Kinderhook). It was no match for "Tippecanoe and Tyler Too" (ex-Virginia Senator John Tyler was the

Whig Vice-Presidential candidate) and "Van! Van! He's a used up man!"

As expected, the New York County Democratic Convention in 1840, anxious to keep the Tammany chieftain in the Great Wigwam on the Potomac, heartily endorsed President Van Buren and Mayor Varian as well. The only surprise of the Convention was a sudden upsurge of support for a twenty-eight-year-old liquor dealer named Fernando Wood, who had taken it into his head to run for the Congress of the United States. His name, which was practically unknown to the City's voters, was put forward by a group of stealthy operators well-dispersed among the delegations of all the wards. The breadth of his backing caught the ruling Sachems off-guard. One by one the delegations were captured by a close majority, and the darkest of horses came loping, then galloping down the homestretch to the nomination. "Fernando for Congress!" the delegates shouted, to which one Sachem replied: "Who is Fernando?"

"Fernando" was the name of the dashing hero in *The Three Spaniards*, a best-selling adventure novel which reached the hands of a pregnant Quaker lady in Philadelphia in the spring of 1812. Having named her previous sons in honor of less secular reading (Benjamin, Isaac, and Zachariah), the lady chose Fernando when she gave birth to another. Fernando was born four days before Congress declared war on Great Britain, the latter event visiting ruination on his father's thriving linen business. The Woods moved from Philadelphia to New York for another start. Young Fernando attended school until he was thirteen, then quit to take a two dollar a week clerk's job followed by a five dollar a week position as a broker's messenger. Through his teens he tried his hand at various trades: actor, wine dealer, auctioneer's clerk, chandler, grocer, cigarmaker, and manager of a tobacco factory.

Fernando grew up to be a handsome, slim, strong-featured six-footer with long black hair, a determined set to the jaw, a stern posture, a low boiling point, and a powerful punch. He embarked upon his first political battle at the age of seventeen during a business trip to Harrisburg. While taking refreshment at a local tavern, he overheard a dissertation by an anti-Jackson Pennsylvania State Senator and chanced to disagree. The Senator came after the young interloper with a bowie knife. Fernando rose to the occasion and to his feet, quickly parried, lifted up a chair and smashed it over the Senator's head with great effect. For his troubles he was whisked off to the Harrisburg Jail for the night, the only recorded imprisonment in a lifetime of keeping an arm's length from the law.

Released from jail the next morning, Fernando headed for home on a stagecoach shared with three dazzling young ladies and an inebriated coachman. A sudden jolt parted the reins from the driver's shaky grip and toppled him into the dust. The horses lunged out of control, placing Fernando and the feminine trio in a classic runaway situation. Sizing up the helpless look of terror on the pretty faces of his companions, Fernando called upon all the adrenalin and élan of his Spanish namesake, pushed open the coach door, pulled himself up onto the driver's seat, stretched down for the dangling reins and yanked the wild-eyed horses to a stop. He was amply rewarded by the grateful ladies and an even more grateful campaign biographer.

The eventful Harrisburg trip led to still more extravagant tales of Fernando's audacity and derring-do, all of which contributed to a general feeling around New York's waterfront bars that one should not mess with Fernando Wood. This lesson was not lost on a would-be thief who followed him home one night as he was returning from the theater. Approaching a deserted street, Fernando heard the footsteps behind him. Swiftly he whirled about with right hand thrust forward in his coat pocket and cautioned the villain, "Follow me one step further and I will blow your brains out." The man turned and ran for his life. Although Fernando modestly credited his own escape to the man's fear of a mock revolver, his admirers claimed that the thief suddenly recognized the face of the dreaded Fernando Wood.

Yet Fernando could be a man of great charm and smooth ways with people. He possessed just the right combination of kindliness and steel nerves that was the makings of a Tammany ward leader. He also owned the right kind of launching pad—a tobacco shop on Pearl Street which he opened at age twenty during the Jackson-Van Buren campaign. Fernando was an instant success with his customers, less for his knowledge of cigars than his great outpourings of devotion to Jackson and Van Buren. It took him no time at all to discover that politics and business mix well.

In 1834 he joined Tammany Hall and was active in the bloody elections which seated Tammany Mayor Cornelius Lawrence. He opened a larger store, with a full line of liquor and a few groceries thrown in, on Washington Street near the Hudson River docks. The store catered to prosperous shipping merchants, seamen, longshore-men, and waterfront toughs. All proved useful to Fernando Wood.

Through his friendship with the shippers, he eventually managed to acquire half-a-dozen sailing vessels and enter the shipping trade. It was later alleged by foes that Fernando's store was a hangout for shipping masters who shanghaied his unsuspecting customers for foreign voyages. Nonetheless, Fernando developed a loyal following among sailors and stevedores, whom he lured to the Tammany cause. Within the Hall he rose to be chairman of the Tammany Young Men's Committee, which gained him considerable influence over Democratic youths in all sections of the City. He was not well-known to the great Council of Sachems, but the young men admired him greatly. Better yet, in his neighborhood he began to make enemies—the first sign of success in politics. They dubbed him "Father of the Dock Rats."

Working through the Young Men's Committee, Wood organized a clandestine association of five loyalists in each ward who gathered each week at a secret meeting place on Chatham Street. The members of this cabal wore masks and disguised their voices so that none was known to the other. This was great fun for budding politicos, and they were anxious to go along with any scheme which Fernando might propose, which turned out to be the capturing of the Congressional nomination at the 1840 New York County Democratic Convention. The basic plot was to infiltrate the delegations without acknowledging fealty to Fernando, then announce for Fernando, issue sweet promises and dire threats to others, run about the convention hall raising a ruckus, shout the name "Fernando Wood" from all corners, join ranks for a great demonstration, and hope for the best. It worked.

On Election Day there was a vast outpouring of immigrants, many of whom had received their naturalization papers in Tammany courts within the week. They were recruited to support the Tammany ticket: President Van Buren, Mayor Varian, and Fernando Wood for Congress. The Whigs charged that Tammany jailors were marching files of convicts from their cells to the polls. Fernando's Whig opponent claimed that riverfront thugs were intimidating voters. The Tammany slate carried the City, which was good enough for Varian and Wood, but outside the City, Martin Van Buren lost the State and the nation, crushed by an electoral vote of 234 to 60.

Personal power in Tammany is never passed instantly. It is lost gradually and gained painstakingly, a see-saw in constant slow motion.

Now the top end of the see-saw began another slow descent as Martin Van Buren left the capital and Fernando Wood, thirty years the President's junior and the victor in a first election, ascended to the capital.

On a windy, rainy afternoon in March, 1841, "Old Kinderhook" Van Buren arrived at Jersey City, beating a slow, ceremonial retreat to the Hudson River town of his youth. Thousands of aging Bucktails and Tammany youths stood shivering in the rain while the ex-President ferried across New York Harbor. A closed barouche awaited him at the foot of Broadway. Van Buren ordered the carriage top down. The cortege, with an escort of lancers, moved up Broadway. Van Buren looked up into the rain, at the women waving handkerchiefs from windows and the damp flags hanging from the buildings. The crowds pressed close to the carriage and slowed the parade. Then Van Buren gave a brief instruction to the driver.

The procession veered east, then south to Frankfort and Nassau Streets. The carriage came to a halt and the Great Grand Sachem stepped out and walked into Tammany Hall for a hero's welcome. The braves cheered wildly as the defeated President shook hands, waved to the crowds, and grinned his familiar smile of serenity. Observers noted that he was dripping wet from the downpour but appeared to be as robust, hearty and cheerful as on his day of triumph in 1836.

Twelve days later President William Henry Harrison died of pneumonia after one month in office.

In Washington, young Fernando made an instant hit with his new colleagues. His theatrical voice charmed fellow orators on both sides of the aisle. After one speech, John Quincy Adams, then in his dotage, tottered up to Fernando, grasped his hand and said, "Young man, when I am gone, you will be one of the foremost men in this country."

The elder solons made a special pet of the twenty-eight-year-old freshman Congressman from New York. Henry Clay was fond of walking the streets with Fernando to show him the sights of Washington. One day the two men wandered into a tobacco shop and watched some craftsmen making cigars. The old Kentuckian was impressed with their skill, but Fernando, who had kept his past a secret, scoffed and proclaimed loudly that anyone could do it. The shopkeeper challenged him to try. Fernando tossed aside his coat, cut a tobacco leaf wrapper, rolled in the tobacco, twisted the end, clipped the pigtail, and waved the perfecto at his astonished audience.

Fernando presented the cigar to Senator Clay, for he himself had given up smoking and other minor vices in preparation for a political career—or, as the tale was told, for religious reasons. An inveterate smoker as a teen-ager, Fernando was leaning against the rail of a steamboat one day smoking his twentieth cigar of the day when a somber Quaker, wearing the broadbrimmed hat of his sect, approached him and announced in a Doomsday voice: "Friend, thee smokes a good deal. Don't thee smoke anymore." The startled Fernando, perhaps sensing a visitation from a deceased ancestor, tossed the cigar into the river and never smoked again.

Clay and Adams were only two of Fernando's many Washington admirers. He won a considerable following as an outspoken member of the House Naval Affairs Committee, in his crusades for Navy drydocks, for full salaries for consuls abroad, for the release of Americans involved in a Canadian border war, and for the cause of an eccentric portrait-painter and New York University professor who came to Washington seeking funds for an improbable experiment with electric wires. It was Professor Morse's claim that if these wires were laid between Baltimore and Washington, signals could be transmitted between the two cities. Congress laughed at the idea of wasting precious tax money on such an absurd scheme. But Fernando insisted that the professor be given a chance. He arranged for the wires to be strung from his committee room to a corresponding room on the other side of Capitol Hill. The experiment was a success; Congress voted Morse thirty thousand dollars to connect the two cities by telegraph, and on May 24, 1844, he sent the first message: "What hath God wrought!" Samuel Morse never forgot that Fernando Wood had wrought the funds.

Having achieved a creditable record in Congress, Wood left his seat to return to the shipping business, establish a string of Southern lotteries with his older brother Benjamin, and assiduously cultivate the City fathers. The Tammany District Attorney became an especially good friend, and a good thing too. One of Fernando's enterprises—the voyage of the good ship *John W. Cater* to California—landed him in court to face a partner who claimed he had been thoroughly swindled. The *Cater*, for which Fernando paid $4,000, carried about $13,000 worth of supplies to the gold prospectors in California. Through nimble penmanship, Fernando presented the cost of the ship as $12,000 and the supplies as $26,000. His partner reimbursed him for half, but later discovered a forged invoice of $112 for thirty-four water casks, when the true facts of the matter were $12 for four casks. An $8,000 judgment was obtained against Fernando but the indictment was not handed up until the exact day that the three-year statute of limitations ran out. The Recorder quashed the indictment. Fernando's enemies claimed that he had prevailed upon his friend the D.A. to delay the indictment, and then sent a $500 check to the Recorder.

Wood's detractors also alleged that he was an executive committee member of the anti-Catholic "Know-Nothings," a charge he vehemently denied. The Know-Nothings spearheaded a nativistic movement which feared the great immigrant invasion of the 1840's and attacked the Catholic Church as an un-American organization. Like Tammany, it began as a secret society (when asked about their organization, the members protested: "I know nothing") and then developed political muscle as the American-Republican Party and later the Native-American Party. In the New York City elections of 1844, the Know-Nothings teamed with the Whigs to win City Hall from Tammany. An anti-Wood pamphleteer charged that Fernando was "quite a spouter" at Know-Nothing political gatherings "from the Battery to Harlem" and "from his first attendance seemed to be particularly desirous to show his utter contempt for the Irish, and more specially for the Catholic priesthood." If there had been truth in this tale, it would have greatly surprised Fernando's large following in Tammany and on the waterfront, for it was among the Irish immigrants that he found his greatest popularity.

During the 1840's an estimated million and a half Europeans arrived in the port of New York. Many moved West to the farms and gold mines, but enough stayed to nearly double the City's population within the decade. Immigrant voters came to outnumber the natives and the vast majority gravitated to the Democratic Party. The Know-Nothings were quite correct on one score: immigrant strength in the Democratic Party was bolstered through illegal naturalization and election frauds. In one year, according to a Whig investigation, at least eleven thousand foreigners were naturalized in violation of the legal time limit and fee.

The Irish rose in the chain of political command by taking over neighborhood saloons as political headquarters; joining the volunteer fire companies (if there was a dearth of fires to keep them busy, the companies sometimes started their own or fought each other with pipe wrenches); and forming neighborhood gangs, which were given semi-official status as ward committees in the party structure. The gangs were particularly effective in working the polls on Election Day, while the police stood by, fearful of both physical violence and political repercussions. The New York *Herald* noted with alarm that "we have a class of municipal legislators forced upon us who have been educated in barrooms, brothels, and political societies."

The most powerful of the gangs had as their patrons important politicians who corresponded to the modern Assembly District leaders. The Dead Rabbits supported ex-Congressman Fernando Wood. The Spartan Gang worked for Tammany Assemblyman Mike Walsh, who frankly maintained that he was well-qualified to be a law-maker because he had so often been a law-breaker. The Empire Club was the enforcement arm of ex-riverboat gambler Captain Isaiah Rynders, an ally of Fernando's and a Tammany Sachem for twenty years. Rynders headquartered his gang in a Park Row saloon across from City Hall and used the boys to keep order at General Committee meetings in Tammany Hall, over which he frequently presided. He himself was adept with fists, pistol, bowie knife, and in real emergencies, a red-hot poker.

While Captain Rynders was fiercely loyal to the Tammany Society, Assemblyman Mike Walsh, a colorful Irish immigrant who once challenged Rynders to a knife duel, was fond of berating his fellow Bucktails on the theory that "Any dead fish can swim with the stream but it takes a real live one to go against the current." Walsh received his nomination for the Assembly despite a resounding rejection by the Tammany nominating committee. He took his case to the seven thousand delegates at the great County Convention in Tammany Hall, as modestly described in his newspaper the *Subterranean:* "I stepped forward, and, after ordering a mock auctioneer from the 17th Ward named Bob something, and one or two other loafers out of the road, so as to have plenty of elbow room, I commenced a speech which was listened to with the most breathless attention for an hour or two, unbroken by any interruptions save the thundergusts of applause with which the close of every paragraph was hailed. Every now and then, three vociferous cheers for 'Mike Walsh' would burst in earthquake tones from the thousands of workingmen present, the misery and depredation of whose condition I brought so vividly before them, that it was impossible to repress them. . . ."

The reporter for the *Herald* was more sympathetic to the plight of Captain Rynders, who was presiding at the meeting: "A low, ruffianly

looking individual pushed himself forward on the platform and took
his seat beside the Chairman. Capt. Rynders immediately seized the
offender, and in true democratic spirit, coolly knocked him down.
(Great confusion, hisses and yells.) The used up man shouted that he
was a full-blooded democrat. Capt. Rynders: 'Well then behave like
one, that's all we want.' (Hurrahs, shouts and deafening cheers. 'Go
it, Rynders—show your authority—hit him again, old boy!—were
among the exclamations which his patriotic sentiment called forth.)"

At that point, in the *Herald's* account, "A very fat, greasy-looking
fellow, with well-plastered soap locks called for three cheers for Mike
Walsh. . . . A fight now took place on the platform—Several men got
on the reporters' table, and their object seemed to be to ascertain who
could yell the loudest. . . . The vast hall was in a state of commotion
—rows, fights and yells, the order of the night. Hats were knocked off
and crushed—noses smashed—eyes blackened, and shins bruised. . . ."

In his speech to the Tammany Convention, Mike Walsh provided
a vivid description of the Tammany nominating process:

"The delegates to nominating committees are chosen not by the
electors of each ward, but generally by a few unprincipled black-
guards, usually office-holders or office-seekers, who meet in the back
room of some low groggery, where they place upon the ticket for
the support of their fellow citizens, a number of wretches of their
own moral calibre whose characters and consciences have been so
long buried that they have become putrid. The formal ceremony of
electing these delegates is always a most ridiculous and insulting
farce. 'A meeting of the democratic electors of the ward' is called
—a number of fellows who either hold or expect office go round
amongst the lowest rum holes in the ward—treat the 'setters' in
addition to which they give the ringleaders a few shillings a piece to
insure the presence of their gangs. Every contractor brings a number
of poor men whose spirits have been broken and whose frames
have been withered and bowed by that worst form of slavery—the
slavery of poverty.

"These, with the city watchmen, lamplighters, police officers and
a number of selected or favored thieves, who receive indulgences
from the police judges and officers to commit a certain number of
crimes without molestation, in consideration of the valuable political services which they render, assemble half an hour before the

time specified in the call—arrange the meeting, cry out 'aye' when the names are called, give three cheers before the 'noes' can be taken, after which the 'contractor' who acts as chairman pronounces everything 'carried unanimously'—then a motion to adjourn is passed, all hands go down and drink, and thus are made nearly all our honorable nominating committees."

If Walsh was to be believed, such was the procedure which in 1841 prefaced the nomination for State Assembly of the bright young politician and Van Buren protégé Sammy Tilden. But Mike Walsh's appeal to the rank-and-file General Committee of Tammany so outraged the wardheelers and frightened the ruling Sachems that Tilden's name was struck and replaced by Mike Walsh. Tilden and Van Buren's high-living son "Prince John" became the leaders in Tammany of the "Barnburner" faction, which fought monopolists and rent gougers in the city and opposed the extension of slavery into new states and territories. "These men are incendiaries," an opponent said; "they are mad; they are like the farmer who, to get the rats out of his granary, sets fire to his own barn."

Martin Van Buren, who opposed annexation of the pro-slavery Republic of Texas, was the hero of the Barnburners. This status ruined his attempt at a political comeback in 1844. At the Democratic National Convention he received the backing of a majority of the delegates, but failed to win the necessary two-thirds (a rule which persisted at Democratic Conventions until 1936). James Polk, ex-Governor of Tennessee and an honorary initiate in the Tammany Society, was nominated and elected to the Presidency by a close vote over Henry Clay. In New York the governorship went to Senator Silas Wright, Van Buren's longtime associate in the Albany Regency.

The slavery issue alienated Van Buren from the bulk of the Democratic Party membership and led to bitter wars within Tammany. Fernando Wood, although known to be a friend to the slave states, straddled the issue by maintaining such good relations with the Van Buren-Tilden faction that he was accused of being a Barnburner. A year before his election to Congress, Fernando had spoken out for emancipation at a meeting of a Broadway abolitionist tabernacle, which earned him the support of wealthy Protestant abolitionists, including the publisher of the *Journal of Commerce*. And now, while Captain Rynders' Empire Club thugs were breaking up abolitionist meetings, Fernando kept on the best of terms with the Captain and at the same time sent out his own Dead Rabbits to assault the Know-Nothings, which was a far more popular struggle in the eyes of the Catholic immigrants. Thus, Fernando, well covered on all sides, began to emerge as a hopeful symbol of unity in Tammany Hall.

Intra-Tammany warring between the Barnburners and the "Hunkers," their conservative adversaries, reached a crescendo at the Democratic National Convention in 1848 when two rival delegations arrived in Baltimore, both professing to speak for the New York Democratic Party. A compromise was effected by which delegates in both factions were given half a vote, but the Barnburners, anticipating a pro-slavery platform, refused to be bound by the decisions of the convention and bolted. They traveled to Buffalo where they joined in convention with the anti-slavery Free Soilers and nominated Van Buren as a third party candidate for the Presidency.

Tammany's allegiance was split. The election results in New York City accurately reflected the nation. Van Buren was the "spoiler" in a three-way race. The Whig candidate, General Zachary Taylor, hero of the Mexican War, beat Michigan Senator Lewis Cass, the regular Democratic candidate, by 9,880 votes in New York City and less than 140,000 in the country. Martin Van Buren's last political act was to run on principle and thereby doom to defeat the party which he had once unified.

Democratic factionalism also enabled the Whigs to win the New York mayoral election. Fernando started a fusion movement within Tammany to bring the groups together, but a segment of die-hard Hunkers refused to join and openly struggled with the Barnburners for control of the Council of Sachems. In 1850, Wood succeeded as a compromise candidate in gaining the barest of majorities on the second ballot of the Tammany nominating convention, and embarked upon his first campaign for Mayor. On the eve of the election the City was rocked by an exposé of Fernando's swindle of his ex-partner with the good ship *Cater* and its high-priced cargo. The Whig candidate for Mayor was given a 2,500-vote victory margin.

In 1850, 212,000 immigrants arrived in the port, including 117,000 Irishmen and 45,000 Germans. Tammany gangs were quick to exploit the sentiments of the newcomers. Posters proclaiming "Workmen, shall Americans or Englishmen rule in this city?" were traced to Captain Rynders' saloon at 25 Park Row, headquarters of the Empire Club.

These posters, and Rynders' inflammatory speeches, were a major factor in inciting the Astor Place Riot, a mass protest by fifteen thousand Anglophobes against the appearance in New York of the English Shakespearean actor William Macready. Gangs of Tammanyites and Know-Nothings joined forces to spoil Macready's performance as Macbeth, capitalizing on the strong feelings of partisans of the American actor Edwin Forrest, Macready's rival on the Shakespearean stage. Macready escaped from the mob, but the mob did not escape from the militia. A warning volley was fired over the heads of the crowd. The leaders shouted: "Don't run! They're only firing blank cartridges. They don't dare shoot anybody." A second volley was fired. Twenty-three were killed and twenty-two wounded.

The spread of violence, the influx of another 289,000 immigrants in 1851, and all the while the continued control of City Hall by the Whigs, prompted Tammany to call a truce within its own ranks and unite solidly behind a slate for the City Council. With the assistance of normal Election Day irregularities, the new policy of peace proved successful and the Tammany aldermen, campaigning for reform, economy, and good government, carried the Council. It was a good year for the Bucktails. Horatio Seymour, who had served as aide to Governor William Marcy, was himself elected Governor and new monarch of the Albany Regency. And in New York City, the President of the new City Council sounded an historic note: "We have been placed here as the representatives and guardians of the Empire City of the Union, to protect its great and increasing interests. . . . We must remember that although our course may soon run in this world, yet our acts will be recorded and they will perhaps be scrutinized by future generations."

It soon appeared that the new aldermen (who included in their midst a fat volunteer fireman from the Seventh Ward named William Marcy Tweed) hungered for something more immediate than immortal honor. One of their first actions was to vote themselves an official Tea Room for intermission refreshments. After one particularly grueling meeting, they submitted a bill to the Comptroller which was duly analyzed by Horace Greeley and his mathematicians at the *Tribune*. It was an open question as to how much padding had gone to the bill and how much to the waistlines of the aldermen, for it seemed that at one sitting *each* alderman had consumed eight pounds of beef, a chicken and a half, 225 oysters, one pound of sausage, two pounds of ham, and more than three loaves of bread, all followed by the smoking of one hundred cigars.

The new City Council soon earned itself the nickname of "The Forty Thieves" as its appetite turned to kickbacks on low-priced City land sales, bribes from contractors and would-be policemen, under-the-table bids for ferry and railroad franchises, and padded bills for patriotic commemorations, such as funeral obsequies for Henry Clay and Fourth of July fireworks ($500 worth for $4,000). The franchise for a new horse-car railway on Third Avenue cost the bidder $18,000 in bribes. Terms were discussed with the aldermen at secret meetings in Tammany Hall. A Council-authorized $600,000 paving job on the Bowery was so shoddy that it had to be torn up and done again. A valuable piece of City-owned waterfront property was sold for $160,000, despite competing bids of up to $300,000. At the same time the City put up more than triple the asking price to purchase land for a paupers' cemetery. The difference was split between aldermen and lobbyists.

Having united for victory behind The Forty Thieves, Tammany renewed its internal warfare with a slight adjustment in factions. The more militant of the Barnburners stayed with the Free Soilers and eventually joined the new Republican Party. Old Guard Hunkers who refused to budge from their rock-bound conservatism became known as "Hardshells." The remaining Barnburners and Hunkers who saw unity as the only alternative to political destruction of Tammany joined together as "Softshells," preaching fusion and compromise. The struggle between the "Hards" and the "Softs" transcended ideology and became a battle for physical possession of the Wigwam. They fought with covenants and leases, but just as often with fists, clubs, and brass cuspidors.

At the January meeting in 1853, two self-proclaimed Tammany General Committees, with a Soft chairman and a Hard chairman sitting side by side, battled to gain control. The Hard faction was outnumbered and stalked out of the Wigwam, whereupon the Council of Sachems recognized the Soft chairman, citing a clause in the old Tammany Society constitution which stated that the Sachems could forbid the use of the Hall to any political party whose principles were inimical to the "general principles of the Democratic-Republican party." The Hards maintained that politics was not at issue because the Society was a patriotic and benevolent association. In replying, the Council of Sachems removed any last lingering doubts about the role of the Tammany Society in New York: "It would be as reasonable to assert at noonday, in the face of the sun, that the orb does not emit light, as to deny that the Tammany Society is a political organization."

At a crucial pre-primary meeting of the Tammany General Committee, the Hards showed up with a majority and appointed the election inspectors, whereupon the Softs, who had been drinking and brooding in the Wigwam's basement tavern, picked up their chairs, and smashed a good number of Hard heads. Several Hard committeemen hastily jumped through windows which they neglected to open. Augustus Schell, the chairman of the General Committee, suffered a severe head wound. Tammany Assemblyman Daniel Edgar Sickles (a friend of Fernando's whose later exploits included murdering the son of Francis Scott Key and losing a leg in the Civil War) was tossed down the well of the Wigwam's massive spiral staircase. He grabbed a bannister in the nick of time, retreated for the night, and thereafter attended all meetings armed with a revolver and a bowie knife.

Even the most diplomatic of the Sachems, such as Chairman Schell, a relatively gentle soul, were unable to avoid continual embroilment in the club-swinging debates between the Hards and Softs. A major factor in the exuberance of the period was the General Committee's habit of gathering before each meeting in the basement of Tammany Hall. There, in an ornate saloon adorned with heavy mirrors, paintings of buxom nudes, and portraits of immortal Bucktails, the Sachems would prepare for the meeting by drinking themselves into a fury. Free drinks were provided for their ward gangs, who were already fighting as they climbed the spiral staircase to the meeting hall.

The Hall became such a dangerous place that a Committee of Conciliation was appointed in the summer of 1852. It met on August 20 in hopes of preventing further bloodshed, but scarcely was the meeting underway when loud sounds were heard from the barroom below. The toughest members of both Hards and Softs were in no mood to be conciliated. After a series of knockdowns, they came up the stairs and assaulted the committeemen in the lobbies and hallways of the Wigwam. One particularly earnest delegation attempted to impress its viewpoint on Fernando's friend Sickles, who was obliged to hold them at bay with his revolver and bowie knife while he climbed out a window and jumped to the street below. The meeting of the Committee of Conciliation continued without success until dawn, at which time its battered members escaped homeward.

As violence became an established way of life in Tammany Hall, the Tammany aldermen politely continued about their business. Prices on police appointments and saloon licenses gradually rose. Arrangements for the latter generally involved contracts with the several aldermen who set themselves up as liquor dealers. Hards and Softs bid for the aldermen's favors after primaries; the aldermen sat as justices on the Mayor's Court, which tried all cases of voting frauds. Newspapers which attacked the City Council promptly lost public notices from the City. Citizens who complained of improprieties in the handling of tax moneys were gently admonished by the President of the Council, a prosperous ice merchant: "We are the treasurers of the people and by an economy in the use of their property we can best testify our appreciation of the honors they have conferred upon us."

The plunderings of The Forty Thieves became so evident, however, that a City Reform Party was established to work toward the defeat of the Tammany aldermen in 1854. Tammany had quite a different idea: to win back the mayoralty from the Whigs and thus assume control of the entire City government. Fernando Wood trotted around town seeking the support of all factions. Despite the business scandals which still plagued him, he was known for his solid Congressional record, his leadership in Tammany as a mediator on the General Committee, and his ability to organize the neighborhood gangs.

After the Know-Nothings nominated a candidate for Mayor, it was charged that Fernando had sought the nomination for himself and lost it by only one vote. He maintained that this was a lie. The secrecy surrounding Know-Nothing proceedings precluded a determination of the truth, but the rumor undoubtedly helped Fernando among the anti-immigrants more than it hurt him among the Irish and German Catholics. He had already established himself in Tammany as an immigrant hero, and few Irishmen believed that he was so foolish a politician as to court Tammany's enemies.

The Hards held their own convention, which was expected to name Augustus Schell. Fernando's gangs infiltrated the delegations, put forth his name, and the meeting ended in an uproar. Schell withdrew in favor of the City Reform Party candidate. The Whigs, who had aided in establishing the City Reformers, broke away to put up their own candidate. Delegates to the Softs' convention in Tammany Hall were terrorized by river front hoodlums who offered them good health in the future should they vote for Fernando Wood. When the convention met, Fernando's men stood about the Hall with fists at the ready, gazing steadily at their assigned charges. Thus was Fernando Wood nominated for Mayor of New York City.

With the Softs behind him, Fernando's chief task in the campaign was to combat a mass defection of the conservative Hards to the City Reform banner. As the four-way race developed, it became apparent that the Whigs were out of the running and the Know-Nothings were showing surprising strength. Fernando was attacked as a swindler, but fortunately for him, his Know-Nothing opponent, a reactionary merchant named James Barker, had few claims on sainthood. Barker was accused of having set fire to his store in order to collect the insurance. The voters were content to accept the fact that none of the candidates was purely honest. One candidate for alderman conducted his campaign from the City Prison, where he was in residence on a charge of stabbing to death a policeman who had dared to arrest a political friend of the alderman. In such an atmosphere, it was quite reasonable for Fernando to raise the battle cry: "The people will elect me Mayor though I should commit a murder between now and the election."

Fernando was correct by the barest plurality. He garnered 19,993 votes against 18,553 for the Know-Nothings, 15,386 for the City Reformers, and 5,712 for the Whigs. Mass protests followed. Ten thousand gathered in City Hall Park to cry fraud. The evidence was impressive. In the Bloody Ould Sixth, 400 more votes were cast than the entire voting population of the ward. But Fernando had at least spared the City from electing a Know-Nothing Mayor.

"Well," said the *Morning Courier and Enquirer*, "it now appears that Mr. Wood is Mayor. With a majority against him, Mr. Wood is Mayor. Supported by none but ignorant foreigners and the most degraded class of Americans, Mr. Wood is Mayor. In spite of the most overwhelming proofs that he is a base defrauder, Mr. Wood is Mayor. Contrary to every precedent in the allotment of honor through a municipal history of nearly two hundred years, Mr. Wood is Mayor. His assertion to us that a murder by his own hands could not prevent his election had reason in it; Fernando Wood is Mayor. On New Year's Day he will go to City Hall, and he will go there to give the lie, in the face of every man, woman and child in this city, to the maxim—that honesty is the best policy."

On New Year's Day, 1855, Fernando Wood did indeed go to City Hall, and there, for the next six months, he astounded his critics with such crusading reforms and visionary public improvements that he attracted national attention as The Model Mayor. Following his inauguration, he delivered a sweeping message to the new City Council (controlled by a City Reform-Whig coalition) in which he thundered against all the evils which New Yorkers had come to accept as the price of existence. He deplored the heavy tax burden, which had increased within ten years from $1,800,000 to $5,000,000, and blamed the rise on municipal corruption and extravagance. He announced a program to abolish and consolidate City departments, particularly those supervising the streets, an area of government which had proved an inexhaustible mine of graft for "clubhouse politicians and greedy contractors." Six separate departments had been responsible for pavement, street lamps, cleaning, removal of dead animals, sewerage, and repair of water mains.

Mayor Wood promised to do away with the system of fees for such offices as County Clerk and Corporation Counsel, and raise salaries instead. "There is no good reason," he said, "to permit a few to amass large fortunes whilst other officials, who perform more labor, are paid one-fifth the sum." He served notice that the City would collect interest on all moneys deposited in banks, much to the sorrow of City bureau heads who were pocketing the interest themselves as a token of the chosen banks' appreciation.

He vowed a crack-down on the letting of contracts through fraudulent bidding. He cut in half the number of stagecoaches on Broadway to reduce the dimensions of New York's "horrendous" traffic problems. And, he said, "The practice of driving cattle through the streets is another evil calling for prompt action." Mayor Wood made dirty streets his special concern. He railed against the contractors who were ignoring their agreements to ensure that "every thoroughfare shall be thoroughly and properly cleaned and swept, and all dirt, manure, ashes, garbage, rubbish and sweepings of every kind removed twice a week and on Broadway and the leading avenues, three times a week."

Assuming full authority in the nation's fastest growing metropolis, the Mayor told the astonished aldermen that he would implement his reforms even if it meant seizing extraordinary powers. "I shall not hesitate," he said, "to exercise even doubtful powers when the honor and the interests of the public is abused. The public good will be sufficient warrant to insure my actions."

In a speech to the Police Department, half pep talk and half tirade, he instructed: "You are to be the eyes through which the theater of my duties is to be observed and the messengers to convey to me, through your officers, faithful and truthful reports." Thereupon he rattled off a twenty-three-point manifesto, including stern warnings to enforce the laws against unlicensed liquor sellers, Sabbath-breaking taverns, prostitutes, the drunk, disorderly and riotous, coachmen who obstruct crossings, and servants who throw ashes and garbage into the streets. He laid down the law that the police were not to enter brothels except on official business, were not to referee street fights, nor were they to accept bribes from those whom they arrested.

The Mayor insisted that the police drill in a military manner, instead of lounging about on the steps of drinking houses. He revolutionized the department by putting the men into uniforms, much against their will. And he announced his intention to place the police under direct control of the Mayor, instead of the then current arrangement of dividing authority with the City Courts, or, as Albany wanted, with a Board of Commissioners.

Fernando's mayoralty began to take on Messianic proportions. Where there had been twenty-three hundred saloons open on the Sunday before his election, a spot check now revealed only twenty, and unlicensed taverns were closed altogether. Fernando struck out at the extortionists who preyed on the immigrants arriving at the docks. He cleared the streets of pickpockets and prostitutes. So vigorous was his war on vice that even the Puritan lawyer George Templeton Strong, an irate diarist of the period, was compelled to speak up in defense of civil liberties: "Chief among the civic notabilia is the Mayor's foray or razzia among the unhappy fallen women who perambulate Broadway, the noctivagous strumpetocracy. . . . He is right in trying to keep vice from proclaiming its allurement in the market place—but are his means legal? I think his policy dangerous and bad. It enables any scoundrel of a policeman to lay hands on any woman, against whose husband he may have a grudge, who may be hurrying home from a day's work, or may have been separated by some accident from her escort, and to consign her for a night to a station house. . . ."

But Fernando balanced his reformist zeal by establishing himself as a civilian review board on everything from charges of police brutality to private grievances between quarreling neighbors. The new Mayor instituted what was then an extraordinary practice of keeping a complaint book at City Hall. It was the forerunner of Robert Wagner's Complaintmobile, which toured the City a century later asking for troubles, and the special Box 100 which received more confidential gripes. Mayors from other cities came to New York to watch the experiment in action as Fernando listened to servants complain of unjust masters, wives of drunken husbands, and mothers of errant daughters. Each day a stream of complainants lectured the Mayor on exorbitant hack rates, littered streets, displaced curbstones, and the dearth of jobs. In response to each grievance, Fernando issued a call for swift action from the appropriate municipal servant, and in some cases took a more direct interest. When a tailor accused a policeman of defaulting on a bill, the Mayor called in the debtor, who pleaded poverty. Fernando paid the bill himself.

The first months of the Wood administration, which the public had anticipated would usher in a new era of civic debauchery, turned out to be a marvel of public relations. The Mayor refused all free tickets, omnibus passes, books and magazine subscriptions. "A gift," he said, quoting King Solomon, "blindeth the eye." But Fernando's regime also became known for achievements of substance. He crusaded for a free City university. And, with the support of Daniel Sickles, he made a proposal for a 776-acre park in the center of Manhattan that would cost three million dollars. Civic groups and economy-minded aldermen sought to cut the park site in half. Taxpayer suits were brought charging that real estate taxes should not be squandered for a massive park.

Fernando was attacked for incurring debts with the park development which would require decades to repay. "Future generations," he replied, "who are to pay this expense would have good reason for reflecting upon the present generation if we permitted the entire island to be taken possession of by the population without some spot like this—devoted to rural beauty, healthful recreation and pure atmosphere." In later years, some charged that Fernando's enthusiasm was less than sincere, that he was motivated by the prospect of collecting a handsome sum from contractors who were to develop the park. True or not, no Mayor since has been able to point to a finer accomplishment than the gift to posterity of Central Park.

"Mayor Wood," wrote an astonished George Templeton Strong, "continues our civic hero—inquiring, reforming, redressing, laboring hard with ample result of good. If he goes on this way he will be a public benefactor, recognized as such and honored with statues. . . . He is the first Mayor, for 30 years at least, who has set himself seriously to the work of giving the civic administration a decent appearance of common honesty. He is a very strange phenomenon."

"Will anyone believe he can walk the streets of New York after nightfall and witness the same order and decency as Berlin and Vienna?" asked the New Bedford *Mercury*, one of many out-of-town newspapers which spread Fernando's fame. "Hercules Wood. He goes into the stymphalic dens of the birds of night and they fall before him; he meets the hydra of Sunday tippling, and down on the hundred heads comes his club with a unanimous thwack. . . ." So far-reaching became Fernando's celebrity that a delegation from Iowa urged him to run for President, promising him support at the 1856 Democratic Convention. Fernando modestly declined.

A more serious effort was made by prohibitionists to nominate their hero for Governor. But Fernando felt assured of re-election as Mayor, even though he could not sustain the pace of virtue through the entire two years of his first term ("A few months of reform dulled the Mayor's love of novelty," the *Herald* observed). The Mayor's candidacy for re-election was complicated by one bombshell, in the form of a pamphlet titled "A Biography of Fernando Wood: A History of the Forgeries, Perjuries and other Crimes of Our Model Mayor." Through an intermediary, Fernando sent five hundred dollars to suppress the document before publication. The author was grateful, pocketed the money as an extra profit, and sent his manuscript on to the printer.

There was actually little new in the pamphlet, but it served to remind the voters of the old Fernando Wood. The story was told once again of the *Cater* swindle, of Fernando's alleged Know-Nothing membership, of his masked men seizing control of the 1840 convention which nominated him for Congress. Other assorted incidents of deviltry included a bank error twenty years before of $1,750 in Fernando's favor, which he had not reported but which he later repaid. The chief intention of the pamphlet, however, was to show that Fernando, champion of the immigrant Catholics, was in fact virulently anti-Catholic and fond of telling jokes about priests, several vulgar samples of which were included in detail even though they were "entirely too disgusting for publication."

The pamphlet had little effect on the Archbishop of New York, who was close to Fernando and advised him on a number of appointments. The valuable site of Saint Patrick's Cathedral was acquired from the City by the Archdiocese for the grand sum of eighty-three dollars. The clergy joined many high-minded civic leaders and reputable businessmen in the ranks of Fernando's supporters as the election of 1856 approached, despite the lurid reminders of past scandals.

The Mayor's greatest troubles were not with the Establishment but with the braves of Tammany Hall. As the leader of the Softs, with a substantial following among the Hards, Fernando was the only legitimate Boss of Tammany. He arranged a ritualistic reconciliation of the two factions by marching the Softs in Indian file from the Hall to the Stuyvesant Institute, Hard headquarters, and bringing both groups back to the Wigwam arm-in-arm. But a new group of rebels arose to plague him. Among its leaders was Peter "Brains" Sweeny, Secretary to the Tammany General Committee, who charged that Tammany had received insufficient patronage from the turncoat reform Mayor. Sweeny was actually the spokesman for Alderman Tweed, who preferred not to risk a public break with the Mayor. Sachems Samuel Tilden, Daniel Tiemann, and James Libby objected to Fernando's one-man rule, particularly his control of Democratic nominations.

At the Tammany convention in 1856, the rebels grouped behind Libby for Mayor. "Honest John" Kelly made the nominating speech for Fernando. He began by drawing unanimous cheers for the Democratic candidate for President, James Buchanan, an Irish Presbyterian. More huzzas greeted Honest John's attack on ex-President Millard Fillmore, the Know-Nothing Party's entry that year, and John Fremont, candidate of the new Republican Party. Then he came to Fernando Wood. The Woodites jumped to their feet and applauded. The Libbyites groaned and hissed.

As the *Times* reported the meeting: "Mr. Kelly could not be heard for some time amid the din and confusion. The Wood men, becoming indignant at the conduct of the Libbyites, pitched into them hot and heavy, and for a time a scene of wildest clamor ensued. Blows were given and exchanged with great spirit, and not a few faces were badly disfigured. The timid fled to corners and mounted the platform in such numbers that great fear of its giving way was felt. Indeed, a few planks of the structure were torn down adding to the confusion. At length victory perched on the party of the Woodites. The great body of Libbyites were kicked out of the room and down the stairs with a velocity proportionate to the expelling force behind."

Fernando won the nomination, the rebels put up Libby, and a five-way race ensued with the Mayor also battling the Know-Nothings, City Reformers, and Republicans. In an effort to secure full Democratic support during the campaign, Fernando allowed saloons to open once again for business on Sundays. This cost him dearly among his newest friends, but he needed the help of the influential saloon-keepers and ward leaders. The Mayor was all for reform up to a point—and that point did not include losing his job.

On Election Day, Fernando's police fanned out to the polls, where they took pains to ensure that Woodites won the fist fights and stole the proper ballot boxes. In the Bloody Ould Sixth, again the scene of the most savage battles, fists were little in evidence. The basic weapons were brickbats, pistols, and axes. Once again Fernando failed to win a majority, but he emerged victorious amidst charges by all four opponents that 10,000 of his ballots had been fraudulently cast. This was approximately the number that separated him from the Know-Nothing candidate, his nearest rival.

The troubles in Tammany prompted The Model Mayor to re-reform. In his second term, Fernando Wood performed another about-face and turned City Hall into an open market place where he sold jobs, contracts, and, ultimately, City Hall itself. This last remarkable transaction came about as the result of the City's agreement to buy a $60,000 lot for $196,000. The City Comptroller, outraged at the price, refused to pay, whereupon the equally outraged realtor obtained a judgment against the City and arranged for the Sheriff to sell City Hall at auction. Alderman Daniel Tiemann, a leader of the anti-Fernando rebels in Tammany, was high bidder. He bought City Hall for $50,000 and sold it back to the City for the same price.

Job-selling also placed Fernando in some embarrassing situations, particularly since he had the habit of collecting on a promise and then re-selling the position to someone else. On one such occasion, the victim was pledged first the Corporation Counsel's office, only to find it had gone to a Tammany Sachem, and then the position of Corporation Attorney, which was given to yet another man for $14,400 and a loan of $1,000 which Fernando later refused to pay. The twice-injured party, armed with a revolver, forced his way into Fernando's home, threatened to shoot off his ears, but departed without violence after pronouncing: "Mr. Wood, I called to say, personally, that you are a scoundrel, a rascal, and a perjured villain."

Fernando was not entirely a selfish grafter. He had a deep affection for his brother Benjamin. When the City purchased four thousand glass ballot boxes, someone commented that only twelve hundred had been needed. The price was fifteen dollars apiece. The supplier, who happened to be Ben Wood, had acquired them wholesale for five dollars apiece. This amounted to a forty-thousand-dollar profit for the Wood family.

Brother Ben, who a short time later became the editor and publisher of the pro-Fernando *Daily News*, played a key role in another contract involving a mysterious $40,000. This was the sum which a bidder on the City's street-cleaning contract was required to transport to City Hall before red tape would miraculously vanish. The Council approved the contract for $279,000 a year, despite another bid of $84,000. The high bidder agreed to give brother Ben a quarter of the contract price each year. If he had encountered bureaucratic delays when he first applied, the street-cleaner found that City government could move with blinding speed once the machinery had been properly greased. The night that the Council approved the contract, Mayor Wood stayed in his office until midnight in order to sign the contract immediately after its passage.

The State Legislature responded to Fernando's chicanery by assuming State power over the Street Cleaning Department and establishing a Metropolitan Police Force which was not responsible to the Mayor. Fernando refused to acknowledge this invasion and retained his own police department. Both police forces claimed jurisdiction and roamed the streets independently, sometimes clashing with each other instead of with the lawless. In his diary, George Templeton Strong viewed the struggle with amusement: "The police bill is to take the power out of the paws of Mayor Wood and get it into the hands of the other scoundrels at Albany . . . [I am] waiting with perfect resignation for the Court of Appeals to decide which horde has the legal right to be supported by public plunder."

A giant tug-of-war between Mayor Wood and Governor John Alsop King (son of Rufus King, the Federalist Senator) was touched off in June, 1857, when the City Street Commissioner died. The Governor

named his own man, Daniel Conover, as successor. An angry Fernando
Wood called the aldermen into session and presented his own choice
for the lucrative job: Andrew Hackley, same contractor who had won
the $279,000 street-cleaning assignment.

On June 15, Daniel Conover and his staff arrived at City Hall to
take possession of his office. He was promptly lifted into the air and
carried out by a dozen of Fernando's police. Early next morning, gangs
of assorted loyalties gathered in City Hall Park, and Tammany thugs
loyal to the Mayor joined his police inside City Hall. At 9 A.M. Conover appeared, entered the Hall, once again presented his papers from
the Governor, and was promptly barred from entering the office of the
Street Commissioner. He took up a position outside his office and
began his work, the first official action being the issuance of a rubbish
removal permit. This may have fired the imagination of the Mayor's
police. Once again they removed Conover from the building.

Conover returned again, this time armed with a warrant for the
Mayor's arrest on charges of inciting to riot. But the Sheriff refused to
serve the warrant. Then came a Captain of the Metropolitan Police to
arrest Fernando. The Mayor turned to his own Municipal Police and
said firmly, "Men, put that man out." This was done. Another warrant
was issued on a charge of resisting arrest. Conover prevailed upon the
City Coroner to serve it, but he could not get into the Mayor's office,
and the party was driven out again.

Meanwhile, City Hall and the park outside were swarming with
what one newspaper called "the most reckless rowdies, thieves, pocket-
book droppers and bloated rummies in the city." More than eight
hundred police, hoodlums, and others of Fernando's palace guard
filled the marble corridors of City Hall. They bolted the gates of the
building to guard against another assault by the Conover forces. Outside, thousands were "hooting and yelling" in the park. "Burly ruffians," the *Tribune* reported, "climbed trees and tore off huge limbs for
clubs, while others gathered up stones and brickbats to use in the
service of the Mayor."

Suddenly the Metropolitan Police appeared at the rear of the building and attempted to force their way in. The Mayor's men rushed
down the stairs and out of the basement doors, and "yelling like fiends,
fell upon them with their clubs."

Inside City Hall, the aldermen were voting to confirm the appointment of Andrew Hackley for the street-cleaning post that commanded

expenditures of some two million dollars a year. "It will look like a farce," one alderman argued, "to place such a man at the head of a bureau of such importance where he is to enforce contracts when he is a contractor himself." The presiding alderman broke in: "The gentleman will confine himself to an explanation of his vote." The appointment passed 17–4, after which one of the dedicated aldermen dashed out and joined the attack on the Metropolitan Police.

The Metros were savagely beaten and forced to retreat. After a breather they re-grouped their forces and raced up the front steps in a determined frontal assault on City Hall. "The scene was a terrible one," said the *Times*. "Blows upon naked heads fell thick and fast, and men rolled helpless down the steps, to be leaped upon and beaten until life seemed extinct." The mob in the park moved in and pinned the police from the rear, kicking at the heads of the fallen.

Fernando remained inside City Hall directing operations while the City verged on anarchy. But it so happened at that moment that troops of the Seventh National Guard Regiment, unaware of the fracas, were marching down Broadway on their way to board ship and sail for Boston. When the Commanding General learned of the local war, he turned his troopers toward the battlefield. The soldiers encircled City Hall and slowly tightened the ring until the mob, staring down the rifle barrels, finally decided to disperse. Fernando surrendered his palace and consented to be arrested. It is questionable whether he would have, had he known that a requisition was only then being dispatched to the Seventh Regiment arsenal for 100 rounds of grape shot and 6,000 ball cartridges. The Guardsmen, in their charge on City Hall, had been carrying empty rifles.

The following morning, rather than Fernando going to court, the court came to him at City Hall. The judge, Fernando's lawyers (including George Barnard, a poker pal of Alderman Tweed's), and an obliging District Attorney by the name of Abraham Oakey "The Elegant One" Hall, filed into the Mayor's office, a bit embarrassed by the whole thing. A writ of habeas corpus was issued, some legal language ensued, and Fernando went back to work a free man.

A month later the courts upheld Albany's right to appoint the police department and the street commissioner. Fernando yielded. Several of the State-appointed policemen who sustained injuries in the City Hall riot were still on the critical list, and George Templeton Strong commented in his diary: "Should one of them be public-spirited enough

to die of his wounds, Fernando may be called on to plead to an indictment for murder. He is an egregious demagogue and a scoundrel, and
it's a great pity his opponents are nearly as bad." The policemen didn't
die. Instead, they sued the Mayor personally for damages and were
awarded thirteen thousand dollars. Fernando turned the bill over to
the taxpayers.

The events of the first six months of Fernando's second mayoralty
spurred the State Legislature to the drastic step of cutting his term in
half. Another mayoral election was set for 1857. Opposition to Fernando's renomination was once again touched off within Tammany
by Samuel Tilden, leader of the Free Soiler faction; Peter Sweeny,
chief of the envious regulars; and James Libby, Fernando's Democratic
rival in the previous year's election. But the Mayor's hold on the
organization was sufficiently strong to win the nomination again.
Tilden, Sweeny, and the reform faction joined with a group of Republicans and Know-Nothings in a Citizens Committee to nominate
paint dealer Daniel Tiemann, the alderman and almshouse governor
who had purchased City Hall.

On Election Day there was a mass defection of Democratic votes.
Alderman Tweed announced publicly that he was voting for the
Mayor only out of loyalty to Tammany, but he enlisted the Bowery
Boys to work for Tiemann at the polls against Fernando's Dead Rab-
bits. The results of the voting were close. Tiemann upset Fernando by
43,216 to 40,889.

The Democratic General Committee met at Tammany Hall on
December 8 to consider expelling the Fernando loyalists. By now even
Captain Rynders, who presided at the meeting, had turned against
The Model Mayor. As Rynders read the Committee's majority report
on seating anti-Woodite Sachems from the Ninth Ward, and ejecting
such close colleagues of the Mayor as Daniel Sickles, there were Bronx
cheers from the old guard. Rynders made a sneering reference to Fernando. A ferocious fist fight broke out between the two groups. The
police piled in and began swinging billy clubs. But Tammany took no
action until the following April when Bill Tweed came into the open
as a reformer and successfully backed a slate of anti-Wood men for
the Society's Council of Sachems. Fernando quit Tammany with a
large band of followers and established a new organization at Mozart
Hall, calling it "the true Democracy."

The reform Mayor, Daniel Tiemann, was an honest but politically naïve public servant. With Fernando and his brother Ben strengthening Mozart Hall for a comeback in the 1859 elections, Tammany bypassed Mayor Tiemann and nominated instead a prominent millionaire, William Havemeyer, to oppose an equally prominent millionaire, the Republican candidate George Opdyke. This was a fine stroke of luck for Mozart Hall. Raging against the aristocrats, Fernando rallied the workingmen behind him and returned to City Hall with an 8,500 vote plurality.

To commemorate the triumph of the masses, Mayor Wood, at forty-seven, took as his third wife the sixteen-year-old daughter of a wealthy merchant. (He had been divorced by his first wife and outlived his second.) Dressed in silk hat and tails, his teen-age bride on his arm, the dashing Fernando became a familiar figure at fashionable social functions, the opera, even an occasional Astor party, though he was never fully accepted by the haughty set. At a meeting in New Rochelle, he delivered a speech that placed him at a safe distance from his humble origins: "What . . . will become of . . . the hundreds of millions of Northern capital invested in Southern productions—the wealth which is now annually accumulated by the people of the North, and especially New York, out of the labor of slavery—the profit, the luxury, the comforts, the necessity, nay, even the very physical existence depending upon products only to be obtained by the continuance of slave labor and the prosperity of the slave master?"

With war clouds on the horizon, Fernando was keeping a watchful eye on the lotteries which he and brother Ben were operating in the South. He was also casting his lot with the Democratic Presidential candidate, Illinois Senator Stephen Douglas, against the Republican whom Douglas had defeated for the Senate, ex-Congressman Abraham Lincoln. The campaign brought Tammany and Mozart Hall together in a common cause. Once the champion of the oppressed, Tammany was far more interested now in preserving property rights and the grand alliance of Northern and Southern Democrats forged by Aaron Burr and Martin Van Buren.

Tammany gangs organized to attack abolitionist meetings. The Sachems campaigned vigorously for Douglas in their districts. Fernando made a personal loan of $60,000 to Douglas for the campaign in exchange for a mortgage on his property in Illinois. With the help of repeaters and fictitious voters, Tammany carried New York City for Douglas by almost 2 to 1. In the nation, Douglas was easily defeated

by Lincoln. He died the following year without repaying his debt to
Fernando. It was charged that the Mayor quietly foreclosed on the land
before Douglas' needy widow could stop him.

The imminent secession of the southern states inspired in Mayor
Wood the most extraordinary proposal of his career. In a message to
the City Council he declared:

> "It would seem that a dissolution of the Federal Union is inevita-
> ble. . . . It cannot be preserved by coercion or held together by
> force. . . . With our aggrieved brethren of the Slave States we have
> friendly relations and a common sympathy. . . . Why should not
> New York City, instead of supporting by her contributions in
> revenue two thirds of the expenses of the United States, become
> also equally independent? As a free city, with but a nominal duty
> on imports, her local government could be supported without taxa-
> tion upon her people. Thus we could live free from taxes, and have
> cheap goods nearly duty free . . . why may not New York disrupt
> the bands which bind her to a venal and corrupt master—to a peo-
> ple and a party that have plundered her revenues, attempted to
> ruin her commerce, taken away the power of self-government, and
> destroyed the Confederacy of which she was the proud Empire
> City?"

Fernando thus became the first of many Mayors to contemplate
the bliss of home rule, free from all interference from Albany, and the
only Mayor to make a serious proposal for an independent state thriving on the Federal customs duties. The threat of a major secession by
the South presented to him the finest opportunity for proposing independence, and the timing of his announcement also placed him in
the forefront of the anti-war Democrats, or Copperheads, who opposed
President Lincoln's military preparations to preserve the Union.

But the firing on Fort Sumter aroused Tammany's old patriotic
wrath. Even Congressman Daniel Sickles, a Southern sympathizer and
Fernando ally, decided the South had gone too far. Sickles helped arm
and train a volunteer brigade which he led down to the front. Tammany itself raised a regiment, the 42nd Infantry, under the command
of Grand Sachem William Kennedy. In Washington, en route to the
field, Kennedy died of a heart attack and a Regular Army officer took
over. The Tammany Regiment fought in thirty-six battles. At Gettys-

burg it suffered heavy losses in the face of Pickett's charge on Cemetery Ridge.

Daniel Sickles' brigade had grown to corps size by the time it reached Gettysburg. At the famous battle of the Peach Orchard the men faced a withering attack from General James Longstreet's Confederate corps. General Sickles, the onetime Hunker who had leaped out of an upper story window in Tammany Hall without injury, lost a leg at Gettysburg and became one of the most controversial figures of the war. Some charged that Sickles had almost lost Gettysyburg for the North by moving his corps to a risky forward position. But others acclaimed him as the hero of the day for absorbing the shock of the rebel attack.

Tammany did not support the anti-slavery policies of the national administration, but its patriotic pride was aroused for the first time since the War of 1812. A banner was hung outside the Wigwam for the duration of the war emblazoned with the words of Andrew Jackson: "The Union must and shall be preserved." Resolutions were passed in support of the Union, repealing previous pronouncements of sympathy for the South. One such resolution condemned Mayor Wood and Mozart Hall for disloyalty to the cause of America. In response, Fernando set about raising a Mozart Regiment. (Apart from a regimental flag which he purchased from contributions, the group never found financial backing.) Fernando's oratory also took another sudden turnabout: "Would that personal and political prejudices were for once laid aside, that all could combine in one common effort to defend and maintain the Government—stand by her with our blood and with our treasure and to avert the blow which a foul conspiracy has leveled against it."

Tammany and Mozart united behind Horatio Seymour in his successful campaign for the governorship in 1861. But the Sachems again balked at nominating Fernando for re-election. In a partial move to breach the rift, they gave the nomination to Godfrey Gunther, one of the staunch Woodites faced with expulsion after Fernando's loss in 1857. Gunther was a fur dealer of good repute, and an excellent choice to face George Opdyke, whose Republican endorsement this time was joined by a group of reform Democrats, under the collective banner of the People's Union of Republicans and Democrats.

The campaign against Mayor Wood was the bitterest of his career, a thorough recitation of all the frauds of a lifetime. The three-way election was so close that a recount was ordered. On the final check, the Republican candidate George Opdyke had 25,380 votes, with Tammany's Gunther trailing by 613, and Fernando Wood behind by another 600. In an election night post-mortem at the Wigwam, a shout of "Three Cheers for Fernando Wood!" brought a water pitcher flying at the head of the lonely enthusiast.

It was now apparent, and most especially to the eminent reformers Bill Tweed and Peter Sweeny, that the reunification of the New York City Democracy would not be achieved unless Fernando Wood were somehow removed from the scene. Fernando ran again and lost to his old friend Gunther by almost 3 to 1. The split in the Democratic vote was therefore not overly serious, but Bill Tweed had plans for New York City which could afford no defections, and which could well utilize the old Tammany gangs over which Fernando still presided. Tweed and Wood met in the fall of 1862 in an effort to bring Mozart back into the Tammany fold. It was decided to split the nominations for City offices between the two Halls. In addition, Fernando was promised local appointments for various friends if he would only pack up and leave town. A simple itinerary was agreed upon: back to the old Congressional seat in Washington.

Fernando was elected to Congress that fall, and re-elected and re-elected. In all, he spent eight terms in Washington, serving until the day he died. He became a leading national spokesman for the Copperheads, the co-organizer of the Peace Democrats with the anti-Lincoln Ohio Congressman Clement Vallandigham. The President banished Vallandigham to Canada, but Fernando stayed in Washington, grew a handlebar mustache, and became "a man of distinction."

He made a few speeches for States' rights and against the tariff, twice tried to impeach President Grant, but in later years he mellowed and said little on the floor. It was, for Fernando Wood, a secure and relaxing period of retirement from the battles of New York City. His attendance was exemplary; he had little interest in returning to New York. For Tammany, however, absence made the hearts grow fonder. The Sachems reappraised their old Boss as a genuine friend who showed steadfast loyalty to the interests of the city. A journalist put it another way: "His patriotism never seemed to reach beyond the limits of Manhattan Island."

At a time when Congress was swarming with unruly legislators, Fernando Wood was the epitome of dignity and decorum, sitting bolt upright in his place, listening attentively to every speaker, his boots shiny as glass, silver hair combed neatly, mustache meticulously trimmed, and all buttons buttoned on his black frock coat. His was an impressive legislative record. "No one," the New York *Herald* reported, "ever saw him put his feet on the desk or spit on the carpet."

Chapter 5

The Great Reformer: William Marcy Tweed

> "The tiger affords a useful lesson for you. The exceeding agility of this creature, the extraordinary quickness of his sight, and above all, his discriminating power in the dark, teach you . . . to look sharp to every engagement you enter into; and to let neither misty days, nor gloomy nights, make you lose sight of the worthy objects of your pursuit."
>
> —*Chief Tamanend* (*attr.*)

New York was a city in crisis. It was overrun by poverty, crime, racial violence, filthy streets, terrible housing. But this was not a Lindsay campaign cry of 1965. This was an accepted fact of life in 1863, the year that Fernando Wood was exiled to Washington.

As the City's population approached one million, about one-fourth of the entire City was Irish-born, a fifth was German. In all, immigrants now formed a majority. Jobs grew scarce, government remained aloof, and the business of exploitation boomed.

One out of every ten New Yorkers had a police record from the previous year. Police now estimated active criminals at 80,000, which did not include those who paid protection, such as saloon keepers and brothel proprietors.

Within the inferno of the Bloody Ould Sixth Ward, foul-smelling, rundown tenements lined such streets as Worth, Park, and Baxter, which came together in the inner ring of the slum: the notorious Five Points. In this and other immigrant ghettos, a family with ten dollars a month could afford a dark attic without windows or chimney to let out the coal fumes. In the cellars, bunks of rotting straw and old rags were available for a nickel a night.

An army of perhaps fifteen thousand vagabond children roamed from river to river, from the Battery to Central Park, sleeping on basement coal piles in the winter and on the docks in the summer. Two orphans were discovered living in a burned-out safe on Wall Street.

Fashionable New Yorkers moved up Fifth Avenue and over to the slopes of Murray Hill as the city stretched inexorably northward. The rural village of Harlem was still somewhat remote, but Yorkville was within hiking distance. Some pedestrian commuters walked to work downtown eight miles each day. This was preferable to the walk to Pennsylvania, where seventeen regiments of Manhattan and Brooklyn volunteers, including the Tammany Regiment, were preparing for the Battle of Gettysburg.

With the advent of the National Conscription Law, prosperous New Yorkers still had few worries. It was legally permissible to purchase an exemption for three hundred dollars, as much money as a City laborer would see in a year. As for the poor, the matter would be decided by chance. On Saturday morning, July 11, a large and sullen crowd gathered outside the Provost Marshal's office on Third Avenue near 46th Street to watch the spinning of a huge drum containing the names of New York City males between 18 and 45 years old. The drum stopped, a blindfolded official reached in and pulled out a slip of paper: "William Jones, 46th Street, corner Tenth Avenue." The draft in New York had begun. By the end of the day, 1,235 more names had been called. The office was closed with the announcement that more names would be drawn on Monday.

The heat and idleness of that July weekend nourished discontent. Men clustered on street corners and in taverns to complain about the draft, and especially the three-hundred-dollar exemption clause. Monday was another blazing hot day. Early in the morning on the West Side, the gangs were coming up from the cellars and down the rickety steps of the tenements. They marched up Eighth and Ninth Avenues and were joined by laborers at work on the streets. They entered factories, urged the workers to join them and thrashed the foremen who tried to stop them. They cut east across Central Park and gathered in a vacant lot off Fifth Avenue with large groups which had come up Third Avenue from the Bowery and the Five Points. Clubs, axes, and rifles were distributed, anti-draft placards were raised, the speakers inflamed the crowd. Then they moved on to Third Avenue and the draft office.

Police and reporters estimated the crowd outside the office at ten thousand, but this was a standard count for nineteenth-century New York mobs. It may have been much higher. One observer noted that the curb-to-curb procession across 47th Street to Third Avenue took twenty-five minutes to pass a given point. As the mob crossed Park Avenue, they hacked down telegraph poles, halted horsecars and carriages, unhitched the teams, and chased away the passengers.

At the draft office, the Provost Marshal pulled out a name from the drum. The crowd pressed in closer to the single line of policemen who stood with drawn clubs in front of the building. In the front rank of the mob was the entire membership of Volunteer Engine Company No. 33, known as the "Black Joke." The leader of the Black Jokesters had been drafted. Someone fired a pistol in the air. The firemen rushed the building, overwhelmed the police, swarmed inside, and wrecked the office and the hated lottery drum. The Provost Marshal managed to escape through a back door with his records just as the volunteer firemen set fire to the building.

Police reinforcements arrived and were thrown back. A detachment of the Invalid Corps, crippled and wounded Civil War veterans, were rushed in from sentry duty. All but three managed to retreat: two were fatally beaten with their own rifles and the third was chased to the East River, caught by the mob, and thrown down to the rocks where he was crushed to death by boulders thrown from above.

Thirty-two policemen were assigned to guard the 21st Street armory. As sledge hammers and tree trunks battered down the doors of the armory, the police escaped through a hole in the rear wall and ran to their station house a block away, but that building was soon in flames. A fresh detachment of police arrived at the armory as boxes of ammunition were being thrown onto the street. Part of the mob barricaded itself in the drill room where the carbines were housed, while the others, driven out by the club-swinging police, set fire to the old wooden building. It was never learned how many, imprisoned in the drill room, died in the flames. Workmen later carted away fifty baskets and barrels of human bones.

Throughout the City, gangs were roaming the streets, looting and burning homes, ransacking stores and taverns, tearing up rails, disabling streetcars, and searching for Negro scapegoats. A group of rioters assembled in front of Republican Mayor George Opdyke's home on Fifth Avenue near 16th Street, but a band of fifty determined neighbors with carbines, swords, and pistols, kept them at bay. The next mass assault, according to police intelligence reports, would be in the downtown commercial district against the banks and the United States Sub-Treasury. But a valiant stand by police on Broadway and a drenching rain after dark saved the financial fortresses of lower Manhattan.

New York's Negro community was not as lucky. Three men were found hanged from trees. Others were beaten and tortured. Homes were burned in the Negro neighborhoods of the Five Points and on the West Side near Hudson Street. One man who tried to defend his home on Clarkson Street was dragged out, hanged, and cremated while the crowd danced around the fire. Uptown on Fifth Avenue, between 43rd and 44th Streets, a mob attacked the Asylum for Colored Orphans. All but one of the 233 Negro children, all under the age of twelve, were hustled out the back door and taken to a police station. The rioters broke in just as the children escaped. They pilfered bedding, clothing, and toys from the rooms. A little girl, left behind in the rush, was found shivering under a bed. They killed her and burned the building to the ground.

Mayor Opdyke sent frantic messages for help to Secretary of War Stanton, Governor Horatio Seymour, West Point, Rochester, Utica, and to the Governors of New Jersey, Connecticut, and Rhode Island. On Tuesday, with the battle still raging, Governor Seymour declared a state of insurrection. But when he appeared on the steps of City Hall, with County Supervisor Bill Tweed at his side, he called the rioters "my friends" and made a tepid plea for order.

As new assaults were mounted against such diverse targets as the Tribune Building and Brooks Brothers clothing store, five regiments of the Union Army were rushed in from the front. Artillery pieces were set up in the streets. On Ninth Avenue, police and soldiers fired grapeshot into the mob. In the East River and the Lower Bay, warships dropped anchor and trained their guns on Wall Street, Broadway, Governor's Island, and the Brooklyn Navy Yard.

Five days passed before the riot was under control. It was one of the bloodiest battles of the Civil War: more than two thousand dead, with no count of the bodies dragged off to the inaccessible neighborhoods of the Five Points. About eight thousand were injured, including virtually every policeman on the force. Seventeen Negroes were found hanged, but seventy more were missing. Fifty soldiers were killed and some three hundred wounded. More than a hundred buildings were destroyed by fire. Trade and commerce had come to a standstill. Property damage totaled about five million dollars.

In the aftermath of the riots, Mayor Opdyke was careful to praise Democratic supervisors and commissioners for being "faithful and courageous advisors" during the emergency. But the Draft Riots were quickly seized upon by Tammany as ammunition against the Mayor and President Lincoln. Tammany aldermen and State legislators called for the immediate withdrawal of armed troops and demanded that the police cease "murdering" their constituents. A Tammany police magistrate ruled the National Conscription Law to be unconstitutional and urged citizen resistance. The City Council appropriated $2,500,000 to enable the poor to buy their way out of the draft just as the rich.

The riots of July 1863, although begun as a protest against the draft law, became an outlet for murder and plunder, an open rebellion against the prosperous lords of the City. They were the symptom of a city swollen with decades of floodtide immigration, ruled by an upstate Legislature callous to its needs, bursting with new forces that cried out to be governed. New York was a city growing without direction, without a centralization of power and services, with poor communications, inadequate protection of health and safety, and little evidence of concern or compassion. It was, in other words, a city that demanded a Boss.

William Marcy Tweed was the great-grandson of a Scottish blacksmith who lived part of his life on the banks of the Tweed River, southeast of Edinburgh, and the remainder in the Manhattan section of Cherry Hill, east of the present City Hall.

William's father, Richard, broke away from the family trade to become a chairmaker, hoping to pattern his life after a prominent neighbor named Thomas Ash who made chairs, but more importantly, was a fire company foreman and Treasurer of the Tammany Society. But Dick Tweed spent all his time on chairmaking to provide for his children, and harbored the hope that one of his sons would eventually make his way into politics. He named his youngest child after Senator William Marcy, the powerful wheeler-dealer in Martin Van Buren's Albany Regency who had uttered the classic defense of patronage: "To the victors belong the spoils."

Tweed was born in a two-story brick house at 1 Cherry Street which was later torn down to make way for the Brooklyn Bridge. Young Bill attended the same elementary school on Chrystie Street that helped shape the artistic talent of Tom Nast, who immortalized the Democratic Donkey, the Republican Elephant, the Tammany Tiger—and Boss Tweed.

At the age of eleven, Bill Tweed, an indifferent student, left school to work in his father's shop. Two years later he took a job with a hardware dealer. Brawling and muscular as a teen-ager, Tweed earned the nickname "Big Bill" following a series of victories against neighborhood adversaries. He fought his way to the leadership of the local gang, the Cherry Hillers, and piloted them through successful campaigns against the rival Henry Street Gang and in the stealing of pigs' tails and potatoes. Dick Tweed, fearing for his son's future, shipped him off to a New Jersey boarding school. Under the tutelage of a genteel minister (whose father had helped found the Society of the Cincinnati) Big Bill gained a solid background in bookkeeping. He became rather handy with numbers.

To prepare professionally for his future, he then clerked two years for a tobacco merchant, after which he kept the books for his father, who had become partner in a brush factory. At twenty-one, Tweed married the boss's daughter, Mary Jane Skaden, whose father was Dick Tweed's principal partner. The newlyweds moved into the top floor of the Skadens' house on Madison Street and Bill Tweed was made a junior partner in the firm. There is no record of the Skadens' wedding gift to their daughter and new son-in-law, but a fair guess would be that a thick carpet was laid on that top floor. Bill Tweed already weighed 270 pounds.

The Boss of the Cherry Hillers could not be content merely with domestic respectability. His position, his wife, his in-laws were all important to success. But to give vent to his animal spirits, and to fulfill the political ambitions that his father had instilled in him, he needed another avenue. He found it at the age of twenty-five when he joined the newly formed "Americus Vespucci" volunteer fire company. The red-shirted men of Americus Engine Company Number Six, known as the Big Six, won a reputation for outracing and outmaneuvering rival firemen. Big Bill, tougher and more bombastic than the clerks and artisans in the outfit, moved up to foreman within two years, to the great delight of his father.

Half the fun of firefighting in the days of the Big Six was beating a rival company to the hydrant. Sometimes, if the race was close, fights would break out enroute. "Crowds gathered to see Big Six and Eight coming downtown," a chronicler of fire lore related. "When they met, the excitement was intense, and the cheering furious as one engine or the other gained in speed." The redshirts, teamed like horses, dragged Big Six through the streets while Big Bill Tweed jogged alongside, blowing a silver trumpet and shouting encouragement: "Jump her, boys! Jump her lively!" Bands of ragtag children, adult firebuffs, and pickpockets tumbled along in the rear. Big Six could always be spotted from blocks away. First, there was Bill, who cut a unique figure. And then, there was the bright emblem painted on the engine box of Big Six: the head of a snarling Bengal tiger.

On occasion, the fire companies would agree to take a sweeping detour to the scene of the blaze. Such pacts made for bigger and better fires, and also provided a longer race. Once on the scene, the men would fight for position while flames consumed the building. Big Bill would usually arrive ahead of Big Six to make sure that an enemy company was not lying in ambush. If he were a few minutes late, he might have to contend with an unfriendly fireman who had planted a barrel over the hydrant and was perched on it awaiting his own company. There was no penalty attached to knocking him off. But the Fire Commissioner did call Big Bill on the carpet once for obstructing an opposition engine enroute to the fire.

Bill Tweed gloried in the life of the fireman, although his wife didn't wholly approve. He stayed home as little as possible, even (and perhaps especially) after three children were added to the household. He paid less and less attention to his father-in-law's business. "Bill," his older brother admonished him, "you always were a loafer and you always will be." He was a coarse, fun-loving man who could roar with laughter at himself. These were the happiest years of his life. He reveled in the race, the fights, the victories. He liked to rub shoulders with Democratic ward leaders. He enjoyed the politics of fire-fighting itself, which involved, for example, negotiating alliances with hose companies that would deny the use of water to other engine companies. And Bill Tweed was always a big hit at the annual Fireman's Ball. Despite his massive physique, he was a "tip-top dancer," according to one onlooker. "He was young and good-looking then, with fine dark brown hair and clear gritty eyes."

The fame of the mighty Big Six spread beyond New York, and Bill took his celebrated company on a junket throughout the East. In each city, the Bix Six was reviewed on parade by the local officials. Tweed and his boys were taken to the White House, where Big Bill was instructed to introduce the Americus Engine Company Number Six to President Millard Fillmore. "Mr. President," Tweed said, in one of his longest public speeches, "these are Big Six's boys." When asked by a reporter how they differed from anyone else's boys, he elaborated: "They don't look like any other redshirts. Does Niagara look like Croton Dam? Not by a damned sight."

New York's volunteer fire department, with its boisterous comraderie and magical hold on youth, was a natural doorway to Tammany politics. Foreman Tweed, lively, shrewd, and immensely popular, was the outstanding exemplar of the new firehouse breed. At the age of twenty-seven, he was approached by Tammany to run for assistant alderman from the Seventh Ward. He made a good race, lost to his Whig opponent by forty-seven votes, took the defeat with good grace, and decided to run again.

The Seventh Ward was a changing neighborhood where professionals, businessmen, and high-wage artisans were gradually giving way to low-income immigrants. Whig and Democratic sentiments were about evenly divided. The year after Tweed's first try for office, he was nominated to face a wealthy Whig alderman and shipbuilder. Tweed viewed the contest as perilous at best, and induced a Whig friend, the popular principal of an East Broadway girls' school, to enter the campaign and split the Whig vote. The tactic succeeded. Tweed's friend siphoned off 206 Whig ballots. Thus was Bill Tweed elected by forty-eight votes to "The Forty Thieves" City Council on Tammany's reform ticket.

Freshman Tweed learned his duties with amazing speed. He was appointed teller of the Council's votes and funds, and chairman of the

Henry Clay funeral committee, which involved outlays of $1,400 for cigars and refreshments and $2,500 for black crepe. He played an active role in the real estate and franchise scandals which led to the formation of the City Reform Party and the passage of a new City Charter stripping the councilmen of their franchising and police powers. The new charter, pushed through by Peter Cooper, the builder of the first American locomotive, took effect only after Tweed had acquired sufficient funds to bankroll a most promising future.

Tweed was also successful, during his second year on the Council, in using his franchise powers to win a seat in the United States Congress. The Democratic leaders in the city of Williamsburgh (not yet a part of Brooklyn) were anxious to secure a ferry franchise to transport their constituents across the East River to Manhattan. It so happened that the Congressional district Bill Tweed was eyeing encompassed Williamsburgh as well as his own Seventh Ward on the Lower East Side. A fairly simple *quid pro quo* came to mind. Tweed promised the franchise in exchange for Williamsburgh backing. Despite this arrangement, Tweed's opponent managed a tie vote at the district's nominating convention. This might have created some problems except that the chairman of the convention was Bill Tweed. In the interest of fair play, he modestly cast the tie-breaking vote with the remark: "Tweedie never goes back on Tweedie."

In Washington, without the exertions of firefighting to keep him in trim, Congressman Tweed, at thirty, became a bit flabby. He had a stomach for rich food but none for such complex national issues as the Kansas-Nebraska Act and slavery in the territories. The members of the new Republican coalition of Whigs, Free Soilers, Barnburners, and ultra-soft-shelled Democrats, seemed to be nice fellows but a little boring in their preoccupations. Tweed spoke on the floor of the House only twice, and, according to one account, "uttered nothing worth listening to." Tweed himself admitted: "I can't talk, and I know it. As to spending my time hearing a lot of snoozers discuss the tariff and the particulars of a contract to carry the mails from Paducah to Schoharie, I don't think I'm doing that just now." He did not run for re-election.

Tweed returned to the City a little short on funds. He had been a heavy spender in the Capital. He was also tying up cash in a rather insecure stock, the Erie Railroad. He joined his father and his brother in a new chairmaking enterprise which quickly went into debt. And he gained a most unlikely position: member of the New York City Board of Education. It all came clear when a later investigation revealed that a lame girl, seeking a $300-a-year teaching job, was required to pay $75 to the Board as tribute. Extortion from prospective teachers provided almost as good an income as the fraudulent sale of textbooks to the city.

A goodly share of his secret take was paid by Tweed to his father, who retired from business after a heart attack. The firm of Richard Tweed and Sons, Chairmakers, was far in the red. Bill's older brother, who had castigated him for "loafing," had gambled away the profits over the years. To shield his father from the failure of the family business, Bill Tweed turned over a monthly share of fictitious "earnings."

Tweed found one other substantial source of income. He became a member of the bi-partisan New York County Board of Supervisors, which was designed to end corruption in elections, contracts, and appropriations. The theory ran that with six Republicans and six Democrats, there would be a pure stand-off. Of course, it only required one swing vote to corrupt the anti-corruption board. Bill Tweed found his man: a Republican supervisor who was willing to accept twenty-five hundred dollars as the price for staying home on the day that election inspectors were named by the Board of Supervisors. Thereafter, the controlling Tammany faction on the board held regular meetings to determine which money bills to pass, how much to increase them, and how to divide the excess. This was the forerunner of the Tweed Ring, but ambitions were then modest. "It was just for making money," Tweed said later, "not for controlling politics."

The chief obstacle to combining those two pleasures was in the person of Mayor Fernando Wood. "I never yet went to get a corner lot that I didn't find Wood had got in ahead of me," Bill Tweed complained. Tweed worked behind the scenes in the Tammany organization, piecing together a coalition powerful enough to drive Fernando out of the Hall. His closest allies in this endeavor were Peter "Brains" Sweeny, a brilliant but tongue-tied attorney; Richard "Slippery Dick" Connolly, a shifty-eyed bookkeeper of considerable mathematical talent; and George Barnard, whose nicknames were usually unprintable. When Tweed had gained sufficient strength for an open break with Fernando, he supported a winning ticket for Tammany's Council of Sachems, forcing Fernando to depart and establish Mozart Hall. Tweed hated Wood, but it was not a personal animosity. Big Bill wanted to reform Tammany Hall. He was afraid there would be nothing left to steal.

In 1859, when Fernando returned to the mayoralty from Mozart Hall, Tweed decided to make his bid for control of Tammany. He offered himself as a candidate for the Council of Sachems. Once seated, he managed to maneuver his poundage into the presiding officer's chair at Tammany conventions and guide the nominations.

George Barnard, a handsome, eccentric dandy with a Yale education, assisted Tweed to his eminence. Barnard, an alumnus of gambling houses and minstrel troupes, had settled into the practice of law in New York and numbered among his former clients Fernando Wood, whom he represented during the struggle with the Metropolitan Police. Tweed decided to nominate Barnard for City Recorder.

"So I took the chair, and wasn't very comfortable in it either. A man from California, by the name of Doyle, was running for Recorder against Barnard," Tweed recounted. "I saw, as the roll call proceeded, that Doyle had the majority of the delegates. Said I to the secretary, 'Have a motion made to dispense with the calling of the roll!' It was done. 'All in favor of Mr. Barnard as the nominee of this body say aye. Carried! The meeting is adjourned!' Well, there was a riot and I was driven into one corner; Isaiah Rynders had a pistol as long as my arm drawn and cocked. Said he, 'I'll pay you for this!' I was scared, but I didn't say so. 'I'm not afraid of the whole ward of you fighting villains,' said I, and we all got out."

Tweed next elevated Barnard to the State Supreme Court despite the warning of Barnard's brother: "George knows about as much law as a yellow dog." Legal circles were treated to a spectacle that was remarkable even in those days of unorthodox jurists. On the bench, Barnard was usually drowsy from all-night poker sessions with Tweed or from risqué adventures with young ladies who ultimately betrayed him to the press. In his more alert moments, the Judge would spice his opinions with obscenities and off-color jokes. And while counsel droned on through lengthy arguments, Barnard would amuse himself by whittling. Each morning his court officer provided him with a bundle of pine sticks and a freshly sharpened knife. At the end of the day, a large pile of shavings was swept up from beneath His Honor's chair by a young attendant named Richard Croker.

By hoisting Barnard to the bench, Bill Tweed cleared the way to establishing his own law firm at 95 Duane Street. Any man could hang out a counselor-at-law shingle with the approval of the courts. George Templeton Strong summed up the state of the judiciary in the 1860's: "The average New York judge is as bad as the alderman, if not worse." Tweed came to control a slew of judges, including Albert Cardozo, a scholarly gentleman whose son, Benjamin Cardozo, fulfilled his father's potential for greatness as a distinguished Justice of the United States Supreme Court.

Sachem, lawyer, Supervisor, ex-Congressman Tweed then spent $100,000 on a campaign for the lucrative post of Sheriff. But his real objective was the defeat of Mayor Wood. He spread before the public all the scandals of Fernando's administration. He charged him with being a dangerous Copperhead and Know-Nothing, an effective issue with Irish Catholics, for Tweed had lost his seat in Congress to a Know-Nothing candidate and was regarded as one of the few trustworthy Protestants in Tammany. The split between Tammany and Mozart brought in Republican Mayor Opdyke. Tweed spent his entire fortune without winning as Sheriff, but Fernando was through.

That was the best $100,000 a young fellow ever lost. It was all recouped quickly, and then some, through sound public service as Supervisor and Deputy Street Commissioner. The latter sounded unimportant, except that Tweed had control over the Commissioner, which meant not only the letting of contracts but the hiring of thousands of maintenance men in exchange for their services on Election Day.

And Bill Tweed became supreme in the City's Democratic machine as chairman of Tammany's Executive Committee. "Boss Tweed" was no insult. He liked to be called "Boss." Tammany and New York were seeking a strong reformer, and Big Bill Tweed was prepared to give the City a thorough reforming.

In 1865, the year of Lincoln's assassination, a popular, pliable lawyer named John Hoffman became Mayor of New York and Grand Sachem of the Tammany Society. He was totally indebted to Bill Tweed.

Each day in the basement of City Hall, Mayor Hoffman ate lunch with Tweed, Peter "Brains" Sweeny, Comptroller Matthew Brennan, and invited guests. These were pleasant social gatherings with a few political overtones which evolved into serious seminars on the conduct of municipal affairs. Gradually, as members of the group were dropped and replaced, there came about the combine which was to become known as the Tweed Ring.

The first cast change was the replacement of Comptroller Brennan with Tweed's henchman "Slippery Dick" Connolly. Brennan had compiled a fairly honest record and wanted to run for re-election as Comptroller, but Tweed turned him down. When pressed for an explanation, the Boss was quite candid: "Because you won't make money yourself, nor let others make any. That's why."

Slippery Dick Connolly, who had left the State Senate to become a bank manager, was more to Tweed's liking. Although Thomas Nast portrayed him later as a surly, squint-eyed creature, he was actually a jovial backslapper and handshaker. He also had a reputation among those who knew him best for political chicanery and a certain carelessness with promises. But he was hailed publicly for his steadfast honesty and perseverance: an Irish immigrant with little formal education who had diligently worked his way up in politics and finance. "Amid all the storms and whirlwind of public suspicion," the *Times* commented at the time of Connolly's election to the State Senate, "he almost alone stands forth untainted by the breath of distrust—the idol and the nominee of every branch of the great Democratic family."

Dick Connolly was known to browbeat his subordinates. But before his superiors, notably Bill Tweed, he was transformed into a fawning, cringing, unctuous little chap. He was clever with figures. All in all, a perfect replacement for Matt Brennan.

Tweed had pushed Connolly along as County Clerk and State Senator. He had also secured the District Attorney's office for Peter "Brains" Sweeny. But Peter Sweeny, a withdrawn and reticent man, broke down while delivering his first speech to the jury, and resigned his office in humiliation. The Tweed-Sweeny alliance was never completely comfortable. Sweeny was a slight man, a graduate of Columbia College, well read, attuned to art and travel. "We were so opposite and unlike that we never got along very well," Bill Tweed said later. He was perhaps the only man that Tweed ever feared. Too many people were calling him the "brains" behind the Boss.

Yet Peter Sweeny had a solid Tammany background: son of an Irish immigrant liquor dealer in the Bloody Ould Sixth Ward; waiter in a Jersey City saloon; lobbyist in Albany for the stage-coach companies. When the Hoffman administration came to power, he sought and received from Tweed one of the most lucrative jobs in city government: the office of City Chamberlain. The Chamberlain was in charge of selecting banks for the deposit of City funds. It was common practice for him to pocket large portions of the interest, estimated at $200,-000 a year, so common in fact that the State Legislature legalized it.

But Peter Sweeny renounced his predecessors: "As a taxpayer, I would not be satisfied that the custodian of the public moneys should reserve, however legally, to his own use, interest or other advantages from such moneys which might be applied to the reduction of taxation." The public was stunned by this outburst of integrity. "With self-denial and a sublime courage never before equaled, he absolutely refuses to touch a dollar of the interest on the city deposits," the *Herald* editorialized. "If this wonderful reform is to be the cue of the Tammany party of the future, we can have no objection to the success of the Tammany nominees."

Thus did Peter Sweeny win for himself a reputation for honesty that was to serve as a valuable shield for future peculations. He also modestly disavowed any great influence that might accrue to him as Secretary of the Tammany General Committee and an aide to Bill Tweed: "I am not and never claimed to be a leader," he said. "I am a sort of adviser. I try to harmonize the interests of the party and endeavor to secure good nominations and sound principles as I understand them. But I do not aspire to the position of leader. I am simply a passenger in the ship with the privilege of going ashore if I do not like its management or its course."

The third member of the Tweed Ring's inner circle was District Attorney Abraham Oakey "The Elegant One" Hall, perhaps the most tragic of the cast, for he had dreams of grandeur for himself and the City which Bill Tweed twisted and exploited. Oakey Hall, playwright, actor, poet, critic, and great raconteur, was a merry showman with twinkling blue eyes, a thick General Grant beard, black-ribboned pince-nez, and almost outrageous sartorial splendor. He delighted in tailor-made frieze coats with velvet collars, stiff-front shirts and silk bow-ties, embroidered vari-colored vests, and expensive jewelry of his own design. Oakey achieved his *chef d'oeuvre* one Saint Patrick's Day when he reviewed the annual parade dressed in green hat, green tie, green tailcoat, green spats, and green kid gloves.

Such an impression did he make that day that the *Sun* speculated: "O'Hall is said to have solemnly assured a committee of Germans that if the French get beaten during the present [Franco-Prussian] war, he will come out immediately in a full suit of Prussian blue. Meanwhile he is having a tri-colored suit made in case of another contingency."

Oakey Hall changed his religion and politics almost as often as his neckties. He was raised a Presbyterian, switched to the Swedenborgian sect, later became a Roman Catholic. In politics, he started as a Whig, became a Know-Nothing, then a Republican, and finally, appalled at the nomination of rustic Abe Lincoln, joined the Democrats. On February 1, 1864, he appeared before the Sachems of Tammany, signed the registration book, and entered a couplet: "Whilst Council fires hold out to burn/The vilest sinner may return."

Hall's period of service as District Attorney was a mixed bag. He prevailed upon Fernando Wood to rotate policemen with an eye toward reducing opportunities for bribery and extortion. It was estimated that in six years he jailed twelve thousand criminals and quashed ten thousand other indictments. He displayed a noticeable lack of interest in liquor violations, and endeared himself to saloonkeepers with the remark: "Somehow the press of business of my office has been so great that I have never yet found time to prosecute a man for taking a drink after 12 o'clock at night."

But Oakey Hall had tremendous energy and capacity to work long hours. Once, after an exhausting day of courtroom appearances in Manhattan and Brooklyn, he gave a political speech in Westchester, then rushed back to the theater to attend a play based on a Dickens novel. After midnight, he returned to his office and wrote a newspaper review. Charles Dickens later described the article as "a wonderfully clever analysis. I have never forgotten some of its peculiar passages."

These three men—Oakey Hall, Peter Sweeny and Dick Connolly —were selected by Bill Tweed for an historic assault on the treasury of New York City. They were all good and necessary choices: the colorful, elegant frontman; the brilliant, secretive attorney with political savvy; the jovial, conscientious bookkeeper. All were men of excellent public reputation and all were respected Sachems of Tammany Hall. If the final, amoral appraisal of a political leader rests on his judgment of the correct means to reach a clear goal, then Bill Tweed, the burly hoodlum of Cherry Hill, must rank very near the top.

Tweed also knew that the key to the treasury would never be secure unless Albany joined his dominion. In 1867, he swung his own election as State Senator. The following year, he moved John Hoffman out of City Hall and into the governorship. At the same time, Tweed replaced

Hoffman as Grand Sachem of Tammany Hall and opened the doors of the Mayor's office for Oakey Hall.

The *Herald* was overjoyed: "It will be a refreshing novelty to have for Mayor of New York a strictly upright, honorable, capable man, and at the same time one who writes a drama or a farce with equal success, acts a part as well as most professionals on the stage, conducts the most difficult cases on the calendar, sings a good song, composes poetry by the yard, makes an effective stump-speech, responds to a toast with remarkable eloquence and taste, mixes a lobster salad as well as Delmonico's head cook, smokes the best cigar in New York, respects old age, and admires youth, as poets and orators invariably do."

The daily luncheons inaugurated by John Hoffman continued without him. Tweed, Sweeny, Connolly and Mayor Oakey Hall gathered 'round the table, and the talk turned from politics to plunder. Peter "Brains" Sweeny resigned from his imposing duties as Chamberlain in favor of the seemingly innocuous post of Parks Commissioner. During one of several junkets to Europe he schooled himself in park management. Angry critics charged that Sweeny had observed some pruning and transplanting of trees in European parks and "returned to prepare for a general onslaught on every grove, shrubbery and tree in the Central Park."

But Sweeny took all criticisms calmly and mildly persisted in being "simply a passenger in the ship"—either a ship to Europe or the luxurious ship he occupied in the new County Courthouse behind City Hall. "The room," a *Herald* reporter said of Sweeny's office, "is handsomely and luxuriantly fitted up with sofas, tempting lounges and soft easy chairs, whereon a sybarite might repose; also a green-baized table, on which were quill pens . . . and all the materials of literary work." Peter Sweeny and his friends were indeed hard at work. The County Courthouse was built but improvements would still be necessary. Nobody know what was transpiring on Peter Sweeny's "green-baized table" and nobody would know for several years.

The public's attention was on Tammany Hall, a new three-hundred-thousand-dollar Tammany Hall on 14th Street between Irving Place and Third Avenue. It was a three-story marble and red brick edifice with arched windows and doors, 30-foot high ceilings, a 20-foot wide central staircase, and on the roof a huge pediment with a niche containing a 12-foot tall statue of Chief Tamanend. Within the palatial Wigwam: a library, concert room, club room, committee rooms, restaurant, the Grand Hall, and circular gallery designed to seat 3,500 Democrats.

Grand Sachem Tweed was the prime force in moving Tammany to 14th Street, then the center of the City. He took office in the year of the Hall's completion and dedication, and in time to lead the braves into the 1868 Democratic National Convention at Tammany Hall. The locale marked the Presidential nominee, ex-Governor Horatio Seymour, as the candidate of the "Big City Bosses." Seymour (who had already suffered heavy political damage by his conciliatory speech to the Draft Rioters) carried New York, New Jersey, and six other states against General Grant. The Democratic National Convention never returned to Tammany Hall.

A Congressional investigating committee, apparently not content to allow Horatio Seymour consolation in defeat, charged that election frauds in New York City that year surpassed any in history ("a systematic plan of gigantic proportions, stealthily prearranged and boldly executed"). Three principal techniques were cited: fraudulence in voting, in vote-counting, and in naturalization.

Indeed, there had been a remarkable increase in naturalization proceedings toward election time. Tweed outdid even Fernando Wood in the craft of high-speed naturalization. The Tammany Society established special naturalization committees in neighborhood offices throughout the City. Fees were paid by the Society, paperwork was expedited, and witnesses were obtained for applicants who pledged to vote Democratic.

The witnesses were important. They did all the talking in court; Tweed's judges ignored the immigrants themselves. When immigrants appeared without witnesses, a call was sent out from the courtroom to round up men from the corridors and streets who would swear to their knowledge of the applicants. There were never enough Bibles to meet the demand for oaths in that fall of 1868. It was a common sight to find a crowd of witnesses gathered about a single Bible, each stretching a fingertip to graze the Good Book. One Tweed judge boasted that he could examine two witnesses a minute, but he was modest. A careful check of the records raised his average to three.

So swamped were the lower courts, working night and day, that Tweed moved his charges into the State Supreme Court, an unprecedented maneuver. Judge Barnard ceased whittling for a while. From October 8 to 23, he naturalized an average of 718 future Democrats per day. On October 19 he hit a peak of 955. In all, it was an impressive showing. The annual average of naturalization ceremonies from 1856 to 1867 was 9,207. In 1868, the total number was 41,112.

Some witnesses at naturalization proceedings appeared up to twenty-five times a night under different names. These were often the same skilled professionals who functioned as "repeaters" at the ballot box. On Election Day, the repeaters were given breakfast at the home of Sheriff Jimmy "The Famous" O'Brien and supplied with fictitious names and addresses that had already been registered falsely. Others were supplied with identification papers of opposition voters who were not expected to appear at the polls. It was estimated that at least 25,000 of the 156,000 votes cast in the city were fraudulent (2,000 in the Sixth Ward alone).

Once the votes were in the ballot box, the responsibility rested with the canvassers and inspectors to calculate the number sufficient to carry New York State for Horatio Seymour and John Hoffman. Oakey Hall had sent confidential letters to the upstate county chairmen (over the signature of Democratic State Chairman Samuel Tilden) requesting them to have local leaders telegraph estimates of the returns immediately after the polls closed. Once these figures were in hand, the Tammany wards would be in a position to know how many upstate Republican votes needed to be offset.

The bi-partisan system of election inspectors and canvassers was only a minor obstacle to Bill Tweed. Shortly before election time, he used the payroll of the Street Department to buy scores of Republican inspectors. He added 600 clerks in his own office. Sheriff O'Brien suddenly took on 400 additional deputies. When Tweed was later asked if he had ever directed these men to alter the bona-fide count of ballots, he replied: "More in the nature of a request than a direction." And he flatly stated his philosophy of democratic action: "The ballots made no result; the counters made the result."

Bill Tweed was convinced that money talked, and who was to prove him wrong? The men of greatest power—men like Jay Gould, Jim Fisk, and Commodore Vanderbilt—were nothing without their money. Tweed did not set the moral standards of his day. He accepted them wholeheartedly, delighted in their ease, and joined in their reinforcement. Property and cash were the gods of America, to be stolen and spent, multiplied and glorified. The only limit was the law, and Tweed found himself admitted to the salons of Gould, Fisk, and Vanderbilt because Tweed was the law.

In Albany, State Senator Tweed spent his springs as drill master of the "Black Horse Cavalry," a band of venal legislators with pretensions far beyond the smalltime Forty Thieves. Legislation was up for sale. "You can't get anything in Albany without paying for it," Bill Tweed said. During the bitter controversy over control of the Erie Railroad, the Black Horsemen demanded $1,000 per vote on bills which would decide the contest between Gould and Vanderbilt for control of the railroad. Vigorous bidding from both camps drove the price as high as $5,000, until a truce was reached by the magnates and the legislative market collapsed. Panicky legislators tried to salvage at least $100 apiece from the wreckage.

During the long negotiations, Democrats and Republicans from all over the State paraded in and out of Bill Tweed's seven-room suite in Delavan House. Canaries chirped amidst flowers and potted palms. Available for the legislators were sideboards of brandy and whiskey, porcelain cuspidors festooned with painted roses, a grand piano, and a private exit. Tweed began his Delavan operations as a Vanderbilt agent, but developed such a rapport with rollicking Jim Fisk that he instructed both legislators and judges to switch sides. Fisk was Jay Gould's financial wizard in wresting control of the Erie from Commodore Vanderbilt.

Those were grand days for Bill Tweed. He and Judge Barnard, who had also been on Vanderbilt's payroll, would join Jim Fisk for poker at the home of Fisk's mistress, Josie Mansfield, on 23rd Street. Tweed and Fisk, portly, brazen, vulgar, genial friends, had genuine affection for each other. Josie Mansfield, on the other hand, eventually turned to another lover and Jim Fisk made the mistake of walking up the stairway of the Grand Central Hotel one evening while his rival was standing at the top with a Colt revolver. The bullet which entered Jim Fisk's belly could not be extracted. "Well, William," Fisk said to Tweed from his deathbed, "you have had a great many false friends in your troubles, but I have always stood by you. I'm afraid that you're going to lose another friend." Jim Fisk had been a friend, a man whom Tweed could understand and respect. "He was a man of broad soul and kindly heart," Tweed mourned. "In his business transactions he was governed by principles which seemed peculiar, without being insincere, and were, perhaps, apparently dishonest, without being otherwise than enterprising."

The Erie Railroad made Boss Tweed a very rich man. He and Peter "Brains" Sweeny joined the Board of Directors. During one three-month period following his elevation to the board, Tweed pocketed Erie profits amounting to $650,000. The railroad's income and the money paid for stocks by the public simply vanished from view. No dividends were declared. Bribes to Tweed and other public officials were written off as legal expenses. Henry Adams called the Erie-Tammany alliance "a combination more powerful than any that has been controlled by mere private citizens in America."

But this was only one aspect of the Tweed Ring's operations. The chief source of income was from the extraction of bribes and kickbacks from public works contractors. Here again, Tweed's role as State Senator was crucial in enacting helpful legislation in Albany. He reportedly paid legislators more than $100,000 to pass the Tax Levy Bill, which gave the City Comptroller the power to raise huge sums for public works through bond issues. The bill was applauded as most beneficial, for among its other provisions was a tax limitation on real estate equal to two percent of assessed valuation. In fact, the tax rate during Boss Tweed's regime actually dropped—as the City debt skyrocketed.

Tweed's next piece of major legislation, a new City Charter, contained such sweeping changes for the public good—increased home rule, centralization of authority, consolidation of departments—that Peter Cooper, Horace Greeley, and other leading reformers endorsed it enthusiastically. Tweed was interested in certain specifics: the Comptroller, rather than being elected, would henceforth be appointed by the Mayor. The Mayor would also appoint all heads of departments. The Street and Water Departments were consolidated under a new Commissioner of Public Works. And, most importantly, the Board of Supervisors was replaced by a Board of Audit which would audit all bills against the City and the county. The Board of Audit was to consist of the Mayor, Oakey Hall; the Comptroller, Slippery Dick Connolly; and the Commissioner of Public Works, who happened to be William Tweed.

The Charter was a little more expensive than the bond issue legislation, but it was a sound investment. Tweed paid five rural Republicans $20,000 each. Several others were a bargain at $2,000. All in all, count-

ing bribes, entertainment, and other expenses, passage of the Charter
cost at least $600,000 by Tweed's own recollection.

But as yet, Tweed's chicanery was a well-kept secret. "Senator
Tweed is in a fair way to distinguish himself as a reformer. Having gone
so far as the champion of the new charter, he seems to have no idea
of turning back," the *Times* said. "He has put the people of Manhattan
under great obligations. His last proposition to abolish the Board of
Supervisors . . . is the crowning act of all. It strikes a blow at one of
the most corrupt departments of a government, and one which is as
useless as a fifth wheel to a coach. We trust that Senator Tweed will
manifest the same energy in the advocacy of this last reform which
marked his action in regard to the charter."

Tweed did not fail his admirers. The Board of Audit, exercising
powers bordering on omnipotence, met regularly, discussed necessary
legislation and how to pay for it, and agreed on how to divide the profits
from excessive bills to the City. Oakey Hall served as chief legal advisor; Dick Connolly handled the finances; Peter Sweeny kept the
judges in line; and Bill Tweed, with overall command, supervised what
might be called political ramifications. The average split on a padded
bill, according to Tweed's later testimony, was: 35 percent to the contractor; 25 to Tweed; 20 to Connolly; 10 to Sweeny; 5 to Hall; and
another 5 percent to minor conspirators who acted as collecting agents
and go-betweens.

The richest vein mined by the Tweed Ring was the new County
Courthouse where Peter Sweeny had his stateroom on the ship of state.
This grim, gray building still stands behind City Hall despite repeated
threats by city planners to plow it under. It is known today as the
Criminal Courts Building, or more affectionately as the "Tweed Building" by the judges and mayoral staff members who rather enjoy sitting
among its pillars and circular staircases in this era of austere architec-
ture. But it is not beautiful nor does it appear to be expensive. Its cost
was originally set at $250,000 in 1858 when Tweed and the Board of
Supervisors approved construction plans.

Work did not begin on the courthouse, however, until four years
later. By that time, curiously, another $800,000 was needed. Year after
year, new appropriations were tendered the courthouse for construction, repairs on construction not yet completed, furnishings, ornaments,
and what must have been a magnificent plastering job. The building
was not completed until 1872. Its cost was sixteen times that of a

similar, just slightly smaller, courthouse in Brooklyn. Somebody noted that the British Parliament had been constructed for one-quarter the price. Somebody else dubbed it the "Palace of Plunder." At any rate, all were agreed that $12,500,000 was a good deal to pay for a new courthouse.

The cuspidors in the Tweed Building were priced at $190 apiece. Thermometers totaled $7,500. There were $404,347 worth of safes. Brooms and other "articles," as they were categorized, cost $41,190. A rug expert estimated that for the amount spent on carpeting the county courthouse, all 8.25 acres of City Hall Park could have been covered three times over.

Perhaps the most enterprising contractor was Andrew Garvey, who became known as The Prince of Plasterers. He had handled other City buildings for a total of one million dollars, but for the courthouse, a very special job, he charged two million dollars. The bill was a catch-all for a number of good deeds, including a one thousand dollar plastering job at Judge Barnard's home. Small wonder that Tammany records describe Andrew Garvey as "one of the enthusiastic braves." Garvey repaid the Society's kindness by donating a walnut case to display Oakey Hall's Indian costumes at Tammany Hall.

The Hall itself was incorporated into the Tweed Ring's field of operations. Rental of the Wigwam's top floor for a year was a fair four thousand dollars. The City took it for thirty-six thousand dollars. Other leases held by the City included an empty loft over a stable and a floor over a larger beer saloon which served as "drill rooms" for troops who mysteriously never appeared. In one instance, the City paid five thousand dollars a year for armory space that was completely non-existent. Meanwhile, real armories on City property were standing vacant.

Tweed had his own private interests distinct from the Board of Audit, including Erie Railroad pay-offs, a quarry which provided marble for the courthouse at exorbitant prices, a $40,000 block of stock on the Brooklyn Bridge, real estate, bank holdings, law fees, printing and stationery companies which did business with the City and with private concerns that needed Tweed's favors, and the *Transcript*, a newspaper of sorts ("whose only constant readers are its proof-readers," said the *Times*) with a circulation of 500 and a near monopoly on City advertising.

The Boss became a walking corporation with holdings and interests of great diversity. He had a deep appreciation of the axiom that spending money is making money. But he did not know when to stop. Like his vest, his empire over-expanded, and it was too late to reduce. He became too Grand a Sachem and the grumblings grew louder in Tammany that Bill Tweed just might have lost the common touch.

Buried beneath the cornerstone of the new Tammany Hall was a casket containing, among other mementos, copies of the Federal Constitution and the Declaration of Independence. It is certain that the Society had more in mind their preservation than their burial. But just as certain among Tammany purists was the notion that Bill Tweed was beginning to look less and less like Tom Jefferson.

Tweed, at forty-seven, had consumed enough ale and duckling at Delmonico's to finally reach 300 pounds. His scrubby whiskers and moustache were beginning to turn gray. His eyes seemed to be sinking more deeply into his skull as he peered out at a hard and corrupt world. He had lost nearly all his hair. He preferred attention to be focused on what he had gained: a big blue-white shirtfront diamond which he wore almost constantly.

The Tweeds—Boss, wife and now eight children—had moved from the Lower East Side to a stylish brownstone at 41 East 36th Street in the Murray Hill section of Manhattan. This sufficed until he graduated from rich to very rich—some said twelve-million-dollars rich, but he claimed never more than three million dollars. Then the Tweeds settled in one of Fifth Avenue's finest mansions at the southeast corner of 43rd Street. He bought a stable on 40th Street, stocked it with horses, carriages, sleighs, fur robes, and gold-plated harnesses. Up in Greenwich, Connecticut, was the Tweed estate, a steam yacht and, it was said, a blonde mistress.

Nearby in Greenwich was the Americus Yacht Club, a summer home for Tammany Sachems. Membership was $1,000 plus another $2,000 for the membership pin: a gold tiger's head with ruby eyes. The 30-bedroom clubhouse was often referred to as "Hotel de Tweed." The reception room was the "Tweed Room." The largest of the three yachts available to club members was the *William M. Tweed.*

Whatever his actual worth, Bill Tweed always had enough money to go around. He was a generous sort: $50,000 for the poor of the Seventh Ward, Christmas, 1870. He had meant it to be $5,000 but a henchman said in jest, "Oh Boss, add another naught to it." "Well, here goes," said Tweed, and he did. Through his efforts, the City contributed $1,400,000 to the Catholic Church in a three-year-period. His political contributions were never accurately assessed. They were, he said, "a continuous dribble."

All this generosity was repaid indirectly when Mary Amelia Tweed, Bill's twenty-one-year-old daughter, received seven hundred thousand dollars' worth of presents on her wedding day. Among the tokens of affection for Mary Amelia were forty thousand dollars worth of gold and diamond jewelry from Peter Sweeny, a five-hundred-dollar silver ice bowl with polar bear handles from Jim Fisk (matched by an embarrassing duplicate from the Police Superintendent), a giant silver coffee urn from the enthusiastic plasterer Andrew Garvey, and sixty diamonds from James Ingersoll, the man who supplied almost twenty-five acres of carpeting for the County Courthouse.

In all fairness, the gifts may have been directed to Mary Amelia after all. She was, at the time, the potential heiress with her seven siblings of two million dollars of New York City real estate. Only two men (John Jacob Astor and Alexander Stewart) owned more of Manhattan than Bill Tweed.

George Templeton Strong, who dubbed Tweed "His Scoundrelism," viewed the limitless ascent of Mary Amelia's father with wonder: "It has been reserved to this age to produce a hero in the department of Larceny and Peculation, corresponding in grade with the Heroes of the Greek Tragedy." In an effort to eternalize these heroic proportions, a group of Tweed's admirers began a campaign to build a statue in his honor. Tweed sensed that it would make him an object of ridicule and put a quick end to the project.

This was an unfair blow to posterity. It would be a delight in these days of the City's transformation to chrome and glass to come upon Bill Tweed on a pedestal in all his corpulence, dressed in Indian finery. Instead, we must rely on the records of Tammany's festive Fourth of July celebration in 1870. On that occasion the braves gathered about their Grand Sachem for a preliminary half-hour of socializing in the committee-room, which Oakey Hall and Andrew Garvey had decked out with Indian costumes and weapons. Then Grand Sachem Tweed held his ceremonial peace pipe to his lips, took a great puff, raised his tomahawk in the air and waddled out the door to the Grand Hall. The others followed behind him, into the Hall which had been the scene of Horatio Seymour's triumph before disaster, and sat amidst red, white, and blue decorations, also supplied by the enthusiastic Mr. Garvey.

In his welcoming address, Boss Tweed hailed the "bright, auspicious day, forerunner of another when the great Democratic Party, through which alone this great country can be properly reconstructed, shall again resume sway, and place us in the condition of constitutional prosperity we were in before the late Civil War."

Then he turned over the rostrum to the Long Talker, a California Senator who was particularly concerned about "the Chinese evil," the introduction of "the degraded cheap labor of Asia" which would "poison our civilization." After appropriate All-American huzzahs, the braves partook of "the usual salt and hominy, with weak firewater." Messages were read from Tweed's old foe, Congressman Fernando Wood; from Tweed's star candidate, Governor John Hoffman, who was then proclaimed "by the help of God and the Democratic party, the next president of the United States"; and from Van Buren's old Regency lieutenant, Edwin Croswell, ex-editor of the *Albany Argus:*

"The Tammany Society stands before the country as the exponent of the principles of civil liberty—as the defender of the Constitution, as a shield against legislative corruption and cupidity, whether in Washington or Albany—as the opponent of monopoly and the class selfishness of designing men—as a protection against excessive and oppressive taxation—as studying the urging of economy in public expenditures—as looking with a single eye to the public welfare, regardless of interested rings and combinations."

Boss Tweed vigorously led the applause. He had every reason to be satisfied on that day. The Ring was prospering well behind the Tammany declaration against "rings and combinations." Tweed was surviving the *Times* editorials which conveyed strong feelings about the new county courthouse but no proof. And within Tammany, he had put down a serious challenge to his power led by Sheriff Jimmy "The Famous" O'Brien, a reformer with a vengeance: he had been blocked by Tweed in an attempt to collect $350,000 in fees.

The O'Brien faction, which called itself the "Young Democracy," had become so confident of gaining majority control of the Tammany General Committee that they sought a meeting to depose Tweed. The Boss obliged them. When the Young Democracy members arrived at the Wigwam, they found the doors locked tight and the building ringed by hundreds of policemen. The officer in charge reported that

Grand Sachem Tweed had, on second thought, determined that the meeting might be conducive to a riot, and had called for police protection in the interest of public safety. When the infuriated Young Democracy reassembled the following day, they found their ranks had thinned considerably. Bill Tweed's power and bankroll seemed insurmountable, and why fight City Hall? A month later, Tweed called a meeting to elect Tammany Sachems. It was reported that all 265 braves who convened that evening were in Tweed's corner. Nonetheless, he allowed (and some claimed he arranged for) twenty-three votes to be cast for the Young Democracy slate before he, Oakey Hall, Peter Sweeny and Dick Connolly received a rousing vote of confidence as Grand Sachem and key Sachems.

Tweed now owned Tammany, City Hall, the State Legislature, two-thirds of the State Supreme Court, and the Governor's mansion in Albany. But the White House was the property of Ulysses Grant, Republican. Surely, the next step would have to be seizing control of the national Democratic hierarchy and nominating Governor John Hoffman for the Presidency. When August Belmont was overthrown as Democratic National Chairman, Thomas Nast drew a cartoon in *Harper's Weekly* of Bill Tweed calling the shots. And when Hoffman and the entire Tweed slate were renominated at the 1870 Democratic State Convention in Rochester, the *Times* warned of national consequences to follow.

Republican leaders, seeking to stop Tweed before he became a figure of national influence, requested President Grant to oversee New York voting practices. The President, hearing reports of hoodlums being imported by Tammany for Election Day duties, dispatched troops to the City and stationed armed ships in the Hudson. At a Tammany Hall rally, Boss Tweed appealed for calm: "We know and feel that although the oppressor's hand is upon our throat, still we must calmly resist and show that the City of New York is a peaceful, law-abiding, and, as the world knows, a well governed city." Outside the Hall a two-mile long parade of Democrats carried high the banner: HOFFMAN FOR PRESIDENT—1872.

"The whole affair," said the *Times* of the rally, "cost the Ring $75,000, but as they have a corporation fund of $1,500,000 stolen from the public treasury which they have laid by for just such emergencies as they are called upon to encounter at this time, they will scarcely feel the loss." The *Times* demanded a thorough investigation of Comptroller Slippery Dick Connolly's financial books.

Tweed sought to quiet the pre-election rumblings by throwing open the books to inspection by a six-man committee headed by John Jacob Astor III. All of the committee members were large property-owners who, it was rumored, had been threatened by the Ring with increased assessment if their findings were less than optimistic. But they were distinguished oligarchs and some credit was placed in their findings that all accounts were in proper order and the City debt would be liquidated within twelve years. "We have come to the conclusion and certify," they reported on the day before election, "that the financial affairs of the City under the charge of the Comptroller are administered in a faithful and correct manner."

Bill Tweed was vindicated. John Hoffman and Oakey Hall were re-elected Governor and Mayor. Tweed's plans for national conquest were proceeding perfectly on schedule—until a wintry night in 1871 when there occurred a fatal confrontation between a man named Jimmy Watson and a runaway horse.

Jimmy Watson was County Auditor, paymaster, and principal go-between for the Tweed Ring. Among his bookkeepers was William Copeland, a protégé of Sheriff Jimmy "The Famous" O'Brien. It so happened one day that Copeland, a seemingly inoffensive accountant, was transcribing figures from a voucher record when suddenly his supervisor snatched the document from him with the warning that only Jimmy Watson and Comptroller Connolly were allowed access to it. Copeland, aware that the Tweed Ring had been cutting out Sheriff O'Brien, became suspicious. He managed to copy the figures secretly and turn them over to O'Brien. They were the incriminating data on the new County Courthouse.

O'Brien contacted Tweed, Connolly, and Sweeny. He would be delighted to forget all he knew, said Jimmy the Famous, if the Ring would only satisfy his claim for $350,000 in unpaid fees. Otherwise, he thought the newspapers might be interested in certain information.

Bill Tweed, reflecting on the daily needles from the *Times* and the savage cartoons of Thomas Nast, decided that $350,000 was a fair price. Comptroller Connolly, who knew just where such a sum could be located, agreed with the Boss. But Peter "Brains" Sweeny, on whom Tweed often relied for sound advice in crises, favored calling O'Brien's bluff. The three men huddled and strong words were exchanged.

O'Brien was asking too much money, Sweeny argued. And he could continue to blackmail indefinitely. It was thereupon decided to send Jimmy Watson to negotiate further with O'Brien.

The two men were to meet at Bertholf's Hotel on Harlem Lane. Jimmy Watson appeared on time but O'Brien was detained, and after a while, Watson decided he had waited long enough. He jumped into his sleigh, grabbed the reins, and began racing home down Eighth Avenue. At the corner of 130th Street, a runaway horse and sleigh with a drunken driver careened out of the northbound lane and crashed into Jimmy Watson's sleigh. The horse leaped up and crushed Watson's forehead with his hoof.

Watson was in a coma for a week. Tweed and his men, fearful of a deathbed confession, hovered about the patient day and night. Watson died without regaining consciousness. Tweed thereupon shook up the County Auditor's office, but in the process he made two mistakes: he retained O'Brien's man Bill Copeland, (he had no knowledge of Copeland's treachery); and he hired an ex-newspaperman named Matthew O'Rourke as chief bookkeeper. Both men were working independently. And both appeared to be extremely diligent. Why else would they stay such long hours into the night?

In the meantime, Sheriff O'Brien awaited a new offer from the Ring following Watson's death. None was forthcoming. Tweed was convinced that the danger was past. Six months passed, and then one hot July night, editor Louis John Jennings was poring over copy on his desk in the *Times* office when Jimmy "The Famous" O'Brien walked in carrying a sheaf of papers.

"You and Nast have had a hard fight," Jimmy O'Brien said.

"Have still," replied Jennings, puzzled by the unexpected visitor.

"I said you *have* had it," Jimmy O'Brien said, and he placed the papers on Jenning's desk. "Here are the proofs of all your charges—exact transcriptions from Dick Connolly's books. The boys will likely murder you when they know you've got 'em, just as they've tried to murder me."

When *Times* reporters began appearing about town to check the addresses of "armories" rented by the City, the "boys" did find out about it. But there were no murders. Instead, Bill Tweed sent Slippery Dick Connolly over to the *Times* to buy the silence of its owner, George Jones, with five million dollars.

"I don't want to see this man," George Jones said when he caught sight of Slippery Dick.

"For God's sake," Dick Connolly said, "let me say one word to you."

Jones listened and then replied: "I don't think the devil will ever make a higher bid for me than that."

"Why, with that sum," Connolly said, "you could go to Europe and live like a prince."

"Yes," said George Jones, "but I should know that I was a rascal."

On July 8, 1871, on an inside page of the New York *Times*, appeared "reliable and incontrovertible evidence of numerous gigantic frauds on the part of the rulers of the city"—specifically, the rental of lofts as armories, and armory repair bills submitted by such enthusiasts as Andrew Garvey. "Who are responsible for these frauds? First, Mayor Hall and Comptroller Connolly, who pass upon these claims and sign checks for their payment—knowing them to be fraudulent. Second, William M. Tweed and Peter B. Sweeny, who pocket their share of the proceeds."

The exposés continued all month, for now the *Times* was also being fed figures from Matthew O'Rourke, the ex-newspaperman whom Bill Tweed thought would make a fine chief bookkeeper. And over at *Harper's Weekly*, Tom Nast's cartoons began to be talked about in a new light. The proof was in. What Jennings and Jones and Nast had protested without the evidence was even more outrageous than they had suspected. The people had been bilked of a sum approaching $200,000,000.

A banker called on Thomas Nast at home. "I hear," he said, "that you have been made an offer to go abroad for art study."

"Yes, but I can't go," Nast replied. "I haven't time."

"But they will pay you for your time," the banker persisted. "I have reason to believe that you could get a hundred thousand dollars for the trip."

"Do you think that I could get two hundred thousand?"

"Well, possibly," the banker said. "I believe from what I have heard in the bank that you might get it. You have great talent, but you need study and you need rest. Besides, this Ring business will get you into trouble. They own all the judges and jurors and can get you locked up for libel. My advice is to take the money and get away."

"Do you think I could get five hundred thousand to make the trip?"

"You can."

"Well, I don't think I'll do it."

Tweed was confused and angered at encountering for the first time in his career men he could not buy. He ordered the Board of Education to throw out all textbooks published by Harper. Board members at Harper tried to persuade Fletcher Harper, founder of *Harper's Weekly*, to discontinue Nast's cartoons, but he refused. Then Tweed attempted to buy majority control of *Times* stock, but within minutes of victory he was outbid by George Jones. Next, he hauled the *Times* into court, claiming the deed on its property was improper and threatening seizure by the City. But the title stood up in court. A reporter finally cornered the Boss and asked for a denial or admission of the charges against the Ring. For the first time in public, Bill Tweed, listening to the recitation of the facts and figures on which his career was built, lost his temper. "Well," he snarled, "what are you going to do about it?"

Four days after the first *Times* exposé in that critical month of July 1871, the City's Irish Protestants marched in the Orange Day Parade despite threats of violence by Catholics. Mayor "O'Hall," at Tweed's urging, had forbidden the march but such a storm was raised by the press and clergy that Governor Hoffman, concerned now with his national image, prevailed upon Tweed not to interfere.

The Governor's lifting of the ban angered Irish Catholics. Fear spread that another Draft Riot was at hand. Only ninety-four Orangemen appeared for the parade, surrounded by a guard of three-thousand police and infantrymen. Marching down Eighth Avenue, the procession was blocked by a crowd of anti-Protestant demonstrators. The police moved in with billy clubs. Somebody fired a shot which hit a National Guardsman. The soldiers fired back into the crowd. When it was over, two soldiers, a policeman, and forty-six civilians, among them onlooking women and children, lay dead.

The Orange Day Riot brought a new sense of urgency to public outrage against the Tweed Ring. Reformers decried a city of lawlessness and began to mobilize their forces for a new order in the fall elections. In a mass meeting at Cooper Union, speakers exclaimed that the City debt had tripled within two years. "This city," said ex-Mayor Havemeyer, "now calls her people to their duty in this time of her humiliation." Resolutions were passed damning Tweed, Hall, Connolly, and

Sweeny, and calling for the repeal of Tweed's City Charter. A Committee of Seventy community leaders was created to head the crusade, under the guidance of the ambitious Samuel Tilden. Three days later, the Committee of Seventy sought an injunction barring any further City expenditures or collections. The matter came before Judge Barnard. And then, suddenly, the first break in the Tweed Ring was at hand. The Judge looked out into the packed courtroom and announced: "I will grant the injunction."

Slippery Dick Connolly was the next defector. First he met with Tweed and Peter Sweeny in search of a stratagem. They had one all prepared: the resignation and disappearance of Comptroller Connolly, thereby taking with him all the blame. But Dick Connolly did not take to the role of scapegoat. He went to Tilden and Havemeyer to offer his help. Tilden instructed him to appoint a reformer as Deputy Comptroller and relinquish all the powers of Comptroller. A furious Mayor Hall wrote Connolly that the appointment was tantamount to Connolly's resignation and would be so considered, but Connolly refused to leave office.

Nast drew a cartoon showing the gallows moving in on Tweed, Hall, Sweeny, and Connolly. But the Ring feigned calm. "In its practical effect," Mayor Hall told a reporter, "the granting of the injunction is one of Judge Barnard's stereotype jokes." And Bill Tweed had a warm smile for the press. "I'm not afraid," he said. "What do I care? I was born in New York and I mean to stay here, too. The *Times* has been saying all along that I have no brains. Well, I'll show Jones that I have brains. I tell you, Sir, if this man Jones would have said all the things he has said about me twenty-five years ago, he wouldn't be alive now. I would have killed him. But, you see, when a man has a wife and children, he can't do such a thing."

Peter "Brains" Sweeny, who had no need to show Jones anything, refrained from comment. He was busy packing his bags. He embarked for France to become a wealthy Paris boulevardier. Soon he had company: Slippery Dick Connolly, who jumped bail after being arrested by the new Sheriff, Matthew Brennan, the man he had replaced as Comptroller. The arrest took place in the presence of Samuel Tilden, a situation of interest to those who draw distinctions between regulars and reformers in the fine art of the doublecross. And along came Tammany brave Andrew Garvey, plasterer *extraordinaire*, to enjoy the sights of Paris, as well as James Ingersoll, who had supplied five million dollars' worth of carpeting for the Tweed Building.

Yet Tweed was still Grand Sachem. He secured his renomination to the State Senate and went downtown to give his acceptance speech to a great rally of the Tammany faithful: "At home again among the friends of my childhood, I feel that I can safely place myself, my record and all that I have performed as a public official, plainly and openly to their gaze. Reviled as man has seldom been, traduced as man has seldom been, maligned as man has seldom been, I point proudly to my record to prove my character, and ask only a fair, a bold and a very impartial investigation at an early day of all my official acts and all the records and acts of my life."

"Tweed is a grand moral spectacle," George Templeton Strong wrote with a new admiration, "statuesque as a demigod in Greek tragedy. Although 'interviewed' and badgered at least nine times a day by 'one of our reporters' (as the vultures interviewed Prometheus), he is always calm and great, if not perfectly grammatical—and that defect may be charged to the reporters."

The Boss's hold on his State Senatorial District still prevailed on Election Day. But it was a personal victory in a lopsided district. Elsewhere in the City, reformers led by Assemblyman-Elect Samuel Tilden won a majority of the State Legislature delegation and the City Council. Judge Barnard was impeached and removed from the bench. Judge Cardozo resigned to avoid the same. Mayor Oakey Hall was indicted for official neglect of duty. He arrived at the courthouse on horseback wearing a top hat. Oakey Hall maintained until his death that he was guilty of negligence but innocent of actually taking part in the vast swindles. The courts upheld his view: a mistrial, a hung jury, and finally acquittal. Oakey then wrote a play called *The Crucible*, in which he appeared as the hero, a man falsely accused of robbery. Subsequently he went to London to practice law and head the British bureau of the New York *Herald*.

Behind public shows of confidence, Bill Tweed now sought desperately to cover his traces. The Comptroller's office was broken into and vouchers disappeared. Real estate holdings changed hands. The Tweed yacht, mansion, and stables were sold. Tweed's bank accounts diminished and his children's funds mysteriously grew.

He was as prepared as he could be for that inevitable moment, as he sat in his office chatting with Jay Gould, when Sheriff Brennan and his deputies appeared at the door.

"Good morning," Bill Tweed said. "Take seats, gentlemen."

"Mr. Tweed," Sheriff Brennan said, "I have an order for your arrest."

Tweed looked at him calmly. "I expected it," he said, "but not quite so soon."

Bail was set at one million dollars and was promptly supplied by Jay Gould.

There was a series of legal maneuvers and trials, including a hung jury which came within a hair's breadth of acquittal. Eventually, Tweed was found guilty on 104 counts. The day of sentencing arrived and Tweed's attorney addressed the court: "Your Honor, we are taught, from the time we enter this world, to ask for mercy; and those prayers which we put in our own behalf must teach us to render deeds of mercy to . . ." The lawyer broke down in sobs. There were tears among the spectators in the courtroom. Bill Tweed quickly covered his face with his hands. He was sentenced to twelve years. They took him to the penitentiary on Blackwell's Island where he listed his occupation as "Statesman."

The Court of Appeals reduced the sentence to one year and Tweed was out after paying a $250 fine. But Samuel Tilden, new member of the Council of Sachems and new Governor of New York State, saw to his re-arrest on a civil suit to recover the stolen City moneys. Again Tweed was imprisoned, this time in the Ludlow Street jail after failure to raise three million dollars bail. Tilden was determined to keep public wrath focused entirely on Tweed. The elaborate Tweed Ring with its leaders but for Boss Tweed scattered to Paris, London, and Canada, was an entity to be forgotten. Tammany and the State Democratic Party must be reformed, but if the finger were pointed at all who had joined with Tweed in the plunder, Governor Tilden would have few supporters left.

Tweed's immediate jailors allowed him to make periodic visits to his family. On one such occasion, he was eating a hearty dinner with his guards in the home of his son, Bill, Jr., on Madison Avenue. When it came time for cigars, Tweed excused himself for a moment and went upstairs. He was not seen again until a Brooklyn fisherman saw a man by the name of "John Secor" who looked a good deal like Boss Tweed minus whiskers. "John Secor" took a series of ships to the Florida keys,

Cuba, and Spain. Spanish authorities recognized him from a Thomas Nast cartoon depicting two young street urchins in the clutches of Bill Tweed. They decided he must be a kidnapper. He was arrested and shipped back to New York. On arrival, Tweed lost his balance coming down the gangplank and landed in a coal pile. He was wiping off the coal dust when his captors moved in.

During his year-long absence, the State had obtained against Tweed a six-million-dollar civil judgment. He was returned to the Ludlow Street jail and kept there as a debtor. Suffering from diabetes and a heart condition, Boss Tweed began to read the Bible. He also wrote a letter to Charles O'Conor, the attorney who was chief prosecutor of the Tweed Ring. Tweed offered to make a full confession in exchange for the freedom to return to his wife and family.

O'Conor was inclined to accept the bargain. The City was being sued by contractors demanding payment of fraudulent bills. Tweed's testimony could save huge sums for the City. Nor did it seem fair to make of Tweed a sad spectacle while the rest of the Ring went free. O'Conor took the letter to Governor Tilden, who promptly refused. He was not interested in Tweed dragging down the entire personnel of the Democratic Party by his confessions. But when the offer was later presented to a new Governor, Lucius Robinson, and to State Attorney General Charles Fairchild, assurances were given to the new Tammany leader John Kelly that Tweed would be freed. On this basis, Tweed gave full testimony before an investigating committee of the Board of Alderman.

But Attorney General Fairchild reneged on his pledge. Tweed, having told all, was to remain in jail until he raised six million dollars. The Boss had nowhere near the sum and no intention of making restitution. Instead, he gave large donations to charity. He sent his wife and children to Europe to avoid humiliation. And, as Christmas approached, he sent for a decorated tree to be presented to the jail warden's family. They kept the star long afterward as a remembrance.

"I never knew him to speak ill of anyone," the warden's daughter said later. She was among those at Tweed's bedside on the morning he complained of a terrible pain in the chest. It was one week after Tweed's fifty-fifth birthday.

Tweed was whispering. He could barely be heard. "Fairchild," he said, "Fairchild and Tilden have killed me." A doctor moved to comfort him. Tweed grasped his hand. "I have tried to do some good, even if I have not had good luck." The sound of the noon bell could be heard in the jail as Big Bill Tweed slumped dead.

In his pocket they found a gold watch with an engraving on the back: "To William Marcy Tweed from the members of Americus Engine Company No. 6."

CHAPTER 6

Family Affairs with "Honest John" Kelly

"I think that you were worse than Tweed, except that he was a larger operator. The public knew that Tweed was a bold, reckless man, making no pretensions to purity. You, on the contrary, were always avowing your honesty and wrapped in the mantle of piety. Men who go about with the prefix 'honest' to their names are often rogues."

—*Mayor William Havemeyer*

"No man was ever esteemed more justly or trusted more entirely by the people of this city than John Kelly. His unswerving and incorruptible honesty made the history of his life a salutary lesson to American youth and a shining example to American manhood."

—*Charles A. Dana*

There is great comfort to be found in scorning Boss Tweed and the Tweed Era, as if the man and his times were entirely remote from the political integrity and well-deserved fortunes of the 1960's. In fact, the attitude of Tweed's contemporaries after his imprisonment was quite similar.

His former associates went free. His former supporters, who were a majority of the New York Democratic Party, quickly shifted allegiance. His former tolerators achieved positions of eminence.

At the time of his death in the Ludlow Street jail, Tweed had already become an absurd curiosity of a bygone era. For seven years his enormous political power had been in the hands of his Tammany successor John Kelly, and with it had gone the homage of most of his "friends." Surrounded in life by thousands of lackeys and sycophants, Bill Tweed had few mourners in death. On the day of the funeral, Mayor Smith Ely, once a servile Tweed lieutenant, busily engaged himself in office chores. Despite a request to the Mayor from Tweed's wife and children, the flag at City Hall was flying at high-mast as Tweed's hearse rolled by on its way to the Hamilton Street ferry.

"Honest John" Kelly, Tweed's long-time enemy, was the only prominent politician to join the short funeral procession. He had come to do penance for a broken promise. It was Kelly who had secured Tweed's confession for the prosecution after being assured by Governor Robinson and Attorney General Fairchild that Tweed would be released from prison.

When the Governor and the Attorney General broke their word, John Kelly was placed in the uncomfortable position of having double-crossed a broken man languishing in jail. Kelly avenged this blotch on his professional honor by denying renomination to Attorney General Fairchild. Two years later, he led the Tammany delegation out of the State Convention to form a rebel ticket, thus splitting the Democratic vote and defeating Governor Robinson.

On March 21, 1878, John Kelly wrote to the new Attorney General: "I feel it to be my duty as an individual and a public officer to urge upon you the discharge of William M. Tweed." Again a promise was secured for Tweed's release, but it was considered the better part of valor to wait until the State Legislature adjourned in May. Bill Tweed died on April 12. And so John Kelly came to the funeral carrying the guilt of betrayal, enraged at the men he had trusted to save Tweed's life, and angered at himself for having naïvely relied upon their pledge.

Kelly had made a serious mistake, but it was neither his first nor last error in gauging the intentions of fellow politicians. He was an impulsive and self-righteous man, deeply religious, painfully sensitive to public criticism, and always susceptible to flattery. His judgment of his fellow men left considerable to be desired. On his way to the summit he chose correctly, but once there, he made the wrong enemies and the wrong friends at the wrong time.

It is no accident, therefore, that John Kelly's most significant contribution to American politics came not in personal leadership but in the form of a blueprint. It was said of Kelly that he found Tammany a horde and he left it an army. The meaning of that achievement has grown with time. In the 1960's, the structure of every major party organization in every city in America is patterned after Kelly's Tammany Hall of nearly a century ago.

If he is the least remembered of the Tammany tigers, John Kelly is clearly the most important. Both his predecessor Tweed and his protégé Croker won more lasting celebrity as flamboyant pirates. Charles Murphy would come the closest to greatness by developing the finest stable of organization candidates in the nation. John Kelly was simply an inventive mechanic, the only true reformer in the annals of Tammany. He *re-formed* the sprawling party network which Tweed and his cronies had all but ignored while pillaging the City. He carefully constructed the detailed and disciplined syntax which would later become the source of Croker's and Murphy's much greater power.

As a boy, John Kelly was pensive and moody. "He thinks a great deal more than he talks," his mother explained, "but be sure he is not dumb."

Born on Hester Street in the Lower East Side's Sixth Ward, he was the oldest son of grocer Hugh Kelly, an immigrant from County Tyrone, and Sarah Donnelly Kelly, a doting mother who insisted on a strict religious upbringing. John Kelly attended the parochial school of the old Saint Patrick's on Mott Street until the age of eight when his father died.

He went to work as an office boy to James Gordon Bennett at the New York *Herald*, then as an apprentice to a soapstone cutter. By the time he was twenty-one, he had established his own grate and soapstone factory on Elizabeth Street. Like Tweed, he was also a volunteer fireman and foreman of his company. He was a captain in the Emmet Guards, a military company. And he displayed dramatic talent at an early age, formed an acting group, and played all the Shakespearean heroes.

John Kelly delighted in reading, especially Shakespeare. He taught himself French, finished secondary school at night, and began a systematic study on his own of scores of textbooks. Horace Greeley once remarked that John Kelly mastered subjects by "throttling them and tearing their vitals out."

For a budding Tammany leader, Kelly spent his youth in relative quiescence. There was, to be sure, an occasional ruckus in the course of fire-fighting duties. And he was seen in prominent taverns wherein gathered young and rising politicians. But it was Kelly's boast that he had only once in his life been in a gambling house, and that was "on business." A friendly biographer noted that young John Kelly "would not loiter with the crowd at street corners of evenings, nor haunt the purlieus of the city where youth loses its innocence, and flaunting vice slopes the way to ruin."

Kelly had dreams of becoming a priest but they were thwarted by the death of his father and the necessity to provide for his mother and her family. He was drawn into politics by his strong attachment to the Church and Ireland and the virulence of the Know-Nothing attacks. The Sixth Ward was largely Irish and German, providing decent margins for the Tammany incumbents, but the anti-Catholic Know-Nothings terrorized many of the election districts. Kelly began his political career by running for alderman in anti-Tammany primaries and castigating the anti-Irish elements both within and outside the Hall. He was twice beaten back.

But his following grew among firemen, local Irish gangs, and immigrant families suffering from discrimination. They were convinced that Tammany election inspectors were voiding Kelly ballots. On his third try for election, at the age of thirty-one, John Kelly vowed that he would personally appear at the polls on Election Day, despite threats on his life from both Tammanyites and Know-Nothings.

The voting took place in a hall at the corner of Elizabeth and Grand Streets. A high partition screened the poll inspectors from the voters, who handed their ballots through a window in the partition. The immigrants were voting heavily for Kelly that day. Once again his campaign had stressed Church, motherland, and outrage at the Know-Nothing menace. But there was no way of determining what happened to the Kelly votes once they disappeared behind the partition.

John Kelly arrived on the scene with a group of hefty supporters. They forced their way past the guarded door and smashed the partition into splinters. A great battle ensued but the Kelly Democrats cleared the room of the opposition. The enemy returned with reinforcements, ship's carpenters from the Delancey Street docks, and waged a mighty counterattack. Again the Kelly forces triumphed. But then a mob of torch-bearing Know-Nothings gathered in the street outside, crying, "Burn 'em down! Smoke 'em out!"

Kelly ran to the doorway, where it was his good fortune to witness the arrival of his reserve platoons. He raced out from the building, divided his men into groups of ten, and dispersed them around the battlefield. The opposition, attacked on all flanks, was decisively beaten. When the votes were counted, John Kelly was elected alderman by 2 to 1 and admitted to the Society of Saint Tammany. The Know-Nothing reign of terror in the Sixth Ward was finished. Thereafter, foreign-born voters held supremacy in the ward and John Kelly was their undisputed leader.

Kelly's fellow aldermen were of old American stock but they admired his spunk and intelligence. He was given excellent committee assignments, providing him with forums for "good government" speeches. Two years after his election as alderman, he had gained sufficient strength to run for Congress against Tammany maverick Mike Walsh. He won by 18 votes out of 6,118 cast, which prompted Mike Walsh to wonder aloud about the possibilities of fraud. Walsh called for an investigation but then the matter was suddenly dropped. It developed that in the interim John Kelly had inquired of Mike Walsh whether the public might be interested in knowing that Walsh had never been naturalized as an American citizen.

Out of 241 members of the United States Congress, John Kelly was the only Roman Catholic. He served in an era when Congressional attacks on Ireland and the Church were frequent and ferocious. Kelly retorted with equally savage attacks on the Know-Nothings. He was the champion of the Irish on Capitol Hill. He became nationally known as a strong advocate of religious tolerance and an open door policy for all immigrants. Kelly was re-elected to a second term by a comfortable margin.

In Tammany Hall, John Kelly was a Softshell, consistently identified with the reform wing. But he was also a strict party man. When his fellow reformers Samuel Tilden and Lucius Robinson followed the Van Buren faction into the Free Soil Convention at Buffalo, Kelly remained loyal to Lewis Cass, the Democratic Presidential nominee. In subsequent quarrels over the Free Soil desertion, he worked to unify the State's Democrats in support of the Franklin Pierce Administration. At the Softshell Convention in Syracuse, where a strong faction denounced the Kansas-Nebraska Bill, Kelly threatened to leave the convention if the "treason of 1848" were repeated. As a result of his vigorous speech, the delegates passed a resolution supporting the policies of outgoing President Pierce, and the State Democratic Party united for the nomination of President James Buchanan.

Following Fernando Wood's astonishing first term of reform in City Hall, it was John Kelly who placed the Mayor's name in nomination for re-election. As we have seen, the meeting was a riotous proceeding but Kelly overcame the Sweeny-Tweed-Tilden opposition to preserve a semblance of party unity in the election. Kelly distrusted Bill Tweed from the outset of the struggle. (He said of Tweed's movement against Fernando, "Some men are bound to rule or ruin.") But when the defections of Tweedites and Tildenites caused Fernando's downfall in the next election, John Kelly did not follow the defeated Mayor to Mozart Hall. Instead, at thirty-six, he resigned from Congress to run successfully for Sheriff on the Tammany slate.

The office of Sheriff of New York County was an unsalaried post coveted for its lucrative fees. It was in this position that Kelly earned the nickname "Honest John," for during his six years as Sheriff he was said to have made about $800,000 "honestly and fairly." The *Times* later charged him with billing the City at 133 percent over the legal rate for transporting prisoners to Blackwell's Island, but the *Tribune* and the *Sun* felt he had shown admirable restraint compared to his predecessors. The *Star* and the *Evening Express* were also complimentary to John Kelly. He was one of their largest stockholders.

In the Tammany tradition, Kelly turned over a large portion of his fees to charities and the Church, particularly to aid student priests. He also had a wife and three children to support, until 1866 when Mrs. Kelly died of consumption, and two years later when his son Hugh died of the same malady at the age of twenty-one.

The second tragedy struck at an especially unfortunate time. Kelly's principles of Tammany regularity were stretched to the breaking point when Tweed assumed control of the Hall. Honest John became a chief lieutenant of Tilden and split away from Tammany with the anti-Tweed reformers. To oppose Tweed's mayoral candidate, Oakey Hall, the reform group needed a good, popular, Irish Tammany name with a reputation for integrity: Honest John Kelly. He was duly selected and began his campaign against Tweed "bossism." But nine days after his nomination for Mayor, John Kelly, heartsick over the death of his only son, suddenly withdrew from the race, pleading poor health, and embarked for Europe. The reform movement was thrown into a shambles. "I am the medical adviser who drove Kelly to Europe," Oakey Hall quipped, with less than his usual good taste.

Honest John was next heard from in Palestine. His letters were filled with introspection and grief. He wrote of his wanderings, of the Way of the Cross, the Mount of Olives, the Holy Sepulchre. Two years passed and a third death struck the Kelly family—that of his daughter Mary. Kelly wrote to Sarah, his only surviving child, that he was contemplating withdrawal to a monastery for the rest of his life. Another year went by and Sarah died. Within the space of six years, Kelly had lost his entire family.

The Tweed Ring scandals were at their height when John Kelly returned to New York carrying with him the "Return of the Prodigal Son" and other paintings for Saint Patrick's Cathedral. He was, he said, still dwelling on the notion of studying for the priesthood. He went calling on Cardinal McCloskey. And then he sat down with Samuel Tilden, Charles O'Conor and a group of leading civic reformers. Out of that meeting came a decision by the strange, sensitive Irishman to become the crusading reform Boss of Tammany Hall.

It was a desperate battle. The Tweed Ring was in its death agony, fighting fiercely for another gasp. But as the Tammany braves began to scurry away from their now tenuous arrangements with Bill Tweed, Kelly picked up sufficient regular support to broaden his reform backing. He was elected County Leader and chairman of the Tammany Committee on Organization. A week after Tweed was indicted, Kelly threw out the Sachems who had dragged Tammany to infamy. On the Council of Sachems he replaced Slippery Dick Connolly with Charles O'Conor, Peter Sweeny with Samuel Tilden, and Oakey Hall with Honest John Kelly. In addition, he brought in Horatio Seymour, August Belmont, Abram Hewitt, and other upright citizens. To succeed Tweed as Grand Sachem, he installed the old Democratic warhorse Augustus Schell, a fine choice, for as author Morris Werner has noted, "The public knew that Mr. Schell was too old to be very actively dishonest whatever his worst inclinations might be."

"Beasts of burden may easily be managed by the new master. But will the wild ass submit to new bonds?" a friend of Tweed's speculated at the time. "The mythological conqueror of the East, whose enchantments reduced wild beasts to the tameness of domestic cattle, and who harnessed lions and tigers to the chariot, is but an imperfect type of the man who can control the wild, whiskey-drinking and fierce spirits that make up the worst elements of this great city. It requires a great man to stand between the City Treasury and this most dangerous mass. It demands courage, activity, energy, wisdom, or vices so splendid and alluring as to resemble virtues. Again we say, dethrone Kelly, and where is the man to succeed him?"

Having selected an impeccable slate of Sachems, Honest John proceeded to cement the structure of Tammany Hall. The basic agencies of this private government were extended and formalized in the neighborhoods. Sacred responsibilities were assigned within an inviolable chain of command.

George Washington Plunkitt, a Kelly district leader who remained on the scene until 1924, described Honest John's organization as "a great big machine, with every part adjusted delicate to do its own particular work. It runs so smooth that you wouldn't think it was a complicated affair, but it is. Every district leader is fitted to the district he runs and he couldn't exactly fit any other district."

The key to Tammany's effectiveness under Boss Kelly was, of course, the ability to win elections by dispensing personal favors to the voters and party workers, thereby controlling more public offices to dispense more favors. This system of self-perpetuation was a smaller and more intimate precursor of the New Deal.

"If a family is burned out," said George Washington Plunkitt, "I don't ask whether they are Republicans or Democrats, and I don't refer them to the Charity Organization Service, which would investigate their case in a month or two and decide they were worthy of help about the time they are dead from starvation. I just get quarters for them, buy clothes for them if their clothes were burned up, and fix them up till they get things runnin' again. It's philanthropy, but it's politics too—mighty good politics. Who can tell how many votes one of these fires bring me?"

Tammany Hall and the Charity Organization Service (forerunner of today's highly esteemed Community Service Society) illustrated completely opposite approaches to the nineteenth-century "war on poverty." The C.O.S. was a private Protestant welfare agency, funded by *noblesse oblige*, which embarked on philanthropic programs to strengthen family life in the neighborhoods. It also crusaded for social legislation to attack the slum conditions which prevailed in the immigrant ghettos, and was ultimately successful in passing the New York State Tenement House Act of 1901, the first major housing legislation in the nation.

This kind of legislation, which set legal standards for maintenance and construction of tenements, was anathema to Tammany. As Plunkitt admitted candidly, a good fire meant more votes for the organization than a program of fire prevention. Human misery was the stuff of Tammany victories. Without the basic conditions that stabilized poverty, Tammany's individual favors would mean little to the recipients.

And Tammany spoke the language of the poor. Its leaders had fought their way up from the bottom. They developed a system of friendly backscratching which was far more palatable to most immigrants than impersonal charity from the old New York families. Honest John's machine had a profound and elaborate understanding of the nature and needs of its constituents. To exploit this insight, an intricate hierarchy was erected which, in its paternalism and design, was strongly influenced by the Roman Catholic Church. It is more than a coincidence that Tammany's greatest structural draftsman was also Tammany's most pious Irish Catholic.

Boss Tweed was the last Protestant to rule Tammany until the installation of Edward Costikyan in 1962. Tweed was prosecuted by Charles O'Conor, the first Catholic candidate for the Presidency. And John Kelly, who took as his second wife the niece of New York's Cardinal McCloskey, became the first Irish Catholic Tammany Boss. He went on to elect New York City's first Irish Catholic Mayor, William Grace, an immigrant singing waiter who made his fortune with the Grace Shipping Line.

Tammany Hall, which had originally barred Irishmen and Catholics from membership, now joined the Church as one of the rare institutions offering rapid advancement to the young Irish-American. If Kelly was not entirely conscious of this parallel, he nonetheless was profoundly affected by the Church's sense of hierarchy and authority in drawing up his plans for Tammany and in maintaining institutional discipline.

At the bottom of the Tammany power structure (see chart on following page) is the voter (parishioner) who depends on the party

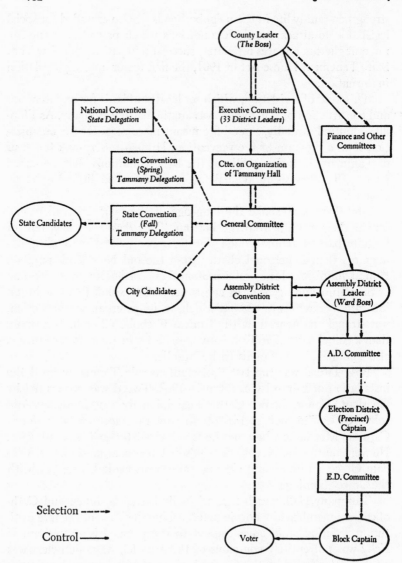

Honest John's Tammany Hall

to care for his needs. He, in turn, confers power on the party through his obedience at the polls. The block captain (parish priest) knows the individual voter and his problems and gives him his personal attention. In the name of the party, he asks only for allegiance in the form of a vote. The block captain is subordinate to the Election District captain (bishop) who administers a larger unit and maintains control by apportioning favors that are passed to him from the next higher level, the Assembly District leader.

The leaders of the Assembly Districts, thirty-three in Kelly's day, comprise the Executive Committee (College of Cardinals) which selects the County Leader (Pope). But once the supreme Boss is chosen, he assumes absolute authority over those who have chosen him.

Barring an election catastrophe reflecting poorly on his leadership, the County Leader, once installed by the Executive Committee, did not have to seek votes of confidence from the committee. On the contrary, the district leaders depended on the Boss for their jobs. Officially, they were picked by the Assembly District Conventions, but these conventions actually ratified the County Leader's choice. In the same way, each district leader was expected to control his Assembly District for the Boss by selecting loyal Election District captains.

Under the later regime of Richard Croker, the district leaders became quasi-independent bosses. This was in part owing to Croker's preoccupation with Wall Street fortune-hunting and foreign travels instead of keeping a close watch on neighborhood politics. He allowed his leaders to handle all local patronage in their districts. But John Kelly, a stickler for the daily details of policy and protocol, funneled all patronage down from the top. Although many voters in the neighborhoods tended to look upon a district leader such as George Washington Plunkitt as an all-powerful boss, the leaders themselves were well aware that their strength to deliver depended on their channel to Kelly.

Thus the voters were as far from the County Leader as the grass roots from the crest of the tree. (The necessity of this arrangement was neatly demonstrated eighty years later when Carmine DeSapio instituted procedures that shortened this distance, thereby hastening his demise.) Support of the individual voter was solicited by the block captains, and even tenement captains, who worked out of the Tammany clubhouses in the neighborhoods. As indicated on the chart, the block captains were members of the Election District Committees, each responsible to an Election District captain. (Election Districts are New York City's equivalent of precincts.) The E.D. captains were members of the Assembly District Committee, responsible to the Assembly District leader. (Assembly Districts are so named because each one elects an Assemblyman to the State Legislature.)

In each Election District, the district and block captains, by offering personal services, favors and jobs, persuaded the voters to elect the Tammany slate of delegates to the Assembly District Convention. This body in turn elected the 4,000 members of the Tammany Hall General Committee, representing all the Assembly Districts in New York County. Usually, about half of these General Committee members would attend its sessions. (Today, the members of the General or County Committee are elected directly at the polls.)

At this point in the hierarchy, the Boss took complete control, mediating the special needs and interests of his district leaders and bringing to bear his perception of the political situation in the City and the State. The General Committee elected officers (in Kelly's time, these were distinguished and untainted leaders like Samuel Tilden and August Belmont) in keeping with the Boss's wishes. These "front men" together with the district leaders constituted the Committee on Organization of Tammany Hall, which took charge of party operations for primary and general elections. The chairman of the Committee on Organization was Boss Kelly.

The mammoth General Committee's main function was to nominate candidates for City offices (a ticket drawn up by the Boss) and select the Tammany delegation to Democratic State Conventions (also dictated from above). In a good year for Tammany, this delegation could heavily influence the outcome of the biennial fall State Convention which selected the State candidates. In Presidential years, the Tammany delegation sought to win control of the spring State Convention in order to swing the New York State delegation at the National Convention. The names of national and State candidates, following their nomination, were brought back to the Tammany General Committee for ratification, which determined whether the precinct workers would give full support in the forthcoming election. Tammany and Kelly were adept at knifing Democratic candidates who failed to meet certain expectations.

New York City's important role in State Conventions, and the size of New York State's delegation to the National Convention, spelled

formidable potential power for Tammany. But apart from the election
as Governor of Tammany Sachem Samuel Tilden, John Kelly was
largely unsuccessful in exercising great influence beyond New York
City. He did, however, establish the machinery for his heirs to do so.
And within the City, through his close supervision of the Executive
Committee and the Committee on Organization, he maintained complete domination of the Tammany organization. He was also chairman
of the all-important Finance Committee, which funded campaign activities for all the district leaders and local candidates. And he appointed himself as the dominant member of all other permanent and
ad hoc committees.

No machine, however well constructed and smoothly run, can function victoriously without enthusiastic support from a broad power
base. Kelly's organization was anything but a fringe movement. It
derived its power, as had Fernando Wood and Bill Tweed, from the
huge immigrant working class, principally Irish and German Catholics.
The Tammany system of Election Districts and saloon-clubhouses
broke down a vast and impersonal city to the warm and familiar level
of the peasant village in the old country.

To the insecure citizen, bewildered by strange customs and the awesome demands of urban life, Tammany was an informal neighborhood
government which dispensed jobs, bail money, rent, coal, clothes, and
Christmas turkeys in exchange for the simple act of casting the right
ballot. Tammany was the trustworthy hearth in a cold and frightening
new world. Its bureaucracy was rigid but intimate, as in an old world
family where the rights and responsibilities of each member are carefully protected. The Boss was the father, who ran the family affairs
fairly and firmly, giving each son his due, teaching and enforcing the
moral lessons of discipline, obedience, and patience. He spanked his
children now and then, but more often he rewarded them for good
behavior. It was all in the family.

"The poor look up to George Washington Plunkitt as a father,"
said George Washington Plunkitt, "and don't forget him on election
day." Plunkitt and most of Kelly's other district leaders were shrewd,
uneducated immigrants with a passion for getting to the top and an
instinctive grasp of practical, personal politics. "There's only one way
to hold a district," Plunkitt said. "You must study human nature and
act accordin' . . . I hear of a young feller that's proud of his voice,
thinks that he can sing fine. I ask him to come around to Washington

Hall and join our Glee Club. He comes and sings, and he's a follower of Plunkitt for life."

In a classic passage from his diary, Plunkitt describes a typical day's work in the life of a Tammany district leader, beginning at 2 A.M. with a message from a bartender to bail him out of jail. Plunkitt returned to bed at 3 A.M., was awakened by fire engines at 6, rushed to the scene to find his Election District captains already there tending to the burned-out tenants. At 8:30, police court opened with six drunk constituents on hand—four released "by a timely word with the judge" and the fines of the other two paid. At 9, Plunkitt went to Municipal Court, where he directed an Election District captain to act as counsel for a widow in danger of dispossession.

Eleven to 3 was spent finding jobs for four men. 3 P.M.: an Italian funeral, with a fast exit to make a Jewish funeral. ("Went conspicuously to the front both in the Catholic church and the synagogue, and later attended the Hebrew confirmation ceremonies in the synagogue.") 7 P.M.: "presided over a meeting of election district captains. Each captain submitted a list of all the voters in his district, reported on their attitude toward Tammany, suggested who might be won over and how they could be won . . ."—the practice first established by Aaron Burr. 8 P.M.: a church fair. ("Took chances on everything, bought ice cream for the young girls . . . and took their fathers out for something down at the corner.") 9 P.M.: back to the clubhouse to hear the complaints of a dozen pushcart peddlers. 10:30 P.M.: attended a Jewish wedding reception. ("Had previously sent a handsome wedding present to the bride.") 12 P.M.: to bed.

This record of an actual day in district leader Plunkitt's career is the definitive treatise on the roots of power in Tammany politics. John Kelly's responsibility was to ensure that this pattern was sustained in all thirty-three districts in the City. Every party organ, from the Election District Committee on up, was expected to function smoothly, and translate neighborhood popularity into victory at the polls and patronage in the backrooms. Kelly had studied Tweed's free-wheeling operations and concluded that personal chicanery simply did not work. He sought to build a Tammany Hall that all men would rally around, one to which they could confidently and sensibly pledge loyalty, and in which there was a place and a duty for each man's particular abilities. Such a machine, Kelly reasoned, could withstand individual setbacks for its members, and even a stunning defeat for the party at large. With proper and stable organization, Tammany's power would be fundamental and invulnerable, "the sea itself" outlasting the waves of opposition.

Kelly believed above all in rules and ritual. In matters of finance, for example, candidates had spent their own money for their campaigns in the time of Boss Tweed, with haphazard assistance for the favored from Tweed's personal treasury and the funds of his wealthy friends. Kelly considered this procedure slipshod and uneconomical. As chairman of the Tammany Finance Committee, he created a system whereby all candidates contributed a fixed sum to the general campaign kitty, and office-holders who owed their jobs to Honest John were assessed a percentage of their salaries. Monday before each election was designated as "Dough Day." The district leaders convened at Tammany Hall to receive their portions of the City-wide campaign fund, under Kelly's close supervision, for Election Day expenses.

Patronage under Boss Tweed had been more of a battle than a procedure. Jobs were fought over and bribes passed freely. It was catch as catch can. Boss Kelly considered this inefficient and damaging to the Tammany system. He set a quota for each Assembly District on municipal jobs to be doled out to captains and constituents. (The available City payroll totaled $12,000,000.) After each election, the leaders submitted their lists of deserving job-seekers to Kelly for his consideration. In consultation with the Executive Committee, he trimmed and adjusted, and passed on the names to the Mayor, who was obliged to repay his debt for election. These appointments extended Tammany's power over the life of the City and its capacity to deliver favors into every center of influence in the municipal government.

In Honest John's Tammany, each political body and each party functionary was delegated explicit functions, prerogatives, and a fixed position in the hierarchy. The formalization of the structure was solidified by Kelly's constant insistence on orderliness—in the broad sense of authorities and duties—at all costs, in all crises. Order is the first priority for permanence, even in—especially in—a democracy. It was a permanent system that Kelly was determined to achieve. What the Federal Constitution had established for the nation, he intended to institute politically for a city of immigrants.

But let there be no impression that Honest John Kelly was an icy technician who flattened and computerized the era of rough-and-tumble politics. The business of winning votes, and jockeying for power, was still carried on in a highly personal fashion within the tight structure that he erected. Efficiency was the concept in the Boss's mind, but loyalty was the emotional word he spoke. Solidarity was the keynote to a successful neighborhood organization; but acts of kindness secured it, and gangs of toughs enforced it. Tammany's primary elections were conducted with full trimmings—broken knuckles, smashed windows, and stuffed ballot boxes. Kelly's regime, which was hailed and assailed in the saloons and streets of the ghettos, did not lack for zest and color and the clash of mischievous Gaelic personalities, though it was remarkably free from financial scandals.

Kelly's Tammany Hall was the Phoenix that arose from the ashes of Tweed's disgrace. It was the most significant of Tammany's many resurrections. For Honest John's essential achievement was to mold the wistful dreams and boisterous spirits of new Americans into a durable force.

In time, Kelly had worked out the lines of control so that he could dictate all nominations for office. Unfortunately, the new reform Mayor he had helped elect after the demise of Oakey Hall, sugar millionaire William Havemeyer, had his own businesslike methods and concepts of government. Mayor Havemeyer failed to comprehend why John Kelly should determine municipal appointments as well as elective posts. And Honest John, in turn, had difficulty understanding why any Mayor would interest himself in such matters. This traditional conflict between executive "ingratitude" and political "bossism" led to a public break in which the eighty-year-old Mayor made some unkind references to Honest John's past achievements as Sheriff.

"In such a matter as conveying convicts to prison, it does seem that you might be satisfied to be honest . . ." the Mayor wrote Kelly in an open letter. "Men who go about with the prefix of 'honest' to their names are often rogues." Honest John swung around and sued the Mayor for libel. The issue was never settled. On the first day of the trial, Mayor Havemeyer dropped dead of apoplexy.

It was the first time that Honest John Kelly's integrity had come under public attack. His next Mayor, William Wickham, was more politic. He appointed Kelly as City Comptroller in recognition of his political services. The *Tribune* highly praised Kelly's discharge of his duties: "He has had to resist in the Board of Apportionment and in the Finance Department the demands of a rapacious horde of office-holders far more numerous than the service required. . . . Nevertheless, in comparison with former administrations . . . he has been economical and conscientious. Under him our city debt has been decreased; our bonds have been advanced in value." During Kelly's five years as Comptroller, the municipal debt was reduced by twelve million dollars.

Mayor Wickham, a lofty businessman, was not popular with the Tammany rank-and-file. John "Old Smoke" Morrissey, leader of Tammany's "Shorthairs" (the workingmen as contrasted with Tilden's wealthy "Swallowtails") discovered shortly after Wickham assumed office that the new Mayor had posted an attendant in City Hall to receive calling cards. Barred from entering the Mayor's office, Morrissey snapped at the attendant: "Well, give my compliments to his honor Mayor Wickham, and ask him to tell Billy Wickham that when John Morrissey has time to put on French airs, he may call again."

The story was told that a few days later Morrissey was seen crossing City Hall Park, wearing patent leather boots, white kid gloves, a swallowtail coat and carrying a French dictionary. "I'm going in full dress to make a call," he told a friend, "for that is the style now at the Hotel Wickham. No Irish need apply."

Old Smoke Morrissey was a knavish Tammany ex-Congressman, holder of a world's heavyweight boxing title, and founder of Saratoga Springs' largest gambling casino. (In June 1966, Morrissey's century-old emporium was the setting for a forum sponsored by Senator Robert Kennedy in which appeared the well-scrubbed candidates for the Democratic gubernatorial nomination.) While Honest John was cultivating the Protestant reformers, Old Smoke Morrissey was gaining popularity among the Shorthairs who resented Kelly's circle of aristocrats. Morrissey taunted Honest John at every turn, and received such cheerful ovations that Kelly had no recourse but to expel him from Tammany Hall.

This action had an invigorating effect on Old Smoke Morrissey, who was known for his vengeful sense of humor. (When the residents of a fancy neighborhood refused to welcome him as a home-owner, he established a soap factory nearby which emitted such horrendous odors that the neighbors were forced to buy it from him at several times its worth.) Old Smoke, who had originally joined the Kelly-Tilden faction against Tweed, decided to test Boss Kelly's strength by running against the Tammany candidate in Tweed's old State Senate district.

He won the contest and proceeded to Albany where he voted against every piece of legislation favored by Honest John Kelly.

Honest John then made the unfortunate remark that only a district which had elected Tweed would also elect Morrissey. This prompted Morrissey to run for his second term in a silk-stocking district against Grand Sachem Augustus Schell. Again he triumphed to the dismay of Honest John. But he campaigned so vigorously to prove his point that he contracted pneumonia and died after the election.

In his disputes with Morrissey, Honest John suffered some damage among the Shorthairs, but he knew that the Swallowtails would be the key to success. They were the face of the New Tammany, the men who had purged the City of Boss Tweed, the leaders who proved that Tammany was an institution of probity and culture.

In 1874, Kelly backed Samuel Tilden, Tammany Sachem and Democratic State Chairman, for the gubernatorial nomination against fierce upstate opposition. Tilden won on the first ballot and went on to victory in November along with Mayor William Wickham. "Tammany," Honest John pronounced on election night, "is the only reform party in existence here today."

Kelly and Mayor Wickham, despite normal patronage disputes, maintained friendly lines of communication. And Honest John was a strong supporter of Tilden's programs in Albany to reform City government, and his crackdown on Tweed's judges and the "Canal Ring," a bi-partisan combine which feasted on the repair bills of the Erie Canal. "Pursue the good work you have commenced," Kelly wrote Governor Tilden, "no matter where the rod will fall, either on friend or foe."

Samuel Tilden was a cold, shrewd politician whose interest in exposés and reforms suggested a sharp eye on the White House rather than a zeal for justice. He was, above all, a man of the party. He had delayed his moves against Tweed until all the evidence was in. And now he welcomed, even depended upon, John Kelly's advice in matters of politics and patronage. The two men were not close friends, for neither knew the meaning of intimate friendship. But they were friendly allies in a common quest for political advancement. Honest John was a frequent guest at the Governor's home. And among Tilden's correspondence, the most confidential letters were addressed to John Kelly.

In the first months of Tilden's term in Albany, Kelly's recommendations for top posts were given the highest priority. ("He is an honest, high-toned gentleman," Honest John wrote of a prospective job-holder, "who will cooperate with you and do credit to himself.") Tilden also paid close heed to Kelly on legislation. ("Do not sign," the Boss wrote, "until I see you. I will be up.")

The incident that suddenly shattered this working relationship was known only to Tilden and Kelly. It may have been a secret patronage quarrel. It may have been a reform bill that stepped on too many Tammany toes. It may have been Tilden's indifference to the humiliating fate of ex-Boss Tweed. Or it may have been the Governor's fear that further association with Tammany Hall would endanger his presidential aspirations. Whatever the event or emotion, it was of such harsh meaning to John Kelly that in 1876 he arrived on a special train in St. Louis, site of the Democratic National Convention, with 150 anti-Tilden workers and a huge banner declaring: "Tilden Can't Carry New York."

Tilden sent an emissary to appease the irate Boss. Kelly sent back the message that he was no longer under any obligations to Samuel Tilden but if by any miracle he were nominated, Tammany Hall would work for his election. Despite Kelly's opposition, Tilden was nominated and Honest John kept his word. In the election, Tilden lost upstate by 25,000 votes but took Manhattan by 55,000. This delivered New York State into his column, making him the apparent victor in the electoral college with a 250,000-vote margin in the national popular vote. But twenty-two electoral votes were in dispute. Instead of throwing the election into the Democratic House of Representatives, Congress established a Republican-dominated Electoral Commission which certified fraudulent returns from Louisiana and Florida, giving the Presidency by one electoral vote to Ohio Governor Rutherford Hayes. Honest John confessed to friends that he was not at all unhappy with the result.

As a result of the Tilden-Kelly split, many of the Tammany Swallowtails left the Wigwam and formed the "Irving Hall Democracy." "You might think," commented George Washington Plunkitt, "that it would cost a lot of money to get up one of these organizations and keep it goin' for even one campaign, but, Lord bless you! it costs next to nothin'. Jimmy O'Brien brought the manufacture of 'Democracies' down to an exact science, and reduced the cost of production so as to bring it within reach of all. Any man with $50 can now have a 'Democracy' of his own."

Irving Hall had no concern about funds. Its leaders were Peter Cooper's son Edward; his co-proprietor of a huge steel company, Congressman Abram Hewitt; William Whitney, financier, Saratoga sportsman, and the "high toned gentleman" whom Honest John recommended to Tilden; and Tilden himself, now in political retirement in Yonkers but burning with energy to rid the New York Democratic Party of Honest John Kelly.

In 1878, Edward Cooper defeated Grand Sachem Augustus Schell for the mayoralty, thus delivering to John Kelly his first serious setback as Tammany Boss. The following year, Honest John led the Tammany delegation into the Democratic State Convention at Syracuse with the goal of denying renomination to Governor Lucius Robinson, the Tilden ally and successor who had broken his promise to free Bill Tweed. Kelly threw his support behind ex-Brooklyn Congressman and Gettysburg hero General Henry Slocum. But when it became apparent that the Robinson-Tilden forces had a majority, Honest John stalked out of the convention hall, followed by Schell, the noted attorney David Dudley Field, and the Tammany Shorthairs. The following night, in a move reminiscent of Aaron Burr's insurgent campaign of 1804, a rump convention met to nominate John Kelly as an independent candidate for Governor. Kelly said publicly that he had no illusions about winning and was frankly out to be a spoiler. He was determined to defeat Governor Robinson at all costs, even through the Tweed precept he despised—"rule or ruin." And in the election, John Kelly won 77,000 votes, enough to split the Democratic Party and swing the victory away from Robinson to the Republican nominee Alonzo Cornell.

Kelly's bolt stirred a national furor among Democrats. He was barred from the party's councils when the 1880 National Convention nominated General Winfield Scott Hancock, another Gettysburg hero. In New York City, a truce was arranged between Tammany Hall and Irving Hall for the duration of the campaign. They agreed to unite behind Hancock. They also met on neutral ground between the two Halls to determine control of the nominations for Congress and the State Legislature. The matter was decided by drawing legislative districts out of a hat. Tammany and Irving joined together to nominate William Grace for Mayor. Grace was a member of yet another reform group, the "County Democracy," founded by former Irvingites Abram

"Stand together," Tamanend told his tribe. "Support each other, and you will be a mountain that nobody can move." ❧ Statue of Chief Tamanend above the old 14th Street Tammany Hall.

THE FUNERAL OF OLD TAMMANY.

"WHAT ARE YOU LAUGHING AT? TO THE VICTOR BELONG THE SPOILS."

There is nothing that Tammany enjoys more than gloating over its own obituaries. ❧ Four of Tammany's many "deaths": 1836 (*upper left*), 1871 (*lower left*), 1901 (*upper right*), and 1933 (*lower right*).

THE WRECK OF THE PIRATE SHIP
HARPER'S WEEKLY

HERE'S HOPING THAT'S ALL!

NEW YORK HERALD TRIBUNE

"There have been seasons of eclipse," the historian wrote, "but after a time, the clouds rolled by, and the old Wigwam came into view." ❧ Four Tammany Wigwams: Martling's "Pig Pen" at Spruce and Nassau Streets (1798–1812, *above left*); the Tammany Hotel at Frankfort and Nassau (1812–1868, *above right*); the 14th Street Hall (1868–1928), scene of the 1868 Democratic National Convention (*below*); the Wigwam at Union Square (1929–1943), today headquarters for Local 90, International Ladies Garment Workers Union (*opposite above*).

Tammany's rites sound little more than collegiate today; but to the early Democrats, they were deeply meaningful symbols. ⧴ A Tammany Fourth of July celebration, 1812 (*below*).

FROM A PAINTING BY WILLIAM P. CHAPPEL, 1869, NEW YORK HISTORICAL SOCIETY

Years later, Aaron Burr told a friend: "Had I read Voltaire less and Sterne more, I might have thought the world wide enough for Hamilton and me." ❧ The Burr-Hamilton duel at Weehawken, New Jersey, 1804.

"The more civilized of the savages," the American Citizen reported, *"are beginning to associate with tamed and tutored men."* ❧ Aaron Burr in a painting by his friend, John Vanderlyn (*left*); Sachem Jacob Barker, a wealthy banker, who helped finance the first Tammany Hall (*center*); Martin Van Buren, "Grand Sachem of the Eagle Tribe" (*right*).

"The meekness of Quakerism,"
Clinton said, "will do in religion,
but not in politics." ❧ DeWitt
Clinton, Scribe of the Society of
Saint Tammany.

"He is an egregious demagogue
and a scoundrel, and it's a great
pity his opponents are nearly as
bad." ❧ Fernando Wood, New
York's "Model Mayor."

It was one of the bloodiest battles of the Civil War: more than two thou-
sand dead, with no count of the bodies dragged off to the inaccessible
neighborhoods of the Five Points. ❧ New York City's draft riots of 1863.
Shown here is the battle between the rioters and the military on First
Avenue.

"WHO STOLE THE PEOPLE'S MONEY?" — DO TELL. N.Y.TIMES 'TWAS HIM

The Tweed Ring: (*front left to right*)
William Marcy Tweed, Peter B. Sweeny,
Richard B. Connolly, and A. Oakey Hall.

*New York was a city that demanded a
boss.* ❧ William Marcy Tweed, in a
photograph taken just after his arrest.

He found Tammany a horde and left it an army. ဦ Honest John Kelly, leader of Tammany Hall, 1872 to 1886.

He was a cold, shrewd politician whose interest in exposés and reforms suggested a sharp eye on the White House rather than a zeal for justice. ဦ Sachem Samuel Tilden, who fought the Tweed Ring.

Morrissey taunted Honest John and received such ovations that Kelly had to expel him from Tammany Hall. ဦ John Morrissey, Tammany Congressman and boxing champion.

Croker confessed that the proudest moment of his life, far above his election victories, was leading Orby past the royal grandstand. ❧ Richard Croker after winning England's classic Epsom Derby, 1907.

He was an American Warwick who knew that his creations would be the true measure of his greatness. ❧ Charles F. Murphy at Tammany Hall. A tiger paperweight rests on his roll-top desk.

Seven months after he took office, there occurred the first of several disasters that were to blight his mayoralty. &❧ The attempted assassination of Mayor Gaynor as caught by the camera of William F. Warnecke of the New York *World* aboard the *Kaiser Wilhelm der Grosse,* August 9, 1910.

Everybody has heard of Tammany and nobody is sure exactly what it is. &❧ Tammany Sachems and other officers, 1935: (*left to right, seated*) John P. O'Brien, William P. Kenneally, James J. Dooling, Jr, Thomas Darlington, Alfred E. Smith, Thomas C. T. Crain, and John F. Curry; (*standing*) Edward J. McCullen, George Gordon Battle, Daniel L. Ryan, George F. Olvany, Daniel E. Finn, Henry V. Unger, James A. Foley, David Knott, Edwin Sohmer, and Sam Waudell.

Will You Love Me in December as You Do in May? ❧ Tammany's Mayor James J. Walker, songwriter and man-about-town, throws out the first ball of a charity baseball game in 1931 (*above*) and faces his inquisitor, Samuel Seabury, the following year (*below*).

He was so much the typical American success story that he would have been a cliché as a literary hero. ॐ Al Smith during the 1928 presidential campaign (*left*) and at the dedication of the Empire State Building in 1931 (*right*).

The Wagners were the last two popular candidates whose careers were spawned in the clubhouses of Tammany. ॐ Senator Wagner and son in 1937 when young Bob was elected to the State Assembly.

Bill-O, they called him, the Democrats' new champion. ॐ Here former Mayor William O'Dwyer appears before the U.S. Senate crime hearing in 1951.

He moved between backrooms of brawling politicos and parlors of wealthy liberals. ᔎ Carmine DeSapio with Mayor-elect Robert Wagner in 1953 (*above left*); at the 1956 Democratic National Convention with Herbert Lehman (*above right*), and James Farley (*below left*); and at the critical 1958 state convention in Buffalo with Averell Harriman (*below right*).

Through him the Negro inherits the scepter once held by the Dutch, the English, the Irish and the Italians. ❧ J. Raymond Jones at a Democratic State Committee meeting in Albany and (*below*) with New York's Senator Robert F. Kennedy.

Hewitt and William Whitney, and growing larger in numbers than Irving Hall.

Despite his agreement to give public support to Hancock, Honest John devoted all his energies in the campaign to pushing the local ticket, with an eye toward making William Grace as much a Tammany man as a product of the County Democracy. Hancock's candidacy was emphasized by both the C.D. and Irving Hall but Kelly gave only token co-operation. As a result, Ohio Congressman James Garfield, the Republican leader of the House, carried New York State and with it the election by 190 to 179 electoral votes. Tammany's lack of interest in the national contest was the decisive factor in the election. Within the City, William Grace was elected as the new Mayor.

The C.D. attempted to oust Kelly the following year when the annual elections were held for the Tammany Society's Council of Sachems. Generally, about 200 braves would appear for these affairs; this year the number quadrupled. The reform slate was distinguished enough, but Kelly's line of voters, which stretched out from Tammany Hall into 14th Street, was insurmountable. By the time many of the C.D. men had inched their way forward, the polls were closed. Honest John remained in control of Tammany Hall.

But the question was raised, when the Democratic State Convention met in Syracuse in September, 1882, as to who and what was the New York County Democratic Party? The Committee on Credentials and the Democratic State Committee ruled that the C.D. was the regular organization. After a lengthy and bitter debate, however, all three factions were recognized: C.D.—38 delegates; Tammany Hall —24; Irving Hall—10. It was a significant tribute to Kelly's political skill that Tammany was recognized at all in the convention. The upstate delegates were still smarting over his knifing of Governor Robinson and Hancock. The Tammany braves were ostracized by most of the other delegations. Whenever they made a motion on the floor, they were booed down from the galleries, which were packed with C.D. supporters.

Kelly was angry but he worked to cultivate all the anti-Tammany factions of the party. He told the upstate leaders that he was "friendly" toward the gubernatorial intentions of Buffalo reform Mayor Stephen Grover Cleveland. As the Cleveland bandwagon began to roll, Honest John persuaded a number of the C.D. delegates to jump aboard, and a temporary union of the warring wings was effected as Grover Cleveland won the nomination and went on to take the governorship by a plurality approaching 200,000 votes. (Tilden, by comparison, had won with 51,000 in 1874.) In the City, Kelly elected a new Mayor, Franklin Edson, and received a vast amount of patronage in return.

Patronage, however, was not the strong point of Governor Grover Cleveland. In his first message to the Legislature, he proposed a thorough overhaul of the State machinery, specifically, the consolidation of agencies and the elimination of no-show politicians. Before he had been three months in office, Cleveland made it plain that Tammany Hall was to have no patronage and that Grover Cleveland might someday be President. "Cleveland and Reform" was the slogan of the day.

"Mr. Cleveland," the *Sun* observed, "possesses valuable and elevated qualities as a public man, but his plan of governing without reference to the party which puts him in office is, in our judgment, quite inconsistent with the theory of free institutions." Tammany charged that Cleveland was a "tool of the corporations," citing his veto of Tammany bills to reduce transit fares and protect the rights of streetcar drivers. To such charges, the Governor replied icily: "God has never failed to make known to me the path of duty."

When the Tammany delegation to the State Senate, led by the popular, bucolic Thomas Francis Grady, blocked confirmation of a Cleveland appointee, the Governor dispatched an ultimatum to Honest John Kelly demanding that Grady "should not be returned to the Senate." This imposition of a political demand by an office-holder who had ignored Kelly's requests was enough to rate Grover Cleveland far above Samuel Tilden, Lucius Robinson, and William Havemeyer on Honest John's list of party traitors who must be purged.

And so once again it was a vengeful John Kelly who led his twenty-five delegates into the Chicago Exposition Hall for the Democratic National Convention of July, 1884. To prevent the nomination of Cleveland for President, he concentrated his attack on the unit rule which would bind a State's entire delegation by the will of its majority. New York had adopted a unit rule at the Democratic State Convention in Saratoga the previous month, but the delegation was still uncommitted, thanks to Kelly's opposition to an upstate resolution favoring Cleveland. As the National Convention came to order, Thomas Grady jumped to his feet to protest the thwarting of the will of the people who had elected the delegates in their various districts.

Grady's impassioned speech angered most of the delegates, who refused to be considered anti-people, and the unit rule was adopted for
the convention by a vote of 463 to 332.

Then Kelly and his Tammany delegates sharpened their knives.
Honest John passed around the letter in which Cleveland had demanded Grady's liquidation, a document which should have given
pause to any politician. Other anti-Cleveland spokesmen told the press
that Cleveland men had been given front seats in the delegations,
which was certainly true in the case of New York. It was charged that
the Mayor of Chicago, a Cleveland backer, had packed the galleries
with his supporters. And the rumor was spread that Grover Cleveland,
whatever virtue might be attached to his record, was virulently anti-
Catholic.

But Kelly's major problem was the lack of positive strength to build
on this base of negative criticism. Cleveland's only serious opponent
was the respected Delaware Senator Thomas Bayard (grandson of the
Federalist Senator who struck the bargain with Jefferson that dashed
Aaron Burr's Presidential hopes). Bayard had broad backing in all
sections of the country but it was short of a majority. The Senator's
floor workers sought to release the Pennsylvania bloc from the grip
of a favorite son who favored Cleveland. Pennsylvania was enough to
give Bayard the nomination, but it would not budge on the first ballot.
The Stop-Cleveland movement was doomed to failure when a Cleveland nominator said of his champion: "They love him most for the
enemies he has made." All eyes followed his gesture toward the Tammany delegation.

Grover Cleveland won on the second ballot with a surplus of 136
votes. But by Labor Day, the odds were favoring a smashing victory by
the Republican nominee James Blaine. Irish Democrats, including
many Tammanyites, were campaigning for Blaine, who was of Irish
descent, son of a devoutly Catholic mother, friend of Irish leaders, and
supporter of the Parnell Home Rule Movement.

In September, 1,387 members of the Tammany General Committee
convened in the Wigwam to ratify Cleveland as the choice of New
York County Democrats. But there were loud boos each time Cleveland's name was mentioned. A compromise resolution was passed by
a vote of 810 to 87: "The candidates of the Democratic Party having
been nominated in the National Convention, we acquiesce in the

will of the majority, although we believe that will to have been un-
wisely expressed."

A Blaine triumph was in the air when the week before election a
group of clergymen called upon the President-apparent at the Fifth
Avenue Hotel to wish him luck. The spokesman for the delegation had
missed his train in Philadelphia, so the committee of clergymen waited
for an hour, then selected the Presbyterian minister, the Reverend Samuel Burchard, to replace him. "We are Republicans," the Reverend
Burchard told Blaine and assembled reporters, "and we do not propose
to identify ourselves with the party whose antecedents have been rum,
Romanism and rebellion."

With that one sentence, every Democrat and every Catholic in
America were gravely offended. The whole campaign suddenly turned
upside down. On election night, 1884, Honest John sat in his office at
Tammany Hall receiving returns on the fate of his nemesis Grover
Cleveland. When it was over, with more than 1,200,000 ballots cast
in New York State, Cleveland had eked out a 1,000-vote plurality,
which gave him the State and thereby the nation.

Honest John Kelly walked out of Tammany Hall that night and
never returned.

Chapter 7

Squire
Croker

> "Richard Croker never said anything to me that was not true unless
> it was a statement for publication . . ."
> —*Lincoln Steffens*

"We don't have any theories at Tammany Hall," Richard Croker said. "I want reports that give me facts and figures. I never went to bed on a theory in my life."

As Honest John Kelly's successor, Boss Croker prided himself on understanding the facts, the workings of the Tammany system, the frailty of his men, the real nature of his times and his world—Old New York during the great burst of merriment known to nostalgia as "The Gay Nineties."

Croker was a squat little pugilist with a keen intelligence and a romantic imagination which he took great pains to deny. When a dedicated reformer asked him if he were working for his own pocket, the Boss growled, "All the time, the same as you." From his early days as an attendant in a corrupt courtroom to his later peerage with the great names of industry, Richard Croker believed that the profit motive ruled the lives of all humanity.

The people followed Croker because they feared he had appraised them correctly; that they were, in fact, self-seeking creatures indifferent to the general welfare. For the reformers, it appeared a futile struggle to bring out of hiding the desperate hope that the people were wrong, that Dick Croker had cheated their destinies.

Croker had famous and powerful enemies, among them Theodore Roosevelt, the Reverend Dr. Charles Parkhurst, the police reporters Jacob Riis and Lincoln Steffens. Throughout his career he was hounded by leading educators, clergymen, and publishers. He was investigated

197

three times by special committees of the State Legislature. Twice he
was defeated by reformers. Once he was tried for murder. Within his
own circle of district leaders—even within his family—he was subject
to sudden attacks whenever his authority appeared vulnerable. Yet for
sixteen years, until he committed the two unpardonable Tammany sins
—pushing too hard and talking too much—he exercised more power
than any Tammany leader before or since.

After scrutinizing Richard Croker's activities, a State committee
concluded with understandable exasperation: "The one clear and distinct fact brought out by this investigation is that we have in this
great city the most perfect instance of a centralized government ever
known. . . . We see that government, no longer responsible to the
people, but to a dictator."

Croker did not consider such attacks unflattering, though he might
have preferred the word "king." The press carried "His Majesty's"
schedule of appointments in a daily "Court Calendar," a taunt as
gratifying to Croker as it was amusing to the public. He could never
understand jokes at his expense. The American industrialists who used
him, and the English nobles to whom he became an unwitting jester,
regarded him as a pretentious hoodlum. Yet he persisted in courting
them, accumulating fortunes of "honest graft," purchasing vast properties, dressing elegantly and affecting ludicrous airs, dedicating his life
to the pursuit of recognition by those born to riches.

Although his father had been a farrier in Ireland, shoeing and doc-
toring horses, Dick Croker was fonder of publicizing his descent from
officers of Oliver Cromwell's forces which brought Ireland under
English rule in the seventeenth century. He also took comfort in the
Scottish lowland origins of his mother's family, the Wellsteads, though
they had been in Ireland for as many generations as the Crokers. This
pedigree was even less successful in impressing the aristocrats than
Croker's attempts to buy his way into pure blood-lines by breeding
prize bulldogs and champion horses.

Given more useful aspirations, Dick Croker's extraordinary political
talents might have carried him past notoriety to greatness. He was
diverted by the distress he felt about his past as a humble Tammany
ruffian. As a boy of three, he had sailed with his parents in the steerage
of the *Henry Clay* bound west from Ireland to New York. It was in the
fall of 1846, the year that blight struck the Irish potato crop. They embarked at Cork Harbour, sixty miles from New Ross where President

Kennedy's great-grandfather Patrick set out for Boston to escape the famine.

In Manhattan the Crokers found shelter in a dilapidated cottage on old Bloomingdale Road in Shanty Town, a settlement of squatters' hovels that sprawled across the western part of what is now Central Park. This was the home of immigrants and outcasts who could find no place in the southern part of the island—the Indians, the Negroes, and the "Shanty Irish." Dick Croker's father, Eyre Coote Croker, registered with the immigrants' caretaker, Tammany Hall, and was eventually appointed assistant veterinarian for the Harlem (horse-car) Railroad. The family moved down to East 28th Street, a better address for immigrant workers which, nonetheless, brought greater tensions to their children.

In Shanty Town there was a huge playground of countryside and open air where the children lived the relatively innocent life of an impoverished rural village. On the East Side there were sidewalks and tenements, the first awareness of anti-Irish prejudice, and the fierce struggle to Get Ahead. The neighborhoods were controlled by powerful and tightly organized gangs, some on the payroll of Fernando Wood, employed to raid the clubhouses of his political rivals in Tammany.

To maintain their strength, the gangs intimidated immigrant children, enforcing affiliation as an obvious necessity for survival. When Dick Croker, at thirteen, dropped out of school to work as a locomotive machinist, he began to devote his off-hours to the affairs of the Fourth Avenue Tunnel Gang, a group of young railroad toughs who met in a saloon down the block from the Crokers'.

The gang was an excellent apprenticeship for Tammany Hall. Its code was Tammany's code: discipline through loyalty, reputation through results, and leadership through strength. Modern sociologists have commented on the superior intelligence and managerial abilities of present-day juvenile gangleaders. In the nineteenth century these talents were considered neither surprising nor wasted. They were well-rewarded by enterprising politicians. One of these was Boss Tweed's thorn-in-the-side Jimmy "The Famous" O'Brien, Tammany alderman and district leader from Dick Croker's neighborhood. "Show me a boy that hustles for the organization on election day," said Jimmy the Famous, "and I'll show you a comin' statesman."

After Dick Croker had knocked out his boxing instructor and gone on to shatter the reputations of several professional prize-fighters, he came to the attention of Jimmy the Famous as a "comin' statesman." By the time he was nineteen, Croker had fought his way to the leadership of the Tunnel Gang and with O'Brien's encouragement made it a subsidiary of the Tammany machine.

"In the year 1864, at the age of twenty-one, I cast my first ballot," Boss Croker later recalled. "I felt then that the Democratic Party was the young man's party; that the young blood of the nation must naturally be drawn toward Democracy, which made a ready place for the newcomers, and welcomed them to a share in the management of the affairs, even into the councils, of the nation." The following year (according to Jimmy the Famous) Croker voted fourteen times for a constable in Brooklyn named William Lyman. But Lyman denied this story. He said it was seventeen times.

The Tunnel Gang, following their leader's example, cast innumerable ballots in Manhattan, Brooklyn, and Philadelphia as well, on a kind of lend-lease arrangement. Jimmy the Famous was so impressed with the ingenuity of his protégé that he made him deputy district leader and introduced him to Comptroller Slippery Dick Connolly. Croker was soon invited to join the Volunteer Fire Department, almost a prerequisite for political advancement, and Slippery Dick gave him his first City job: court attendant to Judge George Barnard, Boss Tweed's poker friend who served the railway interests of Commodore Vanderbilt or Jim Fisk, depending on the highest bid. It was in this hall of justice that Dick Croker gained his first insights into the financial benefits of corporate-governmental conspiracies.

When Jimmy "The Famous" O'Brien was elected Sheriff, Croker succeeded him on the Board of Aldermen. This was a crucial period in his twenty-two-year training for the leadership. Not only did he study the techniques of manipulating the board (he would become the first Tammany Boss to dominate it) but he displayed a shrewd aptitude for the fine art of choosing sides. During the intra-machine struggle against Boss Tweed, he joined the Tammany reform faction led by Jimmy the Famous and Honest John Kelly. Then, after O'Brien had exposed the Tweed larceny to the New York *Times*, Croker turned from his loquacious mentor to back Honest John for the Tammany leadership. He chose correctly. Jimmy the Famous defected, established his own "O'Brien Democracy," and ran a poor third in the mayoral election of 1872. And John Kelly was happy to reciprocate Croker's regard by supporting him in a successful election for Coroner, a position with potential yearly fees of $25,000.

Richard Croker, at thirty, thus achieved sufficient distinction to win the hand of Elizabeth Frazier, a genteel lady whose interests lay in the Church and charitable works. They were married at an important juncture in his career: he was learning from Honest John the maxims of "honest graft" and non-violent leadership. He was improving his syntax, bowing to the ladies, and adopting a reserved, dignified pose. It seems improbable that Elizabeth could have been surprised, as she later professed to be, at the less savory aspects of her husband's political life. More likely, she knew his record and, despite it, responded to the qualities that prompted the philanthropist Nathan Straus to note that under Croker's "stern exterior was an unusual friendliness and a kindness of heart."

If at the time of her wedding Elizabeth did have any illusions about her bridegroom's reputation, they did not survive Election Day of the following year. Jimmy "The Famous" O'Brien was running for Congress against Abram Hewitt, the distinguished industrialist who had the backing of Boss Kelly and Coroner Croker. In the early morning of Election Day, Croker and his Tammany patrol caught up with O'Brien and a group of West Side vote-repeaters on an East Side corner. When Croker inquired of the men their business on the East Side, Jimmy retorted with the epithet "damned loafer," which apparently had strong meaning among Tammany sinecure-holders.

"I am no damned loafer," said Dick Croker.

"You damned cur," said Jimmy the Famous. "I picked you out of the gutter, and now you're supporting a rich man like Hewitt against me for Congress." Jimmy the Famous slugged Croker on the back of the head, and Croker replied with a blow to the jaw.

This dialogue was later recounted to a Grand Jury, inasmuch as a bullet fired in the melee mortally wounded one of O'Brien's men. Croker was indicted by a Grand Jury, imprisoned in the Tombs, and brought to trial for murder. "I never carried a pistol in my life," he told the court, "and never will so long as I can use my hands." His bride Elizabeth sat through the proceedings nervously fluttering her fan, her face pale as death—no paler, however, than the face of George Hickey, a Tammany friend of Croker's who sat next to him during the trial.

The jury, weighing eyewitness testimony that varied according to political allegiance, split 6-6. The District Attorney did not press for a re-trial. In later years it was generally believed that Croker was protecting George Hickey, the actual murderer. The presiding judge acknowledged that post-trial findings had convinced him of Croker's innocence, and the defense attorney said his client had prevented him from introducing evidence of Hickey's guilt. Hickey had been prepared, he said, to immediately confess the killing if the jury had brought in a verdict against Croker.

Public reaction to the trial caused Croker's defeat in a re-election for Coroner. *Munsey's Magazine* reported that for several years he was "in almost abject poverty" and was "shunned by men of his own class." He appealed to Honest John Kelly for a City job. "I've got my district behind me," he told Honest John, "and I go to City Hall every day and hang about and try to see the Mayor. He won't see me. When I speak to him in the hall, he don't notice me."

Boss Kelly and Mayor William Wickham were having patronage disputes at the time so Honest John approached a mutual friend on Croker's behalf. "Now, I know that Richard is a worthy boy," John Kelly said. "I know he means well and is a good party worker. I wish you could help him." The Mayor's friend gave Croker a letter of introduction, but ten minutes later he found him leaning against a lamp-post outside Kelly's office, his hands in his pockets, looking up at the snow beginning to fall in the twilight. Croker confessed he didn't have the fare to deliver the letter to the Mayor. The friend loaned him the money, and, according to *Munsey's*, "Croker returned the loan with interest ten thousandfold."

Apart from supporting his growing family, Croker had squandered a good deal of his Coroner's income at the Saratoga races. From the time of that loan, however, he moved unobtrusively toward a position where there would be no need to curb his extravagance. He received, with little publicity, a series of municipal appointments, and within Tammany became John Kelly's most trusted aide, coming to know better than any other man the detailed operations of Honest John's machine. In any line of succession to Kelly's leadership, Dick Croker was far from the top. Yet through his personal closeness to Honest John, he was the man whom the envious Sachems had to consult on Tammany affairs.

In 1885 Honest John Kelly lay ill after a series of defeats by rival Democrats culminating in Grover Cleveland's Presidential victory.

Croker visited Kelly's home each day to receive directives and, increasingly, to offer advice.

Tammany needed a reputable candidate in the City elections that year to depose Mayor William Grace, the steamship tycoon and leader of the Swallowtails, whom Kelly had originally helped elect but now called an "ingrate." Croker persuaded Honest John to run Hugh Grant, a rich, affable young man with a unique qualification: he was the only alderman who hadn't accepted a bribe. Boss Kelly wanted a stronger candidate, but, convinced that Croker could control Grant, he reluctantly agreed to the choice. Hugh Grant was beaten decisively in the election. John Kelly plunged deeper into disillusionment and died of a broken heart.

The majority of the district leaders immediately demanded that leadership of Tammany be turned over to a ruling committee. The day after the funeral they were still squabbling over seniority when Richard Croker walked into Honest John's office at Tammany Hall and sat down behind the desk.

A British editor once asked Boss Croker to define the fundamental law of the Universe. "Sir," Croker replied gravely, "the law is that although wrongdoing may endure for a season, right must in the long run come to the top. . . . If you put ten honest men into an assembly with 90 thieves, human nature is such that the ten honest men will boss the 90 thieves. . . . Tammany is honest and Tammany is true. And you have only got to go on being honest and true to come out on top."

The editor was sure that Croker was joking until he looked at his face: "His countenance was imperturbable, and I do not believe that he was saying a word in which in some way or other he had not first convinced himself was gospel truth. . . . Mr. Croker is a kind of mundane Pope, with the Executive Committee as his College of Cardinals. To him the new era began with the overthrow of Boss Tweed in 1871— the real Reformation."

This description, of course, was even more applicable to Honest John Kelly, from whom Croker inherited his obedient Cardinals and the air of personal authority which earned their respect. It was Croker's own qualities, however, which broadened the influence of Tammany. "Three things raised Richard Croker to leadership," a Tammany associate wrote years later. "An iron determination, an ability to judge men, and an almost sacred observance of his promise once it was given.

Once he made up his mind, nothing could change it . . . once he gave his word, that word he kept, no matter what the cost or consequences."

Croker was a more rational man than John Kelly. He knew when to compromise and when to strike hard. He was an expert student of the strength of his enemies, therefore less prone to angry disappointment when he lost a battle. Unlike the deeply religious Honest John, he did not fear avenging demons at the polls. He was also slower in assessing his allies; he had watched Kelly fall prey to flattery. John Kelly was a more sensitive man than Croker, but without his judgment or perception. Richard Croker would never be disillusioned.

For his closest aides, the new Boss chose a trio of organization men with virtuous public images: Hugh Grant, the youthful alderman, wealthy, charming—and weak enough for Croker to manipulate; Patrick Gilroy, a boyhood friend and astute master of machine details; and William Bourke Cockran, a colorful hero of the Irish immigrants who had a gift for long-winded purple oratory. (Winston Churchill considered Bourke Cockran to be the greatest American orator.)

A year after assuming command of Tammany, Croker made effective use of this cabinet in winning the county offices from the County Democracy. Bourke Cockran wrote a sparkling campaign platform, Pat Gilroy pushed the Tammany election workers, and Hugh Grant led the ticket, winning election as Sheriff. The following year was Croker's first try for the mayoralty. To consolidate his control over the district leaders, it was essential that he capture City Hall and deliver its patronage. But he faced three formidable enemies: the entrenched anti-Tammany Democrats of the County Democracy; the Republicans, who had a vigorous candidate in twenty-eight-year-old Theodore Roosevelt; and, most importantly, the progressives supporting Henry George, the popular economist whose social welfare and tax programs had won powerful backing from Labor.

Without the support of the Henry George followers, Croker felt that Tammany had little chance. And if he ran a Tammany man, the Democratic vote would be split three ways, thus assuring Teddy Roosevelt of election. Croker decided to offer the Democratic nomination to Henry George. He was abruptly rebuffed. George collected 30,000 signatures and entered as the candidate of the United Labor Party.

Croker's next move was to persuade the wealthy members of the County Democracy that unless they joined with Tammany, the radical doctrines of Henry George would rule New York City. He pleaded with

Congressman Abram Hewitt (who had financed his defense at the murder trial) to take the nomination. Hewitt protested that he was too "old and weary" to run again for office, but Croker succeeded in drafting him on the strength of a truce between Tammany and the C.D.

Abram Hewitt was an honest man, friendly with some Tammany Sachems, and rich enough to make campaign charges against "nihilism" and the "Red Peril" with considerable effect on Republican voters. Hewitt smashed Roosevelt at the polls and defeated Henry George by 20,000 votes. It was charged that Henry George would have won the election but for gangs of repeaters imported by Tammany from Jersey City and Philadelphia.

Once in office, Mayor Hewitt fell out of favor with the public through numerous acts of self-righteousness and quick temper. The Irish were incensed when he broke an old tradition by refusing to review the St. Patrick's Day Parade. He also delivered far less patronage than the Tammany district leaders had been led to expect. The Mayor publicly broke with Croker, attacking him as a "spoilsman," and the C.D. retained its control of City Hall.

In the summer of 1888, Croker engineered a national triumph over the C.D. when he led his elegantly attired Tammany delegation, accompanied by ten marching bands, into the Democratic Convention in St. Louis. For the first time in twelve years, Tammany was cheered on the convention floor. In a press conference, Boss Croker announced his support for Honest John's enemy, President Grover Cleveland: "Tammany Hall this year is going to demonstrate by its united, hearty, and loyal support of the National ticket that it is entitled to be called the exponent of true Democracy; and the results will prove that, as well as being the oldest, it is the strongest and most faithful Democratic organization in the country. We will sink or swim with the National ticket this time, for the day has gone by when any doubt can be raised as to Tammany's loyalty."

It was a sensational turnabout. President Cleveland's civil service reforms had deeply offended the Irish politicians and the word was traveling through the precincts that he was an anglophile. Croker's support for Cleveland was essentially a local power play; he had no interest in national politics. He succeeded in stealing the thunder of the President's real supporters in New York City—the County Democracy—through a strategy which the wrathful Honest John would never have countenanced.

With Tammany established in the public mind as a responsible arm of the national party, Croker set out to overthrow Mayor Hewitt and enforce his thesis that "All the employees of the city government, from the Mayor to the porter who makes the fire in his office, should be members of the Tammany organization." Hugh Grant was nominated for Mayor and Bourke Cockran set the tone of the campaign, railing away at Hewitt as an "Anglomaniac millionaire."

Grant beat the Republican candidate by 40,000 votes. Mayor Hewitt trailed far behind in third place. The County Democracy was finished. On election night 6,000 men streamed into Tammany Hall, prancing through Indian war-dances to Irish melodies. Thirty thousand more were massed in Madison Square to watch the election bulletins at the *Herald*. "The sound of their voices," said the morning edition, "was like the beating of wild waves against a cavern. Along the edges of this vast multitude were the blazing corridors of the hotels, in which half-crazed men with flushed faces and bloodshot eyes waved handfuls of money, and with blasphemous boastings sought out their opponents."

In one of those hotels, the Union Square across the way from Tammany Hall, Richard Croker stood in victory next to his new mayor. "Tammany Hall," he announced, "will be, as it has always been, the only real Democratic organization in the city. When Mr. Grant assumes the reins of government, he will be a reform Mayor in action— not in words or garrulous letters." The cheers from his followers made clear what kind of reform was in the making.

It was not until after midnight that the national returns came in: Grover Cleveland had defeated Benjamin Harrison by more than 100,000 votes. But he had lost New York State and the electoral college. Tammany's winning ballots for Mayor Grant were blank on the Presidential line.

In his first three years as boss of a nationally discredited Tammany Hall, Richard Croker elected two mayors, won the county offices, brought the Board of Aldermen under control, crushed the rival Democratic factions, turned back the strong threat from Henry George, formed lasting alliances with Wall Street contributors, enlisted the support of the hostile upstate Democrats, and earned cheers from the delegates at the Democratic National Convention.

He had proved himself, within the limits of New York politics, to be a superb tactician. In 1889, he celebrated Tammany Hall's centennial by another sweep of county offices, and moved into the "Gay Nineties" with Hugh Grant and then Pat Gilroy as his mayors.

The fundamentals of Richard Croker's Gay Nineties were somewhat different from our Hollywood memories of Lillian Russell riding Diamond Jim Brady's gold-plated bicycle, or mustachioed quartets at Coney Island crooning the wholesome sentiments of Tin Pan Alley. For all the laughter emanating from the brownstones of Fifth Avenue and the saloons of the Tenderloin, this was the City's darkest age. As New York entered the Gay Nineties, there were no public agencies to care for the eighteen thousand immigrants who arrived in the City each month; no shelters or school playgrounds for the thousands of orphans who wandered the streets; no efforts to protect teen-age girls from procurers, small shopkeepers from criminals, or jobless men from police beatings; and, even after a devastating typhus epidemic, only sporadic concern for sanitation and public health.

In such a climate of indifference, with frivolous *nouveau riche* and staid old Knickerbockers exploiting the destitute, it is remarkable that a revolution did not occur. It did not because the institution which protected the masters was the proletariat's own—Croker's Tammany Hall. If the time had ever come, William Allen White maintained, when Tammany's thousands took action "unrestrained by the intervening agency of Croker, or his heirs or assigns, heaven protect wealth and social order in New York City! . . . For Tammany preaches contentment."

Richard Croker was the anti-liberal patriarch of New York's working class. So long as City Hall did not embark on the broad welfare programs urged by Henry George, Tammany's clubhouse favors were desperately and gratefully received. The Boss thereby became both a hero to the mob and an invaluable ally to the aristocracy. "We have thousands of men who are alien born," Croker said. "They are alone, ignorant strangers, a prey to all manner of anarchical and wild notions. Tammany looks after them for the sake of their vote, grafts them upon the Republic . . . and although you may not like our motives or our methods, what other agency is there by which so long a row could have been hoed so quickly or so well?"

The services which Tammany performed for its people, all incidental to the exigencies of New York's social problems, smoothed the way for Croker in his own urgent quest for personal prestige. His criteria for success were absurdly extravagant, but he fulfilled nearly all of them. New Yorkers' esteem for Croker was as great as for any American politician of his time. Thousands of admirers jammed the piers to wave him off on his annual voyages to Europe. On one such occasion, a police boat escorting his ship out of the harbor fired a twenty-one-gun salute. "Why, that's the President's salute," Croker remarked with a smile. On Jefferson's birthday, Croker walked to his seat of honor in the Metropolitan Opera House as the orchestra played "Hail to the Chief." His devotees enjoyed such regal posturing, and many enlightened citizens were amused rather than outraged. More often than not, public curiosity and affection for an eccentric celebrity shielded him from the wrath of the reformers.

Such conscientious muckrakers as William Allen White found the love affair intolerable. "And all this homage," White protested, "all this boot-licking to a mild-mannered, soft-voiced, sad-faced, green-eyed chunk of a man who talks slowly that he may peg in his 'seens' and his 'saws', his 'dones' and his 'dids' where they belong, who has a loggy wit, who cares neither for books, nor music, nor good wine, nor a dinner, nor the society of his kind! All this blind obedience by men of brains and some rudimentary culture to a dull, emotionless prosimian bulk of bone and sinew—a sort of human megatherium, who has come crashing up from the swamps splashed with the slime of pre-Adamite wickedness! And now he sits on a throne and disposes a sort of jungle justice, while civilization knocks its knees together in stupid, terrified adulation!"

Most reporters, however, were as fond of Croker personally as they were antagonistic to the stuffy reformers whose programs they favored. They were grateful for his candor and they valued his gruff sentimentality. "A sweet-faced man he was," Lincoln Steffens said of his first encounter. "His eyes were kind . . . a winning smile spread from his lips up to his eyes." Steffens concluded that Croker was "intellectually and morally a citizen of the civilization of New York" and in many ways a more tolerable symptom of mass dishonesty than the patricians and wardheelers who sustained him. Some journalists even looked upon him as a kind of Robin Hood. "A leader was sure of making a hit with the Boss," said the *Saturday Evening Post,* "by hunting up some boyhood friend of Croker's who was in need of help, particularly if the person had ever done Croker a slight favor."

Croker never stole from the public treasury, as Tweed had done.

His personal code was "honest graft," a term coined by Tammany's forthright philosopher, State Senator George Washington Plunkitt, the district leader who grew up with Croker in Shanty Town. "The politician who steals," said Plunkitt, "is worse than a thief. He is a fool. With the grand opportunities all around for the man with a political pull there's no excuse for stealin' a cent." Plunkitt's espousal of "honest graft" eloquently supported Lincoln Steffens' observation that "hypocrisy is not a Tammany vice." (Today the system is more delicately described as "conflict-of-interest.")

As Croker expanded his power, an increasing number of officials who made decisions on City purchases and contracts, including the letting of the great public service franchises, were indebted to him for their jobs. Businessmen therefore found it prudent to make him a stockholder in their enterprises and to feed him Wall Street speculative tips. To reward loyalty in his organization, Croker spread the winnings. Tammany Sachems became contractors for City projects. Firms that refused to co-operate in their schemes were harassed by municipal ordinances from the Board of Aldermen. And Croker's judges appointed Tammany receivers who appointed Tammany auctioneers.

To anyone watching Dick Croker shake off the dust of Shanty Town, the immense opportunities which "honest graft" afforded were self-evident. At the age of thirty-one, following his murder trial, he and Elizabeth had been living modestly in Harlem. Then, during Honest John's illness, he began to receive money for patronage. He admitted that his infant daughter Flossie received a gift of $10,000 from Hugh Grant, her "godfather" and Croker's star candidate. This was about the time that Croker founded the Meyer & Croker real estate firm, which became the most prosperous auctionhouse in the City.

After the election of Hugh Grant as Mayor, Croker was appointed City Chamberlain. The salary was $25,000 a year and the duties—overseeing the City's investments—assured him of several times that amount in "considerations." He resigned this job after Hugh Grant was re-elected Mayor in 1890. He was never on the municipal payroll again. None of his political activities was salaried. Yet shortly after the 1890 election he moved his family from Harlem to an $80,000-brownstone in the East 70's and refurbished it for $100,000. The following year he was co-purchaser of a $500,000-stock-farm at Richfield Springs, near Utica, and acquired a number of thoroughbreds which ranged up to $30,000 apiece. Two years later he bought a half-interest in the Belle Meade stud farm in Tennessee for $250,000.

Croker traveled in a private Pullman car to national conventions and to his winter estate in Palm Beach, The Wigwam, valued with its long shorefront at $800,000. He much preferred, however, to make sea voyages to Europe, to visit the German spas, the Swiss resorts, and especially the English races, where he spent each summer attempting to persuade British society to allow his horses on the tracks. In England, Croker owned a residence near his stables at Newmarket, a London townhouse, and a huge Berkshire County estate at Wantage.

For a time, the voters of Tammany looked upon the Boss's seven homes with more pride than envy, as though "honest graft" were a rich man's game that did no one any harm. Rewarded by City jobs, peddling licenses, free lawyers, and sumptuous Tammany picnics, most immigrants were bored by abstract reform talk about privileged corporations paying off the City, charging high rates for inadequate service, and providing cheap workmanship that endangered public safety.

"Dirty graft"—extracted by Tammany district leaders through police blackmail of prostitutes, saloonkeepers, criminals, and many innocent persons—hit closer to home. It was the price to be paid for breaking the law or failing to register with Tammany Hall. "Police graft is dirty graft," Croker told Lincoln Steffens. "We have to stand for it. If we get big graft, we can't decently kick at the petty stuff. Can we now? We can't be hypocrites, like the reformers who sometimes seem to me not to know that they live on graft. This I tell you, boy, and don't you ever forget it: I never have touched a cent of the dirty police graft myself."

Steffens insisted on this basis that Croker remained "true to his professional ethics." When he was confronted with exposés of widespread police graft, the Boss remarked confidentially to reporters, "Well, and what are you going to do about it?" One of the men printed the question as a challenge, an echo of Boss Tweed. But Steffens claimed, "The old man, overwhelmed by the evidence produced and knowing how old and established the complicated system of bribery was, really wondered what could be done about it . . . as he used to say it to me, it was an awed, a moral question; and it served a moral purpose."

By allowing his Sachems to pursue their "dirty graft" without interference or taxation, Croker infused great strength into the lower echelons of his organization. The Tammany phalanx which proved unbeatable in the early 1890's consisted of 90,000 precinct workers under thirty-five District leaders responsible to Croker. But Croker allowed his leaders to conduct their business as they wished, on condition that they carry their neighborhoods on Election Day. "He who excuses himself accuses himself," he was fond of reminding those who failed him. Few of them did. When Big Tim Sullivan, Sachem of the Bowery, found one precinct in his district with 388 Democratic votes to 4 Republican votes, he promptly reported to Croker that the Republicans "got one more vote than I expected there, but I'll find that feller."

Croker was the first Tammany Boss to turn over local patronage to the district leaders. This served to pacify men who might otherwise have competed for the main prize. But it also led ultimately to a diffusion of discipline and the creation of intra-Tammany machines which could no longer be controlled from the top. Big Tim Sullivan, whom Croker made Bowery leader in 1890, within a few years came to rule captains and constituents who would follow him for or against Croker. A portrait of Big Tim was hung in nearly every building in his district. The annual picnic of the Timothy D. Sullivan Association (which continued with Little Tim into the twentieth century) was one of the great Democratic functions of the year. And Big Tim, quite independently of Croker, became a partner in a gambling and prostitution ring that grossed three million dollars a year. A journalist who interviewed underworld characters for *McClure's* was told by one: "Croker is Boss on the strength of the understandin' that [New] York is to be open and Tammany is to get the benefit of the police graft. If he should go back on his promises to the boys, he couldn't remain Boss a week."

The close relationship between vice and politics was an immediate fact of life to the immigrants. Yet it was unknown to the bulk of New York's Protestant middle-class until one Sunday morning in February, 1892, when the Reverend Dr. Charles Parkhurst stepped up to his pulpit in the Madison Square Presbyterian Church. In a sermon made public by the *World*, he attacked "the polluted harpies who, under the pretense of governing this city, are feeding day and night on its quivering vitals. They are a lying, perjured, rum-soaked, libidinous lot . . . every effort to make men respectable, honest, temperate, and sexually clean is a direct blow between the eyes of the Mayor and his whole gang of drunken and lecherous subordinates."

Parkhurst had a shrewd sense of publicity as well as an earnest con-

cern for the morals of the community. When a Grand Jury repri-
manded him for failing to support his charges with evidence, he
disguised himself in black-and-white checked trousers and a loud red
tie, and set out on a tour of brothels, flophouses, and dime-whiskey
saloons. He watched a chorus of naked girls playing leap-frog at Hattie
Adams' bagnio, only one of thirty such establishments doing excellent
business within a few blocks of his church. Then he sent out investigators who found two hundred and fifty saloons selling liquor on a typical
Sunday. "Anyone," said Parkhurst, "who, with all the easily ascertaina-
ble facts in view, denies that drunkenness, gambling, and licentiousness
in this town are municipally protected, is either a knave or a fool."

"I have a good deal of respect for any man who tries to do what
he thinks is right," Richard Croker carefully replied. "His methods are
simply a matter of opinion. . . . Of course, he knows, and everybody
else knows, that no man or set of men can eradicate the social evil. All
that anybody can do is to prevent it from annoying and contaminating
respectable people."

Following Parkhurst's charges, some brothels were closed, a few
policemen were demoted, and Croker substituted Pat Gilroy for Hugh
Grant in the mayoral campaign of 1892. Thus far the political damage to Tammany was slight and Gilroy won the election. But the attack
was renewed from an unexpected source.

It is a practical tradition that the Democratic Party in New York
City shares its offices with a few "safe" Republicans. This helps mini-
mize GOP political activity in the City and increases bargaining power
for jobs from a Republican Governor or for Democratic bills in a
Republican State Legislature. In his zeal to assert Tammany's power
over factions within his own party, Richard Croker angered Thomas
Platt, the powerful chairman of the Republican State Committee, by
stalling on GOP patronage. Platt retaliated by moving his lieutenants
into the sluggish Republican political clubs in the City. He became a
prominent member of Dr. Parkhurst's congregation—that is, until the
pastor announced one Sunday morning that one Platt was worse than
five Crokers.

Every Sunday after church, Platt held conferences at the Fifth
Avenue Hotel. He met with his leaders on two sofas in a section of the
hotel lobby still identified today as the "Amen Corner," so rapid was
the nodding of heads at "Platt's Sunday School Classes." Here all the
GOP candidates were selected, State jobs distributed, and orders issued

to the legislators in Albany. One of these directives called for a committee under the chairmanship of State Senator Clarence Lexow ol
Nyack to investigate police corruption in New York City.

Platt intended merely to uncover enough Tammany election frauds
to blackmail Richard Croker into delivering patronage. What Platt had
not anticipated was the great public appetite for tales of evil-doing
which Dr. Parkhurst had whetted. Nor was he aware of the vast extent
of the corruption. In March 1894, the Lexow Committee began hearings on the third floor of the Tweed Courthouse. By the end of the
year, some 6,000 pages of testimony had been recorded, the most detailed accounting of municipal malfeasance in history.

The Lexow report clearly established the responsibility of Tammany district leaders in the vicious circle of police graft. Appointments,
promotions, and transfers in the 4,000-man force were made by a Board
of Police Commissioners, composed of two Democrats and two "safe"
Republicans. By their own testimony, the Commissioners' actions were
guided solely by the recommendations of the district leaders. It took
$300 to buy a patrolman's position from a Sachem, and the fee went
up with each promotion. Captain Alexander "Clubber" Williams, a
wealthy Connecticut commuter, was said to have paid $15,000 for his
transfer to the 19th precinct, a midtown area abounding in fancy brothels that could afford high protection fees. The district received its name
when Clubber Williams remarked to a reporter after his transfer, "I've
had nothin' but chuck steak for a long time, and now I'm going to get
a little of the tenderloin."

Rookie policemen, when they learned that merit was disregarded,
went into debt to finance their promotions. To pay their backers, they
became part of the system of shakedowns which threatened everyone
from the richest madam to the poor shoeshine boy who lacked a sidewalk permit. Once absorbed into the system, the police became more
avaricious and brutal. A veteran of Siberian exile told the committee
he had been safer in the hands of the Czarist police. Another immigrant victim, a woman who operated a small cigar store, had refused to
pay a patrolman fifty dollars. She was arrested as a prostitute and her
children were sent to an asylum.

The Lexow exposés shocked New Yorkers into the first public sense
of outrage since the fall of Boss Tweed. Three months after the hearings opened, Croker resigned as Boss of Tammany and turned over to
his aides what he considered a futile campaign to retain control of City

Hall. He knew that if he lost the next election, he would be finished; but if Tammany lost without him, there would always be the chance of regaining his leadership.

Spurred by Dr. Parkhurst, reform Democrats joined a Fusion movement behind a naïve Republican merchant named William Strong. Tammany nominated Macy's founder Nathan Straus, a candidate of comparable wealth and integrity. Straus, though personally friendly with Croker, became embarrassed defending Tammany and withdrew from the campaign. Hugh Grant was hurried in as the sacrificial lamb. Croker solicited money from his Wall Street friends for the campaign and issued optimistic statements to the press. But he left the responsibility for victory or defeat with the district leaders.

On Election Day the reformers were far from confident. They were a makeshift union of amateurs fighting the most influential Tammany machine in history. Before the ballot-counting began, Croker held an off-the-record press conference. He predicted a large majority for Republican William Strong. The newsmen were astounded. Croker walked over and laid a hand on the shoulder of Lincoln Steffens. "You look flabbergasted," he said. "Why? You knew all along that it was a reform wave, didn't you? . . . Our people could not stand the rotten police corruption. They'll be back at the next election; they can't stand reform either."

William Strong won by 45,000 votes. Richard Croker sailed to England for an exile of three quite comfortable years.

Mr. Dooley, the Irish saloonkeeper created by Peter Finley Dunne, drew this moral from the Lexow hearings: "Niver steal a dure-mat. . . . If ye do, ye'll be investigated, hanged, an' maybe rayformed. Steal a bank, me boy, steal a bank."

While the police were being "rayformed" by the Strong administration, Richard Croker was at the British racetracks enjoying the proceeds of honest graft, and living as a country squire in the splendid mansion on his estate at Wantage, birthplace of King Alfred the Great. Released from the demands of playing the silent, calculating Boss, he relaxed in the company of four-legged animals with fewer expectations, walking his bulldogs, talking for hours with his horses, and feeding his pigs, whom he named after various gluttonous politicians.

Occasionally he received visits from Tammany friends who kept him informed of events in New York. The most dramatic news was

Teddy Roosevelt's installation as president of the police board. Croker prophesied to one visitor that "Roosevelt is all there is to the Strong administration and Roosevelt will make it or break it."

Teddy Roosevelt, a genuinely outraged citizen, demoted or retired the most glaring grafters on the force and insisted on rigid law enforcement. He was an impetuous man of great, good instincts who saw no need to consult his fellow commissioners. As a result, he lost control of the police board. The policemen themselves considered their new orders to be temporary. A reform chief of police picked by Roosevelt told a reporter, "I am willing to play up with T.R., but I cannot help keeping one eye on the signs of the failure of reform and the return of Tammany. Tammany is not a wave; it's the sea itself."

Mayor William Strong proved to be a disappointment to his reform backers. "He was an honest gentleman of sturdy purpose to do the right," Jacob Riis said, "but with an intermittent delusion that he was a shrewd politician." Dr. Parkhurst charged the Mayor with making deals on appointments which impeded the new programs. Nonetheless, the streets were clean for the first time since the Revolution, new schools, playgrounds, and parks were provided, and laws were enforced —more laws than many New Yorkers knew existed, or cared to know.

To thousands of people the word "reform" meant simply that they couldn't buy a drink at the corner saloon on Sunday. As Croker had predicted, the Lexow revelations faded from memory and there was a growing nostalgia for the good old Tammany days. "Dr. Parkhurst and the rest of us exposers and reformers were merely destructive," Lincoln Steffens said. "We were showing up the evils of our police and our Tammany politics and government. Richard Croker's exclamation, the sensation of a day, was a call upon us to do something constructive. What? I mean that I did not find anybody with any intelligent plan for the reform of a city."

On September 7, 1897, Richard Croker sailed into New York harbor on what the press called his "Return from Elba." A reporter on board for the *Tribune* recounted that the Boss was standing on the bow of the ship, leaning on a cane. "His eyes were keen and lively. From under the shaggy brows he shot furtive glances at the city. Those who gazed at the Tammany chief knew that his brain was busy. . . . Mr. Croker's homecoming is fraught with great concern for Tammany Hall." There was no one to meet him at the dock.

Croker was returning for the election of the first Mayor of Greater

New York City. The State Legislature had passed a new city charter, effective January 1, 1898, consolidating Manhattan with Brooklyn, the Bronx, Queens, and Staten Island, almost doubling the City's population. Republicans, reform Democrats, and Tammany men all supported the charter in the Legislature. All were confident that the new boroughs would add to their voting strength.

On his arrival, Croker announced that he was still out of politics, and traveled to his farm at Richfield Springs. There he received confidential aides who filled him in on the "situation": he had lost control of Tammany. During his absence, he had left a lieutenant, John Sheehan, in charge of the holding operation. Sheehan was originally from Buffalo, had little support in the Manhattan districts, and Croker felt this would ease the task of reasserting power. But the lack of authority from the top had bred insurgency. Angered at the lack of patronage and at Croker's foreign residence, the district leaders were massing behind Big Tim Sullivan, who had managed some patronage by working his charms with Teddy Roosevelt. And Sheehan now had no intention of stepping down in favor of either Sullivan or Croker.

With his Bismarckian talent for exploiting weakness, Croker decided to bluff a hunch that the new coalition was still shaky. A meeting of the Tammany Executive Committee had been called for 4 P.M. on October 5, at which time 21 of the 35 district leaders planned to inform the old Boss he was not welcome in the Wigwam. At five minutes before the hour, Croker walked up the steps of Tammany Hall, dressed in a formal black suit and English top hat, a long cigar clenched in his teeth. He stalked past the angry Sachems, feigning complete indifference to their presence, strode into his office, and shut the door. The order came out for the men to come into the office immediately. As one observer described it: "Following the blind, unreasoning instinct of obedience, which is the law of organizational discipline, they came."

"I've heard that some of you have complaints to make," Croker said. He paced back and forth to afford a good view of his costume. "What are those complaints?" There was silence. "None? Well! I just want to say that I'm tired of hearing that certain leaders are dissatisfied. Tim Sullivan, are you dissatisfied? No? Very well, then, there is no dissatisfaction. Now I want you men to go back to your districts and get to work. If you don't, I'll put men in your places who will work. We have a show to carry New York this time, and if you go about it right, we'll do it. But I don't want to hear any more grumbling. We'll meet here Tuesday to perfect plans for the campaign."

One can imagine that after the last district leader had exited meekly from the room, Dick Croker collapsed in his chair with a great sigh of relief, and then burst out laughing to think how his men had mistaken fear for authority. The Boss's personality, or the personality he chooses to display, is a crucial element of his power. In this case, Croker had very little else on his side, and he won. He convinced the Sachems simply by his demeanor that a big game was being played for Greater New York, and that none of them, including Big Tim Sullivan, was worldly enough to lead the team.

Having given an overwhelming impression of strength, Croker was careful to underplay the next hand. John Sheehan, armed with a list of potential candidates for Mayor, went up to Croker's room in the Murray Hill Hotel. Croker tactfully turned down the prospects, but he modestly protested that the final decision must be Sheehan's.

"John," he asked, "have you thought about Van Wyck?"

"No, I never thought of Van Wyck," Sheehan replied.

"He might do," Croker said. "He comes from an old Knickerbocker family, and that would bring in the Dutch and German votes."

Sheehan said he liked Van Wyck "but I don't think he is a vote getter." Croker did not pursue the matter further.

The bi-partisan reformers nominated another Republican to replace Mayor Strong. He was Columbia University president Seth Low, formerly Mayor of Brooklyn. Henry George entered the campaign again on the Labor ticket. The GOP was expected to back Seth Low, as it had Mayor Strong, but Thomas Platt decided to enter his own candidate. It was believed he reached this decision after striking a bargain with Croker.

No word came from Tammany. The *World* held a contest: name the Democratic candidate. Everyone awaited Croker's decision and he continued to insist that John Sheehan was in command. The night before the Tammany nominating convention, Sheehan had dinner with Croker at the Murray Hill. "Well, John," Croker said, "you'll soon have your hands full. The convention is tomorrow and you haven't got your candidate yet. When did you see Van Wyck?" Sheehan replied that he hadn't seen him. "Suppose you see Van Wyck and get him up here tonight," Croker said quietly. A few hours later Judge Robert Van

Wyck presented himself in Croker's hotel room and promised that, if elected, he would let the Boss select 40,000 municipal jobholders.

Nobody won the *World's* contest; nobody had ever heard of Robert Van Wyck. In the election campaign, the reformers made "Crokerism" the central issue. Van Wyck, through sheer force of anonymity, was unassailable. But Croker's palatial residence at Wantage ("New York's wastage is Croker's wantage"), his English valet, and his efforts to lure the Protestant and the growing Jewish and Italian vote by keeping Irish names off the top of his ticket, opened him up to the familiar "anglophile" charge usually reserved for Tammany's opponents. "The best thing Croker can do, if I am elected," Henry George said, "is to take the first ship to England and join the Prince of Wales and his other snob friends."

Tammany's slogan was a frank one: "To Hell with Reform!" The district leaders concentrated on winning back the votes of those who sorely missed their Sunday afternoons at the German beer-garden or the Irish groggery. At the height of the campaign, Henry George collapsed after a strenuous series of speaking engagements. He was stricken with apoplexy and died a week before the election. His son took his place but could not hold the support of the father's huge personal following.

On Election Day the voting was heavy. Croker sat in a room at the Murray Hill receiving returns. His runners brought in reports of a close race. Seth Low was leading in the outlying boroughs and doing better than expected in Manhattan. Then shortly before ten o'clock the lopsided returns began to come in from the tenement districts. Tammany was pouring out the vote as never before. Croker stared at the returns. "I told you three years ago," he said to the waiting reporters, "that when the reformers got into office, they tried to stand so straight that they fell over backward."

Van Wyck was in. Old New York broke loose. Snake-dancers bearing paper Tammany tigers jammed Broadway, chanting, "Well! Well! Well! Reform has gone to Hell!" Richard Croker skirted the throng in Union Square and entered the rear door of the Wigwam's convention hall, where the Tammany workers were listening to exuberant speakers praise the victory. As he emerged slowly onto the back of the stage, the crowd caught sight of him and the orators were drowned out by wild cheers. Croker smiled and nodded. Then he took a small group of district leaders, including George Washington Plunkitt and Charles Murphy, across the street for a drink. Croker ordered vichy and bicarbonate of soda, Plunkitt recalled. "Before midnight we were all in bed, and next mornin' we were up bright and early attendin' to business, while other men were nursin' swelled heads. Is there anything the matter with temperance as a pure business proposition?"

During the month of December, Richard Croker and, quite incidentally, the new Mayor were ensconced at the Lakewood Hotel in New Jersey. Anyone with designs on a City position was obliged to travel out and pay court to the man who was now New York City's single most influential citizen. The trains to Lakewood did record business. Thousands of job-seekers swarmed into the hotel to impress the Boss with their loyalty. This was not as easy as they had anticipated; evening clothes were required at dinnertime. The Boss found great amusement at the spectacle of his ungainly subordinates struggling with bowties and ill-fitting jackets.

Most of the men were well-rewarded for their strenuous efforts. By New Year's Eve the jobs had been dispensed and Croker was back in town for the birth of Greater New York City. Hearst's *Morning Journal*, which sponsored a giant celebration, listed the three gentlemen who made the largest donations to the festivities. They were J. P. Morgan, Jacob Ruppert, and Richard Croker.

Separated from his wife Elizabeth (who had confided financial secrets to members of her family, which were then made public), Croker set up residence at the Democratic Club on Fifth Avenue, where the district leaders were obliged to convene graciously in the evenings. It was quite unlike the old rowdy social events in the Wigwam on Union Square. A doorman barred the entrance of the club to politicians who had forgotten their dress suits. Sachems were expected to dine at the club once a week. No one entered the dining room until Croker was seated, and most ordered the same meal.

Although he told a friend he was aware that much of the homage was insincere, Croker thoroughly enjoyed the "court" atmosphere which attended his victory. And it was an effective aura for extending his influence beyond Manhattan. By shows of personal authority, supported by patronage and a share in "honest graft," he forced the leaders of the other boroughs into submission, notably Brooklyn's Democratic Boss Hugh McLaughlin, who had been in power since the

Civil War. Then, in September 1898, Croker arrived in Syracuse on the eve of the State Convention to make his bid for control of the New York State Democratic Party.

In Syracuse a cheering crowd broke through police lines and mobbed his carriage en route from the railroad station to Yates House. He arrived in the hotel lobby to find the upstate leaders awaiting him, as the angry Tammany Sachems had a year before, determined to prevent him from capturing the party. Within a few minutes he had talked them into supporting his candidate for Governor: another unknown judge named Van Wyck. This time it was Augustus, brother of the Mayor.

Teddy Roosevelt, just returned from the Spanish-American War, was nominated for Governor by the Republicans. Despite his personal fame as the Rough Rider hero of San Juan Hill, he was given little chance against the Croker machine—until Richard Croker, in his initial entry into State politics, made a major political mistake. He refused renomination to Joseph Daly, a State Supreme Court Justice who had rejected a Croker recommendation for court clerk and denied judicial aid to Croker's real estate business.

Two weeks before the election a rally was held at Carnegie Hall to protest "boss rule" of the courts. Croker was astonished at the furor. He considered his action as one of many organizational details which maintained discipline: "Justice Daly was elected by Tammany Hall after he was discovered by Tammany Hall, and Tammany Hall had a right to expect proper consideration at his hands." The issue was developed dramatically and Croker fell into the trap. By publicly defending his blunder, he pinned himself to the classic image of Tammany arrogance.

"My object was to make the people understand," Teddy Roosevelt recalled in his autobiography, "that it was Croker, and not the nominal candidate, who was my real opponent; that the choice lay between Croker and myself. Croker was a powerful and truculent man; the autocrat of his organization, and of a domineering nature. For his own reasons he insisted upon Tammany's turning down an excellent Democratic judge who was up for re-election. This gave me my chance. Under my attack, Croker, who was a stalwart fighting-man and who would not take an attack tamely, himself came to the front. I was able to fix the contest in the public mind as one between himself and myself; and, against all probabilities, I won."

In his first try beyond the borders of New York City, Boss Croker had over-extended himself and lost. Yet he could not now retreat to bind up Tammany's wounds. The momentum of politics demanded that he protect his power in the City by risking everything on his efforts to control the State. In 1900, over the protests of many upstate leaders, he forced the Democratic State Committee to announce for William Jennings Bryan as the next candidate for President. Tammany had unsuccessfully opposed Bryan's nomination four years before, when Croker was in exile at Wantage, and Bryan had lost New York State in that election. Most national observers gave him even less chance of beating William McKinley this time, particularly with Teddy Roosevelt as President McKinley's running-mate.

At the 1900 Democratic National Convention in Chicago, Croker delivered the New York delegation to Bryan, thus assuring his nomination. In addition to placating New York City's liberal Democrats, Croker's intention was to destroy the influence of the upstate leaders who were allied with the anti-Bryan conservative Democrats. He also enjoyed the prospect of emerging as a national power. Should he win the election, Bryan would be heavily indebted to Tammany.

But Croker's prominence in the nomination proved a liability to the national ticket. During the election campaign, Governor Roosevelt and Senator Mark Hanna, McKinley's strategist, taunted the Tammany chief in speeches around the country, drawing angry replies from Croker with each charge. Bryan also suffered great embarrassment during an address in Madison Square Garden three weeks before the election. In a familiar attack on monopolies and McKinley prosperity, he told the crowd, "They say we are prosperous. Who's we?" Somebody yelled "Croker!" and the audience roared with laughter.

Croker had no knowledge of the issues of the campaign. When asked to comment on Free Silver, the cornerstone of Bryan's radical candidacy, he replied impatiently, "What's the use of discussing what's the best kind of money? I'm in favor of all kinds of money—the more the better!" (George Washington Plunkitt commented, "See how a real Tammany statesman can settle in twenty-five words a problem that has monopolized two campaigns!") And amidst widespread predictions of a Republican landslide, Croker began to cover his tracks on his early enthusiastic support for Bryan. "If I had not come out for Bryan," he told a friend, "the rank-and-file would have taken Tammany away from me."

A few days before election, the voters of America were lectured by Tammany Hall. In a widely publicized press conference, Croker charged that the Republicans could win the Presidency only by fraud. "I advise all Democrats to go to the polling places on election night, count noses, and see that they get counted." He shook his fist at the reporters. "If the vote doesn't tally, let them go in, pull out the fellows in charge, and stand them on their heads. I want you to print this!"

William Jennings Bryan carried New York City and the Solid South. He lost nearly every Western state and the entire East, including New York State. Richard Croker was laughed out of the national councils and his grip on the State Democratic Party was severely weakened.

In the City, the reformers mounted a new attack following an investigation of Tammany corruption by Assemblyman Robert Mazet's Committee. This inquiry turned out to be more personally damaging to Croker than the Lexow report. Acting on a series of newspaper exposés, the Mazet Committee produced sound documentation of Tammany's corporate alliances. The most startling revelation was the "Tammany Ice Trust," first brought to light by Hearst's *Morning Journal*. Croker, Mayor Robert Van Wyck, and Dock Commissioner Charles Murphy were found to be substantial shareholders in the American Ice Company, which was granted exclusive rights to use the City's docks. The monopoly was planning to double the cost of ice. This time "honest graft" could be seen as directly affecting the pocketbooks of Tammany's loyal constituents.

The Mazet Committee also showed that "dirty graft" had returned under Mayor Van Wyck to proportions unknown at the time of the Lexow hearings. The Lexow findings had resulted mainly in acquainting Tammany district leaders and high police officials with how much they were missing. Tammany's police chief, Big Bill Devery, told Lincoln Steffens: "I am a credit to you and the rest of the reformers. For you learned me the business. Honest. I never knew it was so good till you showed it all up in black and white. All the matter with the police business was that it was mismanaged, too democratic, every cop on it . . . I'm a-goin' to fix this police graft so you squealers won't get nothin' to squeal it." Devery, a chief target of the Mazet investigation, controlled the City's gambling houses with the Bowery leader Big Tim Sullivan.

New York's Episcopal Bishop Henry Potter wrote an open letter to Mayor Van Wyck condemning the police and politicians for their promotion of gambling and prostitution. As a countermove, Croker established the Committee of Five under the chairmanship of Lewis Nixon to determine for the public whether or not Tammany Hall actually was connected with vice in the City. The reformers charged "whitewash" but Croker was in earnest; he saw the rising of a new wave of discontent in the City.

When Croker called his district leaders together to impress upon them the need to rid Tammany of "dirty grafting," they were shocked by his insistence that the Committee of Five make an honest report of its findings. One Sachem mumbled that nothing could be done, the system was too well-established. Croker leaped up from his chair and ran over to the man.

"If you do nothing except say what you can't do," he shouted, "you can never stop anything. But if the people find anything is wrong, you can be sure that the people can put a stop to it, and will!"

Another leader, who knew Croker better, asked quietly, "Is this a bluff, or is it on the level?"

"It's on the level."

Croker's position in balancing the pressures for and against reform was a perilous one. Initially, for his own safety, he acted forcefully in response to public opinion. "The power of the biggest boss is like chaff in your hands," Jacob Riis said. "You can see his finish. And he knows it. Hence, even he will treat you with respect. The ink was not dry upon Bishop Potter's arraignment of Tammany bestiality before Richard Croker was offering to sacrifice his most faithful henchmen as the price of peace; and he would have done it had the Bishop but crooked his little finger in the direction of any one of them. The boss has the courage of the brute, or he would not be boss; but when it comes to a moral issue he is the biggest coward in the lot. The bigger the brute the more abject its terror at what it does not understand."

A Boss's nightmares are worse than that. When he is threatened from outside his organization, he is in even more danger from within. His district leaders now have the dangerous information that their support is crucial to his survival. After the Bryan defeat, Croker returned to Wantage, leaving behind a Wigwam full of resentful Sachems. They were made no happier the following month when Teddy Roosevelt, just before relinquishing the governorship to assume the

Vice-Presidency, fired off an executive order deposing Tammany's District Attorney for neglect of duty.

Two months later the State Legislature abolished the office of Chief of Police, which removed Big Bill Devery from command. Then a number of gambling dens were raided. Big Tim Sullivan and his supporters were positive that Lewis Nixon's Committee of Five was co-operating in the crackdown. Big Tim cabled Croker at Wantage that unless Devery were reappointed as police chief, ten thousand gamblers in the Sullivan-Devery syndicate would make no further campaign contributions to Tammany.

Croker knew that Devery on the payroll would be a great liability to Tammany in the mayoral election just nine months away. At the same time, he feared he was no longer strong enough to risk an open break with Big Tim Sullivan, his most powerful district leader. Mayor Van Wyck appointed Big Bill Devery with a new title which restored his power over the police. Shocked by the sudden turnabout, Lewis Nixon cabled Wantage to find out if the Mayor had acted, as usual, on Croker's advice. The answer came back: Yes. Two days later Nixon's Committee of Five turned in its report to the Tammany executive committee. It was never made public.

When Croker returned to New York in September, 1901, he was met by "Paddy" Divver, Tammany alderman from the Fourth Ward, a small island surrounded by Tim Sullivan's Bowery empire. Paddy Divver had refused to allow Big Tim's procurers, the "Red-Light Cadets," to steal the daughters of his constituents. Now he was faced with a well-financed primary fight. Paddy asked Croker for help.

The principles of professional politicians hold that a man is loyal when he is needy and beneficent when he is powerful. This places severe limitations on Richard Croker's remark that "Gratitude is the finest word I know. I would much prefer a man to steal from me than to display ingratitude. All there is in life is loyalty to one's family and one's friends." Croker had forgotten his loyalty to Jimmy "The Famous" O'Brien, the man who first sponsored him, when he chose to follow Honest John Kelly, a leader he admired far more than the churlish O'Brien. And he did not show gratitude to Paddy Divver when the embattled loyalist pleaded for support in his struggle against the Sullivan forces. He did give money to Divver for the campaign. But when Tim Sullivan threatened to walk out of Tammany Hall, Croker publicly proclaimed his neutrality.

Sullivan's ally Big Tom Foley (later mentor to Al Smith) was put up against Paddy Divver in the aldermanic primary. Paddy fought bravely: "Don't vote the Red-Lights into the Old Fourth ward!" At 2 a.m. on the day of the primary, a gang of gunmen led by Paul "Kelly" Vaccarelli moved in on the polling stations of the Fourth Ward. When the polls opened at dawn, the Divver supporters were black-jacked as the police stood by. Big Tom Foley won by 3 to 1.

"This wasn't my fight," Paddy Divver told the press, "it was Croker's. That combine is reaching out to control Tammany. I was beaten by these people and by Devery's police. Croker will believe some things now that he didn't believe before." By failing to rescue one of his most faithful district leaders, Croker had acknowledged his loss of supremacy in Tammany. There was no longer any assurance of reward for obedience. Big Tim Sullivan boasted, "Croker ain't the whole thing!"

After Paddy Divver's defeat there were reports that Croker was suffering from insomnia. He would rise in the middle of the night and walk morosely through the empty corridors of the Democratic Club. Each morning he arrived early at Tammany Hall and worked late into the night, feeling out his strength with old political and business friends, questioning, cajoling, frantically maneuvering for position. A 1901 photograph of Richard Croker's round, melancholy face shows the strain. His lips are clamped tightly, his eyelids heavy with fatigue, the eyes cold with fear. He bears a striking resemblance to Ulysses Grant in the old general's last days of cancer and disillusionment.

Croker was still physically strong and far from disillusioned. He was frightened. For the first time in sixteen years he was negotiating from weakness. In the City he had won seventeen elections and lost one. But he had been badly beaten with Augustus Van Wyck in the State and William Jennings Bryan in the nation. He no longer had the stature as kingmaker to force his choice for the Democratic mayoral nomination.

The reformers again named Seth Low, a man of ability and in-tellect, though colorless in personality. This time, however, there was also a popular candidate on the reform ticket. William Travers Jerome, widely admired for his vigorous investigations during the Lexow hear-ings, was running for District Attorney, moving crowds to tears with tales of forced prostitution and police brutality.

Republican leader Thomas Platt, who had assisted in Mayor Robert

Van Wyck's election four years before by splitting the GOP vote, this time joined the Fusion ranks behind Seth Low. The Good Government Clubs ("Goo-Goos") that had installed Mayor Strong, the Committee of Seventy that overthrew Boss Tweed, Henry George's old Labor Party, Dr. Parkhurst's Society for the Prevention of Crime, the City Club, and even disenchanted Tammany lieutenants such as John Sheehan and the fiery orator Bourke Cockran—all were brought together by the Citizens Union in a strong, united reform movement. The theme of the campaign was: "Down with Croker!"

The Boss was well aware that the voters would refuse to accept another "reliable" Mayor on the level of Hugh Grant, Pat Gilroy, or Robert Van Wyck. He was equally sure that Big Tim Sullivan and his associates would not go along with a Manhattan liberal. Croker turned to Hugh McLaughlin, Boss of Brooklyn, who also saw the dangers of an old-line entry. McLaughlin recommended Edward Shepard, a Brooklyn lawyer who could be depended on as a strong contender for the reform vote in all five boroughs. Shepard had been praised by the newspapers for helping uncover election frauds in Brooklyn. He had supported Seth Low against Van Wyck in 1897. In fact, at that time he made a statement which would boomerang in the 1901 campaign: "The most burning and disgraceful blot upon the municipal history of this country is Tammany Hall."

Most of the Tammany leaders fell in behind Shepard. They preferred to follow McLaughlin rather than risk choosing between Richard Croker and Big Tim Sullivan. But they were obviously not happy with the choice. Croker was forced to send his aides into the districts to push the ticket. Shepard conducted his campaign as independently as possible. He did not retract his statements about Tammany. He claimed he could reform City Hall better than Seth Low could. This was the kind of campaign Croker wanted. The Boss stayed in the backroom pushing the election workers.

"The main issue of this campaign," Seth Low charged, "is the wresting of the city from those who permit one man to dominate the organization of his party in the interest of 'his own pocket all the time' and, as if to add insult to injury, to do this from abroad, as though the proud city of New York had been reduced once more to the condition of a crown colony." The "Squire of Wantage" suffered daily onslaughts in newspaper caricatures, variously represented by his pigs, his horses, and his bulldogs. Although Croker remained silent, having learned from Teddy Roosevelt the dangerous consequences of moving to the front lines, it was too late to hide. He had already established himself as New York's most notorious celebrity. The reformers, using the effective strategy that would topple Carmine DeSapio sixty years later, concentrated on the Boss as a personality and a symbol of Tammany corruption.

The vote was predictably large on Election Day. That night the district leaders gathered around the long conference table in the Executive Committee Room, all eyes on Croker, sitting impassively in his armchair next to the ticker. The first returns came in from Brooklyn. Shepard was running behind in his own borough. Croker shifted his cigar to the other side of his mouth. Early returns arrived from Tammany districts in Manhattan. The voters were knifing Shepard. Croker sat up on the arm of his chair and began scratching figures on a piece of paper. "I don't give it up yet," he said. "We always finish well." A newsman reported that Croker's old Mayor Robert Van Wyck was pale as a ghost, and appeared about to collapse. Big Tim Sullivan smiled and walked over to Croker. "Well, Boss," he said, "you see *my* district came through O.K." Croker nodded without looking at him.

By 9:30 Shepard was losing everywhere. Richard Croker stood up slowly and turned to the reporters: "It would appear that Shepard is beaten. A change is a good thing sometimes. But Tammany Hall will be here when we are all gone." He walked past the silent leaders out of Tammany Hall and went to bed.

Reporters talked with Croker again as he stepped on the boat for England. "I am out of politics," he told them, "and now I am going to win the Derby." With him he carried a recently published biography, *Richard Croker*, by the noted journalist Alfred Henry Lewis. Once out to sea, fellow passengers saw Croker begin reading the book in his deckchair: "There was no youth more moral in the city. He drank no liquors, he visited no saloons, he did not set foot in a brothel, and his language was without taint of profanity or violence. These were characteristics of his young manhood; they have found emphasis with every day he has lived." Croker flipped through a few more pages and threw the book into the ocean.

Five years after Croker told reporters he would win the highest honor of a British sportsman, he did it. His favorite horse Orby, a half-American ridden by an American jockey, won the classic Epsom

Derby at odds of 10–1. Croker confessed that the proudest moment of his life, far above his election victories, was leading Orby past the royal grandstand as King Edward VII and his court stood at attention. King Edward, the former Prince of Wales whom the reformers had called a bosom friend of Croker's, was a threetime Derby winner. But the 1907 race went down in impolite history as "The Tammany Derby." In an unprecedented snub, the name of the boy from Shanty Town did not appear on the King's invitation list for the Derby Dinner honoring Orby's victory.

All of Croker's efforts to woo British royalty were ultimately fruitless. Had he been content with success as a famous professional politician, doubtless he could have prolonged his power; he had both the forcefulness and the flexibility to survive the sporadic reform movements. It was his need for nobility, in the shallowest sense, which defeated him. When he should have been tending to his duties, quelling revolts among district leaders, he had been in Wantage campaigning for an election that was lost the day he was born.

At Glencairn, a huge castle he purchased in Ireland after his retirement, Croker was no longer a "character" amusing his betters. He was among Irishmen hungering for freedom and could play his most comfortable role: the wealthy patron of the underdog. He spoke out frequently for the cause of home rule; when the treaty for the Irish Free State was signed, he pledged America's support. The Black and Tans raided Glencairn, but they could never find evidence of Croker's financial aid to the rebels.

In his seventies, Croker married an intriguing young lady named Bula Benton Edmonson, whom he brought to live with him at Glencairn. Bula (who said she was twenty-three) was a thirty-year-old alumna of the University of Chicago who claimed descent on her father's side from a Scottish earl. Her mother's family knew her as Kotaw Kaluntuchy, or Princess Sequoyah, directly descended from the great Cherokee chief Sequoyah. It was in this capacity that Bula startled audiences at the Hippodrome, several months before the wedding, when she dashed across the stage on a horse while singing the Star Spangled Banner in Cherokee. At the wedding, Bula told reporters that "it is the dearest ambition of every Indian girl to win a chief, and I have won the chief of men." Croker's children considered her an adventuress taking advantage of a rich, feeble old man. Bula and "Daddy," as she called him, were inseparable companions for the remainder of his life.

Croker came back to New York in his eightieth year to face a law suit brought by three of his children to prevent him from leaving his fortune to "Princess Sequoyah." Judge Edward McCullen, Secretary of the Tammany Society, remembers Dick Croker's last visit to Tammany Hall: "He came in, a very old man but still amazingly sharp. He was blind then, maybe he could make out a faint shadow, but he looked completely blind. I went up to him and welcomed him back, and he called me by name. He called everybody by name. I asked him how he knew it was me, and he said, 'I remember your voice. I never forget a voice.' "

Although Croker's children were attempting to prove he was senile, doctors testified in court that he had the mind and body of a man twenty years younger. But on the return trip to Ireland, Croker's ship sailed into rough autumn seas, and when he reached Glencairn he was seriously ill with pneumonia. On sunny days he was wheeled out to his stables to watch his horses, and to supervise the final work on a mausoleum built beside a pool under the ancient trees of Glencairn. He instructed the workers to dig up the bones of his Derby winner Orby and bury them near the tomb.

One day, in April, 1922, a cablegram arrived in New York from Bula addressed to the Secretary of Tammany Hall. It said simply: "Mr. Croker passed away suddenly."

Dick Croker, wearing in death his finest evening clothes, was carried from the castle chapel at Glencairn to his mausoleum. His widow was escorted by the Lord Mayor of Dublin. His pallbearers were revolutionary leaders, including the founder of the Sinn Fein. As the coffin reached the mausoleum, soldiers of the IRA snapped to attention and saluted.

Bula Croker inherited an estate worth $5,000,000. Much of it was consumed in continuing court battles with the children. The rest she squandered. Down on her luck, Bula ran unsuccessfully for Congress, later became an avid treasure-hunter, claiming she had maps showing where seventy-six million dollars in pirate gold was buried in Pensacola Bay. She died in Palm Beach on March 16, 1954.

Today in New York, if Boss Croker is remembered at all, he is a sordid afterthought to Boss Tweed. There is a fonder legend in Dublin which tells of a poor boy from Ireland who returned there to die a

Tammany millionaire. The final postscript was written on June 27, 1963, when the Lord Mayor presented the Key to the City to Patrick Kennedy's great-grandson. "John Fitzgerald Kennedy" was engraved alongside "Richard Croker" on the gold-lined roll honoring the immortal Freemen of Dublin.

Chapter 8

Mister Murphy's Golden Years

> "Big Chief sits in his teepee
> Cheering braves to victory
> Tammany, Tammany
> Swamp 'em, swamp 'em
> Get the wampum
> Taammanee!"
> —*Campaign song, 1905*

A reporter once asked Richard Croker how the Boss of Tammany could stay in control of the organization when there were always district leaders plotting to take his place. "Yes, there are combinations constantly being formed," Croker replied, "but when the conspirators or rebels reach as many as five, somebody always gives them away, and then I have no trouble."

At times, as in 1897, Croker was able to crush a cabal by the force of his personality. But in 1901 he compromised with the disaffected leaders and then lost the City election. This defeat came the year after his national repudiation with William Jennings Bryan, so it was no surprise that he resigned his Tammany leadership. To prevent Big

Tim Sullivan from assuming power, he selected Lewis Nixon as the new County Leader.

Croker's intention was to maintain Nixon, who had little support among the Sachems, until the next mayoral election—the tactic that had worked successfully before. Nixon's selection also had the publicity value of bringing in a "reform boss." The trouble was that Nixon took his role seriously. He refused to obey orders from the absentee Croker. The Squire of Wantage had to resort to direct communications with those district leaders who had remained loyal to him.

In May 1902, Lewis Nixon stepped down from his post, remarking that "I could not retain the leadership of Tammany Hall and at the same time retain my self-respect." A troika of Croker's followers was placed in authority. This is a favorite political device to perpetuate a power vacuum. Unless there is a strong presence behind it, however, the risk is run that the strongest man of the three will elevate himself by exploiting his decisive vote. Croker's troika, with its backer three thousand miles away, lasted four months. In September, Charles Francis Murphy, a forty-four-year-old saloonkeeper from Second Avenue, eased out his two co-bosses and became the new leader of Tammany Hall. He remained in that position until his death twenty-two years later.

In a prognosis both false and envious, Croker wrote to a friend, "The Hall will never win under Murphy's management. I hope some good man will get in and drive all them grafter-contractors out." And Big Bill Devery scoffed: "If three lobsters can't run the organization, how can one do it?—and that the one with the least brains?"

"Silent Charlie" Murphy, the stocky, ruddy-faced leader of the Gas House District, had none of the flamboyance and loquaciousness of Dick Croker, Bill Devery, Tim Sullivan, or George Washington Plunkitt. On the contrary, he had perhaps the drabbest, most taciturn personality that ever graced a Tammany clubhouse. What he did have, however, in far greater abundance than his colorful colleagues, was brains.

Mister Murphy (few addressed him otherwise) gradually became known as the most perceptive and intelligent leader in Tammany history, with an unsurpassed feel for power and its uses, a superb instinct for timing, and a remarkable ability to cut through surface personalities and judge the prospects and motives of the men beneath. As a political chess-player, he never met his match. Some of his strongest gains were made during apparent retreats. When a strong Governor disagreed with him, he exercised a strategic withdrawal. When a weak Governor defied him, he had him impeached.

Silence was Murphy's trademark. He recognized that the Boss's worst enemy can be his own public image. He refused to be lured onto the front pages as a target for the opposition. To Murphy, victory was paramount, and the fewer risks the better, no matter how satisfying they might be to the ego. On one occasion, he ordered the rumor spread that he was opposed to a candidate he secretly favored. The candidate won on the basis of his "independence" from Boss domination.

Beyond his uncommon political acumen, Charles Murphy had a quality rarely associated with Tammany Hall: a sense of government's responsibility to the public good. As a young man, he grew rich on "honest graft" and appeased his conscience with clambakes and gifts to the poor. But after the Triangle Shirtwaist Company fire in 1911, he began to recognize the urgent need for social legislation which overshadowed the small favors of the Tammany clubhouse. Frances Perkins, FDR's Secretary of Labor, recalled Murphy saying of an early bill restricting women's work hours to fifty-four hours a week: "It made a lot of votes for us."

Whatever Murphy's motives, it must be said that he anticipated, long before his contemporaries in professional politics, that social welfare programs would be more important to the people than Tammany Hall. He also accommodated himself to that bane of the political machine, the Civil Service, which George Washington Plunkitt called the "biggest fraud of the age . . . the curse of the nation." Instead of fighting the inevitable, Murphy instructed his district leaders to organize classes so that their constituents could pass the Civil Service tests.

Mister Murphy not only tolerated good government, he expected his office-holders to provide it every day of the week. Toward this end he developed Tammany's greatest candidates, a stable of young thoroughbreds who went on to win the Derbys. New York has not seen such men since.

Murphy was the kingmaker of Democratic liberals, an American Warwick who knew that his creations would be the true measure of his greatness. And so Charles Murphy gave to the public a Governor Alfred E. Smith, a Senator Robert F. Wagner, a Surrogate James A. Foley, and a Boss Edward J. Flynn. Had Murphy lived, it is likely he could have disciplined another of his liberal protégés, the brilliant Jimmy Walker.

Franklin Roosevelt called Charles Murphy a "genius." Certainly, he maintained the most powerful and smoothest-running machine in the United States. Under Murphy, the New York Democratic Party was restored for a time to its early role as a dynamic political force in America. His were the Golden Years of Tammany.

Murphy was born three years before the Civil War, one of eight children of Irish immigrant parents. He grew up in a Third Avenue tenement, played ball in empty lots, swam in the East River, attended parochial schools until the age of fourteen when he quit to work as a ship caulker, wire factory worker, and saloon handyman. The Gas House District, in which Murphy lived all his life, was just north of the Lower East Side fiefdom where Tom Foley and Big Tim Sullivan had forced out Croker's man, Paddy Divver. It was a grim stretch of rickety tenements and dreary saloons, peopled primarily by Irish and German immigrants whose lives centered on the neighborhood's chief industry, the giant tanks and stacks of the Consolidated Gas Company.

Young Charles Murphy gained early valuable leadership training as a rough and tumble member of Gas House gangs. At the age of seventeen, he organized the Sylvan Club, a social and athletic association with its own baseball team—the Senators. Murphy, the fastest runner, swimmer, and rower in the neighborhood, was also the best ball player. As captain and catcher of the Senators, he led them to victory each Sunday, winning hundred-dollar stakes. The Senators also traveled outside the City to defeat amateur and semi-pro teams.

Captain Murphy turned down offers to play professional ball, choosing instead year-round employment as a horsecar driver on the 14th Street crosstown line. The story was told that one day a balky horse pulling Murphy's car came to a sudden halt in the midst of the busy intersection of 14th Street and Broadway. No pleas or threats could budge the animal. A policeman drew his revolver and pronounced that the only solution was to shoot the horse and drag it off the street. But Murphy intervened. He removed the harness, then very gently replaced it, shouted at the horse, and slapped its flanks. The horse, thinking it was no longer attached to the streetcar, raced forward at full speed. In later years, Murphy would use the same technique on recalcitrant candidates.

Jobs on the horsecars usually could be obtained only by political wire-pulling. One of their attractions was that the cars had no fare registers. Unreported fares were treated as fringe benefits by some drivers and conductors. There is no evidence, however, that Murphy indulged in this custom. He was a conscientious worker and frugal wage-earner. He spent little, turned over a portion of his salary to his mother, and saved the rest. By 1882, when he reached the age of twenty-four, he had accumulated five hundred dollars—enough to lease a saloon at Avenue A and 19th Street.

"Charlie's Place" featured a sawdust floor, a brass rail, a communal bar towel, a schooner of beer and a bowl of soup for five cents, and plates of free crackers, cheese, and bologna. Behind the bar the Senators' baseball trophies were prominently displayed. The second floor was given over to the Sylvan Club for use as a clubroom to gossip about baseball and politics. Downstairs Murphy attracted a following among stevedores, gas house laborers, neighborhood politicians, and white-collar workers. Patrons knew that they would be safe from the disruptive element that was ruining so many other saloons—women. Murphy was adamant in his refusal to serve them.

Although he never became much of a drinker himself, Murphy acted as his own bartender. He was the great attraction of Charlie's Place, a true friend and confidant, the best sort of person with whom to share one's troubles. He was a patient, attentive listener, offered only a few words of sympathy, and never inflicted advice.

Charlie's Place prospered and Murphy opened three more saloons. He called them "poor men's clubs," although one of them, "The Borough" at Lexington Avenue and 27th Street, was a dazzlingly ornate and pretentious establishment. Another, at 20th Street and Second Avenue, became the headquarters for the Anawanda Club, the local Tammany branch. Murphy joined the club and was installed as a member of Tammany.

Charles Murphy's first political contest took place not at the polls but on the East River. When Barney Biglin, a Republican district leader, boasted that he and his three brothers were the best rowing crew in town, Murphy challenged them and organized a crew of his Sylvanites. The betting was heavy as excited crowds gathered along the banks of the river. Just before the start, the stroke of the Sylvan crew took sick. Fist fights broke out amid charges that the man had been drugged. A full-scale riot was in the making when Murphy slipped into the boat, rowed stroke, and led his crew to victory.

Murphy's political patron was Assemblyman Edward Hagan, Democratic leader of the Gas House District. Eddie Hagan fell out with Dick Croker and was denied renomination to the Assembly. He came to Murphy for advice. Murphy listened to his friend's long tale of woe, reflected a moment, and then said quietly: "Run independent." With Murphy as his campaign manager, Eddie Hagan beat the organization. The prodigals were promptly welcomed back into the Tammany fold. Murphy never again left Tammany. Hagan's deathbed wish in 1902 was that Murphy should succeed him. The wish was honored, and at the age of thirty-four, Charles Murphy became the new leader of the Gas House District.

Despite his sullen demeanor, Murphy was a popular district leader. He had already established a small reputation for charity. From his bar proceeds, he had donated $4,000 to aid the victims of the Great Blizzard of 1888. As district leader, he scrimped on campaign funds and divided the surplus among the three major church groups in his area: Catholic, Lutheran, and Episcopalian. This procedure won unexpected praise from the minister of St. George's Episcopal Church, who preached a sermon one day envisioning an admirable Tammany Hall if all its leaders would emulate Charles Francis Murphy.

Murphy himself was devoutly religious. He attended Mass each Sunday at the Church of the Epiphany (two blocks north of his Anawanda Club saloon) which became known as "The Tammany Church." His other habits found favor with the most thoroughgoing Puritans. He didn't smoke, swear or gamble, drank rarely, and intensely disliked off-color jokes. He looked upon prostitution as an unmitigated evil, and therefore suffered great embarrassment when Big Bill Devery announced that The Borough, Murphy's glittering Lexington Avenue saloon, was frequented by ladies of the evening.

Politics was Murphy's only apparent intellectual interest. He didn't like the theatre. His reading was confined to the newspapers and religious works. His sole pastime was golf. (He built a private golf course on his weekend estate at Good Ground, Long Island.) He retained strong family attachments and remained a bachelor until he was forty-four. His career was untainted by rumors of intrigues with women. In fact, by all appearances, he was the dullest man in town.

Yet scores of loyal constituents crowded the sidewalk each evening, in front of the Anawanda Club saloon, where Charles Murphy held office hours, leaning against a lamppost, nodding and listening. Some of his petitioners were seeking jobs, others City favors, but most wanted only to unburden their problems. Murphy heard them out and closed each discussion with a brief, laconic comment. There were a few complaints that it was impossible to tell whether he was responding favorably. But for most, the Murphy technique only heightened loyalty. He was the master of the old political principle that mystery breeds power.

One year, at a Tammany Fourth of July gathering, a reporter noticed that Murphy had failed to join in singing "The Star-Spangled Banner." He sought an explanation from one of the Boss's aides. "Perhaps," the aide replied, "he didn't want to commit himself."

After the election of Mayor Robert Van Wyck in 1897, Croker rewarded Murphy with a four-year appointment to the Dock Commission, a cornucopia for the party faithful. The Commission let contracts for dock improvements and lucrative franchises to ice companies and other enterprises. The investigations by the State Legislature's Mazet Committee not only established that Murphy, Croker, and Van Wyck were stockholders in the American Ice Company, but also uncovered the leasing of two docks to the New York Contracting and Trucking Company, which had been formed by Murphy's brother John and two political cronies. The company paid the City a yearly rent of $4,800 for the two docks, and sublet them at a $200-a-day profit for an investment return of five thousand percent.

Murphy testified frankly to the Mazet Committee: "When I can do it without violating the law, it is perfectly right to give out contracts to organization men. If I can, I will. I do not excuse myself for anything I have done." Then, in a prepared statement, he gave the rationale behind the issuance of leases without public bidding. If the leases went to the highest bidder, he said, only the biggest corporations could afford them, and the smaller concerns would be driven out of business. Moreover, he said, the high rentals would drive trade and commerce away from the City.

When Murphy took office as Dock Commissioner, his wealth from saloons, stock, and real estate was estimated at $400,000. When he left the Dock Commission four years later, after the election of Mayor Seth Low, he was believed to be a millionaire.

During his period on the Dock Commission, Murphy became even more austere and shy as a person. He never spoke to strangers, except for a mumbled "How do" when forced into an introduction. Once a passerby asked him for the time of day. Murphy, without a word, pulled out his watch and held it up to the questioner's eyes. For the rest of his life, Murphy was addressed only by two salutations: usually "Mister Murphy" and sometimes "Commissioner." He cherished the latter title. Except for his service as a Presidential elector in 1912, it was the only public office he ever held. "Mister" was an even higher compliment. The only other man in New York who commanded a constant "Mister" before his surname was an equally gruff autocrat, John McGraw, manager of the New York Giants.

After Murphy emerged from Croker's triumvirate to become the leader of Tammany in 1901, Big Bill Devery dubbed him "Sir Charles" and took great delight in burlesquing the Tammany chief's new-found respectability. "He's goin' through the bluff of being decent, but look at his record in the old Dock Board!" Devery said. "Since Charlie Murphy has got to running with J. Sergeant Cram, he's turned up his trousers at the bottom, and he's wearing glasses. . . . One of these days one of them panes of glass will fall out, and Charlie'll have only one pane of glass, like Cram, and then it'll be 'Ah, there, chappie,' and when you go to ask him for a job it'll be, 'Ah really cawn't do it, old chappie, don't you know.'"

J. Sergeant Cram, a wealthy Harvard graduate and member of the Peter Cooper clan, was a fellow Dock Commissioner who cultivated Murphy's friendship. The two men became lifelong comrades. It was said that J. Sergeant Cram taught Charles Murphy how to eat peas with a fork.

Big Bill Devery, who had been rejected by both Tammany and Mayor Seth Low's administration, declared war on the Hall and ran a bitter campaign against Murphy's district leader in the Hell's Kitchen neighborhood on the West Side. Just as Murphy kept office hours under a street lamp and George Washington Plunkitt from atop a shoeshine stand, Devery conducted his business in front of a fire hydrant at 28th Street and Eighth Avenue. From that spot he distributed nickels and dimes to children and harangued their parents with charges of Tammany wrong-doing and promises of free vaudeville shows if he should win the election.

The summer before the election, Big Bill, with the aid of the gambling interests which backed him, hosted a mammoth Hudson River outing which required a fleet of nine boats to carry the thousands who attended. The campaign was capped by a barbecue at which twenty thousand glasses of beer were consumed and police had to use rubber hoses to hold the crowd in check. Devery's generosity won him the district leadership but Murphy blocked him from taking a seat on the Tammany Executive Committee by forcing through a rule that barred leaders whom the committee deemed "objectionable."

Fortunately, Murphy did not enforce this regulation against leaders already ensconced, or Tammany's ruling committee would have been all but vacant. Big Tim Sullivan, who controlled the East Side below 14th Street, would have been the next to go. His holdings in gambling and vice dens were probably more extensive than Big Bill Devery's. But Big Tim, who was acknowledged as more powerful than Croker after Paddy Divver's defeat, was Charles Murphy's most valuable ally in the organization. Had he sought it, Big Tim Sullivan could have become the County Leader himself, but he had no interest in the rigorous responsibilities of the job, preferring to throw his support to Murphy and quietly tend to his financial empire.

The Tammany Hall that Murphy inherited was fully as unsavory as in the heyday of Richard Croker, and in some respects more so. Tammany's hoodlums were no longer the brawling youths of the Tunnel Gang and the Cherry Hillers; they were professional gunmen. One of the roots of Big Tim Sullivan's power was his ability to control the vicious Monk Eastman gang and the Antonio ("Paul Kelly") Vaccarelli gang, which had bludgeoned Paddy Divver's supporters. As a Tammany State Senator, Big Tim sponsored an ostensibly anti-gangster law that still bears his name—the Sullivan Law, which forbids the carrying of concealed weapons. In fact, it gave Sullivan and the police the opportunity to plant weapons on disobedient thugs and dispatch them to prison. (To guard against this predicament, one gunman took the precaution of sewing up his pockets and hiring a gun-bearer to accompany him.)

With the support of the Sullivan clan (Big Tim's domain included a number of politically powerful cousins), Charles Murphy took over

the stewardship of Tammany Hall and began once again the task of
face-lifting.

"Now there is a new boss," Lincoln Steffens wrote in 1903, "a
young man, Charles F. Murphy, and unknown to New Yorkers. He
looks dense, but he acts with force, decision, and skill. . . . He may divide with Croker and leave to the 'old man' all his accustomed graft,
but Charlie Murphy will rule Tammany and, if Tammany is elected,
New York also. Lewis Nixon is urging Murphy publicly, as I write, to
declare against the police scandals and all the worst practices of Tammany. . . . Mr. Nixon is a type of the man who thinks Tammany would
be fit to rule New York if the organization would 'reform.' As a New
Yorker, I fear Murphy will prove sagacious enough to do just that: stop
the scandal, put all the graft in the hands of a few tried and true men,
and give the city what it would call good government. Murphy says
he will nominate for mayor a man so 'good' that his goodness will
astonish New York. I don't fear a bad Tammany mayor; I dread the
election of a good one."

Steffens' appraisal of Murphy's sagacity was correct. Mayor Seth
Low's Fusion administration had not been a dramatic success, but the
prospect of a return to Tammany scandals did not excite the voters
as an alternative. To oppose Mayor Low, Murphy looked about for a
loyal Tammanyite who would convey a strong impression of independence and virtue. His choice was Congressman George McClellan,
Jr., son of the Civil War general who had run against Lincoln for the
Presidency.

Young McClellan (he was thirty-eight and looked younger) was a
storybook candidate. He had been in Congress for nine years, and
before that, was the boy-wonder president of the Board of Aldermen.
Handsome and well-mannered, George McClellan was a Sachem in
good standing of the Tammany Society, a reputable lawyer, an ex-
newspaperman, a student of Italian history and art, and an accomplished linguist. At campaign rallies in Italian, German or French
neighborhoods, he planted his men in the audience to shout, "Speak to
us in our own language!" After hesitating long enough for the rest of the
crowd to take up the cry, McClellan would burst forth with an apparently extemporaneous, but actually very carefully prepared, speech in
the appropriate language.

Murphy executed a master stroke in the 1903 campaign by endorsing Seth Low's running-mates for Comptroller and Board of Aldermen president rather than running a full Tammany slate. The two men were delighted to accept places on the McClellan ticket, assuming they would thus be unopposed. But, as Murphy had expected, the Low forces were furious at the betrayal and replaced the two incumbents on the Fusion ticket. Charles Murphy's first City ticket, with heavy campaign backing from local corporations, swept to victory by a decisive majority of 62,000 votes.

The new Mayor's appointments displayed a certain degree of independence, but on the whole were in harmony with Mister Murphy. The most serious problem was a Police Commissioner. Remembering the disasters of the Van Wyck administration, McClellan agonized over the choice. Finally, according to McClellan's memoirs, Murphy said to him, "If you don't find a commissioner pretty soon, I shall have to take the job myself." The Mayor, perhaps thinking the Boss was serious, quickly appointed William McAdoo, a former assistant Secretary of the Navy.

McClellan and McAdoo spiffed up the Police Department by replacing fat, aging policemen in frock coats and helmets with vigorous young rookies in snappy military uniforms. They also established traffic regulations, which were unheard of in New York, where trucks, trolleys and carriages were accustomed to bullying their way through intersections as best they could. But police graft continued. Soon after McClellan's election, reformers claimed, "The lid is off again!" Commissioner McAdoo, although personally honest, seemed unaware of the extent of the system and how to cope with it.

The major accomplishment of the McClellan administration was the opening of New York's first subway line, an S-shaped route running from City Hall up the East Side to 42nd Street, then crosstown to Broadway and north on Broadway to 145th Street, all for a nickel. On the first train run, October 27, 1904, the passengers were Wall Street financiers, and the motorman, who reached speeds up to 45 miles per hour, was Mayor George McClellan. Excavation was also begun at the site of the new Pennsylvania Railroad station. The New York Contracting and Trucking Company, in which Murphy was reputed to be a silent partner, was awarded a two million dollar contract for the job from the railroad, despite another bid which was $400,000 lower. The railroad's choice was a wise one. Difficulties in securing a franchise from the Board of Aldermen for a tunnel approach to the station magically disappeared.

Private control of the subways and utilities was decried by William Randolph Hearst in his lively newspapers the *Morning Journal* and *American*. Hearst was a maverick Democrat with a fanatic hatred of special interest groups, partly motivated by conscience and partly by a desire to promote his own special interest—William Randolph Hearst. Recognizing the power of Hearst's wrath, Murphy gave the publisher a half-hearted endorsement for Congress in 1902, and supported his re-election in 1904. When Mayor McClellan came up for re-election the following year, however, Murphy and Hearst's marriage of convenience was terminated for the political season.

Hearst's passionate conviction that public utilities should be municipally owned, else corrupt elements would bleed the City dry, prompted him to organize the Municipal Ownership League. The League was headed by a brilliant, thirty-one-year-old City Court Judge, Samuel Seabury. Hearst urged Seabury to run against McClellan as an independent. When Seabury declined, Hearst announced that he himself would take on Tammany Hall. The stage was set for one of New York's wildest mayoral elections: "Moiphy voisus Hoist."

The political popularity of William Randolph Hearst astounded Tammany. He was mobbed by admirers on the streets. His rallies overflowed with thousands of shouting enthusiasts. Boss Murphy, Hearst charged, was "The Colossus of Graft." McClellan was "the hireling of Great Britain." George McClellan, running scared, pledged to the voters that if re-elected he would be entirely free of Boss Murphy. The Mayor almost panicked when he learned that a British naval squadron was planning a courtesy visit to New York the day before election. He could see cartoons of himself in the Hearst press, groveling before the British commander. McClellan called Washington and managed to have the visit postponed until after the election.

Hearst's cartoonists were more interested in depicting Murphy in prison stripes. Under one such caricature, the caption read: "Look out, Murphy! It's a short lockstep from Delmonico's to Sing Sing." Charles Murphy had moved his affairs from the Second Avenue street lamp to the second floor of Delmonico's restaurant on Union Square. There he lunched each day with politicians and businessmen, at a table which rested on four carved tigers' paws, in what the press called "The Scarlet Room of Mystery," its door guarded by one of Murphy's boyhood cronies from the Gas House District. The *Evening Post* remarked of the Scarlet Room that "Nearly every important financier in the city is said to have entered it at one time or another."

Hearst made a strong appeal to Irish voters by dwelling on Murphy's aristocratic habits and McClellan's supposedly "pro-British" sentiments. Tammany countered by branding Hearst a socialist and anarchist. Both sides hired toughs to heckle each other's rallies. On Election Day, Tammany repeaters arrived from Philadelphia in full force. Fist and pistol fights erupted at the polls. It was rumored that batches of Hearst ballots were dumped into the East River. George McClellan scraped through by less than 4,000 votes out of 600,000 cast.

The following year, Hearst announced his determination to run for Governor. Mayor McClellan was seeking the Democratic gubernatorial nomination. Murphy recognized that, despite Tammany's effective work in the City election, Hearst was the more popular of the two men. He feared that a Hearst independent candidacy would split the Democratic vote. After months of vitriolic attacks on Murphy by the Hearst press, it came as a surprise to the public when the Boss put through a unit rule for delegates from each Assembly District at the 1906 Democratic State Convention in Buffalo, and delivered the nomination to Hearst. It was charged that Hearst had agreed to give Murphy half a million dollars if he were nominated and elected. Murphy's detractors taunted him with the song, "Waltz me around again, Willie."

But the election was no ball for Hearst. The Republicans nominated Charles Evans Hughes, who had just completed a headline-making investigation of insurance companies as counsel for a State Legislature committee.

Tammany was not united behind Murphy in the election of 1906, and he did not push his luck and risk intra-party disaster by twisting the district leaders' arms in the campaign. He had demonstrated his strength in the State Democratic Party by securing the nomination for Hearst. He considered Hearst the only Democrat with a chance of winning, but he preferred a Republican victory over Hearst on the Democratic ticket to a Hearst "spoiler" victory over Tammany on an independent ticket.

In the closing days of the campaign, President Theodore Roosevelt sent Secretary of State Elihu Root to New York to campaign against Hearst. "With the President's authority I say to you that he greatly desires the election of Mr. Hughes," Root said. "I say to you that he regards Mr. Hearst as wholly unfit to be governor; as an insincere, self-seeking demagogue who is trying to deceive the workingman of New York by false statements and false promises." William Randolph Hearst, the greatest thorn in Tammany's side, lost to Hughes by 58,000 votes. The rest of Murphy's slate, in the State and in the City, was victorious. All in all, it was not a bad election year for Charles Murphy.

The City of Greater New York, which Croker had ruled and now Charles Murphy sought to conquer, was still in its infancy. It burst into the twentieth century with an explosion of movement in all directions.

It reached skyward with towering new office buildings on lower Broadway. Twenty years before, Walt Whitman had looked upon eight-story structures in Manhattan and called them "cloud touching edifices." Now there was the eleven-story Tribune Building, the thirteen-story Tower Building at 50 Broadway, and Joseph Pulitzer's gold-domed, fifteen-story World Building. The first true skyscraper was the twenty-story tower of the American Surety Company, which soon passed the crown to a new champion, the twenty-five-story St. Paul Building. Then the fifty-story bell tower of the Metropolitan Life Insurance Company rose above Madison Square Park on the site of the old Madison Square Presbyterian Church, where Dr. Parkhurst had railed at Richard Croker from the pulpit.

And the City reached northward. The elevated railroads, showering sparks onto pedestrians, steamed up the avenues past the tenements and sweatshops to the once remote areas of Yorkville and the West End, the fashionable neighborhood between Central Park and Riverside Drive. Then came the subway and more street traffic. All of New York society was moving uptown, up Fifth Avenue past Murray Hill, up Park Avenue and Central Park West, where new and stately millionaires' mansions were erected side by side. (Many considered the elegant red-brick mansions of Washington Square as "old-fashioned.")

Lower Manhattan became a patchwork of ethnic neighborhoods, with colonies of Greeks, Turks, Germans, and Hungarians. West of the Bowery, the section once infamous as the Five Points was now called Chinatown. North of Chinatown was an Italian quarter stretching to the south side of Washington Square. The City's Negro population had once lived there, but now nearly all of Manhattan's 40,000 Negroes (mostly Republican) had moved to the West Fifties along

Ninth Avenue. During the first decade of the century, they began to move up to Harlem, after a slump in the real estate market brought down prices in the area.

But New York City was no longer confined to the island of Manhattan. Greater New York now included the borough of the Bronx across the Harlem River, whose Democratic Party was simply a branch of Charles Murphy's Tammany Hall; the borough of Brooklyn, composed of the City of Brooklyn and the rest of Kings County, ruled by Democratic Boss Hugh McLaughlin, whose power passed to Pat McCarren, then to "Uncle John" McCooey; and two boroughs which had no political muscle: Richmond (Staten Island) and Queens borough, which pulled together Flushing, Jamaica, the Rockaways, Newtown, and Long Island City.

Each borough elected a Borough President, and Murphy was careful to ease his allies into these positions, which were then rich with patronage and contracts. The Borough Presidents were therefore natural targets for Mayor McClellan when he broke with Murphy to demonstrate the independence of his second term and his anger over Murphy's support of Hearst for Governor. Through his Commissioner of Accounts, the fierce young reformer John Purroy Mitchel, McClellan launched an investigation of the borough offices. He found that millions of dollars of City funds were being wasted through lax enforcement of contracts, padded payrolls, and fraud in land purchases.

Governor Charles Evans Hughes thereupon removed Manhattan Borough President John Ahearn, a Murphy puppet, and Bronx Borough President Louis Haffen, a Tammany Sachem and one of the triumvirate which had shared party rule with Murphy after Croker's resignation. Hughes also ousted the Queens Borough President on charges of defrauding the City. His successor was similarly removed.

The shake-up appeared to indicate that McClellan had triumphed over Murphy. The Mayor persisted by rejecting nearly all of the names Mister Murphy submitted for City jobs during the second term. When McClellan asked Murphy to supply some alternatives, Murphy snapped, "That's my slate. Take it or leave it. I got no other candidates."

But then Mayor McClellan impulsively moved to wrest control of the Tammany Executive Committee. The Boss blocked him in the same way that he had slammed the door on Big Bill Devery—by changing the rules. The change provided that outgoing members could pass on qualifications of newly elected members. And Murphy invoked an obscure bylaw which allowed the Committee to enlarge itself, in this case with Murphy's friends.

The failure of McClellan's coup within Tammany was politically fatal to him. He never held office again. Years later, when an intermediary tried to interest Murphy in returning McClellan to Congress, the Boss said, "Well, I'd like to do something for George. You know I always was fond of him." Probably he meant it; Murphy often admired his opponents. But when word reached the district leaders that the Boss's old enemy sought a return to office, they declared their objections. Thus, Murphy needed only to shrug off McClellan's prospects as being impossible in the face of such opposition.

In searching for a successor to Mayor McClellan in 1909, Murphy again sought a candidate who could lend an air of virtue to the Mayor's office, and, by association, to Tammany Hall. He selected State Supreme Court Justice William Jay Gaynor, a crusty, irascible jurist with frosty eyes and a gray Vandyke beard. Gaynor, who had a creative flair for original profanity, was a righteous reformer who had, as a young man, overthrown a Brooklyn political boss and sent him to jail for election fraud.

As a judge, Gaynor was detested by lawyers. He called the calendar from the bench in a barely audible whisper. If they failed to respond promptly, he struck their cases. On other occasions he scolded attorneys for ill-prepared arguments and sometimes threw their documents back in their faces. Typical Gaynor decisions read: "The complaint lacks precision, but in its bungling way . . ." or "The facts of this case are simple, once you get through the drudgery of picking them out of the mass of useless matter which counsel on both sides seemed bent on accumulating. . . ."

But although William Gaynor may have lacked judicial temperament, he had a great compassion for the underdog, the helpless citizen caught in the wheels of government and justice. He believed it was his wrathful mission to protect the common man from both the mercantile oppressors and the "do-good" reformers, whom he considered hypocrites and busybodies. Dr. Parkhurst, he said, was a "blatherskite," and as for the great Rabbi Stephen Wise: "He is a man of vast and varied misinformation, of brilliant mental incapacity, and of prodigious moral requirements."

So fiercely independent was Murphy's newest mayoral candidate that he did not hesitate to deride the Tammanyites even after they had tendered him the Democratic nomination. Addressing the braves in the great Wigwam on 14th Street, Gaynor said:

"So this is Tammany Hall. It is the first time I was ever here. I did not even know where it was. I had to telephone before leaving my home to find out exactly how to get here. But if this is Tammany Hall, where is the tiger—that tiger which they say is going to swallow me up? If there happens to be any swallowing up, it is not at all unlikely that I may be on the outside of the tiger."

The puzzled braves laughed nervously. Boss Murphy would have smiled if he had known how. Clearly, he had picked the right man.

William Randolph Hearst, who had supported Gaynor in the past, demanded that the judge reject Murphy's support. Gaynor refused, so Hearst nominated himself as an independent candidate for Mayor. It was another thunderous campaign, with Gaynor waging an onslaught on Hearst in the best Hearstian tradition. He called the Hearst press a bunch of "ragbag newspapers" published by a "liar." "Morally," Gaynor said of Hearst, "his mind is a howling wilderness."

Gaynor won the election by a comfortable margin over Hearst and a relatively ineffective Republican candidate. But Hearst had helped defeat Gaynor's Democratic running-mates. (John Purroy Mitchel, the handsome young Commissioner of Accounts from the McClellan administration, was elected president of the Board of Aldermen on a Fusion ticket.) When asked to what he attributed the defeat of most of his slate, Charles Murphy replied: "We didn't get enough votes."

Gaynor was one of the most awesome and unpredictable creatures ever to sit in the Mayor's chair. Although he was usually unapproachable to newspapermen, the more enterprising reporters learned that productive interviews would ensue if they began the discussion with talk of pigs. The Mayor had grown up on an upstate farm where he proved to be inept, even dangerous, with farm tools in his hands. But he was always fond of the pigs.

Gaynor was an inveterate correspondent, dashing off answers to citizens' letters that came to him at City Hall. Sometimes he was sympathetic (especially to children), sometimes abusive, but always original. He often sprinkled his letters with quotations from favorite authors, like Cervantes or Epictetus. (When he was on the bench,

Judge Gaynor had once quoted Epictetus. Lawyers, seeking to win favor with the judge, looked up everything they could find by that obscure Roman, and soon Gaynor's court echoed with references that began: "Epictetus says . . .")

Charles Murphy had enthroned an uncommon man at City Hall and he soon came to recognize the problems this entailed. Not only did the Mayor ignore Murphy in making appointments, he abolished some jobs that had been filled by Tammany men. When someone asked the Mayor what he planned to give Mister Murphy, Gaynor replied: "Suppose we give him a few kind words." And he did: "I fear there are a good many people in this town who do not know Charles F. Murphy. Some of them seem to think he has horns and hoofs. I can only say of him what I have seen. He fully realizes that a political organization cannot survive and grow broader on patronage alone, without political ideas and virtue, but must shrivel up and die of worse than dry rot."

The Mayor had perceived Murphy's political philosophy. But the Boss wouldn't have minded a little patronage in the bargain. Big Tom Foley of the Lower East Side was horrified. "I will say this about Mayor Gaynor," he later remarked. "He did more to break up the Democratic organization than any other man ever has in the City." When Murphy himself was asked to comment on Gaynor's appointments, he said: "The new officials are all good men—I guess."

With few exceptions, Mayor Gaynor's appointments were good ones, and his first year in office was a success. He received high praise from newspapers, civic groups, and many of his old opponents. (When John Lindsay took office as Mayor in 1966, he cited two predecessors whom he considered models for his administration—Fiorello La-Guardia and William Jay Gaynor.)

Seven months after he took office, there occurred the first of several disasters that were to blight his mayoralty. In August, 1910, Mayor Gaynor boarded the *Kaiser Wilhelm der Grosse* at Hoboken, New Jersey, for a trip to Europe and a much needed rest. It was a festive atmosphere on board the ship, which was decked out with flags and bunting, while reporters and photographers besieged the Mayor and scores of dignitaries. Gaynor had just been introduced to the President of Chile when a disheveled little man, later identified as a discharged Docks Department employee, stepped out of the background and fired a bullet into the Mayor's neck. Mayor Gaynor survived, but never fully recovered. He continued in office with determination, often in pain, more caustic and irritable than ever.

On election night, 1910, Charles Murphy became the first Tammany Boss since Tweed to dominate New York State. The Democrats won control of the State Legislature and Murphy's man, John Alden Dix, was elected Governor. Dix thereafter dutifully followed Murphy's lead. And on Capitol Hill in Albany, Murphy installed as leaders two able, young legislators from Tammany Hall: Robert F. Wagner, Sr., of Yorkville, thirty-three years old, Senate Majority Leader; and Alfred E. Smith of the Lower East Side, thirty-seven, Assembly Majority Leader.

The next order of business was the designation of a United States Senator. At that time (two years before the Seventeenth Amendment), Senators were chosen by the State Legislatures rather than directly by the people. Murphy's candidate was William "Blue-Eyed Billie" Sheehan, a Tammany lawyer who was closely tied to the traction interests. A group of insurgents rejected the choice. They were led by a shrewd and witty twenty-nine-year-old freshman from Dutchess County, State Senator Franklin D. Roosevelt. He rallied nineteen other lawmakers to the cause and they forced the Legislature into a ten-week deadlock.

Edward Shepard, the Brooklyn reformer whom Croker had run unsuccessfully against Seth Low, was the candidate of the Roosevelt forces. (Shepard's father Lorenzo had been a Grand Sachem of the Tammany Society.) The rebels did not have enough votes to put Shepard through, but they were able to block Sheehan by boycotting the Democratic caucus. Roosevelt and his allies (the "Empire State Democracy") met twice a day in his rented house in Albany. The first floor of the home became so choked with cigar smoke that the children's nursery had to be moved to the third floor.

As the weeks wore on, Murphy increased pressure on the twenty insurgents with threats of political reprisals and loss of patronage. After a month had passed, both sides had softened their positions and were offering other candidates. None was mutually acceptable. The struggle continued into March with the Roosevelt camp outnumbered 5 to 1 but refusing to cave in to Murphy. Finally, Murphy submitted the name of James Aloysius O'Gorman, a State Supreme Court Justice of good repute. Roosevelt yielded and O'Gorman was nominated. Years later, FDR reportedly boasted to friends of that "final Murphy surrender." But, in fact, Judge O'Gorman, a former Tammany Grand Sachem, was a loyal friend of Mister Murphy. The Boss was more than happy to let the rebels think they had won by blocking Billie Sheehan.

In that March of 1911, a fire started on the eighth floor of a loft building near Washington Square, sweeping through bolts of cloth and stacks of finished goods at the Triangle Shirtwaist Company. On the floor above, panic broke out. There was no escape except down the stairs and into the fire. An iron grillwork closed off the only stairway to the roof. Frightened women surged toward the grill and crushed each other to death. Some climbed out windows, clung to the cornice, and fell 110 feet to their deaths. In all, 143 persons died in the Triangle Fire.

The City was horrorstruck. A procession of 50,000 mourners marched in the rain for five hours. In Albany, the Legislature established an investigating commission, headed by Smith and Wagner. The result of their state-wide survey of working conditions was a code of fifty-six factory laws, which became models for the nation. Out of tragedy came the first glimmerings of a social conscience in twentieth-century Tammany Hall, and the seeds of the New Deal.

Beneath the liberal candidates and progressive programs of the new Tammany Hall still lurked the old ties between district leaders, gangsters, and police. "Licenses" for illegal gambling operations were granted by some of Murphy's leaders to such powerful racketeers as Arnold Rothstein. For a share in the gambling proceeds, the leaders provided police protection. Unco-operative gamblers were raided by the police Special Squad No. 1, otherwise known as the "Strong-arm Squad." Lieutenant Charles Becker, who had made at least $100,000 on graft and was a special favorite of Police Commissioner Rhinelander Waldo, served as the commander of the Strong-arm Squad.

In April 1912, Lieutenant Becker raided the establishment of a gambler named Herman Rosenthal, who was under the protection of Big Tim Sullivan but had refused a pay-off to Becker. Rosenthal sought advice on the situation from Arnold Rothstein, who suggested he get out of town. Instead, Herman Rosenthal went to District Attorney Charles Whitman and promised to appear before a Grand Jury.

When word of Rosenthal's action reached Lieutenant Becker, he sent word to four professional gunmen that Herman Rosenthal was to be executed. ("Tell them they can shoot him in front of any policeman in town.") About 2 A.M. on July 16, Rosenthal stepped out on the sidewalk in front of the Cafe Metropole on West 43rd Street and was greeted by four simultaneous shots. He died instantly. Seven policemen were within 500 feet of the escaping killers. They jotted down their versions of the license number on the getaway car, all different and all incorrect. When a witness arrived at Police Headquarters with the correct number, he was thrown into a cell. Herbert Bayard Swope of the New York *World* roused District Attorney Whitman from bed and insisted that he take charge of the investigation which the police were blocking. In due course, Becker and his henchmen were arrested, convicted, and sent to the electric chair at Sing Sing.

John Purroy Mitchel, President of the Board of Aldermen, established a committee to investigate "the system" of police graft. The press and public assailed Mayor Gaynor and his hapless Police Commissioner Rhinelander Waldo, a pleasant young socialite who had a naïve faith in the incorruptibility of his police force. "Do not bend a single bit to clamor," Mayor Gaynor told Waldo, "and especially to clamor chiefly created by corrupt newspapers." One newspaper cartoon depicted the Mayor saying to his commissioner, "Waldo, with one exception, I consider you the Creator's noblest work." The Mayor, by way of diverting public attention, instructed Commissioner Waldo to investigate the possible presence of prostitutes at three West 58th Street buildings, which happened to be owned by William Randolph Hearst.

Herman Rosenthal had made out an affidavit before his death describing the network of police, politicians, gamblers, and prostitutes. Among those implicated in the affidavit was Big Tim Sullivan, who had helped finance Rosenthal's operations. "There is only one man in the world can call me off, that is the big fellow, Big Tim Sullivan, and he is as honest as the day is long, and I know he is in sympathy with me," Rosenthal said in his statement. "If I need money I can go to him for it and he will give it to me or get it for me. It is purely a matter of friendship, and he never expects to make a nickel profit out of it. He is the only man that could call me off, and he has told me that he believes I am doing right in trying to protect myself and my home." Rosenthal claimed that Big Tim had loaned him two thousand dollars to start his gambling house "out of pure friendship."

Big Tim Sullivan went insane that year and was placed in a sanitorium, from which he escaped. His body was found on the railroad tracks near the Westchester freight yards. More than 25,000 citizens,

including three Senators and twenty Congressmen, followed Big Tim
Sullivan's coffin to the grave.

Franklin Roosevelt's defiance of Charles Murphy in the 1911 State
Legislature, although it accomplished the immediate goal of blocking
Blue-Eyed Billie Sheehan, was generally considered to mark the be-
ginning of the end for a promising young politician. Going against
Charles Murphy was certain political suicide in New York State.

But the 1912 Democratic National Convention in Baltimore gave
Roosevelt a second chance to battle with Mister Murphy over another
candidate, this time in the national arena. The issue was: who would be
the strongest candidate against GOP President William Howard Taft?
Murphy, although publicly uncommitted, favored the front-runner,
House Speaker James Beauchamp "Champ" Clark. Roosevelt pushed
for New Jersey's favorite son, Governor Thomas Woodrow Wilson.
The contest was decided when William Jennings Bryan, titular head
of the party, backed Wilson. But Murphy could not swing Tammany
to the cause of a diffident ex-history professor. "The boys don't want
him," he explained.

Murphy threw his delegation to Champ Clark and thereby permanently antagonized the eventual nominee, Woodrow Wilson. Teddy
Roosevelt bolted the Republican Party, split the GOP vote, and
Wilson won. After assuming office, President Wilson ignored Murphy
in distributing Federal patronage and, to salt Tammany's wounds,
brought FDR to Washington and made him Assistant Secretary of
the Navy.

Charles Murphy made relatively few mistakes in politics. In 1912 he
made two—both serious. The first was his opposition to Wilson. The
second was the selection of the candidate for Governor: Congressman
William Sulzer, a handsome Narcissus and popular vote-getter who
had been one of the chief ornaments in Dick Croker's collection of
Tammany orators. ("No State, and no country, can long endure half
wet and half dry—RUM—RUM—menaces the progress of the race,
and challenges the advance of civilization.") Sulzer won the governorship by a smashing 200,000-vote plurality. But the whole thing, Charles
Murphy said later, was "the greatest mistake of my life."

Shortly before his inauguration, Governor-elect Sulzer met with
Mister Murphy in the "Scarlet Room of Mystery" at Delmonico's.
"His attitude was very friendly and confidential," Sulzer later recalled.

"He said he was my friend; that he knew of my financial condition and wished to help me out. As he went on I was amazed at his knowledge of my intimate personal affairs. To my astonishment he informed me that he knew that I was heavily in debt. Then he offered me money to pay my debts and have enough left to take things easy while Governor."

Sulzer turned down Murphy's offer and also rejected his recommendations of office-holders, notably Big Jim Gaffney of the New York Contracting and Trucking Company for State Highway Commissioner, and Tammany district leader Eugene "The" McManus for Commissioner of Labor. Sulzer and Murphy met again at the Shoreham Hotel in Washington where they were attending the inauguration of President Wilson.

"I want you to appoint Gaffney," Murphy said. "It is an organization matter and I will appreciate it."

Sulzer said he was thinking about it, and Mister Murphy replied: "I am for Gaffney. The organization demands his appointment and I want you to do it."

"I will make no promise about it," William Sulzer said.

Charles Murphy closed the conversation: "It will be Gaffney or war."

Governor Sulzer did not appoint Big Jim Gaffney as State Highway Commissioner. Instead, he appointed an investigator to probe political corruption in all echelons of the State Government. "As these cases develop," the investigator announced, "the electors of New York State will learn that the political organization, so-called Democratic, captained by Charles F. Murphy in New York City . . . is organized to loot the treasury and regards every honest man as its enemy."

The Governor's next endearing action was to call a special session of the State Legislature to enact a direct primary bill in order to undercut the power of Boss Murphy, whom he compared to William Marcy Tweed. While the legislators met, Sulzer campaigned State-wide attacking Murphy. "The bosses say they will beat me," he told a cheering crowd upstate. "They say they will destroy me, but I tell them that no man can destroy me but William Sulzer."

Mister Murphy was on the phone twice daily with his floor leaders, Al Smith and Robert Wagner. The direct primary bill did not pass. Neither did appropriation bills. State Government came to a standstill.

On May 20, 1913, Charles Murphy met with State Senator Wagner and other Albany leaders in the Scarlet Room at Delmonico's and told them that Governor Sulzer would have to be impeached. Al Smith was given the task of rounding up Assembly votes for the necessary resolutions to put the case before the Court of Impeachment, which was composed of judges and State Senators. It was reported that, at this point, the Governor frantically sent an emissary to see if Murphy would drop the matter in exchange for patronage. Instead, the impeachment proceedings continued.

With summer upon them, Speaker Smith and Majority Leader Aaron Levy had to summon assemblymen from their mountain and seashore retreats. Murphy came in from Good Ground, stayed by the telephone in his town house and kept in touch with Albany. The Assembly remained in special session through the night of August 13, 1913, while Levy filibustered and Smith lined up the votes. When he saw he had the necessary votes, Smith banged the gavel to wake the dozing members, and called the roll. The impeachment resolutions were passed and charges sent from the Assembly to the Court of Impeachment.

The basic case against Sulzer was that he had failed to report campaign contributions from Wall Street financiers and had used the money to speculate on stocks. As a Congressman, Sulzer had spoken out against anti-Semitism in Russia, which earned him the support of such prominent Jewish businessmen as Herbert Lehman, Henry Morgenthau, Sr., and Jacob Schiff. Lehman contributed $12,000 to Sulzer's gubernatorial campaign, $5,000 of it to Sulzer for his personal use. Jacob Schiff gave $2,500. Allan Ryan, son of Thomas Fortune Ryan, the Democratic patron and founder of the American Tobacco Company, turned over $10,000 to Sulzer personally.

On October 17, the Court of Impeachment voted 43 to 12 to remove William Sulzer from office. It was the only time in New York State history that such an action was taken. "From Murphy's High Court of Infamy, I appeal to that higher court—the court of public opinion," Sulzer told a group of loyalists in Albany. "Posterity will do me justice."

Although Murphy, as a matter of course, had made no public statements during the impeachment proceedings, his dominant role was widely publicized. The removal of Sulzer may have eliminated a noisome ingrate, but it also demonstrated too dramatically for self-interest's sake the private power of Charles Murphy. Tammany was

now linked with the assassins of William Sulzer as well as the killers of
Herman Rosenthal.

After the elections of 1913, except in a few "safe" districts in the
City, every legislator who voted for the Sulzer impeachment was out
of office. In the City, Fusion candidate John Purroy Mitchel, with the
endorsement of President Wilson, won the mayoralty over the Tammany candidate, Judge Edward McCall. Mayor Gaynor, charged with
infidelity to the Democratic Party, was denied renomination, though it
was reported that Murphy had a few kind words for him during a
caucus of district leaders. Gaynor, who was in poor health, was nominated by a group of independents. He boarded a ship for a restful cruise
before the campaign. Gaynor died in his deck chair on September 10th.

Each day's events brought worse news to Charles Murphy. Mayor-
elect Mitchel swept out one Tammany job-holder after another. A
Tammany district leader was jailed for his part in a Rockland County
road swindle. The Democratic State Treasurer, under questioning by
District Attorney Whitman in the continuing graft inquiry, slashed
his throat and died in the washroom of a Buffalo hotel. Ex-Governor
Sulzer was elected to the State Assembly and made fresh charges about
contractor kickbacks to Murphy and Big Jim Gaffney's role as Murphy's
"bagman."

President Wilson assigned cabinet members to the task of deposing
Murphy. William Jennings Bryan came to New York to confer with
Dudley Field Malone, Collector of the Port of New York and President Wilson's patronage pipeline for the City. It was reported they
were organizing an insurrection against the Boss at the coming primary
elections. A group of Democrats, calling themselves the Committee of
250, met at the Hotel McAlpin to form a rival organization to Tammany Hall. And at the National Democratic Club, City Judge John
O'Dwyer, the Club President, called Murphy a "corruptionist" and
"the ruin of the party," charges that almost provoked a riot among
club members.

Reports leaked to the newspapers that Murphy was ready to quit.
Murphy called a rare press conference at Tammany Hall. He sat behind his roll-top desk, his small, dull eyes blinking at the unfamiliar
faces of the reporters. "I am the leader of Tammany Hall no matter
what some others may say about it," Mister Murphy said. "I'm going
to stay here as long as I live."

Lieutenant-Governor Martin Glynn, an old friend of Richard

Croker's, succeeded William Sulzer as Governor and soon thereafter joined the Get-Murphy movement. He envisioned himself the leader of the Democratic Party in the State and scurried off to Washington in search of President Wilson's backing. On his return, he issued a statement that contained just enough nonsense to indicate that the White House had turned him down: "There are two kinds of leadership. One is a sort of actual working leadership in the mechanics of politics. With that I want nothing to do. The other is the leadership of ideas, in which I claim a part."

Governor Glynn did say, however, that he favored political party autonomy for each county, thereby refusing the recognize Murphy's authority outside Manhattan. Murphy returned from a weekend at his Long Island estate. He was ambushed by reporters, and his answers were beautifully Murphy.

What about demands for changes in party structure? "I shall be very glad to aid in any effort to uplift the party—if that's the word."

What about charges of graft from contractors? "That's past."

What about re-election for Governor Glynn? "That's future."

What about Glynn's county autonomy policy? "Don't know anything about it."

Murphy was confident he could survive the storm. This was a time for consolidation, not extension. He made no moves to block Glynn from running the gubernatorial race in 1914. There was no need to. The Republican candidate was District Attorney Whitman, prosecutor of Lieutenant Becker, who swept to victory over Glynn on a wave of anti-Tammany sentiment

The expected primary fights against Murphy's district leaders never materialized. Al Smith, Robert Wagner, and Senator James O'Gorman gave their full, public support to the Tammany Boss, which frightened off a number of potential opponents. The anti-Murphy reformers were too busy squabbling among themselves to mount a concerted attack on Tammany Hall. "I see no reason why I should retire from the leadership because groups of men outside of the organization demand it," Charles Murphy said. "The enrolled Democrats have confidence in me. Anytime they have not, all they have to do is cast their votes for a district leader opposed to me."

And that was that. In 1915, Murphy recaptured the Board of Aldermen, the District Attorney's office, and the Sheriff's office. The new Sheriff was Alfred E. Smith.

Edwin P. Kilroe, an officer of the Monongahela Democratic Club in the Columbia University area, was appointed as an Assistant District Attorney. Kilroe was the leading expert on Tammany. As a student at Columbia, he had written his doctoral thesis on the organization and amassed some 60,000 pieces of Tammaniana in a collection that continued to grow for another forty years. (The Kilroe collection is now in Butler Library at Columbia.) In a 1916 letter to a political science professor, Kilroe wrote:

"It must be borne in mind that Charles Francis Murphy, the present leader of Tammany Hall, occupies a unique position in American politics. He is what might be called a natural leader. He occupies no official position in the party organization except that he is the executive member from the 12th Assembly District. He is not an officer of the County Committee, nor of the executive committee, nor is he chairman of a subcommittee of these committees. He is a political Nestor of the organization and because of his rare political judgment and his shrewd manipulation of men, he is enabled to hold a firm control on the party machinery."

To depose Murphy as County Leader, Kilroe explained, "it would be necessary to elect county committeemen and executive committeemen who would refuse to go to Mr. Murphy for advice and refuse to follow his suggestions. Nothing short of a revolution within the party in the County could bring this about."

That revolution did not take place. As Murphy told a friend: "I have allowed them to cut off my right arm. I have allowed them to cut off my left arm. But I have always outwaited them." The Get-Murphy movement collapsed and its leaders began to deal with Charles Murphy as a permanent institution. President Wilson, seeking a second term in 1916, sent Henry Morgenthau, Sr., on a peace mission to Murphy shortly before the Democratic National Convention opened in St. Louis. But "the boys" still didn't want Wilson. Many Irish and German voters were concerned that he was on the verge of enlisting America as a British ally in the World War. Furthermore, it was difficult to believe that after the election he would translate his new overtures into solid Federal patronage for Tammany. The Tammany Executive Committee declined to give the President any delegates from Manhattan or the Bronx.

Wilson's renomination, however, was a foregone conclusion, and Murphy pledged Tammany's support for the election. When the

Democratic National Chairman failed to place a Tammany representative on the President's national campaign committee, the story circulated that Tammany would boycott the campaign. An agreement was then reached between Murphy and the national leaders that Tammany would campaign for the President's re-election and Wilson, who had backed Mitchel in 1913, would keep hands off the mayoral race in 1917.

The 1916 Democratic State Convention was scheduled for August in Saratoga as a convenience for the Tammany delegates who were already there for the races. Faced with a contest against the popular reform Governor Charles Whitman, Mister Murphy reluctantly endorsed Judge Samuel Seabury as the Democratic candidate. Hearst immediately threw his papers' support to Whitman and branded Seabury as "the tool of Murphy." During the campaign, Seabury took great pains to keep Tammany at arm's length. A photograph was published of Seabury and Murphy together on the golf course. Seabury claimed it was all a mistake, that Murphy had just happened to wander by at the moment the camera clicked. On Wall Street the betting odds on Governor Whitman's re-election climbed up to 3 to 1.

Tammany had little enthusiasm for either Seabury or Wilson. But the braves put up an outward show of Democratic solidarity to demonstrate Tammany's strength and responsibility. Just before the November election, the President came to New York to speak at Madison Square Garden, and Tammany whooped it up with a giant parade in his honor. Sheriff Al Smith, Grand Marshal of the parade, marched alongside Mister Murphy and the aging Grand Sachem John Voorhis, all wearing the beribboned sashes and medallions of the Tammany Society. Behind them were more than 12,000 marchers, a dozen bands, and banners proclaiming: "Tammany will give the biggest vote in its history to Woodrow Wilson."

While the Tammany district leaders went through the motions for Wilson, they predicted that he would take New York City by 100,000 votes over Charles Evans Hughes, who had stepped down from the U.S. Supreme Court to head the Republican ticket. On Election Day, however, both Wilson and Seabury were knifed. Wilson had a bare 40,000 margin in the City, Seabury only 21,000, neither enough to offset the traditional upstate Republican lead. Governor Whitman was re-elected by 154,000 votes. President Wilson lost New York State but won California and the election. The following day Mister Murphy refused to receive any visitors at Tammany Hall.

When Carry Nation first looked upon the all-male political clubs of Tammany Hall, she admonished the braves: "Don't you know that God said it isn't good for men to be alone?"

Miss Nation, minus her hatchet, actively supported Big Bill Devery in the earliest struggles against the empire of Charles Murphy the political barkeep. Later, Murphy was beset by lobbyists for women workers, such as the young social worker Frances Perkins, and the Suffragettes who declared: "We are proud to count Mr. Murphy among our enemies." But Murphy surprised the ladies, first, after the Triangle Fire, by acceding to legislation which protected women in factories, and then, as the clamor grew for the Nineteenth Amendment, by recognizing the inevitability of the women's vote and arranging for the appointment of the City's first female judge.

Mrs. Murphy may have had some mellowing effect on the Tammany Boss. She was a widow whom Charles Murphy married when he was forty-four, the year he assumed the leadership of Tammany. It was suggested mysteriously that she had been Charlie's childhood sweetheart and he had waited for her all those years in a state of priestly purity. The Murphys had no children, but Mabel Graham, Mrs. Murphy's daughter from her first marriage, lived with them for many years at their home at 305 East 17th Street until she wed Surrogate James Foley.

Murphy's daily habits were conservative and uncomplicated. Every morning at nine o'clock, dressed in a subdued pinstripe suit, vest and bow tie, he climbed into the same dilapidated hack driven by the same elderly hackman and traveled the short route to Tammany Hall. At noon he lunched in the Scarlet Room at Delmonico's. In the evening he usually arrived home at a reasonable hour. He was not fond of the banquet circuit. Most weekends he went out to his Long Island estate to play golf. At Good Ground, in addition to his private golf course, he had a small farm and a kennel of pure-blood bulldogs. He retained an armed guard to prevent trespassing.

As Mister Murphy aged, he grew stouter and ruddier. He sat at his desk in the Hall looking like a bespectacled Buddha, maintaining the same attentive but impassive expression that had intrigued the customers at Charlie's Place. Murphy rarely talked with reporters, but, unlike the day after Wilson and Seabury lost New York, he customarily gave audience to all members of the organization. He made no promises. He never debated or gave reasons for his decisions. He could take advice and change his mind, but he would not answer arguments. His only answers were: "Yes," "No," or "I'll look into it." He once explained this philosophy to a young protégé, State Senator James J. Walker: "Most of the troubles of the world could be avoided if men opened their minds instead of their mouths."

In 1917, Charles Murphy opened his mind to the possibility that electing William Randolph Hearst as Mayor might swing the Hearst press to the cause of Tammany. Furthermore, Hearst had demonstrated his popularity with the Irish and German rank-and-file in the close 1905 election. A strong vote-getter was needed to topple Fusion Mayor John Purroy Mitchel. Sheriff Al Smith also wanted the job, and he was supported in this quest by the powerful Lower East Side district leader Big Tom Foley. Murphy persuaded Smith to bide his time and await the gubernatorial year of 1918. Smith agreed but refused to accept Hearst for Mayor. The four men—Murphy, Smith, Foley and Hearst—compromised on Judge John F. Hylan of Brooklyn, an ideal candidate of well-known integrity and considerable naïveté. Judge Hylan was a good friend of Hearst's and could honestly tell the voters that he had never met Charles Murphy.

Murphy reportedly met with "Uncle John" McCooey, the pudgy little Boss of Brooklyn, and asked him: "Is Hylan a man we can trust and do business with?"

"He certainly is," Uncle John replied. "Do you want to meet him?"

"No," said Murphy, "I want you to ram him down my throat."

And so a "reluctant" Mister Murphy arranged for Hylan to be nominated untainted by the Boss's public support. Judge Hylan presented a respectable picture of an independent-minded candidate who would oust the incumbent reformers without throwing City Hall to the wolves. To ensure that Tammanyites were not put off by the selection, Murphy gave Al Smith a consolation prize on the ticket as nominee for president of the Board of Aldermen. Smith's popularity with the Irish added great strength to the battle against Mayor Mitchel, who had antagonized many Catholics by criticizing Church-operated institutions and issuing strong statements in support of the Allied war effort.

"Red Mike" Hylan was an amiable, red-headed six-footer who

grew up barefoot on a Catskill Mountain farm, came to Brooklyn at the age of nineteen to study law at night and work days on the elevated railroad. He was fired from the railroad for rounding a curve too fast, but passed his bar exams in the nick of time. Hylan came to Hearst's attention as an outspoken foe of the transit magnates, an issue which he used in the 1917 campaign, although seldom with thoughtful eloquence. A contemporary of Hylan's recalled recently that "his absence of a brain helped him. It made him more congenial." The *Times* called Red Mike a man of "marvelous mental density." Hylan won by 150,000 votes over Mitchel with a Socialist candidate running third. Mitchel enlisted in the Air Corps, although over-age, and fell out of a single-seater training plane to his death.

In theory, Red Mike Hylan was a Tammany Mayor, but his greatest allegiance was always to Hearst. When he appointed a welcoming committee of distinguished citizens to greet returning war heroes, he named Hearst as chairman. Hearst's papers suffered from severe cases of Anglophobia and Germanophilia. Millions of citizens were outraged by Hylan's choice, but the Mayor remained firm.

At the time, Murphy and Hearst were engaged in one of their cyclical love feasts. Hearst, although his control over Hylan was stronger than Murphy's, did not interfere with Tammany patronage demands at City Hall. He needed Murphy's support for the 1918 gubernatorial nomination, which the Boss had implicitly promised Al Smith when sidetracking Smith from the mayoral race. As convention time approached in Saratoga, two rumors were equally insistent about Murphy's choice: he had made another financial deal with Hearst to support him; he had arranged a political *quid pro quo* the previous year with Smith to support *him*. The Boss remained silent.

Charles Murphy was well-recognized as a master of timing, adept at keeping anxious candidates on tenterhooks until the last possible moment. In such manner, he could keep his options broad and put his ultimate choice in eternal debt. The Boss who throws his support at a late enough hour (but not *too* late) to turn the tide is normally the greatest beneficiary of victory. In the case of Smith versus Hearst for the Democratic nomination for Governor, Murphy weighed his alternatives until the convention was underway. In fact, he had not made up his mind.

Some said that Murphy had already decided on Smith and was using his old technique of apparent reluctance in the face of fervent appeal. But Murphy was concerned about the number of anti-Tammany reformers who were pushing the Smith candidacy. One was Judge Samuel Seabury, who said: "Mr. Smith is the best representative of the worst element in the Democratic Party in this State." More importantly, Charles Murphy had strong reservations about Smith's religious credentials in a state-wide race. Edward Staats Luther, a political reporter and later a Tammany committeeman, sought to assure Murphy that Al Smith could win anything. In the midst of one of their discussions, Murphy called out to one of his lieutenants, "Come in here and listen to a man named Luther trying to convince a man named Murphy that a Catholic can be elected Governor of New York State."

Murphy eventually decided to take the gamble. Smith was nominated and elected over Governor Charles Whitman. Boss Murphy and Governor Smith developed a close working relationship on major appointments and governmental policy. The remainder of Murphy's career was devoted mainly to the promotion of Smith as a national figure and as a leader in new concepts of government's responsibility to the people.

Although Charles Murphy developed more popular candidates than any other Tammany leader, he did not concern himself with encouraging heirs to his power in the Manhattan machine. None of his aides earned the trust that Honest John Kelly had in Richard Croker. Murphy had supreme confidence in his own indestructibility. One may speculate that had he lived longer, he would have retired and arranged for an orderly transfer of authority to a capable underling. But then, the story of Democratic politics in the past forty years would have been changed beyond recognition.

Murphy was the only Tammany leader who has ever ruled without rival in the organization, and he did so for twenty-two years. He achieved this not by a dictatorial approach. On the contrary, "iron rule" has always led to rebellion. The best of the Bosses achieve longevity through a wise degree of flexibility. Murphy rarely overplayed his hand. In 1917, he had turned to Brooklyn leader John McCooey for a mayoral candidate. Thenceforth Uncle John was always Charles Murphy's man. So was Arthur Murphy, leader of the Bronx, as well as William Fitzpatrick in Buffalo, and William Kelley in Syracuse.

When Arthur Murphy died in 1922, Edward Flynn, the thirty-year-old Sheriff of the Bronx, let it be known that he would support district leader James Brown for the county leadership. Soon afterward, Flynn received word that Charles Murphy, whom he had never met, wanted to see him.

"I entered Tammany Hall," Flynn wrote in his memoirs, "and one of the secretaries asked me to wait in a very large room. I sat there for some time, wondering what I would be asked or told. Finally Mr. Murphy entered with that dignity which I was to learn was so characteristic of him. I stood up. We exchanged greetings. Then, for want of something better to say, I remarked, 'Commissioner, this is the first time I have ever been in Tammany Hall.' He looked at me quizzically and replied, 'Whose fault is that?' "

It was the first of three meetings between the two men to discuss the political stalemate in the Bronx. At the third session Mr. Murphy said, "Young man, the situation in the Bronx is similar to that which appeared here in Tammany Hall when Mr. Croker resigned." Murphy had decided to appoint a triumvirate, consisting of Flynn and two other leaders, but not Jim Brown. Flynn protested that his constituents would charge him with selling out Brown in order to promote himself. And then, according to Flynn's account, "Mr. Murphy said quietly, 'Mr. Brown will not do.' This was his custom, I learned, when disposing of an unacceptable candidate for office. He never explained why, and few people ever had the temerity to ask."

The troika was selected and "Once a week," Flynn wrote, "we would hire a funeral hack and the three of us would proceed in state to Mr. Murphy's house on East 17th Street. We would be ushered into his overly elegant parlor, where we would sit and wait. After an appropriate pause Mr. Murphy would enter and, with great solemnity, say, 'How are you, Steve?' 'How are you, Tom?' And then to me, 'How are you, young man?' Then he would seat himself with his usual dignity and ask, 'How are conditions in the Bronx?' Each of us in turn would reply, 'Excellent.' This would conclude the conference. We would rise, get our hats, climb into the funeral hack, and proceed solemnly back to the Bronx. This was the sum total of our contacts with the Leader of the party in the City."

After three months of this routine, Flynn finally screwed up the courage to answer Mister Murphy's question about "conditions" with "Rotten!" Murphy replied, "What do you mean?" and Ed Flynn complained that under three-man rule it was impossible to reach decisions. "If that is the way you feel about it, go on up there and select a

Leader," Murphy said. Flynn recalled that the three men rode back to the Bronx in silence, each one trying to figure out how many votes he could muster on the Executive Committee.

The Committee met and was hopelessly deadlocked. This time Ed Flynn drove alone to Tammany Hall in a mood of anger and frustration. "Before the Commissioner could do more than utter an astonished greeting, I blurted out that I intended to call a meeting of my supporters and have myself elected Leader, whether anybody liked it or not. Mr. Murphy, in his benign and fatherly way, tried occasionally to break into my discourse and soothe me. . . . When I was through, the Leader of the Democratic party in the City and State of New York looked at me kindly and said simply, 'There will be a meeting of the committee tomorrow, and you will be elected chairman.' I was elected the morning of May 15, 1922, precisely as he had said. What Mr. Murphy did to bring this about, and to whom he talked, I did not know."

Murphy consolidated Flynn's position in the Bronx by giving the nomination for Secretary of State, which was then an elective office, to a Bronx man at the 1922 Democratic State Convention in Syracuse. It was the first state-wide nomination to go to Bronx County. He also allowed his young protégé to sit quietly in his hotel room to observe the master dealing with the Democratic leaders on the question of the gubernatorial nomination. Once again the two leading candidates were William Randolph Hearst and Alfred Emanuel Smith.

Although relations between Murphy and Hearst underwent convenient reversals year by year, the Smith-Hearst feud was very real and steadfast, dating back to 1907 when Smith backed Big Tom Foley for Sheriff and Hearst opposed him vehemently in his newspapers. Over the years, Hearst attacked Smith for weakness on the issue of municipal ownership and, in general, for being a lackluster office-holder who did Mister Murphy's bidding. After Smith took the gubernatorial nomination over Hearst in 1918, the publisher instructed his reporters to aim their fire at the new State administration on any available issue. The first to arise was the spiraling cost of milk, over which Governor Smith had no regulatory power. Hearst's cartoonists depicted Smith as a friend of the "milk trust barons" and accused him of starving the babies of the poor. Smith challenged Hearst to a debate at Carnegie Hall. Hearst declined, but Governor Smith appeared and treated a full house to a memorable tirade against "cuttlefish" Hearst and his "Mud-gutter Gazette."

In his re-election bid in 1920, Governor Smith ran a million votes ahead of the Democratic national ticket, but it was not enough. Murphy had given critical support at the National Convention in San Francisco to Ohio Governor James Cox, and Al Smith seconded the nomination of Franklin Roosevelt for Vice-President. The Cox-Roosevelt campaign ran counter to the strong isolationist sentiment which was sweeping the country in response to Woodrow Wilson's internationalist policies, particularly the League of Nations. The conservative Republican slate of Ohio Senator Warren Harding and Massachusetts Governor John Calvin Coolidge came in on a landslide, winning every Assembly District in New York City except Al Smith's. Despite his own strong showing, Governor Smith lacked sufficient split ballots to weather the onslaught.

With Smith out of office, and with Mayor Hylan re-elected in 1921, Hearst was sure that his old dream of the governorship was at last at hand. Red Mike Hylan and Uncle John McCooey announced for Hearst. Mister Murphy stayed silent. The normal mystery of his preference was made even more baffling when he refused to give reporters his standard response: "The convention will decide." This time he said, "You never can tell." Whole columns were devoted to dissecting the significance of the new remark.

As the Democratic leaders trooped through Murphy's hotel room in Syracuse on the eve of the convention, it became evident to the young observer Ed Flynn that if Hearst were denied the nomination, the party would be split wide open. "Mr. Murphy would listen until they had concluded their arguments, and then he would simply tell them to call on Smith and repeat to him what they had said. When a delegation arrived and announced support of Smith's position, Mr. Murphy would say nothing. . . . I became convinced, as I watched Mr. Murphy's cautious treatment of the situation, that he and Smith understood each other thoroughly—that Mr. Murphy thought it necessary to maintain the appearance of neutrality while providing Smith with every opportunity to swing doubtful delegations over to his point of view. . . . Mr. Murphy was convinced that Hearst should not be nominated. . . ."

Fearing the import of Murphy's silence, Hearst sought an arrangement whereby he and Smith would share the state-wide ticket, one as a candidate for Senator, the other for Governor. Murphy and Uncle John McCooey were agreeable. Smith was resting a rheumatic foot in his hotel room when he learned of the proposed deal. He removed his cigar, spat into the cuspidor, and barked, "I'm damned if I will." As various leaders came in to plead with him, Smith remained adamant. "Nothing doing. Say, don't you think I have any self-respect? You can tell Murphy I won't run with Hearst on the ticket and that goes."

Hearst finally withdrew after he was allowed to name the Senatorial candidate on Smith's ticket: Dr. Royal S. Copeland, New York City Health Commissioner. Smith and Copeland went on to victory in the fall.

In his first term, Governor Smith had already dispelled the fears that he would be a Tammany hack Governor. He was perhaps the hardest working and most efficient chief executive in the State's history. He performed a major overhauling and streamlining of the bureaucracy, pushed through far-reaching social legislation, and brought in excellent appointees. Among the many in his brain trust were two distinctly non-Tammany intellectuals, the social worker Belle Moskowitz and Judge Joseph Proskauer, who were joshed in the song "Moskie and Proskie are the brains of Tammany Hall." (Robert Moses, also a close friend and advisor to Smith, recalled recently that the Governor had "an exaggerated respect for the learned professions.")

Murphy desired above all that Smith compile a good record for a shot at the Presidency, so he did not load down the Governor with patronage. Ed Flynn wrote that Smith "turned often to 'Boss' Murphy. . . . Mr. Murphy wanted Smith to succeed, and knew he could succeed only by having the widest latitude, by being given a free hand. . . . He could have checkmated the Governor by using his great political power. . . . In fact, Mr. Murphy seemed to me to be more interested in seeing that these political appointments might not affect the policies the Governor was fighting for than in any concern of his own about patronage. I do not think it is generally known, but it is a fact that Mr. Murphy was amazingly well informed about public questions arising in Governor Smith's second term. Mr. Murphy was as vitally interested in Smith's social reforms as anyone around the Governor."

Having accepted the inevitability of a vastly expanded role for government, Charles Murphy was anxious that his party and his "boy" should be the popular instruments for progress. In 1923, Smith and Murphy decided to go for the Presidential nomination which was up the following year. They began analyzing in detail Smith's actions as Governor for their impact on other states. The most ticklish decision came when Smith was faced with signing or vetoing the State Legislature's repeal of a Prohibition enforcement act. Both Murphy and Smith opposed Prohibition and had inserted a plank in the Democratic campaign platform to that effect. Murphy felt that the Governor was honor-bound to fulfill the platform pledge and sign the bill. But Smith feared for his Presidential chances with the "dry" wing of the party in the South and Midwest.

As the deadline neared for action, Governor Smith went to see Murphy at Good Ground. Ed Flynn was in the room when Smith announced he had decided not to sign the bill. "Mr. Murphy seldom lost his temper. His speech was normally economical of words, and he avoided vocal emphasis. But on this occasion he was deeply moved. Quietly but firmly he told Smith, 'Al, you will either sign this bill or I will never support you again, either for the Presidency or for the Governorship.' Whereupon he got up and left the room. Governor Smith sat for some time in silence. . . . Smith signed the bill."

Charles Murphy envisioned Al Smith's elevation to the White House as the final triumph of his own career. In the fall of 1923, he began work on luring the 1924 Democratic National Convention to New York. A series of dinners was held to enlist the financiers who had frequented the Scarlet Room in Delmonico's. Murphy was confident that delegates from throughout the nation would take note of the exuberant crowds which Al Smith collected wherever he went on the streets of New York. A group of prominent New Yorkers was sent to the Democratic National Committee's Washington meeting in January 1924, to propose New York as the convention site. The Democratic National Chairman, Congressman Cordell Hull of Tennessee, was exactly the kind of "dry" whom Smith feared when he repealed New York State's Prohibition enforcement law. It turned out, however, that Hull looked upon Al Smith as a courageous statesman, admired his administration in New York, and was pleased when the National Committee voted to bring the convention to the City.

The convention was scheduled for June 24 in Madison Square Garden. By April, Murphy had lined up nearly 300 delegates for Al Smith and many more were believed ready to hop on the bandwagon. Then suddenly, on the morning of April 25, the bandwagon came screeching to a halt. Charles Murphy awoke that morning at eight o'clock in his home on East 17th Street with an attack of acute indigestion. A doctor was summoned. He found the Boss on the bathroom floor in great agony. Murphy was pronounced dead at 9:05 A.M. He was sixty-five years old.

The Board of Estimate was about to meet when the news reached it. Hylan was speechless. Then he said tearfully and with lips quivering that the Board was too shocked to go on with its business of the day. The flags at City Hall and all borough halls were lowered to half staff.

"In Mr. Murphy's death," Franklin Roosevelt said, "the New York City Democratic organization has lost probably the strongest and wisest Leader it has had in generations. . . . He was a genius who kept harmony, and at the same time recognized that the world moves on. It is well to remember that he had helped to accomplish much in the way of progressive legislation and social welfare in our state."

At Mister Murphy's funeral, fifty thousand New Yorkers lined the sidewalks; six thousand filled St. Patrick's Cathedral; the wreaths at Calvary Cemetery formed a hedge six feet high. Among the pallbearers were J. Sergeant Cram, Red Mike Hylan, Bernard Baruch, and Al Smith. It was, according to one observer, the most impressive funeral since the death of President Grant.

Tammany Hall went into mourning for twenty-five years.

Chapter 9

The Interregnum

"The brains of Tammany Hall lie in Calvary Cemetery."
—*Jimmy Walker at the grave of Charles Murphy*

The 1924 Democratic National Convention—the first in New York in fifty-six years—turned the City into a roaring, steaming carnival. Fifth Avenue was festooned with strings of orange and blue lights, and the flags of the nations and the states. Madison Square Garden (the huge arena in those days actually was at Madison Square) was draped, tier upon tier, with red, white and blue bunting and thirty-five hundred American flags. Lavender and blue lights played upon pictures of Jefferson, Jackson, Cleveland, and Wilson.

As the delegates streamed into the City, they found New York offered much to distract them from platform planks and nominees: the Ziegfeld Follies; a special program of character sketches by Ruth Draper; a Rudolph Valentino movie, *The Sainted Devil*; and on Long Island, Johnny Weismuller swimming in the Olympic trials. The New York Giants were leading the National League, but in the American League, the Yankees, with Babe Ruth in a slump, were in second.

Many of the delegates wandered down to 14th Street to see the fabled Tammany Hall, where New York's last national convention had been held in 1868, when the Wigwam's own Horatio Seymour won the nomination. The awestruck visitors earnestly repeated William Jay Gaynor's mocking remark, "So this is Tammany Hall."

As the June temperature moved into the high 80's the Sunday before the convention, the delegates seemed united on only one mission. They loaded into one bus after another at Times Square and headed for the cool breezes and the apolitical crowds of Coney Island.

Despite Prohibition, Tammany Hall, the gallant host, conspired to make liquor available to the visitors. To the parched delegates from the arid West, New York was an oasis. Mayor Hylan led a Fifth Avenue parade of fifty bands and twenty-five thousand policemen, firemen, streetcleaners, and garbage collectors. In all, everyone was having a fine time, and the night before the convention, Will Rogers pronounced the whole affair a great success: "I would adjourn right now before they nominate someone and spoil it all."

The Democrats unfortunately ignored his advice, and the longest, and perhaps most bitter, convention in the political record book opened on Tuesday June 24. The leading contenders for the nomination were Governor Alfred E. Smith of New York and William G. McAdoo of California, President Wilson's son-in-law and formerly Secretary of the Treasury. The death of Charles Murphy two months earlier had left Tammany without a leader. Mister Murphy had been preparing to storm the White House gates with Al Smith as his candidate. Now Governor Smith, titular head of the party in the State, was left to manage his own floor fight. Babe Ruth gave him a baseball bat and said, "Knock out a nomination," but it wasn't quite that easy.

The convention opened, forty-five minutes late, with a blunder that was a harbinger of far more serious trouble ahead. Cordell Hull, the Democratic National Chairman, stepped forward to introduce Cardinal Hayes to deliver the invocation. He introduced him, instead, as Cardinal Gibbons, a prelate who had died three years earlier. With the audience in stunned silence, Hull corrected himself.

The convention was torn by three issues; Prohibition, the Ku Klux Klan and the League of Nations. Smith opposed Prohibition. McAdoo and his supporters were "drys." The Klan, with its virulent prejudices against Catholics, Jews, and Negroes, was heavily represented at the convention; and so were its opponents, especially the Smith faction, who wanted the party platform to denounce the Klan by name. In the third dispute, admirers of the deceased Woodrow Wilson called for a declaration urging the United States to join the League of Nations immediately; opponents wanted, at the most, to submit the matter to a referendum.

Al Smith, of course, was the popular champion of the galleries. The ovations which greeted each mention of his name would have warmed the heart of Charles Murphy, who had worked to bring the convention to New York in order to impress the delegates with Governor Smith's hold on the crowds. But some of the out-of-state delegates were antagonized by Tammany's attempt to railroad the nomination. Nearly three thousand visitors' passes to the convention mysteriously disappeared, and it was charged that they had found their way to 14th Street and were being distributed by the Tammany district leaders.

In his home territory, Smith was recognized as a kind of urban Abe Lincoln, a man of rough-hewn integrity, innate brilliance, and broad social vision. He was to New Yorkers so much the American success story that he would have been a cliché as a literary hero: born on the Lower East Side, left school at the age of twelve to support his mother, sold newspapers, worked in the Fulton Fish Market, climbed the political ladder, and now a candidate for the Presidential nomination. But in the eyes of many Westerners, and most Southerners, Al Smith was a Big City politician who talked the language of the streets, wore a brown derby, and incessantly smoked a cigar; a Catholic, a "wet," a product of Tammany Hall from beginning to end, the man who had served Boss Murphy in the clubhouse, in the State Assembly, in the Sheriff's office, in City Hall, in the Governor's mansion, and now, would extend the Tammany tentacles into the White House.

The name of William McAdoo, candidate of conservative respectability, was placed in nomination while the convention's resolutions committee struggled in a hotel room with the anti-Klan plank of the platform. The Californian's supporters, wearing "Mc'll Do" slogans on their hatbands, put on a thunderous demonstration. The next day, Franklin Roosevelt, crippled three years earlier by polio, was wheeled to the platform. Roosevelt, whose political career had begun as an anti-Tammany (and anti-Smith) insurgent in the State Legislature, struggled on crutches, to the lectern, gripped it with both hands and held his head high. Then he delivered the memorable speech in which, borrowing from William Wordsworth, he gave to Al Smith his *nom de guerre* "the Happy Warrior of the political battlefield." The previous day's outburst for McAdoo was completely obscured by a seventy-three minute, carefully prepared "spontaneous" demonstration. Amidst a cacophony of sirens, whistles, buzzers, drums, cowbells, and fishhorns, bands played, delegates marched, and an estimated 1,000 Smith zealots outside the building crashed the gate and joined the demonstration. By this time, Madison Square Garden, which was supposed to hold 14,000, was packed with 17,000.

It took three days to put sixteen candidates before the convention. Then came the showdown over the Ku Klux Klan. A proposal early in the evening to denounce the Klan by name touched off a battle that continued until 2 A.M. with William Jennings Bryan pleading throughout for harmony and unity. The anti-Klan plank was defeated by a single vote.

The next Monday, June 30, when the convention was originally to adjourn, the balloting began. On the first ballot, with a two-thirds majority (730) needed to nominate, McAdoo had 431; Smith 305. The next day, by the 30th ballot, McAdoo had 478; Smith, 323. And so it went Wednesday, Thursday, Friday (the Fourth of July), and Saturday, ballot after ballot. The magnolia tones of Alabama's Governor Brandon began each roll call with "Alabama casts 24 votes for Oscar W. Underwood," which was becoming the best known refrain in New York. By the Sunday recess, McAdoo had 513; Smith 367. The dark horses were still in the running and even Will Rogers had picked up two half votes.

Monday, the balloting started all over again. Finally, Roosevelt, representing Smith, proposed a joint resolution freeing pledged delegates. McAdoo refused: "I have never run from a fight." He suggested they switch from a two-thirds to a simple majority rule. Smith refused this. Eventually, they did release their delegates, and on the 103rd ballot on the night of Wednesday, July 9, John W. Davis, ex-Ambassador to England, was nominated as a compromise choice. Will Rogers, who had been writing a daily column on the proceedings, remarked that he would be glad to cover the next war for a fixed fee, but not the next Democratic convention.

The intra-party strife ruined any chance the Democrats might have had to win the election that year. Charles Murphy's absence was crucial. "In my opinion," Ed Flynn commented, "it was a badly managed convention. Had Mr. Murphy lived, it would never have reached the impasse that ultimately developed. I believe that he would have realized early in the convention the hopelessness of nominating Governor Smith, and that some suitable compromise would have been reached. . . . One of the most unfortunate developments was Smith's assumption not long before the convention of the active direction of his own candidacy. I believe it to be axiomatic that the opinion of a man who is a candidate for public office is not dependable in matters of political organization. His ambition gets in the way of his political judgment."

Al Smith was re-nominated for Governor to face Theodore Roosevelt, Jr. He was the only state-wide candidate to win for the Democrats. Calvin Coolidge carried New York State and swept the nation by almost 2 to 1.

After the fiasco of the 1924 convention, Tammany set out to pick a successor to Mister Murphy. The overwhelming choice was Murphy's son-in-law, Surrogate James Foley, whose intelligence and integrity had won the respect of all factions. Al Smith, the real party chief, urged him to take the job, but Foley wanted no part of it. Smith then endorsed Judge George W. Olvany, who resigned from the bench and was promptly elected by the Tammany Executive Committee.

Judge Olvany was chairman of the Tammany law committee and had handled the National Convention arrangements for Tammany after the death of Mister Murphy. With his highbridged nose and copper complexion, he was the only Sachem of the Tammany Society who actually looked like an Indian. Olvany lived in Greenwich Village and had graduated with honors from New York University Law School. (With the exception of the six-month wonder Lewis Nixon, he was the first Tammany Leader to hold a college degree.) During his early years on the Board of Aldermen, Olvany introduced few ordinances but he did achieve a certain distinction. It was said that one day a youngster poked his head into the Aldermen's chamber and shouted, "Alderman, your saloon is on fire!" Olvany was the only one to remain in his seat.

After one term as alderman, Olvany went into private law practice. Later he served as a first deputy fire commissioner and then as counsel to Sheriff Al Smith. In 1923, he was being considered for a Supreme Court judgeship, but there were so many aspirants for the position, he told Mister Murphy to leave him out of it. The Boss was pleased at the sacrifice and he gave Olvany the next available judgeship, a place on the Court of General Sessions. When he left the bench six months later for the Tammany leadership, Olvany formed a law partnership. Asked if the Tammany leadership might help his practice, Olvany replied with a grin, "Well, it won't hurt any." This would prove to be a masterpiece of understatement.

George Olvany was a new (albeit minor) species of Tammany tiger—a congenial "mixer," an effective public speaker, and a prolific writer. Some of his frequent statements were received with less than enthusiasm; for example, in the publication *World's Work:* "The Irish are natural leaders. The strain of Limerick keeps them at the top. They have the ability to handle men. Even the Jewish districts have Irish leaders. The Jews want to be ruled by them." On another occasion, Judge Olvany wrote of New York, in contrast to the scandals of the Harding administration, as "the cleanest and best run city in the world."

Governor Smith was not so sure. Nor did he intend to suffer any longer, now that Mister Murphy was gone, the influence of William Randolph Hearst at City Hall. Mayor Red Mike Hylan was up for re-election to a third term in 1925. Brooklyn Boss Uncle John McCooey saw in Hylan's re-election a chance to step into the power vacuum created by Mister Murphy's death. (The population of Brooklyn was now larger than Manhattan.) Ed Flynn in the Bronx decided that the best strategy to win recognition for *his* borough was to join with Smith and Olvany in running a primary fight against Mayor Hylan.

As he had with the Tammany Leadership vacancy, Governor Smith once more turned to the popular Surrogate James Foley with the offer of the Tammany nomination for Mayor, and again Foley preferred to remain on the bench. Smith then asked Supreme Court Justice Robert Wagner, Sr., who also declined. As a third choice, Flynn and Olvany proposed to Governor Smith the name of one of Mister Murphy's more colorful protégés, the Democratic leader in the State Senate, James J. Walker. Smith had severe reservations about Walker's work habits, but Flynn and Olvany remained firm.

The primary campaign pitted the Manhattan and Bronx organizations against Brooklyn, Queens, and Staten Island. Governor Smith campaigned vigorously for Jimmy Walker, denouncing Hearst at every turn and wringing from the publisher the admission that he was no longer a Democrat. Walker himself was a superb stump speaker. "I have never met a man with greater ability to absorb knowledge and express it to the public," Ed Flynn said. Jimmy Walker won a stunning primary victory, beating Mayor Hylan even in his native Brooklyn. The Republicans nominated Frank D. Waterman, the fountain-pen maker, who was crushed in the general election. After his primary defeat, Mayor Hylan gave begrudging support to Walker against Waterman, and he was rewarded by an appointment as a judge of the Children's Court. Asked why he had appointed his primary foe to this position, Jimmy Walker said, "Now the children can be tried by their peer."

James John Walker, a native of Greenwich Village, was the most dazzling spectacle to enliven the mayoralty since Abraham Oakey Hall. Like the elegant Oakey, "Beau James" was a sartorial delight and an accomplished quipster. Oakey Hall wrote poetry and plays; Jimmy Walker, a fair pianist, turned out lyrics for such forgettable numbers as "After They Gather the Hay" and "In the Valley Where My Sally Said Good-by" before hitting pay dirt with "Will You Love Me in December as You Do in May?" And, like Oakey Hall, Mayor Walker was irresistibly charming and utterly careless, surrounding himself with dangerous friends. The New York *Times* had prophesied at the time of Oakey Hall's downfall that "future Rings will learn by his splendid example how useful it is for a gang of thieves to keep one member of the fraternity to do the ornamental while they do the useful, to cover their swindling with his suavity, and, like another Claude Duval [a gallant highwayman], to lead the fine people gracefully from the coach to dance a corranto upon the heath while the ruder villains search the baggage for plunder at their ease."

Jimmy Walker represented the best and the worst of Tammany. He was a vote-getter and in many ways a compassionate liberal. And he was carefree and irresponsible in both his private and public life. The New York of the 1920's, the City and the time of a rocketing stock market, glittering speakeasies, and jaunty young flappers, welcomed a Jimmy Walker as Mayor. With his dimpled showgirl mistress, Betty Compton, he set the pace for the whole frantic City. "Gentleman Jim" was the beau of New York, who could shoot crap and assemble a municipal budget with equal facility; who eschewed Board of Estimate meetings for boxing matches; who three times daily changed his spats, derbies, and tailored double-breasted jackets; who escaped a gambling raid by donning a waiter's apron; who defined a reformer as "a guy who rides through a sewer in a glass-bottomed boat"—this was the only Mayor for the City in its *Walpurgisnacht*.

In Albany, Al Smith, a man of moderate habits, devoted to church and home, was re-elected to his fourth term as Governor in 1926. He had brought revolutionary changes to the State with bond issues for new hospitals, a vast parks program developed by Robert Moses, liberalized labor laws, a vigorous defense of civil liberties, and other programs which were later extended to the nation in Franklin Roosevelt's New Deal. The celebrated success of Governor Smith's administration overcame the dissension of 1924, and at the 1928 Democratic National Convention in Houston, Al Smith was once again nominated by Franklin Roosevelt as "The Happy Warrior" and this time won on the first ballot.

For the first time since the Tilden campaign, the Democrats chose a Tammany Sachem as their Presidential candidate. But Smith met bitter opposition to his anti-Prohibition stand, his Roman Catholic religion, and his Tammany associations. His appearance before five thousand whooping braves at Tammany Hall on the Fourth of July was well-publicized by the Republicans. In winning the election, Secretary of Commerce Herbert Hoover cracked the "Solid South" and carried Al Smith's home state. But Smith's choice for Governor, Franklin Roosevelt, eked out a victory with his running-mate Herbert Lehman.

Tammany's Independence Day rally in 1928 was the last such occasion at the 14th Street Wigwam. The property was being eyed as a potential office building by its neighbors, the Consolidated Gas Company and the New York Edison Company. Judge Olvany announced that the tribe would move to a building "more adapted to our needs" and word spread that the new site would be on fashionable Fifth or Park avenues. Instead, it was just three blocks north, on 17th Street on the east side of Union Square. "It's been found better for the sake of sentiment," Olvany said, "to remain on the East Side, not too far from the Bowery and close to the poor, hard-working voters." (It became apparent that talk of a fancy uptown location was a ruse to lower the asking price on the property that was really being sought.)

The old Wigwam was purchased for $700,000 by a real estate company which in turn sold it to the Consolidated Gas Company for a $70,000 profit. This maneuver left the Sachems wondering why Tammany could not have reaped that profit by selling directly. After hearing some subtle suggestions, the real estate firm announced, to the astonishment of the business world, that it was returning its profit on the transaction to Tammany.

As they were razing the old building, workmen found beneath a cornerstone the time capsule containing mementos of the 1860's implanted by Boss Tweed. These, together with current newspapers and a sketch of Tammany written by George Olvany, were sealed into the

cornerstone of the new Wigwam on 17th Street. This was and is a
four-story structure of brick with limestone trim, a colonial-style front
with peaked portico and a liberty cap medallion on the upper façade.
It had an 1100-seat auditorium on the ground floor, and a smaller meeting hall on the second floor where there were also offices for the New
York County Democratic Committee, the principal tenant. On the
third floor was an assembly room seating about 250, and a lounge and
offices for the Tammany Society, the building's owner. The whole
shebang cost just under $1,000,000—$600,000 for the site and about
$350,000 for construction—but this was the era of prosperity and
Tammany had more than its share.

The new Wigwam was dedicated on July 4, 1929. The traditional
Long Talks were delivered by Governor Roosevelt, ex-Governor Smith,
and Mayor Walker. Roosevelt warned of danger in the growth of big
business, and was cheered as "the next President of the United States."
Smith warned against encroachment on civil liberties and cited a recent
move to ban smoking in public. And Walker got a laugh by repeating
the Gaynor quip, "So this is Tammany Hall." But the center of attraction was Grand Sachem John R. Voorhis, who was about to celebrate
his 100th birthday.

Obscured throughout the proceedings was George Olvany. On
March 15, Olvany, a robust outdoorsman, had submitted his resignation to the county Executive Committee and given ill health as the
reason. Nobody believed the excuse. A possible explanation emerged
two years later when the Seabury investigation revealed that the law
firm founded by Judge Olvany had deposited more than five million
dollars in five bank accounts over seven years with most of the fees
coming from clients who had dealings with the City. The root of the
Sachems' dissatisfaction with Olvany was not that he had been un-
ethical, but that he had been too greedy. The other Tammany lawyers
wanted him out; he had virtually monopolized the market. His successor, they vowed, must not be a lawyer. And so after five years, it was
the end of the New Tammany and the rebirth of the Old.

Tammany's Big Four at that point were Al Smith, Jimmy Walker,
Surrogate Foley, and Robert F. Wagner, who had been elected to the
U.S. Senate in 1926. Mayor Walker got the jump on the other three
by calling a pow-wow of the district leaders to push his candidate, John
F. Curry. When the leaders met officially on April 23, 1929, they

elected Curry by a close margin over East Side district leader Edward J. Ahearn.

John Curry seemed to fit the mold of old-time Tammany leaders. He was not burdened by a college degree or, for that matter, a high school diploma ("geometry stumped me"). He grew up on the West Side of Manhattan where his father had a farm near what is now 60th Street and Tenth Avenue. Young Curry got his exercise by chasing cows and later ran the 200-yard dash for the West Side Athletic Club, played shortstop for the Palisades Athletic Club, and worked his way up from messenger to accountant at Western Union. He broke into politics under the sponsorship of his district leader Daniel McMahon, who was later a member of the post-Croker triumvirate.

Curry received his first City job in 1897 in the Comptroller's office under the Croker-Van Wyck administration. In 1902, he was elected to the State Assembly and two years later he toppled his aging patron McMahon from the district leadership. Curry maintained a profitable insurance business and plodded along in a series of government jobs until 1929 when he resigned as Commissioner of Records to become the leader of Tammany.

When he took over at Tammany, John Curry was forty-eight, with cold eyes, a square jaw, trim mustache, sparse gray hair, and neat conservative clothes. He didn't drink, didn't swear, and smoked only a few mild cigars a day. Each Wednesday he received Tammany's rank-and-file as he sat behind Mister Murphy's old roll-top desk shielded by a frosted glass screen in the richly paneled second-floor reception room of the new Wigwam. The braves waited in line for up to two hours just to shake hands with "Commissioner Curry" and exchange two or three words. In his background, demeanor and habits, John Curry resembled Charles Murphy—but for one slight detail. He was a political incompetent.

The twilight of the twenties was, for Tammany, the twilight of an era. The first warning was the death of Charles Murphy; then the defeat of Al Smith; and the murder of Arnold Rothstein, which upset an intricate web of arrangements between district leaders and gamblers. Jimmy Walker was dancing with Betty Compton to the music of Vincent Lopez at a Westchester night club when the word reached him that Rothstein had been shot. He was reportedly much disturbed. The Mayor replaced his Police Commissioner, who was also his former law partner, with Grover Whalen, the Wanamaker department store executive. Whalen had a considerable talent for greeting visiting dignitaries but the Rothstein murder was left unsolved.

On October 29, 1929, sixteen million shares of stock changed hands on the New York Stock Exchange with an avalanche of short selling. The fun was over. But New York didn't realize it yet, and Jimmy Walker was re-elected for a second term. His opponent was Republican Congressman Fiorello Henrico LaGuardia, who shouted that there was corruption in high places and no municipal effort to solve the Rothstein case. He was no match for the idol of New York.

At least one LaGuardia accusation was borne out shortly after the election. The bouncy little Congressman had accused Magistrate Albert H. Vitale of underworld connections, specifically of having borrowed $19,600 from Rothstein. A month after the election, Vitale was attending a testimonial dinner in his honor when six masked gunmen entered and stripped the guests of their valuables. Judge Vitale rushed back to his clubhouse and within hours managed to restore the money and jewelry.

Racketeers, emboldened by protection bought from Tammany politicians, were enlarging their jurisdiction. From bootlegging and gambling they moved into legitimate industries to levy tribute. Manhattan's elderly and docile District Attorney, Sachem Thomas C. T. Crain, seemed unable to win indictments despite evidence that mounted on his desk. Perhaps he had become cautious after boasting, upon taking office, that he would solve the Rothstein murder within fifteen days. Scandal rocked the judiciary. Vitale was removed. Magistrate George F. Ewald, who succeeded him, was accused of buying his judgeship from Harlem district leader Martin J. Healy for $10,000. He resigned.

Tammany's greatest mystery, unsolved to this day, began on a hot August day in 1930 when Supreme Court Justice Joseph Force Crater said goodbye to some friends in front of a West 45th Street restaurant, stepped into a taxi-cab, and was never heard from again. Crater had been appointed to the bench on the recommendation of Senator Wagner, for whom he had once worked as law secretary. The investigation into his disappearance revealed various intrigues—an affair with a divorcee, a suspicious real estate deal and a strong implication that he too had purchased his seat on the bench.

Governor Roosevelt called upon the Appellate Division of the State Supreme Court to investigate the Magistrates' Court of the City.

Samuel Seabury was named referee to conduct the investigation. This was the first of three Seabury investigations into the influence of Tammany Hall.

Following his resignation from the Court of Appeals and his defeat for the governorship in 1916, Seabury had turned to private law practice, where he made a fortune. One case alone, the settlement of the Jay Gould estate, which took ten years to resolve, netted him fees totaling one million dollars. Frosty and urbane, Seabury was a masterful advocate who specialized in appeals before the higher courts.

For his investigations, Seabury assembled a team of brilliant, eager young lawyers and named as chief counsel Isidor J. Kresel, who developed the *modus operandi*: a methodical, exhaustive search of a public official's financial records, including bank and brokerage accounts and tax returns, until buried treasure was uncovered. Then the embarrassed office-holder would be called upon for an explanation. After the investigation was underway, Kresel himself was enmeshed in a banking scandal by another skillful lawyer and a long-time enemy, Max D. Steuer, a Tammany stalwart. Kresel resigned as chief counsel to the Seabury investigation but eventually cleared his name.

As a result of the probe of the Magistrates' Court, two judges were removed and three resigned. A sixth died before charges were brought against him. Out of the hearings grew a series of recommendations for court reform, most of which were ultimately adopted.

One of the ousted judges was George Olvany's former co-leader, Jean Norris, who had been Mister Murphy's choice as the City's first woman judge. Judge Norris' jail sentences for prostitutes were the harshest handed down by any magistrate. Her percentage of convictions was the highest also, and toward this end, she displayed an ingenuous faith in the uncorroborated testimony of police officers. In one case, in which the defendant had been framed on a prostitution charge, Magistrate Norris gave the woman a hundred days in the workhouse despite strong evidence pointing to her innocence. It was later revealed that she had altered the official minutes of the trial to remove any hint that she might have violated the rights of the defendant.

Judge Seabury, though a stern moralist himself and the descendant of the first Episcopal bishop in the United States, was especially shocked at one of Judge Norris' rulings, in which a twenty-year-old girl, living in Greenwich Village with a boy friend, was packed off to a home for wayward minors. It was also disclosed that Judge Norris was a stockholder in a bail bond company and had allowed herself to be pictured in her judicial robes, testifying to the value of Fleischmann's Yeast as an aid to digestion.

Seabury's probe of the Magistrates' Court clearly revealed that judgeships were being bought and sold. Far more sensational was the disclosure of a vice ring that trapped both innocent women and prostitutes for purposes of extortion. The scheme involved policemen, bondsmen, lawyers, and a special *agent provocateur*, who would gain entrance to a woman's room, plant marked money, and remove his clothing. Then the vice squad would break into the room, arrest the female victim, and en route to the station house, recommend which bondsman and lawyer to hire. If she complied, the case against her would magically collapse. The most candid details of the vice ring were revealed by a $150-a-week *provocateur*, Chile Mapocha Acuna, later celebrated in song and story as "Chile Acuna, the human spittoona."

The second of the Seabury investigations looked into the affairs of District Attorney Crain in an effort to find out how racketeering and gangsterism could flourish in such unlikely places as the Fulton Fish Market, the garment industry, the kosher butcher business, and a score of other legitimate enterprises. Seabury concluded that although Crain was totally ineffective, he had not acted dishonestly and could not be removed from office.

The third and final act of the Seabury drama was the investigation of city-wide corruption. The sponsor was the Joint Legislative Committee to Investigate the Affairs of the City of New York with State Senator Samuel H. Hofstadter, a Republican, as chairman, and Seabury as chief counsel. After lengthy private hearings, the public hearings began with William "Horse Doctor" Doyle as the first witness. He was a veterinarian with political connections who became inexplicably wealthy not by treating horses and dogs, but by representing numerous two-legged creatures who were seeking zoning variances from the Board of Standards and Appeals. Doyle's only qualification for this service was his intimacy with the members of the Board. "Horse Doctor" Doyle refused to answer questions about alleged fee-splitting on grounds that it might incriminate him. He was then offered immunity from prosecution, but refused it and was sentenced to thirty days in jail for contempt.

At this point, Tammany leader John Curry took an interest in the case and prevailed upon an appellate division judge to grant a stay of the imprisonment order. Curry testified later that he was merely trying to test the immunity-granting powers of the legislative committee. Seabury urged passage of a law giving the committee formal power to grant immunity. Governor Roosevelt, never a warm friend of Tammany's, called a special session of the State Legislature; the law was passed and the hearings resumed.

Tammany's sensitivity to the whole subject of legal immunity gave rise to a lampoon parody by the Inner Circle, an association of City Hall reporters:

Tammany Hall's a patriotic outfit.
Tammany Hall's an old society.
Fourth of July they always wave the flag, boys,
But never will they waive immunity.

Seabury was convinced that corruption in City Government was so widespread that a century of hearings could not root it all out. He therefore went from borough to borough, picking out the major office holders and district leaders. Tammany Sachem Thomas M. Farley, like many of his colleagues, was both. He was Sheriff of New York County and leader of the Fourteenth Assembly District on the upper East Side. His clubhouse had been used as a casino for professional gamblers. Of greater interest to Seabury, Sheriff Farley had deposited $396,000 in his bank account during a six-year period when his salary and other visible income totaled $90,000. On the witness stand, Farley told Seabury that the larger sum represented "savings." Then Seabury inquired:

"Where did you keep these moneys that you had saved?"
"In a safe deposit box at home in the house."
"Whereabouts at home in the house?"
"In a big safe."
"In a little box in a big safe?"
"In a big box in a big safe."
"And, Sheriff, was this big box that was safely kept in the big safe a tin box or a wooden box?"
"A tin box."

Farley's bank deposits, year after year, it developed, came from this same miraculous source. Seabury asked:

"Kind of a magic box, wasn't it, Sheriff?"

"It was a wonderful box."

Seabury's treasure hunt took him to the official City marriage chapel in the Municipal Building, presided over by First Deputy City Clerk James J. McCormick, a Washington Heights district leader. McCormick had a reputation for stinginess, but even that could not explain how he accumulated some $385,000 in thirty banks over six years on an annual salary of $8,500. The secret was all in the marriage ceremony. While McCormick was performing the ceremony, for which the City had already collected the official fee of two dollars, he left open a drawer in his desk in which were displayed bills of various denominations. The bridegroom usually took the hint and happily contributed a few bills of his own, for which the newlyweds received a "God bless you" from Clerk McCormick. If the husband neglected the drawer, McCormick brought him to his senses by pointing to it and asking, "How about it?" When tips were inadequate, McCormick started the young couple out in life with a reprimand: "Cheap skate!"

From Brooklyn, where Uncle John McCooey had been Leader since 1909, a pair of delightful clowns brought more comedy to the Seabury hearings. One was James "Peter-to-Paul" McQuade, the Registrar of Kings County, who had deposited $520,000 in banks over a six-year period on a total salary of less than $50,000. He explained that he had borrowed the money, small sums here and there, to support his many poor relations, "the thirty-four starving McQuades." He repaid his loans with further borrowing, and thus earned his nickname. Unfortunately, he kept no records and could not remember from whom the loans had come.

The other Greenpoint citizen was Deputy Commissioner of Public Works Peter J. McGuinness, who referred to his area of docks and warehouses as "the Garden Spot of America." Seabury was curious about charges that criminals and professional gamblers frequented his clubhouse. McGuinness pleaded ignorance, and even praised the Police Commissioner for raiding the place. "All my congratulations to the Commissioner," he said, "for breaking up this incubator of crime, which flourished under my unconscious aegis."

Some of the subjects of the Seabury probe were punished, others were relatively unaffected. "Tin Box" Farley was removed from office by Governor Roosevelt, who ruled that a public official whose scale of living and assets obviously exceed his public salary, must account for the source of his excess funds. Clerk James McCormick, the high-priced cupid, went to jail for income-tax evasion. But Jim McQuade, saviour of the thirty-four starving McQuades, was rewarded by Mc-Cooey with the Brooklyn Sheriff nomination, and, of course, was elected.

The grand climax of the hearings came on May 25, 1932, in the New York County courthouse. The courtroom was filled, and crowds of disappointed curiosity seekers were turned away and waited outside. At 11 A.M. Chairman Hofstadter gaveled the hearing into session, and Judge Seabury turned to James J. Walker and said, "Mr. Mayor, would you be good enough to take the stand?" The Mayor, nattily attired as always, stepped forward briskly and took the witness' chair. Seabury offered him a waiver of immunity. Walker slipped on a pair of horn-rim glasses, read the document, and signed it. Then Seabury, leaning against the oak railing, began the questioning.

The interrogation of Jimmy Walker continued for two days. Judge Seabury delved into a bus franchise awarded to the Equitable Coach Co., which the Mayor had pushed through the Board of Estimate despite more favorable bids from competitors (and despite the fact that Equitable had no buses). He questioned him about a joint brokerage account he shared with publisher Paul Block, to which Walker had contributed nothing, but from which he netted $246,692. He asked him about a safe deposit box maintained by an accountant who had abruptly fled the city. And he asked about $26,535 in bonds he had received as profits from a transaction in which he had invested nothing.

Through it all, Walker parried wittily, to the delight of the audience. When it was all over, he walked out of the courthouse and a group of excited ladies threw roses at his feet.

Judge Seabury sent a transcript of the testimony to Governor Roosevelt with the recommendation that he remove the Mayor from office. Before the Governor reached a decision, Jimmy Walker and the rest of the Tammany delegation were off to Chicago for the 1932 Democratic National Convention, where two of the principal contenders were Roosevelt and Al Smith. The Empire State Delegation was torn, with Ed Flynn of the Bronx and James Farley of Rockland County fighting for Roosevelt, and John Curry, leading the Tammany contingent, backing Smith. (Curry had no great love for Smith, but he disliked Roosevelt more.) When the New York delegates were polled,

Jimmy Walker, despite Al Smith's coolness toward him, and despite the fact that his fate as Mayor was in Governor Roosevelt's hands, stood up and cast his vote for Smith. Al Smith exclaimed: "Good old Jimsie! Blood is thicker than water."

Roosevelt won on the fourth ballot. His victory was attributed to three main factors: Huey Long's vigorous work in his behalf among the Southern delegations; William Randolph Hearst's longstanding hatred of Smith and his influence in swinging the California and Texas delegations to Roosevelt; and Tammany Hall's fierce opposition to Roosevelt, a fact well-circulated among the other delegates by Farley and Flynn. After the convention swung to FDR, Tammany refused to make the nomination unanimous. Curry and his braves sulked in their seats while the victory parade swept by.

On August 11, the Democratic Presidential candidate, in his capacity as Governor, opened hearings in Albany on removal proceedings against the Mayor of New York City. The nation pondered FDR's predicament. If he removed the popular Mayor, he could alienate the huge City electorate. If he failed to do so, he might be considered soft on Tammany corruption. Walker solved the problem abruptly on the evening of September 1 by resigning as Mayor. Roosevelt declared the removal hearings at an end and the question of whether he would oust Walker was never answered. Jimmy Walker exiled himself to Europe.

Roosevelt and Al Smith united in pushing for the nomination of Lieutenant-Governor Herbert H. Lehman for Governor. Curry, in another display of obstinacy, defied them and opposed Lehman. He yielded, an hour before the balloting, after Smith and Roosevelt had threatened to denounce him on the floor of the State convention. Al Smith said that if Lehman were not nominated to succeed FDR, he would run for Mayor "and take the town away" from Curry. "On what ticket?" Curry asked. "Hell, on a Chinese laundry ticket," Smith replied.

Succeeding Walker as acting Mayor was the president of the Board of Aldermen, Joseph V. McKee, an ex-school teacher who demonstrated real ability and a certain bent for reform. He was from the Bronx and was Ed Flynn's choice for the mayoral nomination the following year. Curry opposed him and named instead Surrogate John P. O'Brien, an apparently capable and honest judge but untested as an executive. O'Brien won the special election to finish Walker's uncompleted term, although Flynn's candidate McKee received an astonishing write-in vote of 335,000. When O'Brien took office, he was asked who his Police Commissioner would be and he replied with characteristic resolve, "I don't know. They haven't told me yet."

The following year, 1933, the full four-year mayoralty was at stake and the election was a wild scramble. Curry forced O'Brien onto the Democrats as the regular party nominee. The Republicans and Independents, led by Seabury, bickered and squabbled, but finally agreed on the irrepressible LaGuardia. And Ed Flynn, with a blessing from Jim Farley and the White House, sent McKee into the arena as the candidate of the hastily assembled Recovery Party. The campaign was both dirty and amusing, with O'Brien, dubbed "the Wild Bull of the China Shop," providing many of the laughs. It was O'Brien who told a Harlem audience, "I may be white but my heart is as black as yours."

LaGuardia, however, was a linguist, and, reminiscent of the McClellan campaigns, spoke Yiddish in one ghetto, Italian in another. McKee accused LaGuardia, who had fought for dramatically progressive social legislation in Congress, of being a Communist. LaGuardia accused McKee of anti-Semitism and unearthed a magazine article that McKee had written thirty-three years earlier which contained a slur against the Jews. President Roosevelt remained silent on the campaign, and both the McKee and LaGuardia forces interpreted this as an endorsement for their man.

On Election Day, LaGuardia was kept busy chasing thugs out of polling places. LaGuardia won, but the combined vote of the other two candidates would have beaten him. The new Mayor turned quickly to the task of rehabilitating a city with an unbalanced budget, a city that couldn't meet its own payroll or market its bonds, combat its racketeers, or fight its way out of the Great Depression.

The press began a new campaign, "Stamp out Curryism!" Tammany faced hostility from LaGuardia in City Hall, Lehman in the Governor's Mansion, and Roosevelt in the White House. With patronage cut off from all three sources, Tammany itself was ready to stamp out Curryism. The district leaders called for his resignation but he refused to quit. One leader, commenting on Curry's attitude toward Roosevelt and Lehman, remarked, "John may be honest, but he doesn't seem to understand politics. Whatever you say about Tweed, Croker and Murphy, they knew a winner when they saw one."

On April 21, 1934, at a night meeting of the Tammany Executive Committee, John Curry was ousted as Leader. It was the first time in

Tammany history that a Chief had been scalped by his own braves. Leaders had fallen, but none had ever been voted out of office. Two months later, after the intractable Judge Foley had again refused the post, James J. Dooling, a forty-one-year-old bachelor, was elected County Leader, till then the youngest ever. Comedian Jack Benny punned his congratulations: "Dooling, we are growing old."

Dooling was a college man and a lawyer, hearkening back to the kind of respectability that Tammany had forsworn five years earlier with the departure of Olvany. But he was careful to point out: "I was always more interested in beer than in Aristotle." Jim Dooling came from the West Side, just above the Hell's Kitchen district, where his father had been a district leader for thirty-nine years. He attended Fordham College and was a star halfback on the football team, which provided him with a frequently broken nose and the proper rough, tough look that was expected of a Tammany leader. Dooling practically grew up in the clubhouse. When his father died, Jim inherited $100,000 and the district leadership.

The new Tammany Leader had a deep resonant voice and flashy dressing habits. One newspaper, observing his first four days in office, noted that Dooling wore four completely different outfits, not quite up to Jimmy Walker's three-a-day. There is no doubt that Dooling was popular and had real ability. He came to office with the backing of Postmaster General Jim Farley, and after a few months had made some progress toward uniting the Hall's rival factions. He seemed to have a promising career, but trouble was ahead.

The Democrats were making one of their periodic attempts to reapportion the State Legislature and break the grip of upstate Republicans. However, because Manhattan had been losing population to the other boroughs, reapportionment could only weaken Tammany. Dooling couldn't deliver the votes from his county for reapportionment, and Farley began looking about for another leader. A movement to oust Dooling began, but the rebels couldn't muster enough votes; and when they thought they had, they couldn't agree on a successor. Then, on July 26, 1937, the youthful, athletic Jim Dooling suffered a stroke and died.

For their new chieftain the Tammany braves returned to an old-style leader: sixty-seven-year-old Christopher D. Sullivan, the last of the old Sullivan clan, one of Tammany's most illustrious families. Christy was a cousin of Big Tim Sullivan, who had ruled the Bowery, and a younger brother of Florrie Sullivan, the ham-handed giant who had fought his way up to Boss of the Eighth Assembly District ("De 'Ate") on the Lower East Side. Christy, who was in the real estate business at the time, took over his brother's district when Florrie died in 1909.

Sullivan was elected to Congress in 1910 and held his seat there until 1940 when he retired to devote full-time to running Tammany Hall. Throughout his years in the House of Representatives, there is no record of his ever having made a speech, a silence worthy of Mister Murphy himself. He was shy and taciturn, cared little for books; in fact, it was almost as if Tammany, in mournful desperation, had chosen the shadow, if not the substance, of the mighty Mister Murphy.

From the golden days of Murphy, Tammany Hall had plummeted into a disastrous Interregnum. For more than two decades, the tigers of Tammany were harmless cubs. Their political judgment was such as to offend the State's leading Democrats. Their allies were racketeers and Communists. Even Al Smith, always proud to be one of "Murphy's boys," could stomach it no longer. Tammany's heroes owed their allegiance to Mister Murphy, not to the Hall. So did many respectable donors, who shifted their coffers to Murphy's political godson, Ed Flynn, Boss of the fast-growing Bronx, confidant of the President and, along with Democratic National Chairman Jim Farley, dispenser of Federal patronage in New York. While Tammany lost election after election, Ed Flynn's Bronx machine never lost one.

LaGuardia had sailed into power after Flynn and Farley conspired to split Mayor O'Brien's vote. And now the "Little Flower" used Tammany as his whipping boy, to the delight of an admiring President Roosevelt. The New Deal compounded Tammany's woes. Already, drastic immigration quotas had cut the supply of Tammany dependents. Immigrants had reached their peak in 1907 with 1,285,000. By 1933 they were down to 23,000. Now began vast welfare programs to displace the baskets of turkeys and bushels of coal. Tammany's very own, Robert Wagner, Sr., pushed his Social Security bill through the Senate, as well as labor laws, unemployment insurance and public works programs. And Senator Wagner, while always loyal to the Hall, maintained neutrality in the duel between Roosevelt and the series of ineffective Tammany leaders. Add to this the shrinkage of Tammany's power base (at the turn of the century, more than half the City's population was in Manhattan; by 1930, only twenty-five percent) and the situation cried out for nothing less than a Mister Murphy. But not even a Richard Croker was at hand.

With the approach of the 1937 mayoral election, Tammany turned to Senator Wagner as the only candidate of stature who could unite the party and win the city back from LaGuardia. He chose to stay in the Senate. There followed a bizarre contest for the Democratic mayoral nomination with Christy Sullivan and the anti-New Dealers supporting Senator Royal S. Copeland, who had turned against the Roosevelt policies, and the other leaders supporting Grover Whelan. Whelan withdrew in favor of Jeremiah T. Mahoney; Copeland entered the Democratic and Republican primaries and lost both. Finally, La-Guardia swept past Mahoney in the general election and carried most of his running mates with him, including the Republican candidate for District Attorney, Thomas E. Dewey. Fiorello LaGuardia was the first Fusion mayor of the century to win a second term. Tammany prepared for four more hungry years.

Among those who had opposed Sullivan for County chieftain was James J. Hines, a muscular ex-blacksmith from the upper West Side. He was a maverick district leader allied with Jim Farley and the New Deal faction. In earlier days, Hines had fought off several of Murphy's challenges for his district, and even came close to beating a Murphy candidate for the Manhattan Borough presidency. After this, Mister Murphy left him alone. Hines was untouched by the Seabury investigations. Speaking frankly to an interviewer, he said he attributed this good fortune to the fact that he kept no bank account. The formula for his political success was a simple one:

"A man comes to me, any man. A man I never saw before or heard of. I don't know whether he's Republican or Democrat, but he wants something, and even before he's through talking, I am trying to see if there isn't some way I can satisfy him. Well, I do satisfy him. He votes for us. So do all his relatives. You know they do. He's grateful. He feels good toward us. We gave him something he wanted."

Hines helped people, and seemed to like doing it. He was enormously popular in his community, and thus it was a sorrowful day when, in 1938, he was indicted for selling protection to Arthur "Dutch

Schultz" Flegenheimer, king of the numbers racket. Dutch Schultz had refined the policy game by pouring huge amounts of money across the pari-mutuel windows and thus manipulating the winning numbers. Hines was alleged to have been paid five hundred to one thousand dollars a week by Schultz for providing an important service—the fixing of police and judges so that Schultz could practice his trade.

District Attorney Tom Dewey, looking older than his thirty-six years with the help of a bristling black mustache, was already being mentioned for the Presidency in 1940, after perhaps a quick sitting in the Governor's chair. He built his case against Hines on testimony primarily from turncoat conspirators. Dutch Schultz had been murdered three years earlier. In fact, of nine persons named in the indictment, eight were dead, missing, or witnesses for the State. Jimmy Hines stood trial alone. Dewey called for a Blue Ribbon jury, and after the lengthy impaneling process, the trial finally began before Supreme Court Justice Ferdinand Pecora, who in 1933 had run for District Attorney and lost to Hines' candidate. Pecora, a respected jurist, declared a mistrial because of a prejudicial question by Dewey. Despite the setback, Dewey won nomination for Governor, but lost to Herbert Lehman in a close race. He returned to his District Attorney chores, prosecuted a new trial against Hines and won a conviction. Jimmy Hines went to jail; Dewey was again on the road to Albany; and the Gallup poll showed him to be the favorite for the presidential nomination. He would have to wait four more years for that prize.

In 1941, Mayor LaGuardia won an unprecedented third term, beating Brooklyn's District Attorney William O'Dwyer. On election night, Christy Sullivan sat in his office at Tammany Hall, with just a few close friends. Unlike the old days, no district leaders, no captains flocked to the Great Wigwam to cheer for victory. Christy slipped out a side door as the returns piled higher on his desk. It was Tammany's third straight city-wide defeat, two of them under Sullivan's stewardship. The inevitable movement to oust Christy Sullivan gained momentum. He refused to resign and on the night of February 6, 1942, the Executive Committee removed him by a close vote. Six months later, the last of the Sullivans died of a heart attack at the age of seventy-two in his clubhouse on Grand Street, over which he had presided for more than thirty years.

Two months after Sullivan's overthrow, the front pages were headlining the siege of Corregidor. On page twenty-two of the New York

Times was the story of a new Tammany leader, Congressman Michael J. Kennedy, who beat former Sheriff Daniel E. Finn, Jr., son of Battery Dan, a downtown leader of legendary proportions. Among the reforms proposed at that Tammany meeting was one by Jeremiah Mahoney for the direct election of district leaders by the rank-and-file voters rather than by the district captains. Mahoney also suggested that the New York County Democratic Committee abandon the name "Tammany." Both proposals died at the time but would soon be raised again.

Michael Kennedy was a likeable, jowly young man from Hell's Kitchen who enjoyed prizefights, but had recently developed more patrician interests. He had a country home up the Hudson River valley in Peekskill where he played golf and raised Irish setters and Airedales. He had been a City Marshal for fifteen years and was now in his second term in Congress, where he was a strong supporter of Roosevelt's program. It was generally assumed that he had Roosevelt's endorsement for the Tammany leadership. After his election, Kennedy issued a prepared statement in which he said, "I am committed to no man or group of men," and pledged that he would seek candidates "of character and ability."

One of his candidates was Thomas A. Aurelio, who had a good record as a magistrate and in August 1943, was nominated by both Democrats and Republicans for the State Supreme Court. Shortly thereafter, Frank Hogan, Dewey's successor as District Attorney, made public the following telephone conversation, which his staff had wire-tapped:

> "When I tell you something is in the bag, you can rest assured."
> "Right now I want to assure you of my loyalty for all you have done. It's undying."

The man pledging his loyalty was Supreme Court nominee Aurelio. The man who put things in the bag was a fifty-two-year-old philanthropist with national business connections named Francisco Costiglia, otherwise known as Frank Costello, ex-convict, bootlegger and slot machine king.

When the news broke, Kennedy asked Aurelio to decline the nomination. Aurelio refused. The Democrats tried to rescind the nomination, but Aurelio blocked the move in court. He survived a disbarment proceeding, and went on to win election to a fourteen-year term on the Supreme Court, where he compiled a creditable record and was retained beyond the statutory retirement age. Meanwhile, at the disbarment hearing, Costello freely admitted that he not only helped Aurelio get his position, but also helped Mike Kennedy get his. He said he had persuaded four district leaders, old friends of his, to vote for Kennedy. Another of his friends in the Wigwam, he said, was Bert Stand, Tammany secretary since the Dooling period.

The Aurelio incident finished Kennedy. He resigned the following January and Edward V. Loughlin of Yorkville, secretary to Judge Pecora, was elected the new Tammany Leader. Loughlin's name was placed in nomination by a young man from Greenwich Village, Carmine DeSapio, who had recently wrested his district leadership from Danny Finn, playboy son of the ex-Sheriff.

Loughlin's first public utterance as the Boss of Tammany had a familiar ring. "I became leader without having made commitments to anyone...." Though Kennedy was out, Costello's other acquaintances remained. Bert Stand continued as secretary and Clarence H. Neal, Jr., one of the four co-operative district leaders, became chairman of the powerful elections committee. Mike Kennedy had made the sacrifice for all. To keep themselves pure, his old friends ostracized him. "He sits in the bedroom crying," said a member of the family. "The phone don't ring no more." During his regime, Michael Kennedy would have been happy if the phone had rung one less time.

Ed Loughlin was a Chief without a Wigwam. Tammany, out of power since 1933, was broke. During the first LaGuardia term alone, membership in Tammany clubs dropped seventy percent. With no jobs in the patronage pipeline, there was little incentive to contribute to the organization. And Manhattan was now polling some 300,000 to 400,000 fewer votes than Brooklyn. In 1943, The Society of Saint Tammany, or the Columbian Order, held its last meeting at 17th Street and Union Square.

The Great Wigwam, which had cost $950,000, was now burdened with a mortgage of $205,000. The Council of Sachems authorized the sale of the building, and Local 91, the children's dress unit of the International Ladies Garment Workers Union, bought it for $250,000. Jimmy Walker remarked, "I never thought I'd live to see the tiger get skinned." The Sachems—Al Smith, Dan Finn, Sr., Jim Foley, Mike Kennedy, John O'Brien, and John Curry among them—trooped up-

town to take up residence with the National Democratic Club in a
Madison Avenue mansion. The New York County Democratic Committee also moved up Madison Avenue, to an efficient eight-room
office suite. A gallery of Tammany pictures, flags, and relics was
loaded into two moving vans and trucked to a warehouse in the Bronx.

In 1945, LaGuardia chose not to run again. The Democrats heaved
a sigh and turned out in massive numbers for Brooklyn's Bill O'Dwyer.
He received some help from a new ally, the American Labor Party,
which had been fostered by Roosevelt and LaGuardia. The best the
Republicans could offer was Judge Jonah Goldstein, an ex-Tammany
man. O'Dwyer won in a landslide. The twelve lean years were over.

Bill-O, they called him, the Democrats' new champion, a six-foot,
200-pound Irish immigrant who landed here in 1910 with $23.35 and
began the upward climb: laborer, ship's stoker, plasterer, longshore-
man, bartender, policeman, lawyer, magistrate, County Court judge,
Brooklyn District Attorney, brigadier general, and the 100th Mayor of
the City of New York.

A feud with Tammany erupted early in his term. The new Mayor
demanded an overhaul of the old sputtering machine and withheld
that valuable lubricant—patronage. Complicating matters was another
power struggle, a revolt by Tammany's new Italian faction led by
Carmine DeSapio against the Irish. DeSapio turned against Loughlin
and joined O'Dwyer to force his resignation. This opened the way
for the election of Frank J. Sampson, O'Dwyer's hand-picked man,
as Tammany Leader. It also meant the end for Bert Stand and
Clarence Neal, who had become as powerful as the Leader himself.
Neal viewed the situation stoically. He reported that he had given this
piece of advice to the new Chief, Sampson:

"I told him he's going to be surrounded by the worst crowd there
is in the world, and for him not to go out for a walk near a cliff, with
any of that crowd near him. . . . Unless he's got a couple of guys around
him that he can trust, he'll have to spend his whole time as leader
walking like this." Neal dramatized the point by spinning around the
room with his hands thrust in his pockets.

Sampson had been a West Side district leader for less than two
years when he found himself in the delicate position of having to support the Mayor and control the district leaders. They resented him
and the Mayor immediately. Their chief act of defiance involved the
coveted office of Surrogate—the judgeship that carries the power to

dispense lucrative estate assignments to lawyers. O'Dwyer favored City Council President Vincent Impellitteri. His opponents, led by De-Sapio, who had switched sides again, proposed Supreme Court Justice Louis A. Valente. When the Bar Association opposed Louis Valente, the DeSapio group switched to his nephew, General Sessions Judge Francis L. Valente.

Eventually the Democrats agreed on a compromise candidate, but a Republican won the election. During the struggle, O'Dwyer threatened to form a rival organization: "Leave Tammany Hall down in the gutter where it belongs." Noting Tammany's enthusiasm for the Surrogate post, he said, "I will have nothing to do with the scavengers who plan to get rich on orphans' money."

Frank Sampson lasted less than a year. In an attempt to bring peace between City Hall and Tammany Hall, the Executive Committee hit on the idea of replacing Sampson with one of O'Dwyer's own running mates, Borough President Hugo Rogers. The committee promptly elected him, then sent a delegation to his office in the Municipal Building to give him the bad news. He was the new leader of Tammany Hall.

Rogers was the first Jewish Leader of Tammany Hall. (Mordecai Noah, a century earlier, was Grand Sachem but not the political leader.) He immediately extended the olive branch, but O'Dwyer spurned it and continued to deal out patronage through Sampson. In July 1949, fifty-three weeks after his sudden rise to the county leadership, Rogers was toppled. The new King of the Hill was Carmine DeSapio.

Hugo Rogers was left without even the borough presidency as a consolation prize. His re-election was coming up that year, but De-Sapio insisted that he withdraw from the race in order that the beleaguered Tammany might find someone more acceptable to the Mayor. Agreement was finally reached on a man with a distinguished name and an unscarred record—the chairman of the City Planning Commission, Robert F. Wagner, Jr.

Chapter 10

Carmine DeSapio in the Smokeless Room

"Sad it is to see the young men of today . . . They don't care no
more for firecrackers on the Fourth of July."
—*George Washington Plunkitt*

Not long before Ed Flynn died, he remarked: "Carmine DeSapio is
the first Tammany man since Murphy who I can sit down with and
not have to talk out of the side of my mouth."

Flynn died in 1953 and his mantle of power in the City was passed
over the East River to DeSapio. Flynn had respected and aided De-
Sapio in much the same manner as he himself had been respected and
aided by Charles Murphy. Each in turn had instinctively recognized
a fellow aristocrat of machine politics.

Carmine Gerald DeSapio, a young second-generation Italian-
American, found a home in the Tammany Hall that had succumbed
to the affluence of the underworld. By dint of character and circumstances, he was purported to be both the last of New York's old-time
political bosses and the first New Leader of the modern machine. His
career was the tragedy of a man broken on the wheel of these two

images, as a Tammany politician and as an anxious seeker struggling toward the elusive American Dream.

Old Chief Tamanend, his feathers drooping sorrowfully, was steered to Madison Avenue by Carmine DeSapio for a new image. The surface rationale was a simple one: dirty teepees lose votes. (Or, in the words of LaGuardia, "Dirty money brings bad luck.") DeSapio sought to gain for Tammany, and for himself, the comforting rewards of acceptance. He took to this task with extraordinary ability. He also displayed the most compelling need for public recognition since Richard Croker. It seems clear that this need was deeply personal, for it led to a fatal political error, and DeSapio worked tirelessly to avoid political errors. By virtue of his total involvement, DeSapio rose rapidly to national prominence and tumbled overnight into oblivion.

Unlike the reclusive Mister Murphy, whose power thrived on secrecy, DeSapio undertook to sell himself, his policies, and his machine to the nation at large. He hired a skilled publicist to write speeches, blanket the press, help map strategy. He became a constant lecturer at banquets, forums, college conferences. "I am the Leader of Tammany Hall," he declared before astonished students at Harvard Law School, "I bear this title with gratitude and pride. I am proud of the tradition, the heritage, the record of Tammany Hall." Profiles of this "new kind of Tammany tiger" (most of them markedly similar) were serialized in newspapers, sent out over the wires, spotlighted in the major magazines. ("Carmine DeSapio," quipped an Ohio daily, "grew up believing that any man could be Postmaster General of the United States.") DeSapio's advance obituary fills six columns in the morgue of the New York *Times*.

The personality sketches followed the pattern of columns on Hollywood stars. He didn't smoke, he drank a scotch or two once in a while, sometimes tea; he really had wanted to play big league ball; he and his family were fond of song fests in the living room; he had bottles of eyewash on all his desks; he bought his conservative $75 dark blue suits at the store of Brooklyn Borough President Abe Stark; he wore banker's striped ties, gleaming cufflinks, starched collar, but seldom a hat; he liked Italian food but didn't speak Italian (once at a dinner he had accepted a diplomat's invitation to visit Italy without realizing it).

"Politics is everybody's business," DeSapio said ten thousand times, and "In business you pay off on performance" and "Every business has a boss." He was a man exhorting the skeptical masses to believe in him as a respectable leader in a respectable profession.

It was an aggressive program, but its substance was defensive. Political machines, once they had ceased to be the welfare centers of urban neighborhoods, were highly vulnerable to the most casual attack. Mayor LaGuardia knew this well. Mayor Robert Wagner, Jr., a product of the Tammany machine, finally got the message. To gain control of a party organization, reformers have learned that the best strategy is to attack its very existence, thus capitalizing on the rebellious emotions of those who feel left out, whether they be ethnic groups, outraged idealists, or frustrated favor-seekers.

In particular, this tactic has worked wonders with the young. DeSapio came to power, and lost his power, partly through the strenuous efforts of hard-working young reformers in the fast-changing Greenwich Village community. When he first ran in a fierce primary fight for Tammany district leader from Greenwich Village in 1939, he was a thirty-year-old insurgent candidate, a rallying point for the burgeoning Italian population in southern Manhattan. His people sought a voice in the Tammany Hall that had been tightly controlled by the Irish since the fall of Boss Tweed. It was a power struggle with little reference to doctrine, similar to that night in 1817 when the Irish forced their way into the Hall and demanded to be seated.

The naked appeal of DeSapio's candidacy in 1939 was his role as the Italian challenger. In the 1950's, the new Greenwich Village insurgency, which sought to unseat DeSapio, was sparked by a militant Jewish middle-class. But this time more was at stake than a subcultural pie-slicing. The latest reformers appeared less concerned with group standing, long since established in professional achievements, than with the implementation of their ethics. Their interest lay more in the realm of ideas and policies than bread and butter. They gave their all for Adlai Stevenson. (Tammany did not.) Their political clubs held panel discussions on international affairs. (Tammany kept the wolf from the door.) They searched out votes in every corner of the precinct. (Tammany relied on its faithful.)

For the anti-DeSapio reformers the day was ultimately carried by the tide of history. After the disillusionment with Jimmy Walker, New York City's voters responded to candidates presenting credentials, however slight, of independence: Fiorello LaGuardia ("I've never belonged to any political party for more than fifteen minutes."); William

O'Dwyer ("This Tammany is nothing but a gutter club"); Vincent Impellitteri ("A vote for me is a vote against Tammany and Frank Costello"); and Robert Wagner, Jr., son of a courageous New Deal Senator, sponsored in 1953 and 1957 by clean-out Carmine DeSapio and the "New Tammany."

Tammany Hall under DeSapio saw the writing on the wall. It supported numerous enlightened municipal programs and appointments. But when Mayor Wagner sought the reform vote for a third term, the machine's ancient evils were uppermost in the minds of the citizenry. Tammany's "secret battalion of corruption," which the Mayor promised to clean out of his own City Hall, was an effective campaign slogan even with sophisticates who might otherwise have smiled at its melodramatic overtones.

We have seen that, given a mighty emperor, the rule of Tammany can reach into the other boroughs of New York City, the Statehouse in Albany, the caucus rooms of the Democratic National Convention, and, with luck, the patronage pantry at 1600 Pennsylvania Avenue. By 1956 it appeared that DeSapio, America's most celebrated Boss, had annexed the boroughs and the Statehouse, was awaited by trembling princemakers in the caucus rooms, and soon would be tasting the meringue on the White House pie.

He had miraculously survived a crow dinner with his first mayoral candidate, Ferdinand Pecora, to feast with his second, Robert Wagner, Jr., on the steak and potatoes of a landslide victory. Better yet, he had claimed a seat at the Governor's table by the difficult feat of delivering that table to Averell Harriman. Said Adlai Stevenson: "If it were my ambition to seek the Democratic presidential nomination, I would welcome the support of Carmine DeSapio and Tammany Hall." Quoth Joseph and Stewart Alsop: "He could name the next president."

It was this omnipotent DeSapio who conquered the cover of *Time* ("the worldly and weighted mien of a Medici"), the rostrums of great universities, and television screens across the nation. His dark glasses and fastidious attire became legendary. His avowed goal—the creation of a modern, moral Tammany Hall to bring the people spotless public servants—was lauded by a wide journalistic spectrum. His reputation for selecting and projecting candidates made him the "politician's politician."

Beyond the respect for DeSapio's skill and influence was a widespread curiosity about his motives and personality. Who was he? He didn't seem to fit into the comfortable stereotypes we assign to public figures. There was something a bit disquieting about the apparent ease with which he moved between backrooms of brawling politicos and parlors of wealthy liberals. His obsessive concern with clothes, grooming, speech, protocol, and courtesy, struck many as incongruous. Was he not, after all, a ruthless politician, spawned in the squalor of New York's Little Italy, catapulted to eminence in a machine well-connected with the underworld? Or was the dignity of his bearing and espoused ideals to be taken at face value? Why did he hide behind those dark glasses? How well did he know racketeer Frank Costello? What caused him to nip in the bud the promising career of a President's son? Was he sincere, as one journal asked, or "sincere"?

On one item there was general agreement. DeSapio was, as Speaker Sam Rayburn once described himself, "a man of considerable power." The emblems of authority he wore gave him apparent command of a vast party structure which affected the lives of millions. At the lowest level, he represented his precinct (Washington Square) as county committeeman. He represented his district (Greenwich Village) as district leader. He was New York County Leader, County Chairman, Executive Committee Chairman, and ex-officio State Committeeman. He was President of the National Democratic Club and at one time Secretary of State in Albany. At the summit he represented New York State on the Democratic National Committee. He was the youngest Tammany Boss in history, the second to install both a Governor and a Mayor, the first ever to sit in the Governor's cabinet, and the first to serve as National Committeeman.

Yet within the space of a few hours on September 7, 1961, Carmine DeSapio was off the throne, rudely yanked to the castle floor in the climax of a frenzied primary election which only conditioned New Yorkers could regard as of this earth. The revolution was led by Robert Wagner, Jr., who aroused the citizenry by pledging to purge New York of his patron DeSapio, and to outdo DeSapio's Mayor—Robert Wagner, Jr. In a bizarre upset, with no precise parallel in modern politics, the Mayor ran against his own record, crushed the political machinery which had supported his City Hall, and emerged as the victorious Reform Mayor. In Greenwich Village, DeSapio lost the district leadership which he had first won twenty-two years before. Ironically, because of party reforms instituted by DeSapio, the drubbing he took in his district automatically ended his twelve-year reign as

Tammany ruler. And as a coup de grâce, the neighbors on his block denied him election as a member of the County Committee numbering 3,328.

It was the worst blow suffered by Tammany Hall since the death of Charles Murphy. For thousands of party regulars it spelled the end to a chapter in the annuals of the Hall which even the enlightened Mister Murphy would not have predicted. By any accounting, Tammany had become under DeSapio the best publicized and least corrupt political machine New York City had ever seen.

It was not, however, without its acts of arrogance, forgotten promises, petty scandals, and "honest graft." Nor, as it turned out, was it what the voters wanted. Tammany's transformation in the 1950's, with DeSapio perched at the pinnacle, was part rhetoric and part reality. Barely had he begun to consolidate his position in the Hall when bright young foes appeared with stronger claims on sainthood. A former insurgent himself, DeSapio sought to keep peace with the strangers in his political household by stealing their thunder on reforms. At the same time, he was obliged to pull along his old supporters, whose reverence for him was tainted by a growing suspicion that maybe he meant what he said.

Politicians, as H. L. Mencken viewed them, are "all scoundrels without exception. Especially that is true of the reformers. I've known politicians by the thousands all my life and I'm here to tell you that the most pleasant men, and on the whole the most honest of 'em, are what are ordinarily looked on as machine politicians." Compared with the Tammany bosses of yesteryear, as well as many of today's reformers, DeSapio may well be remembered in the future as the most pleasant and the kindest of men. He lacked the ruthless strategic genius of Charles Murphy or Aaron Burr. Nor did he have the corrupt audacity of Croker, Tweed, or Fernando Wood. What he shared with them all was a driving ambition to conquer the world from which he was alienated. This same sense of loneliness dominated the lives of all the Tammany Bosses.

In the best and worst sense, Carmine DeSapio was a kind of urban American folk hero, worthy of as much pride as shame. He arose from something in our national character—crude, unkempt, warmly genuine —that is fast disappearing. He strove to secure himself in that segment of our tormented ethos—polite, tidy, chilling,—that may yet do us in. It was his misfortune that, though in both psyches he was made first a hero and later a villain, in neither could he be accepted as a human being.

To the young intelligentsia who fought him with unusual ferocity, DeSapio was that nightmare of the advance guard—the Squarest of Squares. But his real appeal, on the contrary, was as a great outsider. He commanded attention and extremes of emotion because his sense of drama gave force to that role. His thrust to fame—and the consuming anxiety which underlay it—was on a straight line to catastrophe. He was a victim of his own myth, an image of his person and power which he himself came to believe. Those who aided in bringing him low also believed in the myth. It was resented by the old people he left behind, and it was feared by the new people he could never catch up with—the insiders, whose admiration he valued most highly.

On the second floor of the Biltmore Hotel near Grand Central Terminal is a long, empty hallway. In the mid-1950's this corridor was full of life, swarming from dawn to sunset with flocks of chattering pilgrims and supplicants. Many of them had little in common. There were flabby, middle-aged men with strong cigars, mumbling importantly to each other, anxiously keeping vigil on the doors off the corridor. There were young, tight-lipped attorneys with new briefcases, stalking the carpet impatiently, glancing quickly at expensive watches. There were dowdy old women in homemade Sunday best, laughing and gossiping, eyes shining with hope.

All were there for the same reason: to catch one glimpse of a tall, benign-looking man called "The Bishop." The lucky ones would be standing in his path when he walked down the hall. They received warm handshakes from Carmine DeSapio for their troubles and gentle words of reassurance. Others, not so lucky, might kill half the day before he emerged again. But in the end, he would see them, listen sympathetically, and best of all, he would never say no.

Walking down that same hallway in December 1961, three months after the downfall of DeSapio's Tammany, it was quiet as death. You could hear the muffled sound of your own footsteps as you approached a door, unmarked but for a hotel room number. Inside was a small, dusty waiting room, with boxes of old files on the windowsill and in the corners; and one chair—an armchair with a faded print facing a blank wall. On the wall behind was a large oil painting of President Roosevelt. It was in the Biltmore that FDR, with Ed Flynn and Jim

Farley at his side, received the returns which spelled national victory in 1932.

The next room was larger, yet even more austere. Most of it was in shadow. There was one window, its blinds closed. Far across the room, in the center of a wide desk, a small lamp glowed. Coming out from behind the desk to pull up a chair for his visitor was Carmine DeSapio, his face, deeply tanned, indistinct from a distance, placed in darkness by the white shirt, the white suspenders, the tinted glasses, the surrounding gloom. It was surprising to find him in shirt-sleeves— a crack in the sartorial image that decorated his banner—but all buttons were buttoned and a gray silk tie had been knotted with precision.

DeSapio looked, as always, as if he had just got in from the barber-shop. (Enemies say he has enriched both hairdressers and corset-makers.) His jet black hair, beginning to thin in spots, was combed in a high wave, with handsome streaks of silver brushed back carefully along the sides.

He looked to be an inch or two over six feet, a big man, broad-shouldered but trim, maybe 200 pounds. He had the rigid posture that could bump into low doorways, and the graceful movements to duck without your noticing it. His face was long and intense. On that December day, something was gone from the mysterious set of his features which once conveyed potentials of benevolence and ruthless-ness. There was a gentler, tired expression. The hard jaw which alienated the television public was relaxed. But underneath the serenity were hints of a tension that had still to run its course. "No one on this earth," a friend says, "has ever heard him laugh."

Exchanging pleasantries, assessing trust, one noticed that there were no mementos on the desk, only the lamp and a few scattered papers with scribblings of phrases, numbers, and box doodles. There was no ashtray in the room. High on the wall behind the desk was a small photograph of President Kennedy. It bore no inscription.

DeSapio reported with charm that there had been a "temporary slackening of activity." He smiled at this fleeting parody of the terror of defeat. The smile disappeared as he continued in the slow, deferen-tial manner that once infuriated and captivated thousands. "But . . . in spite of everything . . . I must remain a realist . . . This sort of thing . . . it was in the air. It comes in cycles. In the meantime, I'll be watching, and . . . if the wind blows right . . ."

Edward Costikyan, the bright, affable young attorney who succeeded DeSapio, was correct when he said: "Carmine doesn't know
how badly he's been hurt." DeSapio was thinking of another time—
after his defeat with Ferdinand Pecora—when he rose up from the
dead to engineer his greatest triumphs. "You see, it was worse then,"
he recalled. "It was tense, all the time. Now I can relax. I have nothing
to lose." Gradually, he began to warm to his reminiscence of hard
times. It was not nostalgia. Not once did he refer that afternoon to
his days of divinity. It was memory in the present. Always the thought
was with him: Back then is Now. I just might do it again.

From the turn of the twentieth century to the First World War
more than three million Italians, caught in the crush of overpopulation,
emigrated to the New World of Christophe Colombo. Those who
settled in New York came under the immediate care of the Tammany
barkeeps, though their votes were as yet more welcome than their
company. Quick naturalization, weddings, jobs, rooms, coal, food—all
were available for the faithful. "Ninety-nine out of a hundred," Ed
Flynn wrote years later, "want jobs first and political theorizing afterward."

Tammany's district leaders could easily afford such favors in exchange for the votes that put them in reach of the big money for
themselves. But to the lost Italian immigrant, the machine provided,
regardless of its motives, the only helping hand in an indifferent city.
(In Italy itself, the Tammany system of sustenance for votes is the
basis for the enormous Communist Party registration among peasants
who are totally ignorant of Marxist dogma.)

In lower Manhattan, where the rents were cheap, the new immi-
grants moved in on the old Irish strongholds. Into Al Smith's Lower
East Side, eminent domain of Big Tim Sullivan, poured thousands of
Jews, Poles, Lithuanians, Italians, stretching westward into Greenwich
Village and Aaron Burr's Richmond Hill, bailiwick of the Finns and
the Farleys.

Three generations of Dan Finns held the Tammany leadership in
south Greenwich Village. Old Battery Dan was accorded the fanciest
funeral the Village had ever seen. Battery Dan, Jr., ruled the Manhattan Sheriff's office he was to pass on to his playboy son. He presided
over the Huron Club on Spring Street, a combination saloon and
meeting hall where the needs of the poor were tended to while the

liquor flowed. The Huron Club's Election District, a classic piece of gerrymandering, looked like a pigeon perched on Broadway, its back along the Hudson River, its tail feathers reaching down toward the Battery. The head of the pigeon, carved out to escape the wealthier North Village where Tammany's Michael Farley was in trouble, reached up to Charles Street, its eyes looking out on Bleecker Street, its beak jutting out to Seventh Avenue along Christopher Street.

The Finn dynasty watched warily as strangers moved into the brownstones on the old Irish streets running to the Village piers. There were Jewish families from Russia and Poland, a pocket of Lithuanians just above Canal Street, a sprinkling of Portuguese, and, in increasing numbers, the hopeful vanguard of Little Italy. On Van Dam Street, around the corner from the Huron Club, Charles Passanante, a prize fighter from the province of Avellino in southern Italy, had settled down with his bride to nurture five children and a paper supply firm. Three blocks south, on Grand Street, another husky Avellinian married a seventeen-year-old second-generation girl named Marietta Diorio. The Diorios had started a small hauling business and their daughter and son-in-law put a dozen horses in the stable and kept the wheels rolling. Marietta's husband, who sailed over at age ten from the tiny village of Monteforte Irpino, was named Gerald De-Sapio.

In early December 1908, Marietta DeSapio went into labor for nearly a week. From all over the neighborhood, Avellinians came running to the household. Many stayed in the house, bedding down at night, feasting by day, laughing, shouting, shaking the rafters with songs of the old country. On December 10, the infant's cry was heard and the celebration continued for three more days. "When my Carmine came," says Marietta DeSapio, "it was like a king was born."

"In those days . . . I can remember it so . . . well . . ." DeSapio, sitting in the dark hotel room, paused to search for a better word. "Vividly . . . My most vivid memory is of that long line of people— women and children, everybody—standing all the way down the block from the Huron Club, waiting for the baskets of turkey at Christmas-time."

He began to relax and his big hands, tensely folded in his lap, broke apart and cut through the air as his mind turned to a warmer climate, long since grown cold. As he talked, one recognized how deceptive it

would be if words were reported such as "d'toikies in dose days."
DeSapinese is a unique language, merging the dialects of Greenwich
Village with the rambling embellishments of the seminar room. (A
sample public utterance: "You cannot continuously insult the intelligence of the people!" Or: "The employment of semantics in order to
create a gratuitous dichotomy ill becomes the New York *Times*.")

It is always a delight for mortals to discover that one among the
mighty commits Grand Street elisions amidst five-dollar participles. Al
Smith, who grew up at the other end of the Street, numbered it among
his virtues. But DeSapio, uneasy in the high councils, lacked a sense of
humor about it all. DeSapio did not speak from the comic underworld
of Damon Runyon, nor was he comfortable with the social scientific
jargon he painstakingly acquired. On his guard, he treated each syllable
as a word, each word as a sentence. The pattern of dialect changed
with the nature of the subject. In his speech he reflected the "dichotomy," to borrow his word, of his strivings. To his "boys" he could be
a succinct street-talker. To strangers he was charming, soft-spoken,
laboriously articulate. Neither of these could be called an "act." They
were both very much DeSapio, two different but equally honest responses to two worlds of which he was a peripheral inhabitant.

This is not to say that he was no actor; he was an uncommonly
good one. He instinctively communicated with nuance and gesture
to the unconscious mind of the audience. He tested his audience with
indirect forays, sized it up quickly and perceptively, guarded himself
against any uncomfortable demands, and delivered that part of himself
that he could share at that moment, slowly, cautiously, with the
candor of hints. At that moment, having abandoned a short political
science lecture which had not struck home, he was sharing, with little
calculation, that line of women and children waiting for their turkeys
at the Huron Club.

"They were lined up along the sidewalk, a very long line, waiting
for the baskets. They would all pile in there and get the veg-e-ta-bles
and turkeys and clothes and whatever else was in them baskets. It
was fascinating . . . I first went over there before voting age . . . maybe
about seventeen. I would drive around to help deliver the baskets and
the messages. Sometimes, you know, I'd be able to help out. Say, some
family I knew was in trouble, and they might be down at the bottom
of the list submitted by the captains, so I'd put aside a basket for
them, put it over in a corner. Sure. I was a cheat. But they needed help

badly ... I went there every night because of the human aspect. I was fascinated by it. I was always fascinated by *people* ... as far back as I can remember. You just don't see sights like that any more ... This was a way to be close to them and to help them. And being a boy in this neighborhood, I suppose it ... gave me a feeling of ... importance. It was a big thing ..." He smiled with a trace of embarrassment. "Nothing seemed quite so important as telling Mrs. Caruso or Mrs. Jones that there was a message for her husband, or telling somebody in trouble not to be disheartened, things will be looking up, the captain will be around to see you in the morning, and he don't have to worry. Taking messages around and making appointments for people to meet ... it seemed like a big thing ... But I don't want you to misunderstand me. I did it because I liked helping people. I didn't do it to make myself important ... I just don't want you to misunderstand me ..."

There is a photograph of DeSapio at seventeen, the year he went to the Huron Club. Boyhood acquaintances remember him as being no slouch at baseball. (His younger brother Marty signed with a farm team.) But this picture does not show a carefree lad just in from the sandlot. The DeSapio of 1926—handsome, sombre, unsmiling—looked deeply distracted. Wheels were clicking, springs were tensing. You feel that as soon as that photographer stopped wasting young Carmine's time, he'd run out with a message for Mrs. Caruso. Another photograph, taken ten years earlier at first Communion, is an astonishing likeness of the adult DeSapio. This looks like a boy who has already learned something of cruelty. He is braced for the next attack. At seven years of age the proud Roman nose, the hard set of the eyes and mouth, the rigid pose of regality were already established characteristics.

The tension of DeSapio's later plight in Tammany Hall—a struggle to fuse the old and new worlds—was foreshadowed on the sidewalks of his youth. He was an intensely ambitious "guinea" in a "mick" neighborhood. From the taunts of his earliest schoolmates, he found protection in the affectionate bond between Italian families scattered through Greenwich Village. He was a withdrawn child, sensitive to both insult and praise, quietly industrious, determined to please his parents. One may guess from the nature of the household the one daydream that he allowed himself: to be an American. Gerald and Marietta DeSapio came from strong stock. Their life was a warm but a tough one. They minded their p's and q's and expected the same of Carmine. Though

Gerald had difficulty with English, it was the only language permitted
in the house. Hard work was the road to success. Fidelity to one's word
and one's friend was assumed. "That boy never got in one bit of trouble
that I heard of," says an elderly Italian woman. "He was our favorite.
It was us ladies who put him in office, maybe you didn't know. Every
mother on the block wished she had a boy like Marie's son Carmine."

When he was attending parochial school, not yet in his teens,
DeSapio was down on the docks before sunup loading the drays, tending the horses, minding the accounts in the office. After school, Carmine and his brother Marty would take a seventh-inning stretch to
case the neighborhood for prospective customers. Honors were small
but meaningful: a blue ribbon at thirteen in the parade up Fifth Avenue from Washington Square, walking the year's prize work horses.

Life in Greenwich Village was not all libertarian fervor and esthetic
pioneering. For most of the South Village, the Bohemian flowering
was a thing unknown. "North of Bleecker Street," an old-time Villager
recalls, "we never knew what was going on up there. That was another
world. It wasn't just artists on the street, or beatniks, or whatever you
want to call them. There were Republicans behind every bush. A
Democratic assemblyman up there even voted for the Seabury investigation! Naturally, he was taken care of in the next primary. Tom
Curran's club was up there. Herbert Brownell came out of it—Tom
Dewey ran his first campaign. Nothing like that in our neighborhood.
After a while, more of us settled in and all the racialism disappeared—
maybe a little now and then, but the kids grew up together, you understand. It was like a small town. A real village. I can tell you the name
of every family that was on my block and the next one. Not like now,
you understand."

Memory may be a soothing liar on occasion, but there are some
things to be believed. Song, it recalls, was a part of the life, in cold-
water flats and fancy speakeasies. Outside, the sky could still be seen
and the street was a park; you learned to dodge the horse manure.
In the winter, tough Irish cops turned their backs while the small fry
unplugged the fire hydrants and flooded the pavement for skating. In
the spring, baseball started promptly after Mass, Sunday mornings. The
best game to be had was in Hudson Park, on St. Luke's Place, where
Jimmy Walker, pride of the Huron Club, would teeter in from his night
on the town to umpire an inning in his tuxedo before falling into bed.

But there was a harsh vein running through the gaiety of the South

Village which can still be felt today. Someday you were going to grow up. Were you going to boil your water, hang up one suit in the closet, eat a bowl of spaghetti for lunch? Some people seemed to have it made —like those wheels who hung around the Huron Club.

Sheriff Dan Finn built a swanky new clubhouse for his son on Van Dam Street. On the ground floor was a huge meeting hall for Saturday-night dances, beefsteak dinners, and, incidentally, meetings. Upstairs was a three-room apartment for the lucky caretaker, a spacious lounge for the poker-players who canvassed the precincts, a well-stocked bar and kitchen to nurse their spirits when the going was rough, and Finn's private office where father and son kept tabs on confidential woes. The Huron Club was the bastion of the proletarian elite, the only civic center in that small town where you could drink a glass of whiskey with a feeling of deep importance. It was an off-duty haven for stevedores, cops, bootleggers, cobblers, salesmen, and a handful of striving, tenacious puritans like Carmine DeSapio.

"There were good things about him," said Patrick Joseph Sullivan, an early friend who turned against "The Chief." "He was very patient. He had fine manners. He'd never swear, but maybe once or twice at someone, and that when he was alone with me. I've never seen him get angry in public. And there's something crazy about that. Here is a man who for thirty-five years I've never heard so much as whistle or hum. There's something strange about a man like that."

None of DeSapio's friends (Joe Sullivan was the closest) really appeared to know him. They talked of him as if they had watched him on the stage as a character in an unreal drama. Another Village friend turned back the clock: "Even then, he wasn't the kind of guy who would open up to you. I always liked him. He was a very sentimental guy, you wouldn't guess that. Cultured. Kind. But I don't think he'd spill his guts to anybody."

DeSapio's early schooldays were at St. Alphonsus on Thompson Street. Joe Sullivan went to St. Anthony's on McDougal Street. Catholicism was a force in bringing together the Irish and Italian families. St. Anthony's Church, then largely Irish, today has a predominantly Italian congregation.

Yet the real center of the neighborhood—the gateway to America —was an offshoot not of the Vatican, but of Tammany Hall. Prayer was one thing. Worn shoes and overdue doctor's bills were another. And you learned early that for every turkey there was a vulture. The altruism of the South Village, epitomized by the Huron Club, had its darker side: a search for recognition at any cost—if need be, violence. The absurdities of Prohibition, passed down from the hallowed Capitol, heightened the cynicism which Tammany instilled in its followers. Law and justice were fine print taken care of by Mister Murphy's judges and Dan Finn's Deputy Sheriff down the hall. Fiorello LaGuardia, running for Congress as a young man, covered every block in the Village, pilloring sinners in Italian and Yiddish. But the Congressman he could not beat was Michael Farley, president of the National Liquor Dealers Association.

Every immigrant group contributed its share to the underworld of impatience. Irish, Italian, Jewish, German, Anglo-Saxon gangsters roamed the Greenwich Village waterfront, infiltrated the unions, muscled in on downtown political clubs, motored down from Long Island in the night with bootleg for thriving speakeasies. They were powers to deal with, men not easy to ostracize. When the ice broke in the spring, the bodies of unco-operative longshoremen floated up on the Hudson. You didn't forget. On rare occasions, if the press cried aloud long enough, some of these men cooled off in jail. But more of them prospered, invested in gambling and legitimate enterprises, contributed to religious and ethnic charities, became dark princes in the Hall of Tammany. During DeSapio's rise to the top, nearly one-half of Tammany's clubs were controlled by the rackets. When DeSapio and Joe Sullivan attempted to persuade an East Side attorney to run for the State Assembly, he answered fearfully, "They wouldn't give me permission."

Inside the DeSapio home of the 1920's (a groundfloor flat where an occasional horse would cut through the hallway to reach the street) the prey was not so easy. The family was respected in the community. Business was going well and Carmine was sent to Fordham Prep. To the joy of his parents, he brought home honor report cards. "They were close," a family friend recalled. "It was a warm family. His mother wanted him to be a judge. I think she would have preferred that. His father just wanted him to be a success. Carmine teased him a lot. They had fun together. He must be near eighty by now, but I wouldn't want to tangle with him. Strong as an ox." (Gerald DeSapio, a stocky, powerful man, died in early 1966. He would have been cheered to know that a few weeks later, at the annual County Committee Dinner, the loudest and longest round of applause went not to Senator Robert

Kennedy or the host of gubernatorial hopefuls, but to Carmine De-
Sapio.)

But there were two reasons for parental concern about their oldest
son. One was the fierce energy he was burning up on the lower rung
of the political ladder, a ladder which had its treacherous rungs and
uncertain summit. The other was a sudden attack of rheumatic fever.

In the dark hotel room at the Biltmore, where there was no ashtray
in sight, DeSapio, staring, unblinking, tried to recall. "I don't remember exactly when. It was long before the new drugs . . . I remember
it hit all over the body. There was no heat in the house, of course, so
we put hot bricks under the mattress and I slept on top of them. You
had to keep the whole body warm . . . The eyes are the weakest part
of the body. They had to suffer the most . . . I'm always aware of them.
The pain comes and goes, but there is a constant feeling. When I go
down to Florida, it's very relaxing . . . swimming . . . the salt water,
you know, is good for my eyes . . . Now, like this morning, I had a few
dates around town, I was out in the open, that's when I feel it the
most . . . For a period of ten years . . . until seven or eight years ago
. . . I was in the hospital three or four times a year. Today, with the
new drugs, it isn't so bad. I carry it with me wherever I go . . . But in
the sun out there, I really feel it. My eyes will redden . . . you wouldn't
notice it, you couldn't see it from over there . . . My glasses will get
misty. I have to change them every couple of hours."

He leaned onto the desk and pulled up the lampshade slightly.
"I read like this, you see." He pulled it up farther so the beam covered
the papers before him. "You would read like this, but that's too bright
for me. Now, if . . ." He pulled up the shade and the light glared full
in his face. For a long moment he held it there, his face only a few
inches from the lamp, staring hard into the harsh ray of the bulb, the
spotlight, the cameras, the Eye. "I couldn't . . . take that for very long."

Through the eyes, perceivers and betrayers, the world comes in,
the self goes out. In an arena of smoke and bright lights, DeSapio's
iritis provided a tidy angle of incongruity for the press. Yet he appeared
to be painfully aware there was a psychogenesis to his affliction. The
nerves are sensitive not only to surface irritants, but to the tensions
of his life. When the pressures are greatest, the pain mounts. It is a
measure of the cross-currents which beset DeSapio that he was forced

to protect his eyes from the glare of his surroundings. From behind the shaded glasses, he watched.

Those currents conjoined to torment in college—that point where the generation is suddenly torn from its past. At Fordham University, DeSapio took well to the humanities, poorly to the sciences. His iritis erupted and he withdrew. Later he tried again with night classes at Brooklyn Law School. DeSapio's interests narrowed to the perilous, yet comforting, game of grass-roots politics. Throughout his career he read rarely, avoided theatres, relaxed infrequently with a swim or a night at the prize fights.

Two years before City Hall fell to LaGuardia, the first Italian district leader, Al Marinelli, was seated by Tammany Hall. The primary election on the East Side was a bitter one, marked by torn ballots and broken jaws, but when it was over, the first foot was in the door. In Greenwich Village, Sheriff Finn was preparing to pass on his kingdom to his son. Charles Passanante was forming the rival Manhattes Club on Houston Street. DeSapio's friend Joe Sullivan had left the docks for the police force. The DeSapios had sold their firm to American Express, shifted into real estate, moved from Grand Street to Dominick Street. DeSapo was now twenty-two, his dreams of hanging out a shingle shattered.

Henry Ford had provided a boon to canvassers as well as bootleggers. DeSapio tore through the streets of Manhattan, sometimes as chauffeur for a Tammany law clerk, more often to deliver those baskets of turkey. He was the youngest precinct captain in the city. His personal following grew larger, and more expectant, each year.

The first offer of solid financial support—to run for the State Senate—came from unsavory elements on the East Side. DeSapio turned it down. Aside from the mobster taint, there was the unhappy prospect of certain defeat. A man with secret aspirations, dangerous ones if known, had best stick to home base. DeSapio stood close to the Finns and the Huron Club. Danny Finn came up for his father's shoes in the primary election for Tammany district leader from Greenwich Village. He was opposed by a corps of young Italian lawyers grouped around Charles Passanante at the Manhattes Club, but the Irish hierarchy was still all-powerful. Danny Finn entered the Hall and captain DeSapio was rewarded for his loyalty with a $3,500-court job.

There was reason for the Finns to be generous. The DeSapio and the Passanante families were close friends. (Charles Passanante had

given young Carmine his first job in a warehouse on Varick Street.)
Passanante's Manhattes Club was drawing a good share of the educated
Italian community which was disgruntled with the Irish Tammany
machine. And the most popular precinct captain in Greenwich Village
was the Huron Club's Carmine DeSapio, an energetic worker for that
machine. His defection to the reformers would have meant the loss
of a large following.

Passanante's Manhattes Club became a spearhead for a reform
movement which was sponsored by Governor Lehman and President
Roosevelt through Ed Flynn. They did manage to defeat Tammany's
candidate for Mayor in the 1937 primary election (Senator Royal
Copeland), thus giving re-election to LaGuardia, a nominal Republican.

This was an omen of the schism that divided New York Democrats
in the political wars of the Kennedy-Johnson era. The old-time Tammany regulars were split from the young reformers who triumphed over
DeSapio in 1961 under the sponsorship of Mrs. Eleanor Roosevelt and
the same Herbert Lehman. In 1962, however, Herbert Lehman, then
eighty-four and still active and exceedingly influential with the voters,
surprised the Greenwich Village reformers who were opposing the
re-election of Tammany State Assemblyman William Passanante, De-
Sapio's godchild and son of Charles Passanante. Perhaps remembering
the early role of the Passanantes in the reform movement of the
1930's, and the liberal record compiled by young William, Lehman
publicly announced for the Tammany candidate. This played a decisive
role in preventing reformers from their goal of ousting all of DeSapio's
associates regardless of ability.

The Finns' worry in the 1930's that DeSapio would defect to the
Manhattes Club was misplaced. He was busy cultivating the Irish
regulars. He would need them when the time came. And there was
another reason for waiting his turn. The year he was rewarded by the
Finns with the court job, he fell in love with a girl he met at a dance.
She was Theresa Natale, a lively, attractive secretary from across the
Hudson. They were married in Hoboken on the last day in January
1937, and settled down in a modest apartment on Charlton Street in
the Village. The older DeSapios were now doing comfortably in real
estate, having opened a batch of summer cottages on Long Island.
DeSapio helped out in the business, but he was now firmly committed
to a political career. "The Bishop"—as he became known owing to the

gravity of his dress and demeanor—supported Finn against the Man-hattes reformers once again in the primary that fall. He was rewarded with a secular title—Deputy Sheriff at five-dollars-a-day. He lost his more lucrative court job when his judge lost the election. But he continued to pick up support for his personal banner.

Danny Finn, DeSapio's leader, was two generations away from the legendary Battery Dan, with little taste for the rough old world of Tammany. Jimmy Walker set the style for Danny Finn's brand of politics, though Finn lacked the wit to be more than a dilettante. The Huron Club gave way to Times Square. Whenever Danny dropped in on Van Dam Street for a drink with dull company, he found his affairs in order. The Bishop had seen to everything. In the neighborhood the word was changing to: "Go see Carmine." This kind of gossip has put ideas into many a shrewd political head. (When young LaGuardia discovered that a Tammany Congressman was neglecting to treat the Greenwich Village boys to their usual rounds, he nearly took his seat in the House on that issue.) And so it was that one spring evening in 1939, Danny Finn was calling his Huron loyalists to order while Carmine was out working the neighborhood. Old Dan Finn looked anxiously around the room and interrupted his son: "Better hold up the meeting, Dan. Till Carmine gets here."

It was time for The Bishop to gather his flock. DeSapio resigned in June as Tammany Deputy Sheriff, left the Huron Club, established his own headquarters in Greenwich Village's Sheridan Square, and set his sights on Danny Finn's district leadership. He called his insurgent club Tamawa (a fictitious Indian name of his invention) and welcomed allies in and out of the Huron and Manhattes Clubs. Enthusiastic support came from the women, grateful to be included in the smoke-filled world of their husbands. The campaign was vituperative and widely publicized. So distraught was Danny Finn that when primary day rolled around in September, he barred Tamawa's pollwatchers from the voting stations. He also called police headquarters and had DeSapio's aide Joe Sullivan put on a beat far across town from the furor. Finn won. Tamawa cried foul, took Finn to the courts, and forced Tammany to run off a special election in one disputed precinct. DeSapio won by fifty-one votes.

"There's an important distinction to be made," DeSapio said twenty-two years later. "This was done on the inside. The 1961 primary was from the outside. . . . Ideological." He intones the word as a faint oath. "And also . . . ironically, it was really the Irish who were behind me."

DeSapio's support soon crossed factional lines. He attracted knowledgeable men from both the Huron and Manhattes Clubs. But Tammany denied DeSapio a seat as district leader at the County Convention, thus boosting his popularity with reformers. Dan Finn controlled some 150 jobs in the Sheriff's office and Tammany was not about to lose them over a Young Turk.

At the January 1940 County Convention, pickets with DeSapio placards ("The Friend of the People") paraded angrily outside, chanting: "To hell with Tammany Hall! To hell with Tammany Hall!" Dan Finn sniffed the atmosphere: "It smells strongly of Communism." Inside, The Bishop's county committeemen, steered by his Tamawa organizer George Tombini (uncle of Theresa DeSapio), shouted for recognition by the Chair. They were ignored. Tombini furiously raced to the platform. The lights went out and a riot ensued.

Tammany has never lacked for sergeants-at-arms. DeSapio's small army was vanquished. A few days later, Finn pacified him with another court job. As a man who saw his future in Tammany, DeSapio (who now had a two-year-old daughter to consider) was highly vulnerable to such a truce. The uproarious and frustrating battle within the Hall probably served as much to restore the regular in him as it did to incense his followers. For all the energy and devotion he had inspired in the outsiders, he had not in the end received acceptance from Inside.

Finn's strategy was clearer to the men around DeSapio than to their beleaguered leader. Danny Finn was simply guarding against future fires by buying off the arsonist. Tamawa would collapse without its hero. And Finn could drop him from the court job at any time with no friends left in either camp. It was this last piece of information that Finn inadvertently dropped in the ears of the wrong people. When word reached DeSapio's aides that he'd be off the payroll soon, they held what amounted to a hearing of the revolutionary court. DeSapio, confronted with an informal subpoena, appeared to face the wrath of his supporters. One of those present says that as the charge of treason was recited against him, The Bishop burst into tears.

Small wonder, for DeSapio faced the dilemma of the rebellious regular. He had run out on Dan Finn to little avail. Now he had moved back toward Finn for his own survival, thus repudiating the friends who expected gratitude for their risks. If Finn would have his scalp

within a month anyway, the gambit was a doubly disastrous one—
expedient and unsuccessful. DeSapio quit the payroll after two weeks
and ran in the primary for the State Senate. The New York *World-
Telegram* was elated: "That is startling indeed—an insurgent defying
the organization from some motive higher than personal gain. Here is
a man who wasn't to be bought off. If this sort of thing is to continue,
what can become of Tammany Hall?" The senatorial election went
heavily against DeSapio but the halo was back in place and the following year Tamawa closed ranks to draw a bead once more on Danny
Finn's seat in Tammany. Finn beat DeSapio six precincts to five in a
contest which, contrary to later publicity, observers recall as being
passably honest in its mathematics.

New Yorkers kept an appreciative eye on the determined challenger
to the old guard of Tammany. Three months later their attention
shifted to the news from Pearl Harbor. The war broke out three days
before DeSapio's thirty-third birthday. He was deferred from the draft.
The iritis was a lingering problem, and, more pertinent to the intricate
wheels of the law, he was married, a father, and working to support his
parents' real estate business. (In Greenwich Village subway stations in
the early 1960's there were still angry scrawls in yellow chalk: "DeSapio
is a Draft Dodger.") After V-E day, one friend recalls, DeSapio confided that he was about to be called up and that he hoped his aides
would keep watch on his constituency. But the war ended and his
political career was climbing steadily.

While the news was focused on Italy's surrender in September of
1943, Tammany Hall was negotiating its surrender to that hapless
nation's second generation in America. Carmine DeSapio outdid Dan
Finn for the last time and was finally acknowledged his place on the
inner circle of the Democratic County Executive Committee. Finn
had become expendable. His sheriff post had been abolished. He had
beaten DeSapio once by fraud, twice by an edge; twice he had lost to
him. Clearly, his grip on Greenwich Village lacked the iron of the
Battery Dans of yore. Furthermore, the public outrage over the Irish
machine's affronts to outsiders was growing. LaGuardia's victory over
William O'Dwyer in 1941 indicated the Mayor's steady pulling power
with all ethnic groups, including the bulging sector of Italian-Americans.

The tales of DeSapio's climb to power during the 1940's are contradictory, stemming from the cynicism of his Irish foes and the senti-

mentality of his Italian admirers. "Just luck," his enemies say, as if seizing the breaks were not the indispensable skill of politics. "Just a nice guy," his friends say, as if backroom wars were a popularity contest. One deduction which does not appear in either accounting is that DeSapio was an astute infighter. During the last years of the Interregnum, as the heads of leaders rolled frequently, he stood each time on the good side of the guillotine.

He gained the confidence of Clarence Neal by helping to overthrow Michael Kennedy. Shortly thereafter, he was instrumental in vanquishing the Loughlin-Neal-Stand leadership, for which he was recognized by a twelve-thousand-dollar job on the Board of Elections. In 1949, he capitalized on the humiliation suffered by Tammany at the hands of Franklin Roosevelt, Jr., who won a spring election to Congress backed by a group of Tammany insurgents and Liberal Party leader Alex Rose. It was election year for Mayor O'Dwyer, who did not relish the idea of support from a Tammany Hall that could not elect its own Congressman. O'Dwyer determined that Tammany Leader Hugo Rogers had to go. DeSapio led the coup within Tammany and Rogers was toppled. The press charged that the decisive influence in this last maneuver was exercised by Frank Costello.

Costello, wrote *Times* reporter Warren Moscow, "hoped that De-Sapio would make a good, respectable leader, that the public would forget about Costello, while Costello enjoyed his golf and his friends in respectable retirement, free from politics and racket connections." On the other hand, one Tammany politician remembers Costello as being opposed to DeSapio until he was persuaded to accede by another mobster. In a Tammany Hall repudiated by the State and National Democratic Parties, its treasury empty, its leadership adolescent, its potential reformers away at war, the political vacuum could be filled to a large extent by criminals, but they engaged in as much political disagreement as law-abiding Republicans.

Tammany had deteriorated into a loose, ineffective coalition of selfish factions. Political intriguing not only involved underworld wings, but purely ethnic and geographic power struggles. Added to this was the strenuous effort of Mayor O'Dwyer to build Tammany into his own personal machine. Costello, who had financial and coercive power which rivaled Jim Fisk's in the Tweed era, undoubtedly influenced more Tammany decisions and nominations than have been revealed to date. But he was only one of many forces which shaped the election on July 20, 1949, of his well-scrubbed compatriot Carmine DeSapio as leader of Tammany Hall.

DeSapio won unopposed. Ten Irish district leaders abstained. After the vote, DeSapio, totally contained, wearing a loud checked tie, stood up, and thanked one and all for being so pleasant. The Tammany Executive Committee thereupon renominated Mayor O'Dwyer, Council President Vincent Impellitteri and District Attorney Frank Hogan. All went on to victory in November, with an assist from the famous name of Robert Wagner, Jr., candidate for Manhattan Borough President. O'Dwyer hailed DeSapio, the newest Tammany tiger, as a man of "matchless leadership."

But consider: DeSapio's Mayor was a gregarious Irishman who had already overthrown four County Leaders. The Governor was Thomas E. Dewey, who had sent Jimmy Hines of Tammany Hall to the penitentiary. The Senators were Irving Ives, a Republican, and Herbert Lehman, a liberal Democrat with an independent following. The District Attorney was Frank Hogan, who had wire-tapped at least one Tammany transaction. The president of the City Council was Vincent Impellitteri, who despised Tammany Hall. The President of the United States was Harry Truman, who came from Missouri. All told, the situation was not a comfortable one.

There were compensations. Paul Fitzpatrick, the Democratic State Chairman, took a liking to DeSapio. So did National Committeeman Ed Flynn, the Leader of the Bronx. Flynn was a cultivated man with a good record for playing hunches on cultivated candidates (FDR and Herbert Lehman). Only two of his underlings had been caught in the Seabury investigation, a piece of discipline in which he took great pride. When, in 1950, a Brooklyn bookmaker announced with equal pride that he, Harry Gross, listed some 300 New York City policemen on his payroll, Ed Flynn dropped in on Harry Truman to pass the time of day. Not long thereafter a new ambassador appeared in Mexico: William O'Dwyer.

The interim Mayor was by right of succession Vincent Impellitteri. Flynn looked about for a cultivated alternative, and in consultation with Carmine DeSapio, who was eager for cultivation, he found one: Ferdinand Pecora, State Supreme Court Justice and former counsel for the Securities and Exchange Commission, who had scored headlines with his investigation of shady Wall Street practices. Tammany split again. The anti-DeSapio Sachems joined Brooklyn in supporting

Impellitteri as an independent candidate. Governor Dewey backed liberal Republican Edward Corsi, a third Sicilian.

In DeSapio's first critical campaign, as in his last, his candidate was badly managed. Pecora did not come across. Impellitteri did. With the aid of Sydney Baron, a facile, twenty-six-year-old speechwriter who was at odds with Ed Flynn, "Impy" launched a virulent attack on the "Pecora-DeSapio-Costello" trinity. Impy and Baron, cobblers' sons on the warpath, overcame the disparity between the candidates' qualifications by presenting a sharp image of virtue versus Tammany: "If Pecora is elected, Frank Costello will be your Mayor. . . . Carmine DeSapio, the Tammany leader, and others allied with him in this campaign take their orders from Frank Costello, directly or indirectly." Impellitteri won a smashing upset victory, the only independent in New York history to crush both Democrats and Republicans in the race for Mayor.

Tom Dewey stole a page from Impy's book, attacking the "Flynn-Tammany-Costello slate," and won a third term in Albany. And into City Hall as the Mayor's patronage secretary came an angry Frank Sampson, leader of the anti-DeSapio group in Tammany Hall. But for his alliance with Flynn, DeSapio's status was, at best, precarious. His only achievement in the eyes of the Democratic Party was helping rid it of two left-wing embarrassments as the shadow of Joe McCarthy fell across the land: Benjamin Davis had lost his City Council seat in the 1949 election; and Congressman Vito Marcantonio died of a heart attack in the face of a DeSapio-engineered coalition in East Harlem. (The price was another Republican in Congress.)

For DeSapio, the worst was yet to come. Three lean years stretched ahead before the next crack at City Hall. Enemies surrounded him in Tammany. The knives were flashing. "I went to see him in the hospital," a friend recalls. "He couldn't see. His eyes were all bandaged over. He had his ear to the telephone. Another petition to dump him was going the rounds of the district leaders. He held on by one vote." DeSapio was figured for a one-year mediocrity, another weak link in the long chain leading back to Mister Murphy's grave.

Then one day he had a visit from Impy's speechwriter, young Sydney Baron.

"I wanted to meet him because I had a feeling of remorse."

Syd Baron swung around in his reclining chair away from a question.

The phone rang and he turned to a complicated looking switchboard which appeared to be the apple of his eye. He handled the call and swung back.

"Remorse, that's what it was. I didn't know anything about bosses. I'd never met them. I'd written some lousy things about DeSapio. So some guy—"

The phone rang again, and first irritated, then soothing words were imparted to the caller. Baron apologized for the interruption.

"A friend comes to me and says, 'Syd, you ought to meet Carmine. He's really not a bad guy.' So I talked with him and I had this feeling of remorse."

An aide entered with coffee and Baron popped a pill into his mouth. Just like the movies.

"I wrote his speeches, that's all. I'll tell you what finished him. He reformed himself out of business. He wasn't a backroom boy and that's where he made his mistake. And the Buffalo thing. And his name, you know. The dark glasses. A perfect target."

Baron had the press agent's habit of dealing out well-known cards with a confidential air, quite disarming in its innocence. One had the feeling that he would sincerely like to be *entre nous* with the world.

The phone rang again and there was a chance to walk about the spacious room, done up by an interior decorator who must have been sent to one of those movies, with crystal decanters peeking out from behind sliding doors, ashtrays marked "Syd," the kind of room where time and money could pass very painlessly. Smack in the middle of the room was a string bass. (One of the axioms of the Madison Avenue movie is that the big boss must have big idiosyncrasies.)

There was also an electric Menorah. It was the seventh day of Chanukah, 1961, three months after the fall of Carmine DeSapio in the primary fight with his old friend Mayor Robert Wagner.

Did DeSapio, like Richard Croker in his battle against Theodore Roosevelt, put himself too much in the forefront in that election?

"What do you mean? He issued two statements. If he'd been more vigorous in the primary, he would've won. What's he supposed to do —hide in his toilet?"

The most striking thing about Sydney Baron, who was widely considered to be the Dr. Frankenstein of DeSapio's Tammany Hall, was his vulnerability. He was an open wound. He darted from one concept to the next (DeSapio lost because he was too much in the public eye; too little in the public eye) with all the consistency of a Presidential candidate wooing North and South. His anxiety to please, his sensitivity to his own afflictions, the childlike relish with which he enjoyed the fruits of commercial victory—these are the qualities which have opened him up to cruel treatment by journalists. They also make him a very likeable fellow.

On the wall was a photograph of Carmine DeSapio (*To Sydney— A Sincere Friend*). "He's my closest friend. Look over there. That's the only picture in my office. And now he's out of politics."

DeSapio and Baron rose to eminence through a long struggle, much of it shared together, the complexities of its compromise more freely confided than was possible with either Tammanymen or reformers. Baron's closest friend was an ideal account. DeSapio's closest friend was a man with whom he could talk *realpolitik*.

Sydney Baron first came to public attention at age twenty-two when he blew the whistle on Ed Flynn. It was in 1943, when Flynn was Democratic National Chairman and FDR planned to name him Minister to Australia. The nomination was withdrawn when Baron testified in Washington concerning, among other things, the "Belgian paving block scandal" (a driveway built by City labor and materials at Flynn's country home in Putnam County). Baron also revived the charge that Flynn had once made Arthur Flegenheimer (Dutch Schultz) an Honorary Deputy Sheriff. Both statements were correct, though there is little evidence that Schultz was important in Bronx politics. (When Schultz was murdered in a Newark tavern by the avengers of Vincent "Mad Dog" Coll, his intriguing last words shed little light on his activities: "A boy has never wept, nor dashed a thousand kin.")

Ed Flynn wrote in his memoirs: "Senator Styles Bridges of New Hampshire, a Republican, on January 14 submitted a list of charges against me. These charges had been, in large part, supplied to the Senator by one Sydney S. Baron of Brooklyn. It might be noted here that later, when young Baron was testifying under oath, the extent of his 'personal knowledge' turned out to be that he had 'read the newspapers,' having been all of six years old when the incident of which he was speaking had occurred."

"Now, Ed Flynn was not a bad guy," said Sydney Baron, swiveling away. "But, frankly, he wasn't very bright. Look at it this way. Suppose you found out that twenty, twenty-five years ago, I gave Frank Costello a job, and now I'm going to be made an ambassador. Would it matter how old you were when I knew Costello? See what I mean?"

The analogy is a curious one, for Baron's political role changed sharply in the service of DeSapio, a name most Americans first heard on the lips of Frank Costello at the Kefauver hearings in 1951: "I know him three, four, five years." It was Baron's mission to eradicate the implications of that terse statement. Even more challenging was District Attorney Frank Hogan's charge the following year that an anti-DeSapio district leader was voted out of office by his committee-men after the defeat of Pecora, while Harlem allies of Dutch Schultz watched the proceedings, hands in their pockets.

"Sometimes I had to get a little rough," Carmine DeSapio said of the three-year period when Mayor Impellitteri and Sampson cut him off from all City patronage. While he was waiting for the election year of 1953, a second chance to install his own Mayor, he developed a number of techniques to purge his opponents within Tammany. One was to merge two districts, thus forcing a primary between two of his enemies. Another was to tolerate the election of reform candidates over old-line anti-DeSapio district leaders. The most ingenious was the "reverse gerrymander"—changing district lines *after* the primaries and thus ousting the winners—which was used against old foes and new reformers who had defeated pro-DeSapio Sachems. (It was through this tactic that DeSapio finally rid himself of district leader Frank Sampson.)

More often than not, DeSapio's purges were aimed at friends of Costello whose presence hindered a great renovation of Tammany Hall in the public mind. DeSapio was most anxious to earn the admiration of Ed Flynn and State Chairman Paul Fitzpatrick, who were coming to recognize him as a figure of real stature in the Democratic Party. His association with party leaders was helpful to intra-Tammany prestige and rank-and-file dreams of future glory.

Bert Stand circulated another petition to dump DeSapio. It failed. Impellitteri tried to deprive DeSapio of his job as Elections Commissioner. The County Committee retained him. DeSapio pursued his crusade for the sanctification of Tammany Hall. He traveled to club-houses throughout Manhattan to urge them to unite behind him and renounce the racketeers. He made contact with civic reform groups, entreating them to bring their issues to the New Tammany Hall. He publicly urged election reforms—permanent personal registration, voting machines, direct election of district leaders, and equal recognition of women co-leaders. He gathered about him a group of young lawyers, who sat at the master's feet to discuss the future of the Democratic Party. And he worked probably the longest hours of any Tammany leader in history.

DeSapio's personality—his courtesy, his patience, his air of mystery —was a major factor in his survival during years when most leaders would have died of patronage-starvation. It was essential that he convince his nervous followers that he had the ability to win City Hall in 1953 and bounty for all. One of his chief skills was to convey *impression* without making commitments.

"I want to show you something." Sydney Baron walked to an outer office and pulled open three packed file drawers of speeches by Carmine DeSapio. Their labels were a cross-section of universities and civic organizations. "I wrote his speeches," Sydney Baron said, "that's all I did."

One of Baron's proudest moments came when he was teaching a course at New York University night school where the highlight of the semester would be a guest lecture by Carmine "The Bishop" DeSapio. On the day of the scheduled appearance, an aide to The Bishop received a frantic call from Baron.

"I just realized," Baron said, "it's *Yom Kippur* eve! The classroom will be almost empty! What am I going to do?"

"Don't worry about it," the DeSapio lieutenant replied, "I'll handle it."

The next day, Baron phoned again. He was ecstatic. The lecture had gone superbly. The room had been packed with attentive scholars. And DeSapio was delighted.

"How did you do it?" Baron asked.

"Easy," the aide replied. "I made them all get crewcuts and put a little spring in their step."

"But who were they?"

"Sanitation workers."

In 1951, Sydney Baron was working to cleanse the DeSapio image as industriously as he had muddied it the year before. First he sought a reconciliation between his old and new employers, but he failed to impress DeSapio's true nature upon Mayor Impellitteri. After all, the Mayor had once refused to shake hands with Frank Costello himself. Borough President Robert Wagner, in his capacity as chairman of the annual Tammany dinner, sent an invitation to Impellitteri. The Mayor muttered something about not being caught dead there.

But New Yorkers expected more than anti-Tammanyism from the Mayor's office. And it was now coming clear why a friend had remarked to Impellitteri, on the night he celebrated his election victory at the Stork Club: "My God, Vincent, why aren't you on your knees in Saint Patrick's?" Impellitteri's victory had not been a fluke. He discovered a powerful public response to his portrayal of a fighting underdog in a duel to the death with the Tammany underworld. But no one bothered to ask him along the way what he planned to do as Mayor of the City of New York.

The new administration's honeymoon with the press and public was the shortest on record. The question more and more came to be asked: where is the Mayor today? It was almost certain that he was not at City Hall. Between junkets and vacations, Impellitteri unleashed brief attacks on municipal problems, including Carmine DeSapio, but none were sustained. That was his misfortune. DeSapio prepared a postcard and sent it to three mail-order houses with instructions to scatter it among 41,000 Democrats in New York City. The postcard inquired whether Vincent Impellitteri should be re-elected as Mayor in 1953. The answer came back "No" by 4 to 1.

In July 1953, Ed Flynn announced the Bronx's support for Robert Wagner for Mayor. Carmine DeSapio joined in the endorsement; Brooklyn, Queens, and Staten Island stayed with Impellitteri. A few days after the announcement, a dozen Tammany district leaders appeared at City Hall to pledge their loyalty to Impy. Another petition to depose DeSapio was circulated but the signatures fell short of a majority. A Wagner-Impellitteri primary election was set for September.

Robert Wagner had proven himself as a vote-getter in the 1950 contest for Manhattan Borough President. He had been reared by his father. Some of his earliest baby sitters were election district captains. He knew the men and manners of urban politics better than any of his contemporaries. He had stayed honest as an assemblyman and in a series of important City positions. He was a strong choice for the general election, but a decided gamble in a primary against an incumbent Mayor who was supported by three boroughs and an angry group of dissidents in Tammany Hall.

The stakes for DeSapio were all-or-nothing. He could not survive another Impellitteri victory. But should he unseat the Mayor, his Tammany leadership would at last be supreme. DeSapio moved to liquidate the district leaders who had deserted him. Two of the most troublesome were disqualified in advance of the primary for non-residence in their districts. Others were beset by insurgents.

In August, Ed Flynn died. Carmine DeSapio was left alone to face triumph or disaster.

Robert Wagner defeated Vincent Impellitteri by 169,000 votes. He went on to win election as Mayor by 400,000 votes. Carmine DeSapio was recognized by the new Mayor as the City's foremost party leader.

DeSapio moved to extend his influence to the State of New York. He toured the upstate counties seeking support for the post of National Committeeman left vacant by the death of Ed Flynn. In December he became the first Tammany Boss to sit on the Democratic National Committee.

Although he had previously exercised minor patronage powers for the courts, and, through Ed Flynn, for a few Federal posts, DeSapio for the first time now had access to City Hall. Many observers feared the worst. A horde of corrupt Tammanyites, they predicted, would infiltrate the City bureaucracy.

But Wagner's major appointments astonished New York. He named first-rate experts to the commissionerships, including such distinguished ladies as Health Commissioner Leona Baumgartner and Corrections Commissioner Anna Kross. Unlike Honest John Kelly and Richard Croker, who had bitterly fought their Mayors whenever expertise was placed above political performance, Carmine DeSapio recognized the value of these appointments. Good government was good politics. He wanted to demonstrate that Tammany could not only win but Tammany could support a classy administration.

The opposition of three counties in the mayoral primary was helpful in opening up jobs. DeSapio and Wagner, for example, replaced Queens Boss James Roe's loyalists with appointees from other boroughs and with anti-Roe Queens Democrats. This served both to foster rebellion against Roe and to improve the quality of municipal government. The Corrections Commissioner had been a Queens man. So had the Commissioner of Investigations, the Commissioner of Purchase, the City Treasurer, and a number of deputy commissioners.

There were, of course, a few new jobholders whose qualifications were doubtful. The Director of the Bureau of Real Estate, another Queens appointee, was replaced by the husband of DeSapio's secretary (a most knowledgeable and efficient lady whom he had inherited from Ed Flynn). He resigned after his chief accountant was arrested for grand larceny.

And there was a new expert on the airways and seaways, the Deputy Commissioner of Marine and Aviation, Sydney Baron.

In 1954, DeSapio and Baron prepared another postcard. This one was sent to five percent of New York State's enrolled Democratic voters. On it were a dozen potential candidates for Governor, including Congressman Franklin D. Roosevelt, Jr., and Ambassador Averell Harriman, who was then running America's foreign-aid program. The results of this poll were never released.

Roosevelt was barnstorming the State. He was the front-runner with strong support in such upstate Democratic bastions as Buffalo and Albany. Upstaters and New York City reformers felt his 1949 victory against Tammany Hall would draw Republican votes this year. His name was magic. His delegate pledges mounted into the hundreds. It would take just such a powerhouse to defeat the Republican candidate Irving Ives, who had been elected to the Senate in 1952 by a record plurality.

Averell Harriman, whom New York had supported for the Presidential nomination in 1952, was making no moves toward the governorship. He had never held elective office. He was not a back-slapper. He had, however, helped formulate Lend Lease and the Marshall Plan, served as Secretary of Commerce, ambassador to Great Britain and to the Soviet Union, Director of the Mutual Security Administration, and held more important Federal positions than any American in history.

DeSapio remained neutral as the delegates lined up for the candidates. Then, suddenly, following the lead of Herbert Lehman, he declared for Harriman. Most delegates were amazed. Harriman could not possibly win. It could only be that Carmine DeSapio was continuing his search for respectability by sponsoring a distinguished statesman. But the price was bound to be continued Republican rule in Albany.

Yet DeSapio was not a man to ignore in safety. He had elected a

Mayor and controlled City patronage. He was the National Committeeman. The delegates fell in line. The September State Convention, as best described by columnist Murray Kempton, was a contest between DeSapio, "a political boss with aspirations to be a liberal idol, and FDR, Jr., a slightly tarnished liberal idol with aspirations to be a political boss. . . . DeSapio had the votes but he wanted so much to possess the sense of virtue. Roosevelt was offered the sense of virtue and he obviously would have preferred the votes."

"Ives, Schmives!" the delegates shouted, with some prompting. "Dewey, Phooey! We Crave Ave!" But, truth be known, Carmine DeSapio was one of the few who actually believed that Averell Harriman could win. A basic element in his decision was his conviction that Franklin Roosevelt could *not* win. The postcard poll, whatever its exact figures may have been, showed that Roosevelt was in trouble in districts which were heavily Irish Catholic. This was attributed in part to disputes between Eleanor Roosevelt and Francis Cardinal Spellman.

DeSapio also knew that endorsement of the Roosevelt candidacy by Alex Rose and David Dubinsky, leaders of the Liberal Party which had originally sponsored the President's son, was all but impossible. They liked Harriman and were disillusioned with young Roosevelt. Apart from this, there was no advantage to DeSapio in backing a front-runner. If his decision were to be the crucial one, it would have to be in behalf of a candidate who needed his support. And what better candidate than Averell Harriman, a man of international reputation but little local power, an eminent supporter of Robert Wagner in the 1953 campaign which exalted Carmine DeSapio.

Five million voters turned out for the 1954 New York State gubernatorial election. Averell Harriman won by 11,125 votes. Franklin Roosevelt, Jr., running for State Attorney General on the same ticket, was decisively beaten by Jacob Javits.

On election night, Carmine DeSapio held Eleanor Roosevelt's hand for the photographers. "Franklin has a great future," he said. Roosevelt went into political exile for twelve years until he returned to New York in a second fruitless quest for the governorship in 1966.

If that November night in 1954 marked the low point for Franklin Roosevelt, from which he might never recover politically, it was also the apex of Carmine DeSapio's career. The two highest Democratic officials in America—the Governor of the largest State and the Mayor of the largest city—owed their election to him. Only Charles Murphy had done it before. It appeared that at long last Mister Murphy had found a successor.

The election of Averell Harriman, who had little experience in party politics, dramatically boosted DeSapio's standing in the party. The Governor appointed him to his cabinet as Secretary of State, a post roughly analogous in its political duties to the U.S. Postmaster General. (Al Smith had given the job to Robert Moses, Governor Roosevelt to Ed Flynn, and Tom Dewey to Tom Curran, Republican leader of New York City.)

For the next four years, he operated out of four offices—a lavish government suite in the State Office Building in the City, a second Secretary of State's office in Albany, the National Committeeman's quarters in the Biltmore Hotel, and the Tammany Hall suite at 331 Madison Avenue. DeSapio was also seen more and more at social functions in the Governor's mansion and at the Harriman town house in the East 80's. (The invitations did not include his Tammany entourage.)

In matters of organization and patronage, the liaison between Governor Harriman and Boss DeSapio was George Backer, a witty, urbane realtor, novelist, and ex-publisher of the New York *Post*, who made the transition from the literary set of the twenties to the Tammany exigencies of the fifties with gusto. DeSapio and Backer were on good terms. They worked out specific patronage matters with the Governor's aide Milton D. Stewart, who funneled New York City appointments through DeSapio. In general, a program of compromise was followed similar to the relationship between Tammany and the Al Smith administration, with certain posts going to the party faithful and a number of key policy-making positions allotted to experts less politically inclined.

A study by Daniel Patrick Moynihan and James Wilson of Harriman's appointments shows DeSapio's influence in the process: in New York City, high recognition of the Manhattan organization compared to Brooklyn and the Bronx, but a disproportionate number of upstate job-holders from counties where DeSapio sought to assert himself as a State leader. At least twenty County Leaders were placed on the State's payroll. From an intermeshing of partisanship and statesmanship came a State administration which, in contrast to its Republican predecessor and successor, was notably scandal-free.

DeSapio and his new friends were also at work on a national project: securing the Democratic Presidential nomination for Averell Harriman. The press's appetite for DeSapio yarns, whetted by his duo-image as an associate of idealists and rowdies, was entirely tantalized by the possibility that the man in the dark glasses might be the kingmaker for America. In fact, DeSapio did not so much launch the Harriman Presidential campaign train as hitch himself to it. Harriman had been bitten by the White House bug four years before, with the encouragement of President Truman, after Adlai Stevenson had publicly closed the door on himself. What Averell Harriman had not anticipated was Stevenson's failure to turn the key in the lock, and as the 1952 convention approached, the door had slowly inched open. The lasting result was a certain coolness between Harriman and Stevenson, and between Harriman and such Stevenson enthusiasts as Senator Lehman and Mrs. Roosevelt.

Stevenson was again the front-runner for 1956—a perfect set-up, some columnists speculated, for Boss DeSapio, who had stopped FDR, Jr., in his tracks. Or perhaps, the Alsops wrote, there was significance in DeSapio's growing friendship with Kentucky Senator Earle Clements—perhaps a Southerner as President with Robert Wagner as Vice-President? DeSapio was watched closely by reporters, but the trail led them nowhere: each morning a drive uptown to one of his offices in Sydney Baron's car or a chauffeur-driven State limousine; every other day to the eye doctor on East 79th Street; on Tuesdays to Albany. There were few surprises in the names of his office visitors.

In November 1955, Stevenson announced that he was available. Democratic national leaders convened in Chicago to assess the situation. DeSapio was conspicuous in his absence. He let it be known that he was holding New York's 94 delegates for Harriman. He was, he said, receiving 750 phone calls a day, taking a good ten percent himself; clearly, great things were in the wind. And he had a new postcard poll on the presidential mood of New York Democrats: seventy-six percent for Harriman, nineteen percent for Stevenson, one percent for Jim Farley. Then Harry Truman announced for Averell Harriman.

DeSapio's prospects were heady. "Today," he told Local 15 of the Bartenders Union, "all Americans realize that a Republican national administration stands for government by deception, government by secret council, government by expedient slogan, government by proxy, government by almost everything, indeed, but principle." Averell Harriman would turn that administration out of office and bring to the nation government of vision and substance, supported by an enlightened Tammany Hall.

Throughout the pre-convention period, newspapers reported DeSapio rounding up more delegates for Harriman. But then a well-kept secret began to make the rounds. The delegates encountered around the country by Harriman advance men said they were offended by the reports of DeSapio's activity—not because of undue pressure from Tammany Hall, but because they had never met DeSapio and wanted to know why, if he was conferring with other delegates, they were not on the honored list. Who was he talking with, anyway? And in the summer of 1956, the national Governors Conference, traditionally heavy with Presidential politicking, convened in Atlantic City. New York City and Washington newsmen scoured Atlantic City to solve the greatest mystery of the conference: where was the hotel room with Carmine DeSapio meeting with governors and party officials from across the nation to push Harriman's candidacy? For a week, the press reported rumors of the results of DeSapio's meetings and speculation as to why he was avoiding newspapermen in Atlantic City. But no newspaper reported the real story: Carmine DeSapio was nowhere near Atlantic City. He simply did not know enough Governors or party leaders from other states to make his entrance. His national power was a creature of publicity.

Averell Harriman once again saw Adlai Stevenson take the Democratic nomination. In the campaign that followed, Stevenson's supporters in the City were even more dedicated and fervent than in 1952. They charged that Tammany was knifing their candidate, and established their own independent Citizens for Stevenson campaign committee. The charge had merit. DeSapio was aware that Eisenhower would carry New York by a large margin. His district leaders worked to save as many local candidates as possible by campaigning "from right to left," that is, by concentrating on close-to-home offices on the right side of the Democratic voting line. There were also efforts to save one candidate who was third from the left—Mayor Robert Wagner, running against Jacob Javits for the Senate. In the election, Wagner ran far ahead of Stevenson, but he was plowed under nonetheless. The liberal establishment, with which DeSapio had earlier put together a proud but tenuous alliance, never forgave him for his parochial concerns in 1956. For the many young people whom Stevenson had attracted to politics, this was their first encounter with Carmine DeSapio, and they determined that it would not be their last.

The energetic group of young Democrats, largely middle-class, who were active in Citizens for Stevenson stayed in politics after their first taste of defeat. In Greenwich Village, they formed a rival club to DeSapio's Tamawa called the Village Independent Democrats, and in 1957 they mounted a primary against him for district leader. This effort was viewed with amusement within Tammany Hall; The Chief would slaughter the affronters. But that year, a relatively unknown Greenwich Village lawyer took more than one-third of the vote away from DeSapio, a portent of things to come.

Mayor Wagner, pledging to serve a full term, was re-elected in 1957, this time with full support from the county organizations and press. The following year, Governor Harriman was up for re-election and a vacant Senate seat was to be filled. DeSapio and Harriman, concerned about the razor-thin margin in 1954 for a state-wide ticket which had lacked an Irish Catholic, were convinced that this situation should be rectified in 1958. Stevenson liberals were pushing the candidacy of former Air Secretary Thomas K. Finletter, who had been chairman of Harriman's campaign in 1954 and chairman of New York Citizens for Stevenson in 1956. DeSapio was pushing District Attorney Frank Hogan. Harriman proposed Thomas Murray, the former chairman of the Atomic Energy Commission, but at the same time he encouraged Finletter to go around the State and meet the County Leaders.

When the convention opened in Buffalo, the real desire of the leaders was to unite behind Robert Wagner for Senator. At a hotel room meeting, Wagner said No, but everyone in the room was convinced he meant Yes. Harriman was renominated for Governor and then the convention came to a halt while the conferences continued on the Senate seat. Wagner returned from a trip to Niagara Falls with his family and said that he really did mean No. It was reported that Mrs. Wagner had reminded him of his pledge to the people of New York City that he would serve out his full term as Mayor.

Announcements were made: the convention will be delayed another hour, then another hour and another hour. Finally, Averell Harriman and Carmine DeSapio, grim and tight-lipped, emerged from the hotel room in the Statler-Hilton ready for a floor fight. The leader of Tammany Hall had broken with his Governor. In so doing, both men displayed their political weakness. Harriman could not make up his mind on full support for Murray or Finletter, and DeSapio was not strong enough in his own right to alter the pro-Hogan position which was the consensus of other County Leaders whom he was now treating as equals.

A convention is normally controlled by less than half a dozen men. New York City has approximately one-half the delegates at a State Convention. By placing Buffalo leader Peter Crotty on the ticket as the Attorney General nominee, DeSapio secured more than enough delegates to offset the pro-Finletter insurgents in the City. To the very end, it was reported that Governor Harriman never reached a firm decision. The message passed to pro-Harriman delegates was, "If you are with the Governor, vote for *either* Finletter *or* Murray." Upstaters voted for Murray; New York City Stevensonians voted for Finletter. Hogan won the Senate nomination.

During the same week, the Republicans meeting at their State Convention were thus far confident that Harriman was a shoo-in for re-election. They nominated a political neophyte who could afford to bankroll his own campaign—Nelson Aldrich Rockefeller. The "boss-ism" issue was handed to Rockefeller. Millions of New Yorkers had witnessed the Buffalo fiasco on television. Newsreels of the Democratic Bosses emerging from the hotel room were played again and again as Republican commercials. The Democratic State ticket, with the exception of Comptroller Arthur Levitt, went down to defeat.

In 1959 the Stevenson liberals formed a city-wide organization called the Committee for Democratic Voters, dedicated to the reform of the Democratic Party at the precinct level and the elimination of the Boss of "bossism," Carmine DeSapio. An office for the CDV was organized by George Backer. Among the leaders of the group were Senator Lehman, Mrs. Roosevelt, and Thomas Finletter. Since the early 1950's, insurgent candidates for district leaderships had sought money and advice from liberal party leaders. Now there was an organization, with telephones, secretaries, funds, and famous names.

Robert Kennedy came to meet with a group of the reformers during the 1960 campaign. "I'm not interested in your fight with DeSapio," he reportedly told them. "As between you and DeSapio, I don't care if blood runs in the streets. I want to elect my brother." Following the Stevenson pattern, the 1960 Presidential campaign in New York was run by both the party organization and a citizens committee. However, the Kennedys took the precaution of setting up various mediators and boards of conciliation to settle disputes. This system worked relatively well until a rally at the New York City Coliseum the Saturday night preceding the election. Democratic State Chairman Michael Prendergast broke a mediated agreement and refused to allow Senator Lehman and Mrs. Roosevelt to sit on the speakers' platform. The audience was buzzing with this news when John Kennedy arrived to deliver his address.

Kennedy was furious at this incident. When he assumed the Presidency, both Prendergast and DeSapio were by-passed. Federal patronage was funneled through Mayor Robert Wagner. The stage was now set for Wagner's public break with Tammany Hall. He did it first by successfully opposing DeSapio's candidate for a vacancy in the Manhattan Borough Presidency. Then the Mayor publicly denounced DeSapio and, after some unsuccessful negotiations with the County Leaders, announced that he would name his own running-mates in the mayoral election of 1961, regardless of what the Bosses said.

The reformers were reticent to endorse the Mayor whose fortunes had been advanced by Carmine DeSapio, but when they failed to come up with their own candidate, such respected realists as Herbert Lehman convinced them that City Hall and Tammany Hall must be treated as separate entities. Carmine DeSapio, Congressman Charles Buckley (Ed Flynn's powerful successor in the Bronx) and Brooklyn leader Joseph Sharkey picked State Comptroller Arthur Levitt as the organization candidate. There was nothing in the record to indicate that Levitt would not have made an admirable Mayor, but he was handicapped by an aroused public revulsion toward Tammany Hall. The primary fight was essentially between Robert Wagner and Carmine DeSapio. "This primary," said the Mayor on election eve, "can be a call to greatness or it can be a return to the dark ages of sinister boss corruption."

The Village Independent Democrats nominated James Lanigan, a young attorney who had been active in the Stevenson movement, to run for district leader against DeSapio. Lanigan had previously predicted that a Wagner victory would be "disastrous for the reform movement," but the new allies moved forward toward the dawn. And a third candidate was in the Village race: Joe Sullivan, DeSapio's boyhood friend, who had fallen out with the Chief over some kind of "broken promise." But the "real issue to be resolved," said Carmine DeSapio gravely, "is whether the Democratic Party is to reflect the responsible leadership of the elected majority or be subjected to the quick cure-alls peddled by a willful minority which is determined to rule or ruin the party organization."

On primary night, Arthur Levitt, addressing a small crowd of stragglers, conceded at 11:40 P.M. He had lost to Wagner by 160,000 votes. Down at the Tamawa Club in Greenwich Village, in a dingy clubroom above a cut-rate drug store, Carmine DeSapio stood smiling before his followers, mortally wounded. Voting had been unusually heavy in the newer high-income buildings of the Village. And in his strongest district in Little Italy, DeSapio, who had been away for awhile, won by a tiny margin. With only five election districts missing, he was trailing by an insurmountable thousand votes.

"You and I have not lost this contest with any degree of shame," Carmine DeSapio said. "It may be disappointing to you because this is the first contest we've lost since 1939. But I don't concede that this is a defeat on any level except for a personality. I'm not indispensible or immortal. If I've let you down, I'm sorry."

DeSapio's voice broke and someone shouted: "You're too soft, Carmine!" Then he walked around the room shaking hands and kissing the ladies. Election District captains were arguing in a corner, blaming each other for the loss. But most of the members of Tamawa slowly trailed out of the room, weeping.

Murray Kempton, one of the more sensitive columnists since the death of Bolitho, wrote bitterly of the evening's end: "[I] walked out onto the streets and noticed that there were no slums anymore, and no landlords, and the Age of Pericles was upon us because at last we were rid of Carmine DeSapio. One had to step carefully to avoid being stabbed by the lilies bursting through the pavement."

DeSapio left Tamawa to visit his Fifth Avenue headquarters, across the pavement from 11 Fifth Avenue, site of the deceased Hotel Brevoort which once housed Fiorello LaGuardia and celebrated artists and writers of the 1920's. Nineteen floors up is the penthouse of Carmine DeSapio. When it came his turn to face the street, DeSapio, smiling grimly, wended his way through the lilies to that new home—an elegant dormitory of the new bourgeoisie which had just thrown his life back in his face.

Chapter 11

A Fox among the Tigers: J. Raymond Jones

"Ray Jones is a man of distinguished mind and great learning. He can play it rough, or way up high where men speak of America's ultimate purpose. How he uses the power of the Negro in American politics may determine our culture for years to come."
—*Theodore H. White*

The Leader sipped a tall, frosty rum drink and waved his cigar toward a memory.

"Down there," he said. "That's where I was born. And over there is where I almost drowned. I was on that rock. The wave went down and I reached for a shellfish. I didn't have sense enough to know that what goes down comes back up."

He stared out to sea. "The wave knocked me off. I was more worried about the beating I would get at home from my father . . ." His voice trailed off.

The Boss of Tammany Hall was sitting on the shaded porch of his Virgin Island home, high atop Raphune Hill. It was a fairy-tale house, pink with red shutters, with walks of blue-gray stone. All around were the blazing colors of tropical plants—red and orange bougainvillaea, red and white poinsettias, yellow-green crotons, flamboyants, papayas, and mampoo trees.

Down the green hillside was the town of Charlotte Amalie, quaint and bustling, with its old Danish villas and faceless public housing, duty-free bazaars, a cruise ship docked at the deep-water pier, red and blue and yellow sailboats at anchor in the harbor, waves rolling in from a freighter's wake to the rocks of childhood.

J. Raymond Jones was recuperating from defeat. Dressed in blue linen shirt, white shorts, and blue slippers, he settled comfortably into his chaise longue and surveyed the scene of his youth. The night before, on a nearby island, John Lindsay, Republican Mayor-elect of the City of New York, had breezed into the Rockefeller resort at Caneel Bay Plantation. Excited vacationers scurried down the beach to greet the victor. A salesman from Toledo assured Lindsay that he had voted for him. Ray Jones smiled when he heard about the scene.

"Yes, everyone voted for the winner. It's very hard to find someone who didn't."

Next to him was a tape recorder. He had no intention of being misquoted. He turned on the recorder to clear the tape. Over the amplifier came the high-pitched voices of his grandchildren. He smiled and switched it off.

"Well, we can talk without it."

Ray Jones is the first Negro to head Tammany Hall, and the only Negro county leader in America. Through him the Negro inherits the scepter once held by the Dutch, the English, the Irish and the Italians. It has come to mean the power of the underprivileged.

"It means," he said, "that the other groups have become less rugged. They're better educated. They have better jobs. They've moved into better areas of the community. They leave the rugged, day-to-day politics to those who are not so well off. The political leaders come from the most mobile group of the community. They're economically down but they're moving.

"But there's a difference, between a Negro leader and a leader of Negroes. It's difficult for a leader who comes from a minority to adjust and realize he must lead a whole community.

"Adam Powell is a leader of Negroes, not a Negro leader. He's very parochial. He couldn't get elected outside of Harlem. That's the problem with the Negroes. The leadership is parochial. Martin Luther

King tried to break out of that, and got involved in foreign affairs. He would have been better off if he had left foreign affairs alone. His leadership had already been accepted by whites and Negroes. King is both a Negro leader and a leader of Negroes."

Jones speaks and moves like a wise old chief, slowly, precisely, powerfully. In an era wracked by the war whoops of paleface reformers, Ray Jones, unlike DeSapio, had no need to resurrect myths of Chief Tamanend. He *is* Tamanend. George Olvany and Richard Croker (in his beardless days) could be mistaken on sight for Delaware braves. Ray Jones could only be the Grand Sachem of all the tribes, somber as Murphy, impassive as Burr, suspicious as Geronimo. Seeing him for the first time, a reporter remarked: "He makes Carmine look like a lamb."

He is a 200-pound six-footer with gray, close-cropped hair and a thin mustache. Away from his Virgin Islands retreat, he dresses somewhere between formality and flash, usually gray silk suits, white handkerchiefs, too-light ties. His fingernails, once grimy with the residue of labor, are elaborately manicured. It is difficult to imagine Ray Jones as a boisterous youth on the high seas. Instead of laughter, there is the trace of an ironic smile. Instead of anger, there is the slash of a carefully composed phrase, its implications left to the listener. For Jones's responses are never visceral. He hears and reacts with his intellect.

"Everything has changed. The clubs don't serve the same purpose anymore. They grew on the economic and social needs of the times. They were the welfare bureaus and social service agencies of those days. But no longer. The government has taken over. There's only one old-line organization left, the Buckley machine in the Bronx. They no longer have the close contact they had with the families, though many people still go to the clubs for help.

"The role of the political club has become one of community action—another school for the neighborhood, another traffic light, and so on—not individual service. But a political organization should not be a pressure group. That's a mistake the reform people make. I don't agree. It should be responsive to community demands. Any community program is a matter of priorities. What determines these priorities? Community pressures. The councilman doesn't create these pressures, but responds to them. And it's the duty of the political unit to get the community needs moved up on the priority scale.

"I don't know if the local clubs have a future, but it would be tragic if they don't. The political unit has discipline. If groups without discipline take over, the result will be demagoguery and chaos."

Sitting on his island sundeck, Jones squinted down at the sunbaked road that coiled its way up Raphune Hill. A car, straining in low gear, was slowly climbing the hill.

"I favored the reforms brought about under Carmine," Jones said slowly watching the car. "No district leader can exist today unless he is responsive to the thrusts of the community.

"But Mayor Lindsay's plan [to bar district leaders from public office]—it's a good slogan, but it doesn't mean much. And from the political standpoint, it's not justified, nor is it a service to the people.

"I would ask whether the leaders are performing in their jobs, not whether they are leaders. If you have a party, the people want rewards. They won't work without them. Otherwise, do away with the party. But the history of the United States shows that the two-party system is desirable.

"Anyway, there aren't enough jobs on a political basis now to sustain a leader."

The car pulled into the driveway. It was Ruth Jones, United States Collector of Customs for the Port of St. Thomas.

"Hello, colored girl," Ray Jones called out.

Mrs. Jones appeared in a flowered print dress, looking very cool after a drive in the tropical heat. She was pleasant, brisk and businesslike. She reminded her husband it was time for his insulin. Jones has had diabetes since 1945. Aside from insulin treatment and the need for bland meals at regular hours, he said it has not been an inconvenience.

Jones eased himself up and out of his chair and went inside. A few minutes later he returned to the porch and to politics.

"Under Mayor Wagner, no district leader could go to a commissioner for anything, or he did so at his peril." Mayor Wagner, he said, had led the way in establishing a non-political government, one in which top-grade professionals were at the head of City departments. Jones's loyalty to Wagner seemed genuine. He spoke bitterly about the Mayor's critics.

"Newspapers reserve the right to apply one standard to politicians and another to themselves. They're not after truth. They're out to prove a viewpoint, a pre-conceived notion. That may sound pretty rough, but I'm sixty-seven years old, and I can say it.

"They were absolutely unfair to Bob Wagner. As far as motivation and results, he did an excellent job. New York has its problems, the movement of millions of people, the constant shifting, adjusting. The solution of one problem raises two or three others. You can't push a magic button and solve them all. It's unfair to hang a man from the yardarm who devoted twelve years to trying to solve these problems.

"The Mayor's mistake was getting involved in party matters. There should be complete separation between party organization and elected officials. The Mayor should set party policy, but stay clear of its administration. He realized this too late."

The house inside was a soft blend of brown wood paneling, pink beams, and gray tile. One wall of the living room was pink and gray stone. Inset bookshelves lined another: Chekhov, Shakespeare, Ian Fleming, and Kenneth Clark's *Youth in the Ghetto*, the program document of Harlem Youth Opportunities Unlimited, Inc., whose chief political sponsor was J. Raymond Jones.

"I read a lot of the lighter fiction these days. I've stopped reading the heavier stuff," Jones said. "And I play chess with my wife."

Jones married Ruth Holloway in 1935, his second marriage. He has a son, a daughter, and six grandchildren. Mrs. Jones was a career worker for the Internal Revenue Service before her appointment in 1961 as Collector of Customs. In a patronage-packed field which has improved only slightly since the days of Samuel Swartwout, Ruth Jones may be over-qualified. She has a Ph.D. in economics.

Most of the year the Joneses are apart. In New York, Jones lives alone in a Convent Avenue apartment in Harlem while attending to politics and real estate. He tries to spend three or four months a year in his sanctuary on St. Thomas in the Virgin Islands. He plans to retire there, though "the timetable isn't fixed."

"I'm happiest when I'm here. I like to work with my hands." He gestured at the panels, sliding doors, bookshelves, closets. "And I designed all the landscaping outside. It was about four years work."

He opened one door to a display of glittering power tools. "My workshop." He opened another. "And a guest room for my grandchildren."

"What lies ahead for me? You're looking at it. My big problem in living here—my only one—will be to stay out of the politics of the island. They think I'm a snob, but I know the dangers."

New York's Negro population once clustered between Chinatown and Washington Square, the area that later became Little Italy. But by the 1890's, most of the City's 40,000 Negroes had shifted to the West Fifties along Ninth Avenue, a stretch of tenements flanking the elevated line. The avenue rose to a crest there called San Juan Hill, some say because of the heroism of Negro soldiers in the Spanish-American War, others say because the Negroes fought off whites who swarmed up the hill to attack them.

San Juan Hill was solidly Republican. Dick Croker made an effort to lure Negro voters from the party of Lincoln by establishing the United Colored Democracy. Its leader, Edward "Chief" Lee, a hotel bellman, had a voice but not a vote in Tammany Hall. Charles Murphy worked to strengthen the UCD with City jobs. By the end of World War I, about 1,000 of New York's 150,000 Negroes were employed by the City. With the exception of teachers, most held menial positions. There were only fifty Negro policemen.

Chief Lee's retirement set off a violent power struggle in the UCD. When the new leader, Caleb Simms, was murdered by a political opponent, Murphy prescribed his favorite sedative—the triumvirate. It lasted no longer than the troika from which Murphy himself had emerged. One leader followed another. Chief Lee made a comeback and then was sent into permanent retirement by an insurgent.

In 1915, Ferdinand Q. Morton took control of the UCD, and for years reigned as New York's highest ranking Negro office holder. On Murphy's recommendation, he was appointed a member of the Municipal Civil Service Commission where he served under Mayors Hylan, Walker, LaGuardia and O'Dwyer, and retired as president of the commission in 1948. Meanwhile, the United Colored Democracy withered and died in the 1930's as Negroes pressed for direct representation in the district organizations. The Irish leaders still controlled Harlem. In 1935, Morton tried to unseat a Tammany district leader in Harlem, Martin Healy of the Cayuga Club. Morton lost. In the meeting of district committeemen that followed the primary, fistfights erupted between Negroes and whites, and police were called in to restore order.

But that same year another Harlem district elected a Negro leader, the first in Tammany history. He was Herbert Bruce, a former redcap who found the same doorway into politics that the Irish had before him—the saloon. Bruce was the proprietor of a tavern at Seventh

Avenue and 137th Street, which became a celebrated gathering place for Harlem politicians.

Harlem, once a remote country village, had developed into a fashionable, high-rent suburb around the turn of the century. Plans for subway service set off a wave of real estate speculation. Houses were built faster than the demand, until realtors decided to introduce Negro tenants rather than let properties stand vacant. During the first decade of the century, "block-busting" landlords placed families from San Juan Hill in all-white Harlem blocks, and the now-familiar pattern was established of a white neighborhood gradually developing into a black ghetto through panic selling. By 1915, fifty thousand Negroes lived within a twenty-three block area in Harlem. Within the next five years, the area spread as another thirty thousand Negroes moved in, many of them migrants from the South.

Segregation stiffened during the 1920's and the Depression struck hard at the majority of Negroes, who depended on laboring and service jobs. New Deal relief projects helped encourage Negro allegiance to the Democratic Party. Traditionally Republican Negroes switched over to support President Roosevelt and Governor Lehman.

The prospect of defense employment brought thousands of Negroes to New York during World War II but discrimination in hiring was rampant and the rolls of the Negro unemployed grew longer. As Harlem expanded into the nation's largest ghetto, Negro enclaves developed in Brooklyn, the Bronx, and Queens. By 1950, the Negro population had swelled to 800,000, and to more than one million by 1960, nearly one-seventh of the City's total residents. Potentially, the Negro was now as powerful a political force, and as needy a constituency, as any in the history of Tammany.

New York's Negro "community" has always had a shared culture of adversities and humiliations, but at the same time a sensitive awareness of different backgrounds and status: old stock Negroes whose ancestors date back to the Revolutionary War; recent migrants from the South, whose immediate heritage is caste oppression; Negroes from Central America and the West Indies who speak French, Spanish, and British-accented English.

Unlike Southern Negroes, many of the West Indians came from societies where they could hold high positions and accumulate wealth. West Indians generally arrived in New York already well-educated, highly motivated, and skillful in buying and investing. Some became labor leaders. Some became militant Black Nationalists (Marcus Garvey). Others entered business and the professions. A few were prominent in the rackets. (The numbers game, before Dutch Schultz took it over, was run by West Indians.) And some went into politics.

John Raymond Jones was the son of a no-nonsense West Indian school teacher. He was born on St. Thomas six weeks before the turn of the century. At sixteen, he stowed away on a schooner bound for Puerto Rico. He arrived in New York at the age of eighteen. Big and tough, he worked as a factory hand, seaman, redcap at Pennsylvania Station, and iceman. He earned enough to establish his own ice company and a bicycle renting service.

Jones once gave this account of his start in politics at Martin Healy's Cayuga Club in Harlem: "In 1921 somebody discovered much to their surprise that I could write. I was asked to keep custody of the enrollment books. I walked in brazen as you please and was told I should go to the bottom door where the Negro club was. I determined then to go into politics and eliminate that kind of club from the American scene."

Ray Jones became a Harlem district leader in 1944. He was appointed a Deputy U.S. Marshal and held various other patronage jobs. By 1945, he was recognized as a power in Harlem, and Mayor O'Dwyer appointed him Deputy Buildings Commissioner under Commissioner Robert Wagner, Jr.

The Valente-Impellitteri battle for the Surrogate's Court was Ray Jones's first full-scale political brawl. He sided with DeSapio, who was backing Judge Francis Valente against Mayor O'Dwyer's nominee, City Council President Vincent Impellitteri. Jones was among the district leaders questioned by District Attorney Frank Hogan in an investigation of alleged bribery to obtain votes for Valente. Jones was cleared but because he was defying the Mayor, who had appointed him to his City job, he submitted his resignation as Deputy Commissioner. ("It was the only honorable thing to do.")

O'Dwyer accepted the resignation but reappointed him a few months later. Jones soon left his job and his district leadership to become secretary first to General Sessions Judge Harold Stevens (later a Supreme Court Justice) and then to General Sessions Judge Gerald Culkin. "Working for Judge Culkin was the only job I ever thoroughly enjoyed," Jones says. "Judge Culkin is an artist. He paints and loves flowers as I do. We built a roof garden on the seventeenth floor of the Criminal Courts Building."

In 1958, Jones bade farewell to Judge Culkin and their roof garden retreat to return to the harsh world of Harlem politics. He was summoned by Congressman Adam Clayton Powell, who was running for re-election after bolting the party's national ticket two years earlier to support President Eisenhower. Carmine DeSapio was seeking to purge Powell as a traitor to the party. Jones served as Powell's campaign manager in the primary fight against DeSapio's candidate Earl Brown (who had run errands as a boy for Ferdinand Q. Morton). Jones and Powell polarized the contest as a death struggle between the Negro of Harlem and Plantation Boss Carmine DeSapio. Earl Brown was all but forgotten. He was beaten at the polls by 3 to 1.

Jones and Powell both won district leaderships in 1959 against Tammany regulars, as did two of their allies, leaving DeSapio with only one leader in the five Harlem districts—the popular West Indian politician, Hulan Jack. The four anti-DeSapio leaders banded together in the "United Democratic Leadership Team," pledging to join in making Harlem a powerful voice in City politics. The following year, Hulan Jack, who had been installed by DeSapio as Manhattan Borough President, also cast his lot with the Jones team. Ray Jones was now recognized as an important power center in the party. His successful political footwork had earned him the nickname "The Fox." He had also become "Emperor Jones," and "the man to see" in Harlem. But he shared his throne with Powell. A break was inevitable.

Two housing projects, which were to be aided with public money, provided the first battleground for J. Raymond Jones and Adam Clayton Powell: the $3,000,000 Clayton Apartments on the site of an abandoned public school at Seventh Avenue and 135th Street; and the $40,000,000 Esplanade Gardens, which would replace obsolete subway yards at Lenox Avenue and 145th Street. Rival front groups for Jones and Powell struggled to gain sponsorship of the lucrative developments. Charges of political interference were raised by both sides over a period of several years. Earl Brown—Powell's and Jones's opponent in 1958— was eventually drawn into the fight. He had become a member of the City Housing and Redevolpment Board, the agency which had to approve the projects.

The feud between Jones and Brown was one of persistent animosity. There was never room between the two men for political accommodation. But the Jones-Powell relationship changed swiftly from bitter to sweet and back again depending on the needs of the moment. In 1960, the two men joined together in active support of the Kennedy ticket, although neither had been an early JFK supporter. Powell was initially a backer of Stuart Symington. Jones was one of four New York delegates to cast his vote for Lyndon B. Johnson for the 1960 Presidential nomination.

But in 1961, strange, new alliances were formed and marriages of convenience severed. The political year for Harlem began with the search for a Negro successor to Borough President Hulan Jack, who resigned after being charged with a minor conflict of interest. In a mayoral election year, the identity of his successor was less important than who would name him.

Jones allied himself with Mayor Wagner to support Edward Dudley, a distinguished Domestic Relations Court Justice and former ambassador to Liberia. A majority of the Manhattan delegation on the City Council was expected to follow DeSapio's lead and elect one of his Harlem allies to the Borough President vacancy. But Wagner and Jones applied sufficient pressure on the councilmen to bring about key defections and a victory for Dudley. It was the opening shot of Wagner's Holy War against the Bosses.

When the Tammany Executive Committee met to nominate Arthur Levitt as the organization candidate for Mayor, Ray Jones was the only old-line leader to support Mayor Robert Wagner for a third term. The Reverend Adam Clayton Powell, who had called DeSapio every name not in the Good Book, was now his admiring friend (and a foe of old friend Jones) as he saw the opportunity to oust Wagner and win recognition from City Hall. Powell and Jones engaged in a great tug-of-war for control of the uptown democracy. Handbills were distributed from Ray Jones's Carver Democratic Club with an injunction held over from the Powell-DeSapio struggle of 1958: "Stay Off DeSapio's Plantation." Pictured on the sheet was Kentucky Colonel Carmine DeSapio, complete with goatee, broadbrimmed hat, and bullwhip dripping blood.

On the night of September 7, 1961, as DeSapio stood in defeat before his Tamawa supporters, 125 blocks to the north the scene at the Carver Club was joyous. The crowd in the clubroom pushed close to the blackboard to watch the figures climb. Every vote for Wagner was a vote for J. Raymond Jones. Election District captains rushed in with lopsided totals on their tally sheets. They were invited into Leader Jones's inner office to receive expense money for the day.

Jones left his desk to go downtown to the Astor Ballroom. There he stood on the stage next to Robert Wagner, the victorious, all-new Reform Mayor. Everyone was claiming he had put Wagner over: reformers, Puerto Ricans, unions, civil servants, Wagner himself. But Ray Jones knew at that moment that Harlem voters had backed his judgment against Adam Powell's. He was, therefore, no longer a Harlem leader. He was the only Tammany regular whom the Mayor could trust. To him, by all that's just, must now come the crown torn from the head of Carmine DeSapio.

When the cheering died down that night, Ray Jones and Adam Powell were on the telephone. All was forgiven. It had been, said Powell, just one of those things.

Three weeks after the primary, Jones faced a tumultuous meeting of the nearly 2,500 members of the Democratic County Committee and made it clear to reformers and regulars alike that he was the Mayor's Man.

The reformers were still in a warring mood. Their candidate for County Chairman, Arnold Fein, the head of the city-wide reform group, had withdrawn his name in the interest of party unity after conferring with Wagner and Jones. And now Ray Jones stood at the rostrum to convey the word from the Mayor: the new chairman would be Fire Commissioner Edward Cavanagh, a close friend of Wagner's. Jones spoke strongly, in a tone which dared any delegate to contradict him. Many did with boos and catcalls. Other reformers sat silently, smiling knowingly to each other "I told you so." It was clear that the Mayor had no intention of replacing DeSapio with a simon-pure reformer.

Wagner's move was a characteristic holding operation to last until he had weighed the strength of factional pressures. Arnold Fein assured his reform colleagues that he had withdrawn only after the Mayor guaranteed to him that real action would be taken within three months. At that, Ray Jones led the applause.

But four months later, Tammany was still leaderless as the County Committee convention met again, no bridge in sight to span the canyon between regulars and reformers. No further word had come from the Mayor, who was now in fact of power, the new Tammany tiger.

The January convention developed into a spirited debate on party rules. As the evening wore on, regular delegates, remembering the September convention which had dragged on for seven hours, began to file out the doors, leaving proxies with their district leaders. The reformers charged that only committeemen who were actually present could vote on the motions. And so Ray Jones took to the floor once again in behalf of the Harlem delegates in the balconies whose employers might not be so forgiving of absenteeism in the morning as the law partners of Greenwich Village reformers.

"You are putting the mock in 'democracy,'" he cried. "Do not disenfranchise the poor people. If you say that they will have no voice because they can't stay until four o'clock in the morning, you are driving people out of the Democratic Party." Applause swept the balconies and the next speaker conceded: "Many of our best Democrats are working people."

The reformers were justified in their fear that voting by proxy might not represent the precise vote of the rank-and-file. But their penchant for squabbling away the night appeared this time to be a tactic to reduce the regulars' voting strength. The most important result of the night was their achievement in pushing J. Raymond Jones, the first lieutenant of the Wagner reform victory, further to the wall of regularity, his chances dimmed for the Tammany leadership. In the primary, he had worked against the regulars without gaining the trust of the reformers. Now he was a rallying point of the surviving regulars who were anxious to recultivate City Hall.

Nearly one-half of the Tammany Executive Committee was now in the hands of the reformers, who were pushing several candidates for the leadership. In other circumstances, Jones might well have been Wagner's immediate choice. He was the proud recipient of a letter from the Mayor which read: "Without prejudicing the privilege of organization leaders to have direct access to me, you will be the ordinary channel of communications between me and that leadership on city-wide matters." But unlike earlier insurgents, the new reformers did not consider themselves "organization" leaders, nor were they interested in channeling their views through the Mayor's political-secretary-without-portfolio.

Tammany was still Tammany so long as it embraced any leaders who had brushed fingertips with Carmine DeSapio. And it was still Tammany despite the Executive Committee's move from Madison Avenue to the Chatham Hotel on East 48th Street. The leaders began to talk of "Chatham Hall" and the "New Wagner" as reformers moved into positions in City Hall. But many of the newly elected district leaders continued to doubt the reform credentials of J. Raymond Jones and Robert Wagner.

"I believe that I deserve consideration," Jones said politely, "because of my service in the campaign for the Mayor and my record of forty years of service to the Party." Negro leaders characterized reform opposition to Jones as inspired by "racism." The *Amsterdam News*, an influential New York Negro weekly, claimed that "The only thing standing between J. Raymond Jones and the leadership of Tammany Hall is the color of his skin."

City College psychology Professor Kenneth Clark, a respected Jones ally, charged that the snubbing of Jones to appease reformers was "racism under the guise of expediency and I call upon the Mayor and all so-called liberals and reform Democrats to repudiate this immediately." Roy Wilkins the NAACP Executive Secretary, issued a temperate statement: "It is regrettable that ethnic considerations have entered into the discussions." And Adam Powell, the primary defeat behind him, came running to Jones's defense: "If Ray Jones were a white man, he would be County Leader by now, whether he was from the regular or reform clubs."

Jones was given a big testimonial dinner featuring Wagner, Mrs. Roosevelt, Herbert Lehman, Jim Farley, and a telegram from President Kennedy. But he was not given the leadership. It went instead to the Mayor's compromise candidate, Edward Costikyan, thirty-seven-year-old son of an Armenian rug dealer, the first Protestant Leader of Tammany Hall since Boss Tweed. Costikyan, a partner in Adlai Stevenson's law firm, had become an East Side reform leader when he upset a DeSapio district leader in 1955. He was an excellent choice for the Tammany leadership under any circumstances, and the only possible choice in the aftermath of the 1961 reform victory. His word was trusted by the regulars, and, despite opposition from militant West Side and Village reformers, he had more strength than Ray Jones among the early anti-DeSapio leaders.

The most important political fact about both Jones and Costikyan was their fealty to Robert Wagner. Jones had been the Mayor's only

loyalist among the regulars and Costikyan his first booster among reform leaders before the blessings of Herbert Lehman and Eleanor
Roosevelt assured Wagner of widespread reform support. Wagner
now reigned supreme in the City and the State. He was not anxious to
share power. Party responsibilities in Manhattan were split among
Jones, Costikyan, Cavanagh (who became Deputy Mayor), and a
number of others, but Robert Wagner was at all times the party chief.
Carmine DeSapio's remaining position as National Committeeman
was without meaning after his ouster from Tammany. His erratic ally,
State Chairman Michael Prendergast, stood by helplessly while the
White House funneled Federal patronage for New York State through
the Mayor of New York City.

Eddie Costikyan viewed the 1961 election as a triumph for Wagner,
who, he said, had pulled in the reformers, not the other way around.
"My notion all along," said the new Tammany Leader, "has been that
the only way for the Reform Movement to succeed is to get the leadership of competent public office holders."

But he had not bargained for the brand of leadership offered by
the New Wagner. The Wagner style, as Costikyan described it in his
political memoirs, was: "create no potential opponents, eliminate those
who appear, take care of yourself, and never make a decision until it
can't be avoided." Some of this style Wagner picked up from his
father, a master of delayed timing, and some from DeSapio, whose
record for developing bright new candidates was considerably short
of Charles Murphy's.

The Wagner style was much in evidence during the pre-convention
maneuvering for the 1962 gubernatorial nomination. Governor Rockefeller's first term in office, according to Democratic polls, had created
a potential liberal backlash in the City among the "swing" Democrats
who had supported him in 1958. Some felt that Rockefeller had given
more attention to Republican delegates for the Presidency than to the
problems of New York. A hike in the income tax, a sudden divorce,
and a host of other warm issues were waiting to be heated up further
by a strong Democratic candidate. Buffalo chieftain Peter Crotty and
Long Island leader John English were confident they had such a candidate in Frank O'Connor, the District Attorney of Queens County,
whose earlier exploits as a defense attorney had been recounted in
Alfred Hitchcock's *The Wrong Man*.

O'Connor was indeed the wrong man for Robert Wagner. First, he was a potential rival for leadership of the State Democratic Party. Second, his early record as a State Senator was too conservative for Wagner's allies in the Liberal Party. And third, a poll had apparently convinced Wagner, Jones, and Attorney General Kennedy in Washington that it was the Jewish vote, not the Catholic, that needed heavy courting.

Shortly before the State Convention met in Syracuse, Ray Jones announced his support for United States Attorney Robert Morgenthau, son of FDR's Treasury Secretary. The announcement, assumed to be "the word" from the Mayor, followed a series of newspaper accounts concerning the Democrats' hunt for a Jewish candidate to win back Jews who had defected to Rockefeller in 1958. With White House and City Hall backing, Morgenthau was able to win a second ballot victory over O'Connor despite a fervent floor fight by upstate delegates who had never heard of him.

But Rockefeller's Democratic voters had obviously demonstrated by their independent action at the polls in 1958 that they were not to be wooed as a voting bloc. If one could characterize the liberal Jewish vote, the key word would be "liberal" and not "Jewish." One of the least important political facts about Herbert Lehman, who rallied many Jews to the reform banner in 1961, was that he was Jewish. The name Lehman meant liberalism, progressivism, reform. The Morgenthau family name did not carry those qualities. And, worst of all, Robert Morgenthau, although a prosecutor of exceptional skills, proved to be a shy and uncomfortable candidate with a distinct distaste for political combat.

Nelson Rockefeller was once again handed the issue of a "bossed" Democratic convention. He romped to victory by nearly half a million votes, substantially increasing his 1958 showing in New York City. His state-wide drop from the 573,000 plurality of four years before was caused by anti-Rockefeller feeling in Buffalo and inroads by a Conservative Party candidate. But within New York City, the Governor was aided by his liberal running-mate Senator Jacob Javits, whose Democratic opponent was James Donovan, the attorney who arranged the Gary Powers-Rudolph Abel spy exchange. Again, the important fact was not that Donovan was a relatively unknown Catholic pitted against a prominent Jew. Donovan's conservative posture on social welfare issues alienated many of the voters whom the Morgenthau candidacy was designed to attract.

The Democratic debacle weakened Wagner's standing as a political soothsayer. Ray Jones had privately predicted the results, but he remained loyal to the Mayor. His eye was still on the Tammany leadership held by Costikyan. Although rivals for the Mayor's affections, the two leaders did share a growing irritation with the strident tones of the new reformers who were claiming, with some justification, that Tammany Hall had merely changed its name to City Hall.

"There is a new order, but the shape of the new order is not yet clear," said Herbert Lehman, the patient statesman. But a younger reformer, the president of the Village Independent Democrats, felt it was quite clear: "We feel that what the Mayor is doing is substituting himself for DeSapio." Wagner now had well nigh complete control of the City's machinery, including a rubber-stamp City Council. When a vacancy occurred on the Council in the spring of 1963, the legislators dutifully invited Ray Jones to join the club.

Councilman Jones was an imposing figure at City Hall. From the first day there was about him an aura of power and knowledge which overshadowed his more vociferous colleagues. He was an Administration Man, oriented to both mayoral and Presidential policies. When Adam Powell stood beside Malcolm X and berated "white" civil rights groups, Ray Jones's Carver Club passed a resolution: "We cannot call for integration while advocating segregation." Jones announced that he was buying a lifetime NAACP membership for his grandson. The action was typical of Jones the pragmatist. "How he uses the power of the Negro in American politics may determine our culture for years to come," Theodore White predicted. "Yet all he wants at the moment is fair shares of education and schooling, of patronage and public jobs."

Ray Jones was determined to be a leader among whites as well as Negroes, and thereby to better the lot of his constituency and himself. In a white man's City Council (the Caucasian margin was 33–2), he was highly respected by both regulars and reformers, not as a Negro politician but as a smart politician. And in a council known for the constant eruption of petty feuds, no one ever tangled with J. Raymond Jones.

As a freshman councilman, Jones immediately assumed the demeanor of an old pro legislator. The Council Room was silent when he spoke, for he addressed himself to only a few subjects, and he did so carefully, with precision and economy, in a deep, soft voice. If his grasp of an issue were less than solid, he left the talking to others less troubled by ignorance.

"I have enjoyed the Council," Ray Jones said in his Virgin Islands home. "I found you must be selective in what subjects to be concerned with. I'll be articulate for four more years on certain subjects." Generally, those subjects were housing, fiscal matters, and civil rights. On the latter, he left the histrionics to the whites, contenting himself to add a brief reminder of what it means to be a Ray Jones constitutent in the Harlem ghetto. At one meeting, Theodore Weiss, a firebrand reform councilman, charged that a resolution supporting a pro-Administration parade on Vietnam was beyond Council jurisdiction. Jones replied quietly: "In the past, we have welcomed Mr. Weiss' support on other matters outside the purview of the Council, such as resolutions on civil rights marches in the South."

The Civil Rights March on Washington in August 1963, indirectly led to an all-out assault on Jones's council seat and district leadership by his friendly enemy Adam Clayton Powell. Leaders of the March did not invite Powell (who had been courting the followers of the Black Nationalist, Malcolm X) to participate in planning the March or exhorting the marchers at the Lincoln Memorial.

This was a damaging setback for the absentee Congressman. Ray Jones was maintaining a good attendance record in the City's legislature and strengthening his hold on the people of Harlem. The two men were also locked in a legal battle over the sponsorship of Esplanade Gardens. And Powell had chosen wrong with DeSapio and Levitt in 1961; Jones had chosen right with Wagner, who carried Harlem by 2 to 1. Little admired among political professionals, Adam Powell had now been ignored by civil rights leaders in a national arena where he could have soared above Jones of Tammany Hall.

Powell returned to New York, humiliated and angered at being an eminent spectator at the March, and grabbed the nearest headline by declaring war on Ray Jones. Powell's name had already been printed on campaign literature as an honorary chairman of the citizens committee backing Jones for a full term on the City Council. But five days before the primary election, the Congressman announced his support for insurgent candidates attempting to oust Jones from both the City Council and the Tammany Executive Committee.

Five days was a short time, even for Adam Clayton Powell, but he made the most of them: Ray Jones was "a traitor to the black revolution," "a Wagner puppet" backed by "a flood of white money . . . only white votes could elect him."

"Powell can dish it out," Ray Jones noted. "Now we'll see if he can take it . . . Powell is no longer considered a national leader of any importance in the civil rights movement . . . Adam is contemptuous of Negroes. He has nothing but contempt for the Negro masses. In relaxed moments, Powell refers to Negroes as 'my slaves.' " The venom spewed back and forth in Harlem, all in good fun, and on Election Day, Jones turned back the Powell threat by 5 to 1.

A few days later, Eddie Costikyan let it be known that he was anxious to resign from the Tammany Leadership and return to full-time law practice. Increasingly, he had found the Mayor too busy to come to the phone. And the reformers had worn down his patience: "These reformers have walked all over me and I don't intend to be walked over any longer. The reformers have done nothing on any issues. The old-line leaders are warm, genuine people. They're friendly to people and that's how they win votes. The reformers could learn something from them."

The assassination of President Kennedy, as it stunned the nation, sent shock waves into the structure of the Democratic Party in every section of America. John Kennedy had been, to a greater degree than most Presidents, the leader of his party. Tammany Hall, which had originally viewed him as an upstart lacking proper respect for the traditions and prerogatives of the political machine, had come to respect him as a shrewd and insightful politician. Early in 1963, Kennedy had sent his brother-in-law Stephen Smith to New York to establish channels with old-line leaders and attempt to unite the warring factions in the City party for a Kennedy victory in 1964. Now the political goals of Washington were unknown and the entire future of the party filled with uncertainty. Costikyan announced that he would stay on as Tammany Leader until the shape of the crisis had been determined and met.

Costikyan and Jones were successful early in 1964 in securing the nomination of Constance Baker Motley, Associate Counsel of the Legal Defense Fund of the NAACP, for a vacant seat in the State Senate. Mrs. Motley was Jones's choice over the West Side Reform candidate, a dry cleaning store operator who had been convicted on a numbers racket charge. The alignments left the public wondering about the relative ability of Tammany and its insurgent foes to pick candidates of merit.

But while Ray Jones the district leader gained new stature as a sponsor of distinguished candidates, old doubts arose about Ray Jones the businessman. A law suit was brought against Jones and nine others by a consulting management firm, whose vice-president was a former secretary to Congressman Powell and whose attorney was the Powell-backed candidate for Jones's council seat the year before. The suit charged that Jones, who had once been an officer of this concern, had used confidential information to take the Clayton Apartments and Esplanade Gardens away from the firm, deprive it of its fees, and deliver the projects into the hands of favored friends. Jones denied the allegations and charged that the lawsuit was politically inspired by Adam Clayton Powell.

As the suit followed a tortuous path through motions and cross-motions, it was learned that the State Investigation Commission was conducting a probe of possible conflict-of-interest. The Powell camp took this opportunity to call for Jones's resignation from the board of directors of the Harlem anti-poverty program. The program was to be operated by a new agency, HarYou-Act, a merger of Harlem Youth Opportunities Unlimited, with which Jones had been affiliated, and Associated Community Teams, of which Powell was a sponsor. The merger provoked a new power struggle between the two Harlem leaders. Each accused the other of attempting to control the more than $100,000,000 in Federal money to be poured into Harlem's war on poverty.

Slum housing, severe unemployment, ennui, and all the degrading conditions which plague the Harlem resident, did not cease their pressure to await the outcome of the Jones-Powell rivalries. On July 16, 1964 an off-duty policeman, attempting to break up a disturbance, shot and killed a fifteen-year-old Negro who, the policeman said, had attacked him with a knife. Two nights later, Harlem exploded into rioting that lasted for five nights.

Negroes battled police on the streets and hurled missiles from the rooftops. Police fought back with clubs and fired their pistols into the air. When it was over, 140 persons were injured, 520 had been arrested, and one man was dead, shot by a policeman. Throughout the rioting, Harlem's top elected officials maintained an uncharacteristic silence. Neither Ray Jones nor Borough President Dudley appealed for calm.

Congressman Powell was off on a European junket. It was perhaps clear to all three that their entreaties in the face of Harlem's overwhelming frustrations would have been branded as soothing words from the mouth of Uncle Tom.

Barry Goldwater's prescription for the Harlem riots—more police and fewer civil rights statutes—produced a massive vote in Harlem, with an organizational assist from Ray Jones, for President Johnson and Senatorial candidate Robert Kennedy in November. After the election, Eddie Costikyan announced that he would definitely step down as County Leader, thus bringing to a close Tammany's brief Aremenian Era. Costikyan designated Mrs. Charlotte Spiegel, a petite Lower East Side co-leader, to assume his duties until his resignation took effect thirty days hence. For the first time in its history, Tammany was in the gentle hands of a female Boss. Under the delicate gavel of a pretty brunette, Tammany's meetings were somewhat more orderly than in the days of Isaiah Rynders and Mike Walsh. As one district leader explained: "It's hard to be rude to a woman."

Mrs. Spiegel was holding the line until Mayor Wagner settled on a successor to Costikyan. In private talks with the district leaders, Wagner suggested that a troika be installed—a technique that the Mayor had recently attempted with little success in his efforts to conquer Brooklyn. The leaders balked at this prospect, and on December 6, 1964, New York County's sixty-six district leaders, who form the Tammany Executive Committee, gathered to take action at the National Democratic Club, where the remains of the Tammany Society are enshrined. For six hours they wrangled over the choice of a new Leader. The impasse was broken by a phone call from City Hall in which Mayor Wagner passed down the word that Ray Jones had been awaiting for three years. With only two dissenters, Tammany inaugurated its first Negro Boss. "It's just possible," said J. Raymond Jones, "that the ancient Sachems of Tammany Hall are turning over in their graves."

One of Boss Jones's first moves was to travel to Washington for a public display of friendship with Adam Clayton Powell. "We've never been opponents," Congressman Powell said as the two men posed together for photographers. "We merely differed once on a candidate. Ray and I have been close together all our lives." (Only a year before, after he had defeated a Powell candidate for his City Council seat,

Ray Jones had ruled out any possibility of a reconciliation: "You can forgive everything except ingratitude.")

Jones had first demonstrated his strong alliance with Mayor Wagner in their battle against Carmine DeSapio over the Manhattan Borough President vacancy in early 1961. Another vacancy in the same office was created by the election of Borough President Dudley to the State Supreme Court in 1964. Deputy Borough President Earl Brown, Jones's old enemy, was in line for the job. He was favored by a majority of the Manhattan City Councilmen. To assert his power, Jones held a secret caucus in which those who attended agreed to be bound by the majority vote. Three indignant councilmen refused to participate in such proceedings and boycotted the caucus. It was a grave error. The vote in the caucus was 3 to 2 for Jones's choice, State Senator Constance Baker Motley, thus pledging all five votes. And so, while the actual sentiments of the councilmen lined up 5 to 3 for Brown, the final vote was 5 to 3 for Mrs. Motley, an impressive victory for "The Fox" in his first exhibition of cunning as the Boss of Tammany.

In Albany, Jones demonstrated his skill at achieving victory with a minority of votes during the legislative marathon of 1965, which rivaled in its long weeks of deadlock and bitter debate the struggle between Mister Murphy and Franklin Roosevelt over Blue-Eyed Billie Sheehan in 1912. This time the issue was the choice of Democratic legislative leaders, for the Democrats had won control of both the Senate and Assembly for the first time in nearly thirty years. It was well recognized that the Democratic minority leaders, who were loyal to Mayor Wagner, would be as majority leaders several notches below Mister Murphy's men, Al Smith and Robert Wagner, Sr. Furthermore, both were from New York City, at a time when the balance of Democratic strength was beginning to lean to the upstate areas. Stanley Steingut, the leader of Brooklyn, Democratic State Chairman William McKeon, and the upstate allies of Senator Robert Kennedy, decided to oppose Wagner's choices. Steingut was proposed for the Assembly Speakership which had been held with distinction during the 1930's by his late father Irwin Steingut. For Senate Majority Leader, the insurgents backed Julian Erway, a conservative State Senator from Albany, perhaps hoping to exploit the friendship of Mayor Wagner with Albany Boss Daniel O'Connell.

The choice of Erway was a naïve political error which gave Ray Jones a perfect opening to transform the power struggle into a conflict between liberals and right-wingers. Just as the the pro-Wagner legislators appeared to be on the brink of defeat, with a majority aligned against them, Jones rallied the Manhattan State Senatorial delegation and branded Erway as a "Goldwater Democrat." Leading Negro spokesmen charged that Erway had resisted civil rights legislation. Support for Erway crumbled and a deadlock ensued in which the anti-Wagner rebels were unable to muster enough votes for a series of compromise candidates.

Both sides finally agreed to a secret ballot for the two leadership posts with all Democrats to support the winners. Once more the upstaters were lulled into a mood of imminent victory. Then, before the balloting took place, Ray Jones reported to Mayor Wagner that State Chairman McKeon had attempted to "bribe" two senators with "public money" to secure votes for the upstate candidates, specifically, the offer of extra "lulus," a term coined by Al Smith meaning payments in lieu of expenses, a traditional fringe benefit for State legislators. The offer was supposedly made to Jones in a smoke-filled room at the DeWitt Clinton Hotel in Albany. Wagner announced the accusation publicly and the State Investigation Commission decided to hold public hearings on the incident.

The hearings produced only more confusion but gave the charge the kind of publicity that Jones and Wagner were seeking. Jones appeared as a witness to verify the Mayor's account of the transaction. State Chairman McKeon was adamant in his denial. The others who were in the hotel room had apparently been stricken by temporary deafness during the conversation. The hearings ended inconclusively and the legislative fight continued with Jones and Wagner still holding only a minority of the Democratic votes but having swung public opinion to their side.

The battle was decided by a simple, heretical maneuver. The legislative leaders had to be elected by a majority vote of both parties; traditionally, the minority party endorsed the majority party's choices. But now the Republican legislators, voicing frustration over the long delay in getting on with the real business of the Legislature, joined with the Wagner group and elected the Mayor's choices. It was suggested that Mayor Wagner's end of the bargain was support for Governor Rockefeller's proposed sales tax, which he did indeed deliver, and which earned the Mayor the enmity of every Democratic County

Leader north of the New York City line and canceled him out as a gubernatorial prospect for 1966.

Wagner's next political bombshell was his announcement that he would not seek a fourth term as Mayor in the 1965 fall elections. In the primary to choose the Democratic candidate, he and Ray Jones threw their support to City Council President Paul Screvane, a thoroughgoing Wagner loyalist. Queens District Attorney Frank O'Connor and Brooklyn's Abraham Beame, the City's expert Comptroller, announced their candidacies to oppose the Mayor's choice. Then O'Connor withdrew to support Beame, reputedly at the urging of Brooklyn leader Stanley Steingut and Charles Buckley in the Bronx, who were prepared to support O'Connor for the Governorship the following year. The move was reminiscent of Al Smith's brief mayoral candidacy in 1917, when Mister Murphy persuaded him to await the gubernatorial convention of 1918 and accept a place on the City ticket for president of the Board of Aldermen.

Comptroller Beame, with the support of the Brooklyn and Bronx organizations, won the primary over Jones's candidate Screvane, but went on to lose the election to Republican Congressman John Lindsay. Frank O'Connor survived the Lindsay victory, easily winning the City Council presidency and placing himself in the front rank of contenders for the Democratic nomination for Governor. There remained eight months between O'Connor's assumption of office in City Hall and the Democratic State Convention in Buffalo. He decided to delay formal announcement of his higher aspirations until he had convinced City voters that he was not using his new City Council office as a springboard to Albany.

The race for Governor began in February 1966, with the announced candidacy of Eugene Nickerson, chief executive of the populous suburban county of Nassau on Long Island. Nickerson was an articulate intellectual, with a speaking style reminiscent of the late President Kennedy, and had twice won election in the traditionally Republican stronghold of Nassau. The County Leader of Nassau, John English, had been instrumental in securing the New York Senatorial nomination for Robert Kennedy in 1964, and it was widely assumed that Nickerson was now Kennedy's choice for Governor. Many County Leaders, impressed with Nickerson's reform of a relatively ineffective county government, were convinced of his strong credentials for the governorship and awaited the word from Senator Kennedy.

Ray Jones acknowledged privately that he was committed to former Mayor Wagner for the nomination, but if Wagner had no interest in it, the Tammany Leader had an "open mind" toward all candidates. The gubernatorial contest was not Jones's chief preoccupation in the early months of 1966. In February, the State Investigation Commission opened hearings on political influence in publicly-aided housing projects. Amidst volleys of charges and countercharges, and a few rounds of choice name-calling, the only certain fact to emerge was that political influence was a more important ingredient in the construction of housing than concrete and steel.

Earl Brown testified that early in 1962, when he was a member of the City's Housing and Redevelopment Board, Jones had invited him to his Convent Avenue apartment and in the course of a conversation there showed "an unusual interest in Esplanade Gardens." According to Brown, Jones said: "Any member of the board who supports this project ought never to want for money again. . . . You commissioners ought to make millions with all the housing involved in New York City."

Jackie Robinson, one-time Brooklyn Dodgers star and an active Rockefeller Republican, recalled on the witness stand that he had applied for sponsorship of Esplanade Gardens but was told by a high official of the Housing Board that the project was "reserved for Powell and Jones." Another witness, whose construction firm had built Clayton Apartments, testified that William Hampton, a former secretary to Powell, had demanded $75,000 in fees or "I could pick up my marbles and go home . . . it was a shakedown, pure and simple." Hampton denied this. Daniel Burrows, former president of Jones's Carver Democratic Club and a sponsor of Esplanade Gardens, confirmed as a witness that he had received a performance bond commission on the Clayton project, and at about the same time had purchased stock in Jones's Sea-Ray Development Company in the Virgin Islands. And Harlem real estate broker Clarence King testified that Jones had sought insurance commissions on the Clayton Apartments.

When Ray Jones took the stand, he denied the alleged conversation with Earl Brown, called him "malicious and vindictive" and countered that Brown had sought the meeting in order to win Jones's support for a housing developer. As for Clarence King's testimony, it was a "vicious and deliberate lie."

Reformers on the Tammany Executive Committee doubted Jones's veracity. They attempted to round up votes to depose the Boss, but they could not agree on a replacement. In late May, however, they were successful in securing Senator Robert Kennedy's support for a primary fight against Jones's choice for Manhattan Surrogate. The campaign was managed by Kennedy's brother-in-law Stephen Smith. Some observers felt that Kennedy's chief interest in the Surrogate race was to eradicate the stain on his "good government" image which had resulted from his support of a controversial Massachusetts judge for the Federal bench. But it was also recognized that if Kennedy could beat Ray Jones and Tammany Hall, he would be in a strong position to move on and name the Democratic candidate for Governor.

Jones made Kennedy the chief issue of the Surrogate campaign: "Characters have been wrongfully maligned, the Supreme Court has been demeaned, integrity of commitments is shown without value— and for what? To satisfy a combination of boundless and burning ambitions, the ruthless court quest for power, a vendetta to seize control. . . . He who seeks to conquer aims at me, the office, the Court—all principle is shoved under the rug." A group of Negro legislators and district leaders charged that Kennedy's intervention was "aimed solely at J. Raymond Jones, because he is a Negro." In another statement, two respected Negro spokesmen, Professor Kenneth Clark and James Dumpson, former City Welfare Commissioner, declared: "The issue of the selection of a surrogate was not made a major inter or intraparty fight until a Negro became chairman of the New York County Democratic Committee and played a crucial role in the selection process." (In fact, the Valente-Impellitteri Surrogate battle in 1948, by which Carmine DeSapio came to prominence, was a major battle.)

Meanwhile, Franklin Roosevelt, Jr., had announced his candidacy for the Democratic gubernatorial nomination. Anxious to gain Senator Kennedy's support, he opposed the Jones camp in the Surrogate primary fight. Roosevelt's major rivals, Frank O'Connor and Eugene Nickerson, proclaimed neutrality because of non-residency in Manhattan, but Nickerson's County Leader John English sent scores of campaign workers into the primary on the Kennedy side. English refused to call them off when Jones heard of the subterfuge, and the Tammany Leader closed his mind to the Nickerson candidacy. In the meantime, Kennedy's Surrogate candidate, Justice Samuel Silverman, and Jones's candidate, Justice Arthur Klein, both almost lost in the shuffle, expressed regret that politics had become the main order of the day in a campaign which was ostensibly aimed at ridding the courts of politics.

Kenneth Clark's assertion that Kennedy had "injured his vote-getting power in New York City among Negroes and Puerto Ricans" was not borne out on Primary Day, June 28. As the vote tallies came in from Harlem, it became apparent that Kennedy's civil rights posture was a durable one, and that the Jones forces had erred in concentrating their attack on the popular brother of a beloved President. "Bobby's Boston Brains, a hard core of highly paid professionals, the standing army of Kennedy mercenaries"—as characterized in the Tammany literature—won a surprising upset victory for Justice Silverman, who was thus safely assured of triumph in the general election of November 1966.

The movement was renewed to oust Jones from the Tammany Leadership, but again, no district leader was strong enough to replace him. Jones shrugged off the discontent and announced that the Manhattan delegation would support Mayor Wagner as a favorite son for Governor at the State Convention in September. But as O'Connor's and Nickerson's strength grew among upstate delegates, Wagner's prospects diminished and Jones mailed out a postcard poll to his delegates before going to the Virgin Islands for a vacation.

All eyes were now on Robert Kennedy, the new Boss of the New York State Democratic Party. In April he had privately told party leaders that he would express his own personal choice for the governorship. Background news stories emanating from the Senator's Washington office indicated that this choice would not be Frank O'Connor, a rival Irish Catholic, an old face, and a candidate who needed only Kennedy neutrality, not Kennedy backing, to win the nomination. O'Connor was in the dangerous front-running position that Franklin Roosevelt, Jr., had occupied in 1954 before being blocked by DeSapio, Lehman, and the Liberal Party leaders. Moreover, O'Connor reportedly had the commitments from the previous year of Charles Buckley in the Bronx and Stanley Steingut in Brooklyn, two of the leaders who had supported Kennedy for the Senatorial nomination in 1964. Senator Kennedy, riding the wave of his reform victory with Justice Silverman, was reported anxious to rid himself of the "Boss-picked" image just as he had overcome his "politics-in-the-courts-of-our-land" tarnish.

As the weeks went by, however, the Senator's continued public

neutrality strengthened the belief that the traditional Kennedy disinterest in the condition of State Democratic parties, already well demonstrated in Massachusetts, would also apply to Robert Kennedy's
adopted state of New York. If John Kennedy, working outside the
organizations in Massachusetts, New York and elsewhere, could reach
the White House, why not also Robert Kennedy, whose magnetic
presence never failed to gather huge crowds on the streets? Some observers began to reason that Nelson Rockefeller's re-election to a third
term in November 1966, would strengthen Senator Kennedy as New
York's top Democrat far more than victory for a Democratic Governor
with whom he would have to share party leadership.

The gubernatorial race was enlivened by Franklin Roosevelt's public airing of charges of a deal between the Bosses in Brooklyn and the
Bronx in 1965 to support Frank O'Connor for Governor in 1966. It
was a magnificent election issue but fatal in a pre-convention campaign,
which must be geared to party leaders and not to the voters at large.
The ten delegates already pledged to Roosevelt deserted him. And far
from hurting O'Connor, the charge confirmed the suspicions of upstate
leaders that the City Council president *did* have the support of more
than 250 delegates in Brooklyn and the Bronx. With 573 delegates
needed to nominate, a bandwagon was now in the making. O'Connor
aides traveled throughout the State issuing bright promises to delegations that announced early and dark threats to those that delayed.

O'Connor's strategy was to convince Kennedy that the tide was too
strong, that a Kennedy intervention in behalf of another candidate
would split the party and hurt the public's picture of the Senator as a
strong leader and, ultimately, as a Presidential contender. A majority
of the delegates, however, remained uncommitted, particularly after
national columnists reported that Kennedy was on the verge of supporting Eugene Nickerson. An unpublished poll showed Nickerson
running the strongest against Rockefeller in key "swing" districts which
would decide a close election. Other polls gave Nickerson substantial
delegate strength among Manhattan reformers, a majority in upstate
counties including suburban Westchester and Broome, home county
of State Democratic Chairman John Burns, but only 126 were publicly
pledged and O'Connor maintained a decisive lead.

In July, Nickerson aides were authorized to tell delegates that Kennedy was "inclined" to support Nickerson if sufficient pledges were
announced publicly. But party leaders cautiously insisted on awaiting

word from Kennedy himself. Said one county chairman: "God hasn't called me yet." Kennedy's last chance came when Liberal Party leaders announced that they could not endorse Frank O'Connor, the same opportunity which Carmine DeSapio had seized to block Franklin Roosevelt twelve years before. The Liberal Party, which broke off from the Communist-infiltrated American Labor Party in 1942, had provided the winning margin for President Kennedy in New York State in 1960. No state-wide Democratic candidate had carried New York without Liberal endorsement during the party's twenty-four years. It was believed that up to 400,000 votes for the Democratic candidate were now in jeopardy.

But the Liberal announcement provoked a backlash among many upstate Democrats. How long would the Liberal tail be permitted to wag the Democratic dog? The feeling ran high that a Democratic victory without Liberal assistance would be sweet. This sentiment, and a strong antagonism toward Senator Kennedy, was the prevailing mood when delegates in Suffolk County, neighboring county to Nickerson's Nassau on Long Island, met on Friday night, August 12, to name their choice for Governor. A majority voted for O'Connor and against their neighbor. The next day, Kennedy told the Nickerson camp that it was "too late" for the Senator to enter into the governorship contest. It was indeed. That night the Syracuse delegation voted overwhelmingly for O'Connor and on Monday night, as Westchester County began to caucus, Nickerson released his delegates and withdrew from the race. Two days later Kennedy announced his neutrality.

J. Raymond Jones returned from the Virgin Islands to pick up his postcards from the Manhattan delegates. O'Connor was nearing a majority of the delegates and former Mayor Wagner was without visible support. Standing on the steps of City Hall, Leader Jones announced that 75 New York County delegates would support O'Connor, thus putting him over the top. Having lost one round in the Surrogate primary to Kennedy, Jones had now demonstrated in the second round a simple matter of timing: being on the right side at the right time.

Round three opened on September 7, 1966, in Buffalo, scene of the 1958 split between DeSapio and Harriman. The convention got underway with a notable lack of spirit. Many delegates were deeply troubled about the news from two other conventions taking place at the same time. Nelson Rockefeller was accepting the Republican nomination with an attack on the "Big City Bosses," the same charge which had paid him splendid dividends in 1958 and 1962. And Franklin Roosevelt, Jr., having withdrawn from the Democratic contest with the helpful statement that "O'Connor can't win," was accepting the nomination of the Liberal Party. The Liberal leaders, who needed more votes than the growing Conservative Party to stay on the third party voting line, had swallowed their dissatisfaction with Roosevelt's past performance and nominated the only name that could bring them a large vote. In the process, they hoped to teach the Democrats a lesson about the necessity for Liberal endorsement.

Before the balloting began in Buffalo, feelers were extended by Ray Jones and others loyal to Robert Wagner in a last-minute search for delegates who realized the Liberal threat to O'Connor. Wagner's ties to Liberal leaders Alex Rose and David Dubinsky were the firmest of any Democrat. But he now had virtually no support within his own party for the governorship. The Wagner balloon never left the ground, Jones maintained his public support for O'Connor, and the City Council president was nominated with little ceremony on the first ballot. Then Senator Robert Kennedy, who had been boxed into the same passive position as his brother Ted in the Massachusetts State Convention, decided to assert his leadership in naming the rest of the State ticket.

It was, of course, a necessity for the Senator thus to display some influence in the party councils, having lost the governorship by default. But he underestimated both the memory and the power of J. Raymond Jones. The party leaders sat around a table in the traditional smoke-filled room to determine the nominations for Lieutenant-Governor, Attorney General, and state-wide delegates to the April 1967, Constitutional Convention. Senator Kennedy entered the room and State Chairman Burns, sitting at the head of the table, rose to greet him. Kennedy thereupon took Burns's chair.

When the delegates re-convened in the auditorium on Thursday afternoon, September 8, the word was passed down: Orin Lehman, grand-nephew of the late Herbert Lehman, for Lieutenant-Governor, and Buffalo Mayor Frank Sedita for Attorney General. Sedita's name came as no surprise. He satisfied the ticket's need for an upstate Italian-American. Lehman, however, was considered by the delegates to be Kennedy's candidate. He had been induced by the Senator earlier in the year to run for the Congressional seat vacated by John Lindsay, and he had lost after Kennedy put on a vigorous campaign for him. Orin Lehman was also a resident of the island of Manhattan. "Does the junior Senator think that he is the Leader of New York County?" Ray Jones asked, in a spirit of subdued profanity. "As long as I am County Leader, nobody will put anybody from New York County on any ticket without consulting me. That will happen at this convention over my dead body."

Suddenly, from all corners of the auditorium, the chant began: "We Want Howard!" Placards were raised displaying the features of liberal industrialist Howard Samuels, known to housewives as the inventor of "baggies" and plastic clothes lines, and to reformers and many upstaters as a two-time unsuccessful but spirited candidate for the gubernatorial nomination. New York County would fight for Samuels on the floor and would support him unanimously, Ray Jones said. Tammany Hall and the reformers were at last united.

Now there was a Democratic Convention. The delegates, frustrated by the lack of conflict for the first spot on the ticket, gave full vent to the hostile spirits which Democrats can only satisfy against Democrats. The hall was in an uproar. Senator Kennedy had left Buffalo by plane. It was reported that he could not be reached on the telephone. Finally, Frank O'Connor appeared at the rostrum and threw the convention open to the delegates' choice. Howard Samuels won in a breeze.

Reformers and most upstate counties then united behind Supervisor Michael Petito of Oyster Bay in Nassau County to oppose Buffalo Mayor Sedita for Attorney General. Ray Jones did not join in the second heresy. "I am under no obligation," he said, "to support a man from the county whose Leader opposed me in the Surrogate primary. This is an entirely different matter." Petito made a good showing around the State, picking up most of the delegates who had privately favored Nickerson for Governor. But the City organizations rode Sedita in successfully.

Ray Jones now sat tight in his seat awaiting the vote on the delegates to the 1967 State Constitutional Convention. "I am very tired," he said. "I am waiting only to hear two names—Roy Wilkins and Judge Bernard Botein. I have now been promised I will hear those names. When I hear them, I am going back to the hotel to bed."

The names were read and duly passed. Ray Jones stood up and left the hall. He could feel secure in these contingencies: If the Liberal party defection should cause Frank O'Connor's defeat, Jones could point to the man he had favored, Robert Wagner, as one who could have wooed the Liberals. Another, Eugene Nickerson, had been ignored by Kennedy. And if Frank O'Connor should defeat Nelson Rockefeller, it would be no thanks to Robert Kennedy and no grudges against Ray Jones.

At ten o'clock that night, J. Raymond Jones, looking fit and well-rested, benign and serene, entered a Buffalo restaurant far from the cocktail lounges where the chattering ward-heelers of the New York Democratic Party were gathered. There he enjoyed a quiet victory dinner in the peace and dignity befitting a true tiger of Tammany.

Is Tammany still alive? Nelson Rockefeller found many believers. In October he charged that the election of O'Connor would mean a "Tammany take-over" by "Big City Bosses." On November 8, 1966, Rockefeller won Tammany's old stronghold of Manhattan and coasted to a third term victory.

A few days earlier, James Driscoll, National Democratic Club secretary, met a visitor at the club's Madison Avenue mansion, and led him past a lobby portrait of Charles Murphy, up a marble staircase and into a small dark room. The light switch was broken. While rain splashed a dirt-streaked window, an extension lamp cast rays of light on a tiger skin, Liberty Caps, Tammany flags, a painting of Richard Croker, a black-ball ballot box, pictures, clippings, ledgers and a facsimile of the treaty between William Penn and Tamanend.

Jim Driscoll, florid-faced veteran of old Tammany wars, surveyed the dusty artifacts. "You'll probably write that this is all that remains of Tammany. But something that's lasted so long can't be dead. Tammany will revive."

Acknowledgments

This book was written to reach readers who find living history instructive, and to whom an abundance of footnotes and references might be a deterrent. The authors wish in this space, and in the partial bibliography, to acknowledge their debt to those who provided a great mass of material.

We are grateful to many politicians in and around Tammany Hall who were most helpful and co-operative, in particular: Sydney S. Baron, president of Baron Public Relations Corporation; Earl Brown, editor of the *Amsterdam News*; Edward J. Costikyan, former Leader of Tammany Hall; Carmine G. DeSapio, former Leader of Tammany Hall; Hulan Jack, former Borough President of Manhattan; J. Raymond Jones, Leader of Tammany Hall; James Lanigan, former district leader, First Assembly District South; Judge Edward J. McCullen, Scribe of the Society of Saint Tammany; Assemblyman William Passanante and Marie Passanante; Police Lieutenant (ret.) Patrick Joseph Sullivan; Leonard Wallstein, Commissioner of Accounts (1914–17); and James Driscoll, secretary of the National Democratic Club.

The authors deeply appreciate the counsel of: Paul Crowell, former City Hall reporter for the New York *Times*; Ed Edwin, formerly of NBC News; the late Leo Egan, gentleman and scholar, of the *Times*; Clayton Knowles, political reporter for the *Times*; Tom O'Hara, political reporter for the New York *World Journal Tribune*; Richard Severo, reporter for the Washington *Post*; and Morris Werner, author of *Tammany Hall* (1928).

For research assistance we are especially indebted to Roland O. Baughman, head librarian, Kenneth A. Lohf, assistant librarian, Bernard Crystal, reference librarian, and their staff at the Department of Special Collections of the Columbia University Libraries; Robert Grayson and his staff at the *Herald Tribune* reference library; and Eugene J. Bockman and his staff at the City of New York Municipal Reference Library.

Our very special thanks go to our agent Miss Lynn Nesbit for her belief in this book; to our editor Tom Wallace for patience and fortitude; to Mrs. Carolyn Sims for her painstaking marginalia; to our designer Ernst Reichl and to Miss Mary Sherman Parsons and Ben Price for pictorial assistance; to Mrs. Susan Rosenfeld and Fred Gluck for typing assistance; and to Miss Anne Luetkemeyer for proofreading.

Bibliography

General

Much of the material in this book was culled from the remarkable Edwin Patrick Kilroe Collection of Tammaniana in the Department of Special Collections, Columbia University. The authors also frequently consulted M. R. Werner's authoritative *Tammany Hall* (Garden City, Doubleday & Co., Inc., 1928) and Gustavus Myers' *The History of Tammany Hall* (New York, 1901; revised, Boni & Liveright, 1917). The Tammany Society's self-admiring official history, compiled by Mrs. Euphemia Vale Blake, and published under the direction of Fred Feigl, editor of *The Tammany Times*, is *History of the Tammany Society or Columbian Order from its Organization to the Present Time* (New York, 1901).

Two other valuable works referred to throughout the writing of this book were Frederick Shaw's *History of the New York City Legislature* (New York, Columbia University Press, 1954) and *A Short History of New York State*, by David M. Ellis, James A. Frost, Harold C. Syrett, and Harry J. Carman (Ithaca, Cornell University Press, 1957). An attractive introduction to the history of New York City is Susan Elizabeth Lyman's *The Story of New York* (New York, Crown, 1964). Also, *Incredible New York*, by Lloyd R. Morris (New York, Random House, 1951) is an unusual and lively treatment of the City's history.

The most entertaining account of Tammany politics is William L. Riordan's *Plunkitt of Tammany Hall* (New York, 1905; reissued in paperback, E. P. Dutton & Co., Inc., 1963). For a good picture of the radical changes in Tammany politicking during the twentieth century, readers are invited to compare the last chapter of Plunkitt, "Strenuous Life of the Tammany District Leader," with Frances H. Costikyan's essay "The Captain in the Election District" in *Behind Closed Doors* by Edward N. Costikyan (New York, Harcourt, Brace & World, Inc., 1966). Also highly recommended is Edward J. Flynn's *You're the Boss* (New York, The Viking Press, Inc., 1947).

Extensive use was made for this book of clipping files, microfilms and back issues of New York newspapers, including the *American, Daily Advertiser, Daily Mirror, Daily News, Evening Journal, Evening Post, Herald, Herald Tribune, Journal-American, Mail, Morning Chronicle, Morning Courier and Enquirer, Sun, Times, Tribune, World,* and *World-Telegram and Sun.*

367

Chapter 1   Tamanend and the Evil Spirit

The romantic legends of Tamanend were most vividly described by Samuel Latham Mitchill in *The Life, Exploits and Precepts of Tammany, the Famous Indian Chief, Being the Anniversary Oration before the Tammany Society in Old Presbyterian Church, New York, Tuesday, May 12, 1795* (New York, 1795). Drawing from Greek tragedy, and anticipating Victor Herbert, Ann Julia Patton wrote *The Songs of Tammany; or, The Indian Chief. A Serious Opera* (New York, 1794), which was performed each year by members of the Society.

Annual Register, or a View of the History, Politicks, and Literature of the Year 1759. London, 1760.

Charter and Bye-laws of Tammany Society or Columbian Order in the City of New York. (unpublished volume, probably 1805, with bylaw amendments by Tammany Committee of Revision, December 16, 1833, donated to Columbia University by the New York County Democratic Committee on February 5, 1965)

Cooper, James Fenimore, *The Last of the Mohicans.* New York, Charles Scribner's Sons, 1919.

Johnson, John B., *An oration on Union, delivered in New Dutch church, in the city of New York, on May 12, 1794, The anniversary of the Tammany Society or Columbian Order.* New York, 1794.

Josephy, Alvin M., Jr.; Brandon, William, and the editors of American Heritage, *The American Heritage Book of Indians.* New York, American Heritage, 1961.

Journal and Rules of the Council of Sachems of Saint Tammany's Society, 1789–1796. (unpublished minutes from first meeting through seventh year)

Kilroe, Edwin P., *Saint Tammany and the Origin of the Society of Tammany or Columbian Order in the City of New York.* (Ph.D. thesis, Columbia University) New York, 1913.

Linn, William, D.D., *The Blessings of America, A Sermon preached in the Middle Dutch Church on the Fourth of July, 1791, Being the Anniversary of the Independence of America, at the request of the Tammany Society.* New York, 1791.

Miller, Samuel, *A Sermon preached in New York, July 4, 1793, being the anniversary of the Independence of America, at the request of the Tammany Society, or Columbian Order.* New York, 1793.

Murphy, Charles Francis, "History of the Tammany Society or Columbian Order." *The Encyclopedia Americana,* 1906.

Plan of the Tammanial Tontine Association. New York, 1792.

Receipts and Expenditures of Saint Tammany's Society, 1789–1795. (unpublished ledger book)

White, Theodore H., *The Making of the President 1960.* New York Atheneum Pub., 1961.

Wortman, Tuenis, *An oration on the influence of social institutions upon human morals and happiness, delivered before the Tammany Society at its anniversary on May 12, 1796.* New York, 1796.

Chapter 2   The First Hurrah: Aaron Burr's "Little Band"

A sympathetic biography is Nathan Schachner's *Aaron Burr* (New York, A. S. Barnes, 1961). Most other sources are uncomplimentary, especially James Cheetham's *A View of the Political Conduct of Aaron Burr, Esq., Vice-President of the United States* (New York, 1802), which proposed dumping Burr from the national ticket in the 1804 election. Contradictory accounts of the Burr-Hamilton duel are contained in Hamilton's *Evening Post* (July 19, 1804); Burr's *Morning Chronicle* (July 18, 1804 and subsequent issues in July and August, 1804); and William Coleman's *A Collection of the Facts and Documents Relative to the Death of Alexander Hamilton* (New York, 1804).

Abernethy, Thomas P., *The Burr Conspiracy.* New York, Oxford University Press, 1954.

Alexander, Holmes, *Aaron Burr, the Proud Pretender.* New York, Harper, 1937.

Beirne, Francis F., *Shout Treason: The Trial of Aaron Burr.* New York, Hastings House, 1959.

Cheetham, James, *A Narrative of the Suppression by Col. Burr of the History of the Administration of John Adams, Late President of the United States.* New York, 1802.

Clinton, George, *An oration delivered on the Fourth of July, 1798, before the General Society of Mechanics and Tradesmen, The Democratic Society, The Tammany Society or Columbian Order, The New York Cooper's Society,* and a numerous concourse of other citizens. New York, 1798.

Colver, Anne. *Thedosia.* New York, Farrar, 1941.

Davis, Matthew L., *Aaron Burr.* New York, 1838.

Jefferson, Thomas, *Autobiography.* New York, Capricorn, 1959.

Parton, James, *The Life and Times of Aaron Burr.* New York, 1858.

Wood, John, *A correct statement of the various sources from which the history of the administration of John Adams was compiled, and the motives for its suppression by Col. Burr.* New York, 1802.

Wood, John, *A full exposition of the Clintonian faction.* New York, 1802.

Chapter 3   Tammany Takes the White House: The Van Buren Regency

The Kilroe Collection contains numerous pamphlets, "Long Talks," and letters of interest to students of this era. Two essential books are Dixon Ryan Fox's *The Decline of Aristocracy in the Politics of New York, 1801–1840* (New York, Columbia University Press, 1919; revised, Harper & Row,

1965, ed. by Robert V. Remini) and Remini's *Martin Van Buren and the Making of the Democratic Party* (New York, Columbia University Press, 1959).

Butler, William Allen, *Martin Van Buren, Lawyer, Statesman and Man.* New York, 1862.

Hammond, Jabez D., *The History of Political Parties in the State of New York.* New York, 1846.

Lynch, Denis Tilden, *An Epoch and a Man: Martin Van Buren and His Times.* New York, Horace Liveright, 1929.

Remini, Robert V., "The Albany Regency," *New York History*, October, 1958.

Shepard, Edward M., *Martin Van Buren.* Boston, 1899.

Van Buren, Martin, "Autobiography," *American Historical Association Annual Report*, 1918.

Watson, John F., *Annals and Occurrences of New York City and State in the Olden Time.* New York, 1846.

Chapter 4   Fernando Wood, The "Model Mayor"

Mayor Wood's escapades were extensively reported in the *Herald* and the *Tribune*. Readers may also take their choice of two campaign biographies: Donald MacLeod's enthusiastic *Biography of Hon. Fernando Wood, Mayor of the City of New York* (New York, 1858) and Abijah A. Ingraham's unsigned pamphlet *A Biography of Fernando Wood, A History of the Forgeries, Perjuries, and Other Crimes of Our "Model" Mayor* (New York, 1856).

A Model Mayor, Early Life, Congressional Career and Triumphant Municipal Administration of the Hon. Fernando Wood. (Anon.) New York, 1855.

Asbury, Herbert, *The Gangs of New York.* Garden City, Garden City Publishing Co., 1928.

Byrdsall, F., *The History of the Loco Foco or Equal Rights Party.* New York, 1842.

Courtney, Calvin, "New York's Worst Mayor," *American Mercury*, September, 1951.

Grand Council of the Tammany Society or Columbian Order, *Address Relative to the Political Use of Tammany Hall, February 4, 1853.* New York, 1853.

Hendley, J. T., *The Great Riots of New York, 1712 to 1873.* New York, 1873.

Lease of Tammany Hall, December 22, 1842, between the Tammany Society and Joseph W. Howard, innkeeper. (unpublished document)

Nichols, Roy Franklin, "The Democratic Machine, 1850–1854," *Columbia University Studies in History, Economics and Public Law.* New York, 1923.

Pinchon, Edgcumb, *Dan Sickles, Hero of Gettysburg and Yankee King of Spain*. Garden City, Doubleday & Co., 1945.

Pleasants, Samuel Augustus, *Fernando Wood of New York*. New York, Columbia University Press, 1948.

Purdy, Bartholomew B., *Affidavits before the Recorder relative to abuses in the city government*. New York, 1854.

Strong, George Templeton, *Diary, 1820–1875*, Vol. I and II, ed. by Allan Nevins and Milton Halsey Thomas. New York, Macmillan Co., 1952.

Swanberg, W. A., *Sickles the Incredible*. New York, Charles Scribner's Sons, 1956.

Walsh, Mike, *Sketches of the Speeches and Writings of Michael Walsh, Including His Poems and Correspondence, Compiled by a Committee of the Spartan Association*. New York, 1843.

Chapter 5   The Great Reformer: William Marcy Tweed

In addition to stories in the *Times, Sun, Daily Tribune,* and *Herald,* good contemporary accounts are in Matthew P. Breen's *Thirty Years of New York Politics Up-To-Date* (New York, 1899), Samuel J. Tilden's *The New York City Ring, Its Origin, Maturity and Fall* (New York, 1873) and Volumes III and IV of George Templeton Strong's *Diary, 1820–1875,* edited by Nevins and Thomas. An interesting treatment of Mayor Hall is Croswell Bowen's *The Elegant Oakey* (New York, Oxford University Press, 1956).

Bales, William Alan, *Tiger in the Streets*. New York, Dodd, Mead & Co., 1962.

Barnes, David M., *The Draft Riots in New York*. New York, 1863.

Board of Aldermen, *Report of the Special Committee Appointed to Investigate the "Ring Frauds," Together with the Testimony Elicited during the Investigation*. New York, January 4, 1878.

Citizens Association of New York, *Items of Abuse in the Government of the City of New York*. New York, 1866.

"Confession of William Marcy Tweed," New York *Herald*, October 10, 1877.

Davenport, John I., *The Election and Naturalization Frauds in New York City, 1860–1870*. New York, 1894.

Executive Committee of Citizens and Taxpayers for the Financial Reform of the City and County of New York, *Appeal to the People of the State of New York*. New York, 1871.

Gunther, C. Godfrey, Mayor of the City of New York, letter to the Board of Supervisors dated April 4, 1864.

Hirsch, Mark D., "More Light on Boss Tweed," *Political Science Quarterly*, June, 1945.

Hirsch, Mark D., *William C. Whitney, Modern Warwick*. New York, Dodd, Mead & Co., 1948.

Hudson, William C., *Random Recollections of an Old Political Reporter*. New York, Cupples & Leon Co., 1911.

Life Sketches of Executive Officers and Members of the Legislature of the State of New York. Albany, 1863, 1867, 1870, 1873.

Lynch, Denis Tilden, *Boss Tweed, The Story of a Grim Generation*. New York, Boni & Liveright, 1927.

Mandelbaum, Seymour J., *Boss Tweed's New York*. New York, John Wiley & Sons, Inc., 1965.

New York Times, How New York City Is Governed. (pamphlet). New York, 1871.

Opdyke, George, Mayor of the City of New York, official addresses, letters, and other documents, 1862, 1863.

Roosevelt, Robert B., *Political Corruption in New York* (speech). New York, September 4, 1871, pamphlet, New York, Journeymen Printers' Cooperative Association, 1871.

Select Committee of the Senate of the State of New York, Appointed to Investigate Various Departments of the Government of the City of New York, *Proceedings, February 9, 1865*. Albany, 1865.

Sheldon, George W., *The Story of the Volunteer Fire Department of the City of New York*. New York, 1882.

Swanberg, W. A., *Jim Fisk, The Career of an Improbable Rascal*. New York, Charles Scribner's Sons, 1959.

Union League Club, *Report of the Committee on Municipal Reform*. New York, 1862.

U. S. House of Representatives, *Report of the Select Committee on alleged New York election frauds*. Washington, 1869.

Wingate, Charles F., "How The Times Broke the Ring," *North American Review*, July, 1875.

Chapter 6   Family Affairs with "Honest John" Kelly

Talcott Williams' essay "Tammany Hall" (*Historic New York, Being the Second Series of the Half Moon Papers*, New York, 1899) is appreciative of Kelly's contribution. Werner's "Honest John' Kelly," Chapter V in *Tammany Hall*, is more critical. *The Life and Times of John Kelly, Tribune of the People* (New York, 1885), by J. Fairfax McLaughlin, an associate of Kelly's, should be taken with a large grain of salt.

"Calm Death of John Kelly," New York *Tribune*, June 2, 1886.

Fiske, Stephen, *Off-hand Portraits of Prominent New Yorkers*. New York, 1884.

Flick, Alexander Clarence (assisted by Gustav S. Lobrano), *Samuel Jones Tilden: A Study in Political Sagacity*. New York, Dodd, 1939.

Grover, William C., *The Tammany Hall Democracy of the City of New York, and the General Committee for 1875*. New York, 1875.

Moynihan, Daniel P., "When the Irish Ran New York," *The Reporter*, June 8, 1961.

Riordan, William L., *Plunkitt of Tammany Hall, A Series of Very Plain Talks on Very Practical Politics, Delivered by Ex-Senator George Washington Plunkitt, the Tammany Philosopher, from His Rostrum—the New York County Court-house Bootblack Stand—and Recorded by William L. Riordan.* New York, 1905; Dutton, 1963.

Shannon, William, *The American Irish.* New York, Macmillan Co., 1963.

Tilden, Samuel J., *Letters and Literary Memorials,* ed. by John Bigelow. New York, 1908.

Tilden, Samuel Jones, *Public Papers,* ed. by John Van Buren. New York, 1866.

Wittke, Carl F., *The Irish in America.* Baton Rouge, Louisiana State University Press, 1956.

Chapter 7   Squire Croker

Steffens and his fellow muckrakers were all intrigued by Croker as a personality. Elements of this fascination even creep into William Allen White's angry "Croker" (*McClure's Magazine,* February, 1901). Croker was followed closely throughout his reign by various reporters for the *Tribune* and by Walter S. Edwards of the *Commercial Advertiser.* William T. Stead's lengthy interview ("Mr. Richard Croker and Greater New York," *Review of Reviews,* London, October 17, 1897) contains inaccuracies but reflects Croker's opinions at the climax of his career. A first-hand account by a Croker intimate is Louis Seibold's "Richard Croker" (*Munsey's Magazine,* August, 1901). Croker is defended in Lothrop Stoddard's *Master of Manhattan: The Life of Richard Croker* (New York, Longmans, Green, 1931) and idealized in Alfred Henry Lewis' *Richard Croker* (New York, 1901). Lewis' novel, *The Boss and How He Came to Rule New York* (New York, 1903) is a blending of the lives of Croker and John Kelly.

Jacob A. Riis' self-righteous autobiography *The Making of an American* (New York, 1901) describes immigrant conditions under Tammany rule. First-person accounts of Tammany's alliance with criminals are recorded in Josiah Flint's "Interviews with the Underworld" (*McClure's Magazine,* April, 1901). An amusing commentary on graft under Croker is Finley Peter Dunne's essay "Lexow" in *Mr. Dooley in the Hearts of His Countrymen* (Boston, 1899). See also M. R. Werner's excellent "Dr. Parkhurst's Crusade," originally published in the *New Yorker* (*It Happened in New York,* New York, Coward-McCann 1957). Another valuable essay is "The Reformer in Politics" in William Bennett Munro's *Personality in Politics: A Study of Three Types in American Public Life* (New York, Macmillan Co., 1934). Edwin Lawrence Godkin's *The Triumph of Reform: November 6, 1894* (New York, 1895) is a detailed analysis of the 1894 mayoral election.

Barker, Charles Albro, *Henry George.* New York, Oxford University Press, 1955.

City Club of New York, *Some Things Richard Croker Has Said and Done*. New York, July, 1901.

Hodder, Alfred, *A Fight for the City*. New York, 1903.

McGurrin, James, *Bourke Cockran: A Free Lance in American Politics*. New York, Charles Scribner's Sons, 1958.

"Mr. Richard Croker in His English Home," *Black and White*, London, November 10, 1900.

Parkhurst, Rev. Charles H., *Our Fight with Tammany*. New York, 1895.

Platt, Thomas Collier, *Autobiography*, ed. by Louis J. Lang. New York, 1910.

Report and Proceedings of the Senate Committee Appointed to Investigate the Police Department of the City of New York. (Lexow investigation) Albany, 1895.

Report of the Special Committee of the Assembly Appointed to Investigate the Public Offices and Departments of the City of New York and of the Counties Therein Included. (Mazet investigation) Albany, 1900.

Roosevelt, Theodore, *Autobiography*. New York, Charles Scribner's Sons, 1958.

Roosevelt, Theodore, *Essays on Practical Politics*. New York, 1887.

Schurze, Carl, "Our New Monarchy," *Harper's Weekly*, January 29, 1898.

Steffens, Lincoln, *Autobiography*. New York, Harcourt, 1931.

Steffens, Lincoln, *The Shame of the Cities*. New York, 1904; Sagamore Press, 1948.

Testimony Taken Before the Senate Committee on Cities Pursuant to Resolution Adopted January 20, 1890. (Fassett investigation) Albany, 1890.

Chapter 8   Mister Murphy's Golden Years

Considerable material on Murphy is in clippings of the *Herald Tribune, Mail, Sun, Times,* and *World*. No biography exists. This is a much-needed book which should be undertaken before the last of Murphy's old acquaintances depart. He left few words behind him. Many memoirs in the Oral History Collection, Columbia University Libraries, shed light on these years and those covered in Chapter 9.

Brooks, Sidney, "Tammany Again," *The Fortnightly Review*, London, December, 1903.

Flynn, Edward J., *You're the Boss*. New York, The Viking Press, Inc., 1947.

Forrest, Jay W. and James Malcolm, *Tammany's Treason*. Albany, 1913.

Gaynor, William Jay, *Letters and Speeches*. New York, Greaves, 1913.

Handlin, Oscar, *Al Smith and his America*. Boston, Little, 1958.

Harlow, Alvin F., *Old Bowery Days*. New York, Appleton, 1931.

Hylan, John Francis, *Autobiography*. New York, Rotary Press, 1922.

Koenig, Samuel S., memoirs, Oral History Collection, Columbia University Libraries.

McClellan, George B., Jr., *The Gentleman and The Tiger: The Auto-biography of George B. McClellan, Jr.,* ed. by Harold C. Syrett. Philadelphia, Lippincott, 1956.

Paterson, Isabel, "Murphy," *American Mercury,* July, 1928.

Perkins, Frances, *The Roosevelt I Knew.* New York, The Viking Press, Inc., 1946.

Pink, Louis Heaton, *Gaynor: The Tammany Mayor Who Swallowed the Tiger.* New York, International Press, 1931.

Pringle, Henry F., *Alfred E. Smith: A Critical Study.* New York, Macy-Masius, 1927.

Proceedings of the Court for the Trial of Impeachments, The People of the State of New York by the Assembly Thereof Against William Sulzer as Governor. Albany, 1913.

Report of the Special Committee of the Board of Aldermen of the City of New York, appointed August 5, 1912, to investigate the Police Department. New York, 1912.

Smith, Alfred E., *Up to Now: An Autobiography.* New York, The Viking Press, Inc., 1929.

Smith, Mortimer, *William Jay Gaynor: Mayor of New York.* Chicago, Henry Regnery, 1951.

Steffens, Lincoln, "New York: Good Government to the Test," *McClure's Magazine,* November, 1903.

Stein, Leon, *The Triangle Fire.* Philadelphia, Lippincott, 1962.

Swanberg, W. A., *Citizen Hearst.* New York, Charles Scribner's Sons, 1961.

Swope, Herbert Bayard, "First Complete Story of New York's Amazing Murder: How Police Lieutenant Becker Plotted the Death of Gambler Rosenthal to Stop His Exposé," *New York World,* October 27, 1912.

Walker, H. W., "The Trail of the Tammany Tiger," *Saturday Evening Post* (series), March, April, 1914.

Warner, Emily Smith (with Hawthorne Daniel), *Happy Warrior.* Garden City, Doubleday & Co., Inc., 1956.

Zink, Harold, *City Bosses in the United States: A Study of Twenty Municipal Bosses.* Durham, Duke University Press, 1930.

Chapter 9 The Interregnum

Milton Mackaye's *The Tin Box Parade* (New York, McBride, 1934) is an acrid and witty description of the Walker administration. Good coverage was given to the period by the *Herald Tribune, Post, Times* and *World-Telegram and Sun.* Among especially enjoyable and informative sources are: Charles Garrett's *The LaGuardia Years* (New Brunswick, Rutgers University Press, 1961), Joseph McGoldrick's "The New Tammany" (*American Mercury,* September, 1928), Herbert Mitgang's *The Man Who Rode the Tiger: The Life and Times of Samuel Seabury* (Philadelphia, Lippincott, 1963), Warren Moscow's *Politics in the Empire State* (New York, Knopf, 1948), and Charles W. Van Devander's *The Big Bosses* (New York, Howell, Soskin, 1944).

Allen, William Harvey, *Al Smith's Tammany Hall, Champion Political Vampire*. New York, Institute For Public Service, 1928.

Allen, William Harvey, *Why Tammanies Revive*. New York, Institute For Public Service, 1937.

Farley, James A., *Behind the Ballots*. New York, Harcourt, 1938.

Finegan, James E., *Tammany at Bay*. New York, Dodd, 1933.

Fowler, Gene, *Beau James: The Life and Times of Jimmy Walker*. New York, The Viking Press, Inc., 1949.

LaGuardia, Mrs. Fiorello H., memoirs, Oral History Collection, Columbia University Libraries.

Lavine, Emanuel H., *Gimme—or How Public Officials Get Rich*. New York, The Vanguard Press, Inc., 1931.

Minutes of public hearing of the Magistrates' Courts investigation (conducted by Samuel Seabury), Sept. 29, 1930 to May 14, 1931.

Minutes of public hearing of the investigation of the departments of government of the City of New York by the Joint Legislative Committee (with Samuel Seabury), July 21, 1931 to June 1, 1932.

Minutes of public hearing before Governor Franklin D. Roosevelt of charges against Mayor James J. Walker brought by Samuel Seabury and others, Aug. 11, 1932 to Sept. 2, 1932.

Moscow, Warren, memoirs, Oral History Collection, Columbia University Libraries.

Seabury, Samuel, report of the investigation of District Attorney Thomas C. T. Crain of New York County (by commission of the Governor of the State of New York), Aug. 31, 1931.

Seabury, Samuel, report of the investigation of the Magistrates' Courts (by the Supreme Court, Appellate Division, First Judicial Department), March 28, 1932.

Seabury, Samuel, report of the investigation of the departments of government of the City of New York (by the Joint Legislative Committee), Jan. 25, 1932, Dec. 19, 1932, and Dec. 27, 1932.

Chapter 10   Carmine DeSapio in the Smokeless Room

Governing New York City (New York, Russell Sage Foundation, 1960), by Wallace S. Sayre and Herbert Kaufman is a first-rate treatise on the workings of political and governmental structures in New York. See also Nathan Glazer's "Is New York City Ungovernable?" (*Commentary*, September, 1961). Some of the leading characters in this period are dealt with harshly in "The Shame of New York" by Fred J. Cook and Gene Gleason (*The Nation*, October 31, 1959), which has some inaccuracies but draws important conclusions. An excellent analysis of DeSapio as a County Leader is in Meg Greenfield's "The Decline and Fall of Tammany Hall" (*The Reporter*, February 15, 1962). Numerous sympathetic close-ups of DeSapio by Murray Kempton appeared in the *Post*, especially a series of columns in June, 1960.

Profiles of DeSapio appeared in *Harper's* (Robert Heilbroner's "The Smile on the Face of the Tiger," July, 1954); *Daily Mirror* (series by William Henderson in November, 1954); *Look* ("Tammany Hall Comes Back," December 28, 1954); New York *Post* (series by Irwin Ross in January, 1955); *World-Telegram and Sun* (series by Luman Long in January, 1955); *Saturday Evening Post* (Joseph and Stewart Alsop's "The Tiger Who Looks Like a Banker," April 23, 1955); *Life* (Cameron Hawley's "New-Style Boss," June 6, 1955); *Time* (August 22, 1955 cover story); *Newsweek* (September 8, 1958); New York *Times Magazine* (Leo Egan's "How and Why of DeSapio," September 14, 1958).

Burns, James McGregor, "DeSapio at the Village Barricades," New York *Times Magazine*, August 27, 1961.
Egan, Leo, "The Political Boss: Going, Going—" New York *Times Magazine*, January 8, 1961.
Greenfield, Meg, "Tammany Hall in Search of a Boss," *The Reporter*, April 13, 1961.
Kempton, Murray, "New York's Political Zoo is Open Again," *Life*, September 1, 1961.
Moynihan, Daniel P., "Bosses and Reformers," *Commentary*, June, 1961.
Moynihan, Daniel P., and Wilson, James Q., "Patronage in New York State, 1955–1959," *American Political Science Review*, June, 1964.
Nevins, Allan, "The Last Good Fight," Chapt. XIX of *Herbert H. Lehman and His Era*. New York, Charles Scribner's Sons, 1963.
Ottenberg, James S., *The Lexington Democratic Club Story*. (pamphlet) New York, 1960.
Talese, Gay, "The Ethnics of Frank Costello," *Esquire*, September, 1961.
Tamawa Club, Inc., *The People Themselves: A Manual for Democrats*. (pamphlet) New York, 1959.
Wakefield, Dan, "The Village and the Tiger," essay in *Between the Lines*. New York, New American Library, 1966.
Wilson, James Q., *The Amateur Democrat: Club Politics in Three Cities*. Chicago, University of Chicago Press, 1962.

Chapter 11 A Fox among the Tigers: J. Raymond Jones

This chapter, like the preceding, is based largely upon interviews and personal observation. A somewhat exasperated view of political trends in the City during this period is well-expressed by Edward N. Costikyan in *Behind Closed Doors: Politics in the Public Interest* (New York, Harcourt, Brace & World, 1966). The problems of Harlem are set forth compellingly by Kenneth B. Clark in *Youth in the Ghetto: A Study of the Consequences of Powerlessness and a Blueprint for Change* (New York, Harlem Youth Opportunities Unlimited, Inc., 1964). See also *Beyond the Melting Pot: The Negroes, Puerto Ricans, Jews, Italians, and Irish of New York City* (Cambridge, Mass., M.I.T. Press, 1964), by Nathan Glazer and Daniel Patrick Moynihan.

The Jones-Powell relationship is traced in *Adam Clayton Powell and the Politics of Race* (New York, Fleet, 1965), by Neil Hickey and Ed Edwin. A colorful account of the 1965 mayoral election is "The Fight for City Hall," by Peter Maas and Nick Thimmesch (*New York, Sunday Herald Tribune Magazine*, January 2, 1966). Well worth reading is "City Bosses and Political Machines," edited by Lee S. Greene, comprising the May, 1964, issue of *The Annals* of the American Academy of Political and Social Science. See also Roma Lipsky's "Electioneering Among the Minorities" (*Commentary*, May, 1961); Richard Armstrong's "Bobby Kennedy and the Fight for New York" (*Saturday Evening Post*, November 6, 1965); and the memoirs of Samuel J. Battle in the Oral History Collection, Columbia University Libraries. Much material on Harlem politics and the Negro in New York is in the Schomburg Collection of the New York Public Library.

Index